SLOW TRAVEL

Sussex
South Downs, Weald & Coast

Local, characterful guides to Britain's special places

Tim Locke
Updated by Emma Gregg

T0182502

EDITION 3
Bradt Guides Ltd, UK
The Globe Pequot Press Inc, USA

Third edition published July 2024
First published 2011
Bradt Travel Guides Ltd
31a High Street, Chesham, Buckinghamshire, HP5 1BW, England
www.bradtguides.com
Print edition published in the USA by The Globe Pequot Press Inc, PO Box 480, Guilford,
Connecticut 06437-0480

Text copyright © Bradt Travel Guides Ltd, 2024
Maps copyright © Bradt Travel Guides Ltd, 2024; includes map data
© OpenStreetMap contributors
Photographs copyright © Individual photographers (see below), 2024
Project Manager: Samantha Fletcher
Cover research: Pepi Bluck

ISBN: 9781804690109

British Library Cataloguing in Publication Data
A catalogue record for this book is available from the British Library

Photographs © individual photographers and organisations credited beside images &
also those from picture libraries credited as follows: Alamy.com (A), AWL Images (AWL),
Dreamstime.com (D), Shutterstock.com (S), Superstock (SS)

Front cover Birling Gap (www.mjt.photography/A)
Back cover Rye (Helen Hotson/S)
Title page The Sussex Weald (SuxxesPhoto/S)

Maps David McCutcheon FBCart.S. FRGS

Typeset by Ian Spick, Bradt Travel Guides
Production managed by Gutenberg Press Ltd; printed in Malta
Digital conversion by www.dataworks.co.in

Paper used for this product comes from sustainably managed forests, recycled and
controlled sources.

AUTHOR

Tim Locke lives in Lewes in East Sussex. He began his work in freelance travel writing in the 1980s when he was commissioned to write guidebooks on walking and various national parks in Britain. He specialises in travel writing about Britain but has variously branched out into other areas, including consultancy work on sustainable tourism, children's history books and guidebooks. He has been the project manager of Bradt's Slow Travel guides and continues to be involved with the series. He is an Honorary Life Member of the British Guild of Travel Writers. Visit his Slow Sussex Facebook page f slowsussex.

UPDATER

Emma Gregg (⊘ emmagregg.com) is an award-winning travel journalist, specialising in responsible tourism and sustainable travel. Keen on walking, wildlife and culture, she has travelled all over Sussex and the South Downs. Originally a Londoner, she fell for Brighton more than 20 years ago and it's been her base ever since. She's also very fond of the Cuckmere Valley, where, as a labour of love, she and her husband have renovated a 17th-century cottage with a flint-walled garden full of roses and birdsong.

AUTHOR'S STORY

As a child living in London, Sussex and the South Downs seemed to me a far-flung, exotic destination, less accessible than Kent or Surrey for our car-free family. Occasionally we ventured by train or bus and picnicked on Beachy Head, steamed along on the Bluebell Railway to Sheffield Park or got extremely but happily lost in the wilds of Ashdown Forest. At the age of 14 I decided to devise my own Michelin Green Guide to our own house, with star ratings for everything including the cat; such measurements of quality evidently must have gripped my imagination, as I urged my parents to take us on the train to Lewes, for the simple reason that it got a glowing write-up in the *Shell Guide to Britain*. The book didn't let us down in that respect, and some years down the line I joined the ranks of the DFLs ('Down From London') in that very town. I do think living in a place from where you can see straight into the hills is very special, and the relationship between Lewes and the South Downs that surround it is very much cherished by both residents and visitors.

The area covered by this book is simply made for seeing with a Slow attitude. I'm still nosing out new places within a cycle ride of my house, and as far as walking goes the landscape has such variety and a perfect sense of scale that there's a freakishly wide range of exceptional walks. The last research trip for this book took me to the eco-friendly Secret Campsite, all of five miles from home, where my wife and I found walks I'd never known about, and wandered nocturnally back from the pub through moonlit woods, with owls for company, then lit up a campfire and sat under the stars. This seems to sum up the essence of Slow travel: taking time to enjoy the details, and experiencing the pleasure of being immersed in a landscape. It is very much what I feel 21st-century travel should be about.

ACKNOWLEDGEMENTS

Huge thanks to all those who chatted to us and showed us around their museums, vineyards, B&Bs, campsites, cottages, farm attractions, nature reserves or generally helped us during our research for this book. Specific thanks to (in no particular order) the staff at Sussex Past, the Weald & Downland Living Museum, Anna Zeuner from the Pallant House Gallery, Emily Bamber at the British Airways i360, Georgia Mallinson at Rathfinny Estate, Adrian at the English Martyrs' Church in Goring, Jo Seaman at Eastbourne Borough Council, Ami Bouhassane at Farleys House and Gallery, Jenny Passmore from Church Farm, Anna Moores and all the other wonderful staff at Bradt Guides, Andy the volunteer National Trust minibus driver, Natasha Williams at Battle Abbey, Lauren Hoskin at the National Trust Press Office, Dawn Champion of English Heritage, the Brighton Sea Life Centre, Pat Warren of the Arundel Wetland Centre, Bridget Gladwyn of Nutbourne Vineyard, and the many others who helped out on the way. Apologies to any we've missed out, and sorry we weren't able to squeeze in every bit of information gleaned from our travels.

FEEDBACK REQUEST

At Bradt Guides we're aware that guidebooks start to go out of date on the day they're published – and that you, our readers, are out there in the field doing research of your own. You'll find out before us when a fine new family-run hotel opens or a favourite restaurant changes hands and goes downhill. So why not tell us about your experiences? Contact us on ✆ 01753 893444 or ✉ info@bradtguides.com. We will forward emails to the author who may post updates on the Bradt website at ⌂ bradtguides.com/updates. Alternatively, you can add a review of the book to Amazon, or share your adventures with us on social:

f BradtGuides, SlowSussex & timlocke73

𝕏 BradtGuides, TimLocke83 & Emma_Gregg

◙ BradtGuides

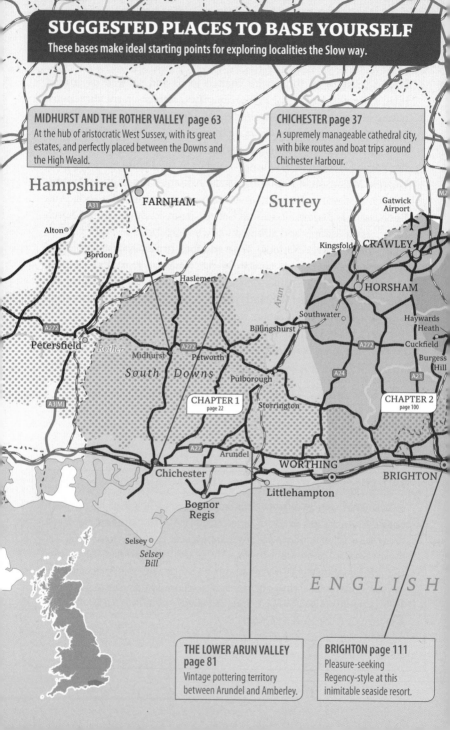

SUGGESTED PLACES TO BASE YOURSELF

These bases make ideal starting points for exploring localities the Slow way.

MIDHURST AND THE ROTHER VALLEY page 63
At the hub of aristocratic West Sussex, with its great estates, and perfectly placed between the Downs and the High Weald.

CHICHESTER page 37
A supremely manageable cathedral city, with bike routes and boat trips around Chichester Harbour.

Hampshire

Surrey

FARNHAM

Gatwick Airport

Alton

Bordon

Kingsfold   CRAWLEY

Haslemere

HORSHAM

Arun

Southwater

Haywards Heath

A272

Billingshurst

Petersfield   Rother

Midhurst   Petworth

South Downs

Cuckfield

Burgess Hill

A24

Pulborough

A3(M)

CHAPTER 1
page 22

Storrington

CHAPTER 2
page 100

A27   Arundel

WORTHING

Chichester

Littlehampton

BRIGHTON

Bognor Regis

Selsey

Selsey Bill

ENGLISH

THE LOWER ARUN VALLEY page 81
Vintage pottering territory between Arundel and Amberley.

BRIGHTON page 111
Pleasure-seeking Regency-style at this inimitable seaside resort.

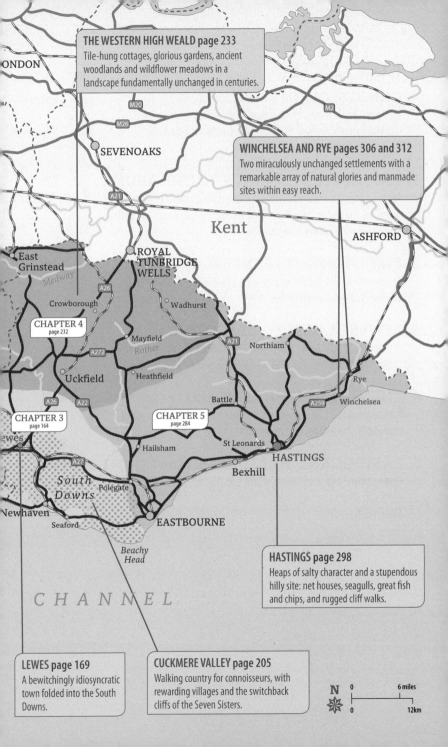

THE WESTERN HIGH WEALD page 233
Tile-hung cottages, glorious gardens, ancient woodlands and wildflower meadows in a landscape fundamentally unchanged in centuries.

WINCHELSEA AND RYE pages 306 and 312
Two miraculously unchanged settlements with a remarkable array of natural glories and manmade sites within easy reach.

LONDON

SEVENOAKS

M20

M26

M2

ASHFORD

Kent

East Grinstead

Medway

ROYAL TUNBRIDGE WELLS

A26

Crowborough

Wadhurst

CHAPTER 4
page 232

Mayfield

Rother

A272

A21

Northiam

Uckfield

Heathfield

Rye

A26

A22

Battle

Winchelsea

CHAPTER 3
page 164

CHAPTER 5
page 284

A259

Hailsham

St Leonards

Lewes

A27

Bexhill

HASTINGS

South Downs

Polegate

EASTBOURNE

Newhaven

Seaford

Beachy Head

HASTINGS page 298
Heaps of salty character and a stupendous hilly site: net houses, seagulls, great fish and chips, and rugged cliff walks.

CHANNEL

LEWES page 169
A bewitchingly idiosyncratic town folded into the South Downs.

CUCKMERE VALLEY page 205
Walking country for connoisseurs, with rewarding villages and the switchback cliffs of the Seven Sisters.

N

0   6 miles
0   12km

CONTENTS

GOING SLOW IN
SUSSEX

A couple of things about the title of this guide need explaining at the outset. First, this book covers my favourite parts of Sussex and not the whole of it; it's more an anthology of handpicked favourites than an exhaustive guidebook. Then there's that word 'Slow'. This is one of a series of Slow guides written by local authors. It's more than Slow food or Slow cities – it's more an attitude, taking time to ponder, savour, explore and reflect. Slow tourism is about changing down a gear and enjoying the essence of a place, rather than a headlong, high-carbon, non-sustainable, superficial dash around. Ultimately it's a realisation that one can often get a fuller picture by immersing oneself in a small area.

In this book I have attempted a Slow, sideways look at the familiar as well as the little known, celebrating the present as much as the past. I hope it goes beyond the obvious and will appeal to seasoned residents as well as newcomers. It is very much a selection of aspects that make the region special and I apologise to those places that haven't made it into these pages. I have lingered in a scattering of locales that struck me for their sense of place.

The Slow concept tunes in to a reaction against 'clone-town' Britain in an age of increasing standardisation, with the realisation that it makes no sense to travel without an awareness of one's surroundings. I feel that personal contact is one of the most rewarding aspects of travel, so I've chatted to local people including garden owners, craftsmen, curators of rural museums, shopkeepers and wildlife experts – among many others.

I do hope this book inspires you to encounter some of those special qualities of Sussex and the South Downs National Park. Perhaps to mingle among locals at a farmers' market and nibble a few samples of Sussex cheese, to become a volunteer at the likes of the Weald & Downland Living Museum or the Bluebell Railway, to take a guided walk with a naturalist to find wildflowers or butterflies on the grasslands

of the Downs, to drink a pint of Harvey's bitter after a walk on the heathy heights of the Ashdown Forest, to munch a fresh crab sandwich on the beach amid Brighton's wonderful seaside paraphernalia, or to go mushroom spotting in the woodlands of the Weald. There are endless ways to make the most of pottering around in the Slow lane.

I have lived in Lewes for over 20 years, and while researching this book realised that this wonderfully diverse corner of southeast England seems to expand as you get to know it. For all its centuries of civilisation this mere smudge at the bottom of the map of Britain is quite extraordinarily hard to know in its entirety. For me Sussex and the South Downs have no equal among lowland landscapes – seemingly made for savouring slowly and returning to again and again.

THE DOWNS, WEALD & COAST

The idea of Slow may have connotations of exploring rural places, but it also embraces the built-up environment. This is a long-settled area with distinctive historic towns and cities such as Chichester, Lewes, Rye, Petworth, Hastings, Midhurst, Brighton, Eastbourne and Arundel. Some of it feels hundreds of miles from London, yet the capital's proximity drew many here, and still does: it is dotted with country retreats ranging from diminutive beach houses to great rural estates. In the railway age, new money was tastefully deployed into creating some of the finest gardens in the country, with a notable concentration on the acid soils of the High Weald. Literary and artistic figures such as Henry James, Rudyard Kipling, Duncan Grant, Virginia Woolf, Eric Ravilious, Hilaire Belloc and Alfred Lord Tennyson revelled in the beauty of the countryside and attracted others to visit or join them.

This book includes the Sussex portion of the **South Downs National Park** – which in its entirety extends from the brink of Winchester in eastern Hampshire to Beachy Head, just above Eastbourne, and covers a good deal of the Weald in West Sussex, not geologically part of the South Downs but of very high landscape quality. Despite the massive pressures from the modern world and towns and cities that lie at close range, it's a remarkably rural area. In 2016 the national

◄ **1** The South Downs Way passes fields that bloom with poppies in summer (page 13).
2 The magnificent 15th-century Herstmonceux Castle (page 328).

THE SLOW MINDSET

Hilary Bradt, Founder, Bradt Guides

> We shall not cease from exploration
> And the end of all our exploring
> Will be to arrive where we started
> And know the place for the first time.
>
> T S Eliot, 'Little Gidding', *Four Quartets*

This series evolved, slowly, from a Bradt editorial meeting when we started to explore ideas for guides to our favourite part of the world – Great Britain. We wanted to get away from the usual 'top sights' formula and encourage our authors to bring out the nuances and local differences that make up a sense of place – such things as food, building styles, nature, geology, or local people and what makes them tick. Our aim was to create a series that celebrates the present, focusing on sustainable tourism, rather than taking a nostalgic wallow in the past.

So without our realising it at the time, we had defined 'Slow Travel', or at least our concept of it. For the beauty of the Slow movement is that there is no fixed definition; we adapt the philosophy to fit our individual needs and aspirations. Thus Carl Honoré, author of *In Praise of Slow*, writes: 'The Slow Movement is a cultural revolution against the notion that faster is always better. It's not about doing everything at a snail's pace, it's about seeking to do everything at the right speed. Savouring the hours and minutes rather than just counting them. Doing everything as well as possible, instead of as fast as possible. It's about quality over quantity in everything from work to food to parenting.' And travel.

So take time to explore. Don't rush it, get to know an area – and the people who live there – and you'll be as delighted as the authors by what you find.

park was designated a Dark Sky Reserve. The unifying feature of the South Downs themselves is chalk: they rise to no great height but have the knack of looking much larger than they are, and have a huge significance for the entire region. You can hardly fail to notice them – a long, sparsely populated range running west to east, with a steep escarpment along much of their northern sides, and shelving gently to the sea to the south. World War II propaganda posters exclaiming 'Britain: fight for it now' harnessed the emotional impact of the South Downs, the most English of landscapes – variously depicting the old village of Alfriston and a shepherd guarding the cliffs towards Belle Tout lighthouse in East Sussex.

The South Downs are the southernmost segment of the area's symmetrical geology. North to south it's basically an end-on sandwich of chalk, clay, sandstone, clay, and chalk again, with a few intervening complexities too: the northern layer of chalk is the North Downs, across Surrey and Kent, and the area between – known as the **Weald** – includes sandstone hills, huge country estates and an endless patchwork of hedge-lined fields and woodlands. The effect of this is that the area can show great unity if you travel west to east, but go north to south and it changes astonishingly fast. The coastal strip, hugely built up and suburban for the most part, has its great landmarks. Up on the South Downs, it is a land of dry valleys, rolling cornfields flecked with poppies, windblown hawthorn trees beside lone dew ponds and with skylarks and blue butterflies for company. Further into the Low Weald and High Weald it's a different world: convoluted heathlands, tile-hung cottages around triangular greens in woodland clearings, grand country houses set in sweeping parkland behind estate walls, and some of the lushest gardens you will find anywhere on this planet.

Sussex's best-known feature, its **coast**, is mostly built up, but is hugely rewarding if you pick your way around it carefully. Facing France and a potential invasion site for centuries, it has impressive and abundant relics from the Roman period to World War II that indicate its former defensive importance. Brighton, Eastbourne and Hastings each have their own personality, and less fêted spots like Shoreham and Bexhill deserve seeking out too. The shores reveal great beauty in the marshy expanses of Chichester Harbour and Rye Harbour, the sandy beaches at either end of Sussex (West Wittering and Camber Sands), the dizzying chalk cliffs between Seaford and Eastbourne, and the rugged sandstone heights east of Hastings.

SKYLARKS & DRAGONFLIES

I ventured to Woods Mill, the headquarters of the **Sussex Wildlife Trust**, and asked Mike Russell about wildlife in this area. 'The great thing about Sussex is its variety. It has the largest coverage of deciduous woodland in England, while the chalk grasslands harbour a range of blue butterflies. If there's one species that is the essence of the Downs, it's the skylark. Its UK population declined massively in the 1970s and 80s because of agricultural change, but many spots along the Downs are the best place

ROGER WILMSHURST/SUSSEX WILDLIFE TRUST

LAURENCE GOUGH/S

IAN STEWART/S

to hear it. Then the heathlands have many scarce specialities like black darter dragonflies, keeled skimmer dragonflies or small red damselflies, and attract special birds like nightjars and Dartford warblers. On the other hand, Rye Harbour, Pagham Harbour and Chichester Harbour are internationally important for migrating birds'.

LEARNING THE SLOW WAY

The variety of courses with a Slow theme really struck me while researching this book. Rural crafts and countryside skills can be learnt at the **Weald & Downland Living Museum** (wealddown.co.uk) near Chichester. **Plumpton College** (plumpton.ac.uk) and its Stanmer Park outpost, One Garden Brighton (onegardenbrighton.com), offer the chance to develop pastimes such as beekeeping, floristry, baking, pollinator-friendly gardening and fly fishing. The **Sussex Wildlife Trust** (sussexwildlifetrust.org.uk) has lively calendars of events including courses on nature and wildlife such as bushcraft, plant and tree identification and fungus forays. Another leading centre for nature, **WWT Arundel** (wwt.org.uk), runs courses on wildlife identification and much else. A number of businesses teach woodland and survival skills such as foraging, wild herbalism, astronomy and tracking animals, including **Wilderness Wood** (Hadlow Down wildernesswood.org), **Bison Bushcraft** (near Heathfield bisonbushcraft.co.uk), **So Sussex** (various locations near Brighton and Lewes sosussex.co.uk) and **Wowo** (near Sheffield Park wowo.co.uk).

DIGGING UP THE PAST

I've spent many hours with a trowel in hand exploring Sussex's archaeological secrets. The first time I went out was exactly as I'd hoped it would be – scraping and brushing away soft sand to reveal a huge Romano-British storage pot almost exactly as it had been left in the ground. It isn't always like that though: a whole week up on **Mount**

◀ **1** Ardingly Reservoir is one of the few large expanses of water in the southeast (page 240). **2** Sussex encompasses some of the best places to hear skylarks (page 13). **3** The South Downs has one of England's densest network of bridleways, making it prime territory for horseriders and mountain bikers. **4** The exceptional mosaics at Bignor Roman Villa (page 61).

Caburn near Lewes yielded only a single pottery sherd a little smaller than my thumbnail. The great thing about this area is that any interested novice can join in, through one of its very active archaeological societies. Along with the chalklands of Wessex, the South Downs were the birthplace of British archaeology in the late 19th century, and the tradition has continued. Modern excavations have shown that prehistoric people weren't in fact concentrated on the Downs – it's just easier to see the remains in the thin-soiled, grassy landscape – but you can't help imagining them striding along enjoying the same views, and if you know what to look for (page 139) you can easily find their flint tools just lying on the surface.

A TASTE OF SUSSEX

It's not hard to find high-quality locally produced food and drink in Sussex. On the coast, Hastings Old Town, for instance, has become a byword for fresh **fish**, and for fish and chips, and the recent proliferation of **farmers' markets** and **farm shops** has brought local food and its producers to the people. **Food festivals** have sprung up all over Sussex and there's something food- or drink-related somewhere in the county in every month of the year, including the Rye Bay Scallop Week in February (⊘ scallop.org.uk) and the Chilli Fiesta at West Dean College (near Chichester ⊘ westdean.org.uk) in early August, as well as various events in Brighton and Hove, Ardingly College, Lewes, Horsham and many other places.

A hundred years ago, pretty much every town in Sussex would have produced **beer**, with at least one brewery in operation, but things declined rapidly with takeovers by big breweries in the 1960s and 1970s. Harvey's Brewery (⊘ harveys.org.uk) in Lewes managed to weather that particular storm and is very much flourishing. The head brewer, Miles Jenner Miles, confesses to giving a daily prayer of thanks to the existence of the Campaign for Real Ale, without which many small breweries like his might have disappeared. And happily numerous other breweries

---

1 A swathe of wheat fields beneath the Downs near Amberley (page 84). **2** Sussex's wine scene is booming: sample local produce at vineyards such as Sedlescombe (page 327). **3** Harvey's has been brewing beer in Lewes since 1838 (page 178). **4** There are plenty of food markets and festivals to enjoy, including Rye Bay Scallop Week (see above). ▶

have opened in recent decades, including Beak (𝒸 beakbrewery.com) in Lewes and the Long Man Brewery (𝒸 longmanbrewery.com) in the Cuckmere Valley.

Cider is produced too, though not on the scale of the West Country. The best selection is at Middle Farm (near Firle 𝒸 middlefarm.com), where barrels are laid out in rows, according to sweetness.

A bigger story is Sussex's upward surge as a **wine** producer, with a great number of vineyards appearing in the last couple of decades. In 2023, a quarter of the wine produced in the UK was made in West and East Sussex. The soil in places, particularly near the Downs, is similar to that of the Champagne region in France. And the Sussex vineyards such as Ridgeview and Bolney are producing some exceptionally classy stuff, winning the major awards and, as one wine seller was happy to tell me, 'trouncing the French at their own game'. Rathfinny Wine Estate (𝒸 rathfinnyestate.com), just outside Alfriston, is on track to overtake the Kent-based big-hitters as the biggest wine producer in Britain.

HOW THIS BOOK IS ARRANGED

I have covered Sussex in five chapters that define themselves well geographically. Though it's tempting to stray over county boundaries, I've kept it strictly in Sussex. The coast, South Downs National Park and High and Low Weald are shared between chapters. The book begins with the major chunk of West Sussex, from Chichester Harbour to the Arun, and taking in the western Sussex Downs and the Weald as far as the Hampshire border; the next chapter follows the coastal strip through the main Sussex conurbation around Brighton, together with its hinterland in the Downs and picking out a few of the less-celebrated places further north. The third chapter focuses on Lewes, the Ouse and Cuckmere valleys and the best-known part of the undeveloped coast, past the Seven Sisters to Beachy Head. The fourth chapter explores the very different world of the High Weald, including Ashdown Forest and the world-famous gardens of the Weald, then the final chapter takes in the coast east of the national park, from Eastbourne to Hastings, and inland through 1066 Country and some other very rewarding parts of the High Weald.

Tourist information centres (alas, a threatened breed – most have now been replaced by websites) are listed at the beginning of each chapter along with other useful information sources.

MAPS

Each of the five chapters begins with a map, with places **numbered** on it to coincide with numbered headings in the text. The relevant Ordnance Survey maps and their grid references, marked ♀, are given for the detailed walks within the chapters, which also have sketch maps. Walks are indicated on the chapter maps via the ♀ symbol.

ACCOMMODATION, FOOD & DRINK

The places to stay reviewed in this book are a very small, personal selection of bed and breakfasts, campsites, self-catering cottages and hotels – places that struck me for their location, friendliness or character, or a mixture of all three.

The hotels, bed and breakfasts and hostels are indicated by the symbol ♠ under the heading for the nearest town or village in which they are located; self-catering options by 🏠. Camping options, which cover everything from full-on glamping to no-frills pitches, are indicated with a ▲ symbol.

I also recommend a number of favourite **cafés, pubs and restaurants** that specialise in locally sourced, sustainability-conscious meals and drinks, plus notable **food shops and markets**.

No charges have been made for inclusion of businesses in this guide.

PRACTICAL INFORMATION

Telephone numbers, marked with the symbol ♪, along with **websites** marked ♂, are included where I've thought it helpful. **Opening times** are susceptible to change, so rather than misleading you with specific times that might go out of date, I've kept this information very general, highlighting general periods of closure, for instance, flagged with the symbol ☺. **Postcodes** are given where possible; for places that don't have postcodes (including starting points for walks) I've given **grid references**, marked ♀.

GETTING THERE & AROUND

Sussex is quite a mixed bag when it comes to finding ways of reaching it. For **driving**, the A27 provides the easiest west–east route, but the A259 and A272 are much more fun; the latter has even inspired Dutchman Pieter Boogart to write a book (*A272, An Ode to a Road*) in homage to its glories. If venturing from London or further north, the A23/M23 make a practical if unlovely entrance, but there are plenty of more appetising, slower alternatives through the high ground of the Weald and over Ashdown Forest. In this book I've picked out some useful ways of **exploring areas without a car** – this can work very well in some parts, less so in others. When describing places of interest, I've mentioned how to get there by public transport wherever practical. For **bus** timetables, ⌀ traveline.info is handy. Most local bus operators offer day tickets, giving scope to visit a huge range of places for a fixed fare, though requiring a lot of careful reading of bus timetables. For **train travel**, the coast is mostly well served, and a handful of lines lead northwards to give a decent set of options: the regional map at the front of this book shows rail routes. DaySave tickets give unlimited travel on Southern rail services. Beware that at weekends services can often be subject to engineering works, and trains replaced by buses, which can be much slower.

WALKING & CYCLING

Here and there I have described and mapped out ten of my favourite **walks** in the region. I have also suggested others that are well publicised through websites or are ready-made trails. Sussex and the South Downs are extraordinarily rich in good walks – I've written numerous walking guides in the past, and this area really stands out for walks worth travelling across the country to do. Somehow the excellent rights-of-way network and diversity of the scenery, with a good smattering of viewpoints and manmade and natural places to discover, all combine to make this high-quality walking terrain.

The clearly marked **South Downs Way** is a source of many outstanding strolls and longer hikes from the Hampshire border to Beachy Head. Another waymarked National Trail, the new **King Charles III England Coast Path**, follows the shoreline of the English Channel. It's a work in progress; in Sussex, at the time of writing, the section from Wittering to Eastbourne is already open.

I've also highlighted some of the joys and logistics of cycling onroad and offroad in each chapter. You can cycle (or ride a horse) along the entire South Downs Way, for example, except the section down the Cuckmere Valley and along the Seven Sisters.

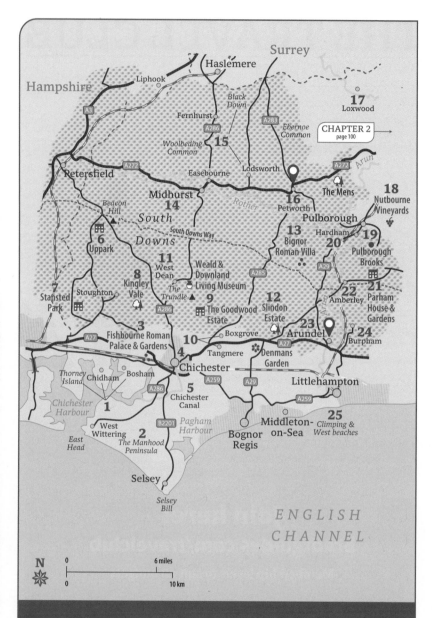

Surrey

Hampshire

Liphook

Haslemere

Black Down

17
Loxwood

Fernhurst

A286

A283

Ebernoe Common

CHAPTER 2
page 100

Woolbeding Common

15

Lodsworth

A272

Arun

Petersfield

A272

Easebourne

16

The Mens

Midhurst

14

Rother

Petworth

18
Nutbourne Vineyards

Beacon Hill

South

Pulborough

Hardham

19

Downs

South Downs Way

13
Bignor Roman Villa

20

6
Uppark

A285

A29

Pulborough Brooks

11
West Dean

Weald & Downland Living Museum

8
Kingley Vale

The Trundle

9
The Goodwood Estate

12
Slindon Estate

22
Amberley

21
Parham House & Gardens

7
Stansted Park

Stoughton

A286

23
Arundel

24
Burpham

3
Fishbourne Roman Palace & Gardens

10

Boxgrove

A27

Thorney Island

Chidham

Bosham

4

Tangmere

Denmans Garden

Chichester

A27

1

A286

5
Chichester Canal

A259

A29

Littlehampton

Pagham Harbour

West Wittering

B2201

25
Climping & West beaches

East Head

2
The Manhood Peninsula

Middleton-on-Sea

Bognor Regis

A259

Selsey

Selsey Bill

ENGLISH CHANNEL

N

| 0 | | 6 miles |
| 0 | | 10 km |

CHICHESTER HARBOUR TO THE ARUN

1
CHICHESTER HARBOUR TO THE ARUN

I have a soft spot for **Kingley Vale**, the mysterious yew forest on the Downs. No-one knows why it's there, and it's enough of a trek to mean that only the most dedicated get to it. From the top, the view is utterly sublime, far over **Chichester Harbour**, Sussex's answer to East Anglia – a lowland of great water channels and saltmarshes. This waterscape could hardly be more different from the South Downs, and makes best sense explored by boat; I particularly like the solar-powered catamaran that glides silently and slowly around the harbour – the perfect way of slowing down. At its northern end, Chichester is one of a quartet of sharply contrasting historic centres in this corner of Sussex, which along with Midhurst, Petworth and Arundel all have their special places to savour – the **Bishop's Palace Gardens** forming an unexpected haven in the heart of Chichester, Midhurst with its melodramatic **Cowdray Ruins**, Petworth for its juxtaposition with a huge park and house, and Arundel, where you can swim in a lido with a view of the castle or encounter the wildlife at the Wetland Centre.

Art is particularly strong here, with **Pallant House** in Chichester being home to one of the country's top modern art collections. **Petworth House** has the foremost art collection of any National Trust house – though for me the **Grinling Gibbons carvings** steal the show. **Stansted Park** and **Uppark** are fascinating houses to visit and compare, each destroyed by fire and rebuilt at either end of the 20th century. And more ancient offerings are there in the form of exceptional mosaics at **Bignor Roman Villa** and **Fishbourne Roman Palace**, and a host of the churches with medieval wall paintings, such as at Clayton, Hardham and Trotton.

In Loxwood and Chichester you can travel slowly by **canal boat** on a short cruise along canals being rescued by volunteers. The same spirit of voluntary dedication has gone wholeheartedly into two of the finest rural museums in this book – the **Weald & Downland Living Museum** in Singleton, and the **Amberley Museum**; both are in choice settings in the South Downs, with plenty else to justify staying and exploring. Amberley village is a picture of perfection with its thatched houses and views across **Amberley Wildbrooks Nature Reserve**, part of a watermeadows wetland that merges into **Pulborough Brooks RSPB reserve**.

Walking on the Downs escarpment is boosted by some glorious greensand countryside immediately north – as at **Bignor** for instance. But if there's a favourite view here, for me it is further north, in the High Weald, from the heights of **Black Down** or from the obscurity of **Woolbeding Common**, where you look to the Downs across a foreground of heather – a scene that almost appears too wild to be in Sussex.

Between 2014 and 2017, the Heritage Lottery-funded Secrets of the High Woods project, led by the South Downs National Park Authority, made a sensational **archaeological discovery** in this much-wooded part of the Sussex Downs, between the Hampshire border and the Arun. Lidar topographic scanning – which uses an aircraft-mounted laser-guided beam that can penetrate tree cover – helped the team reveal traces of a long-lost Roman road from Chichester to Arundel, and a huge, continuous system of Iron Age fields, some 600 sq miles in extent. The forest had protected their outlines for centuries; in a more open landscape, they would have been obliterated. Previously, it was thought that large-scale, organised cultivation had begun with the advent of the Romans, but this find took the story back many centuries earlier. So prehistoric does not necessarily equate to primitive.

GETTING AROUND

The hectic A27 and the more leisurely A272 form the main west–east routes. For a wonderful cross-section of West Sussex, drive along the A272 from the Hampshire border to **Midhurst** and **Petworth**, then pick up the A283 as it skirts **Pulborough Brooks**, **Parham Park** and **Steyning**.

TRAINS

The **West Coastway Line** between Southampton and Brighton stops at Havant (for Stansted Park), Emsworth, Nutbourne and Bosham (for Thorney Island, Chidham and Bosham Quay), Fishbourne (for the Roman Palace) and Chichester, with a branch to Littlehampton (handy for getting to the beach at Climping). The **Arun Valley Line**, which connects the central and western part of the West Coastway Line to the Brighton Main Line, stops at Arundel, Amberley, Pulborough and Horsham. It's very rewarding to walk between them and get the train back. The **Portsmouth Direct Line** from Woking follows the Hampshire–Sussex border and joins the West Coastway Line at Havant. Haslemere and Petersfield stations lie on the region's northwest doorstep; they're each around ten miles from Midhurst which, despite being a notable market town, lost all three of its railway lines in the mid-20th century.

BUSES

Chichester is a regional transport hub, with Stagecoach bus 60 running twice hourly to West Dean, the Weald & Downland Living Museum and Midhurst, and decent Stagecoach and Compass services to Pagham Harbour, West Wittering, Uppark, Petworth, Tangmere, Littlehampton and Arundel. **Midhurst** stands at a crossroads: as well as Stagecoach bus 60 running south, it has a useful southeast-bound service, Stagecoach bus 1, to Lodsworth (for Langham Brewery), Petworth, Pulborough (for Stopham and Nutbourne vineyards), Cootham (for Parham House), Findon (near Cissbury Ring) and Worthing. There are also Stagecoach buses from Midhurst heading north (70 to Haslemere station and Guildford) and west (92 to Petersfield station).

CYCLING

You can see quite a lot of the area **around Chichester** by using the city as a base and cycling out along designated routes that avoid the busy A27 (a no-go for cyclists). Several leisure routes start from the Chichester Cross: the **Salterns Way** (to West Wittering for East Head), the **Itchenor to Bosham Circular**, the **Bill Way** (to Pagham Harbour) and the **Centurion Way** (to West Dean). Visit ⥾ chichester.gov.uk/cycling for a route planner and downloadable maps.

Starting westwards, you can cycle along **Sustrans Route 2** via West Street, Westgate and an A27 underpass to Fishbourne Road (West), for **Fishbourne Roman Palace**. Next, carry on towards Broadbridge, turning south off Route 2 into the **Chichester Harbour Area of Outstanding National Beauty**. After Bosham and the seasonal ferry to

West Itchenor, you can explore the east side of the harbour to East Head via upgraded public footpaths and quiet lanes – handy for beating the traffic queues at summer weekends. The 12-mile **Salterns Way** follows the same route out of town, then turns south towards Apuldram and Birdham, before winding southwest to West Wittering. Meanwhile, Sustrans Route 2 continues west to Havant, then south to Hayling Island, where you can loop around the coast for views of Langstone Harbour, the Solent and the Isle of Wight.

Heading south, the **Bill Way** through North Mundham to **Sidlesham** has less going for it scenically but is a handy way to reach Pagham Harbour, from where you can explore **Selsey Bill** and **Bracklesham Bay** beach. There's also the **Chichester Canal towpath,** which heads south from Chichester canal basin (near the station), then west at Hunston to reach the marina at Birdham Pool.

Eastwards, the A259 between Chichester and Bognor Regis has a dedicated cycle path – no fun at all, but useful if you need to come that way.

Northwards, the **Centurion Way**, a route for cyclists and walkers, runs 6½ miles from Chichester to West Dean with wacky and entertaining **artworks** along the route. Some reflect the area's Roman heritage like the 'amphitheatre', while others are just plain quirky – such as a bridge hung with bits of dangling metal. Local schoolchildren helped in the making of a triumphal Roman Archway, topped by a prancing bull, a ship and various other devices. Start by heading west along West Street and Westgate, then turn north up Centurion Way, which follows the track bed of a long-defunct railway that ran between Chichester and Midhurst. After passing through Mid Lavant, the path continues to West Dean; from here, you could easily visit West Dean Gardens or the Weald & Downland Living Museum, and take a more energetic return route up to The Trundle and downhill for a glorious if bumpy mile to East Lavant.

Heading **into the South Downs**, cycling is particularly lovely west of the busy A283, where you're on to lush, forgotten country lanes that are too crooked and narrow for much traffic to bother with – I particularly enjoy the ride out past Bignor to Sutton, then north to Burton Mill and past an unexpected tract of heathland known as Lord's Piece. It's very sandy hereabouts, so the off-road cycling is completely useless – the only time I tried it, my bike sank into the sand after about 30 seconds,

TOURIST INFORMATION

General information ⟨ thegreatsussexway.org, sussexbythesea.com
Arundel ⟨ visitarundel.co.uk
Chichester Novium Museum, Tower St PO19 1QH ⟨ 01243 775888 ⟨ thenovium.org/chitic
Littlehampton ⟨ visitlittlehampton.co.uk
Midhurst ⟨ visitmidhurst.com
The South Downs Centre (South Downs National Park) North St, Midhurst GU29 9DH
⟨ 01730 814810 ⟨ southdowns.gov.uk

and I got off and pushed the rest. Up on the Downs, as usual, off-road is much better, with long lonely bridleways in all directions; as well as the **South Downs Way**, the **Monarch's Way** up from Houghton through Houghton Forest and along **The Denture** is a nice, steady way up, and Stane Street (page 62) is a Roman road cutting dead straight through the trees.

BIKE HIRE

App-Bike Chichester ⟨ app-bike.co.uk. Self-service bike hire.
Southern E-Bike Rentals Gravel Hill, Horndean PO8 0QE ⟨ 023 9241 4624
⟨ southernebikerentals.co.uk. Delivery available on request.
Southwater Cycles Bonnington Farm, nr Loxwood RH14 0RS ⟨ 01403 701002
⟨ southwatercycles.com. By the Wey and Arun cycle route and close to the Downs Link (page 104).

CHICHESTER HARBOUR & CHICHESTER

Forming the smallest **Area of Outstanding Natural Beauty** in the southeast, Chichester Harbour has a watery beauty that is unlike anywhere else in Sussex. Footpaths skirt parts of its shores, but it all makes best sense from the water – most easily done by taking a harbour boat tour from **West Itchenor**. Boating has been the thing in these parts for many centuries, with four broad water channels providing safe haven and trading routes. Fourteen villages dot the coast on the peninsulas that jut into the harbour. Nowadays leisure boating is very popular here: of 10,000 boats registered in the harbour, only 30 or 40 are working boats.

The water, intertidal mudflats and long coastline with its hinterland form a cherished site for wildlife. It encompasses the seventh largest **saltmarsh** in Britain, and the waters are home to more than 40 species of fish in addition to limpets, sponges, anemones, crabs and worms, while in excess of 55,000 birds are resident or pass through. The local **seal population** is particularly visible at low tide: their movements are tracked as they are fitted with GPS devices, with numbers generally in the 23–25 range; each seal has different markings, and their colourings are variously black, brown, tan or grey.

The boating routes are along four channels, running a total of 17 miles; around them are 53 miles of coastline, 33 of which are defended from coastal erosion by stone walls.

The **Chichester Harbour Conservancy** (⌗ conservancy.co.uk) undertakes the work of conservation, maintenance and improvement of the harbour. Its website is full of information about boat trips, nature events, talks, bird-watching, water sports and recommended walks, including downloadable route maps. By the waterside, the scenery is utterly beautiful; inland it's flat and arable. Some paths may be submerged at very high tides; phone the Harbour Office, Itchenor (⌗ 01243 512301) for information.

 ## BOATING IN CHICHESTER HARBOUR

The sheltered waters are superb boating territory, with several ways of taking to the water, including:

Chichester Harbour Water Tours The St, Itchenor PO20 7AW ⌗ 01243 672088 ⌗ chichesterharbourwatertours.co.uk. Trips around the harbour, with seal-watching year-round and birdwatching in winter. You can charter an entire boat for your own party.
Chichester Watersports Coach Rd, Westhampnett PO18 0NX ⌗ 01243 776439 ⌗ chichesterwatersports.co.uk ⌗ Apr–Oct. The main watersports centre in the area, offering kayaking, wakeboarding, waterskiing and stand-up paddleboarding on a lake.
Oyster Boat *Terror* Thorney Rd, Emsworth PO10 9BP ⌗ oysterboatterror.org.uk ⌗ summer only. This ominous-sounding offering is in fact a very lovely way of passing a couple of hours: the vintage 1890s oyster boat *Terror* tours the most beautiful parts of Emsworth Harbour, and is available for charter.
Solar Heritage Boat Tours The St, Itchenor PO20 7AW ⌗ 01243 513275 ⌗ conservancy. co.uk ⌗ see website. Excellent value, 90-minute general, birdwatching, history and nature tours of Chichester Harbour on a solar-powered catamaran. This is the essence of Slow travel:

you glide across the water in a stable, fume-free, environmentally friendly boat. There's commentary from the crew, and binoculars are passed around as you travel. Powered by solar panels attached to the roof, this was one of three craft once used to ferry people to an alternative-energy exhibition in the Three Lakes region in Switzerland. 'She's quiet, doesn't scare wildlife, uses no oil or lubricants and doesn't cause a wake,' said my guide. One of the other craft crossed the Atlantic to the US, where it faces retirement in a museum; I think this one's fared better. It's available for charter.

1 THORNEY ISLAND, CHIDHAM & BOSHAM

Train to Emsworth, Nutbourne or Bosham, West Coastway Line (Southampton–Brighton); Stagecoach Coastliner bus 700 (Portsmouth–Chichester; three per hour Mon–Sat, less frequent Sun)

Chichester Harbour comprises four peninsulas with relatively limited road access. T-shaped **Hayling Island**, a centre of yachting and windsurfing, bounds the west side and is linked to the mainland by Langstone Bridge and by ferry to Portsea. It lies in Hampshire, with a three-mile beach along its southern end; the Hayling Island Sailing Club (HISC) is the largest such club in the harbour.

At the western end of Sussex's coastline, **Thorney Island**, joined to the mainland by a land reclamation project, was taken over by the RAF as an airfield in the 1930s. Then the village of West Thorney was closed, including its 13th-century church. The RAF moved out in 1976 and for a while it became a haven for the Vietnamese 'boat people' fleeing turmoil in their country at the end of the Vietnam War. It remains MOD property,

"It's an outstandingly scenic and very easily followed coastal walk which you can start from just south of Emsworth."

with the Royal Artillery now in possession of a peninsula, and is largely Ministry of Defence land and out of bounds because of its Royal Artillery base. Happily, its shores are accessible by the Sussex Border Path which runs the entire way around the 8½-mile perimeter, giving an outstandingly scenic and very easily followed coastal walk which you can start from just south of Emsworth (which is on the Southampton–Brighton West Coastway railway), and you can look in on West Thorney Church. The military establishment gives it an intriguingly sinister ambience: you press a buzzer to gain permission to enter, a camera zooms in to identify you and a voice asks you for your name, address and purpose of visit. The southerly extremity, Longmere Point, gives an exhilarating sense of being alone with the elements right in the middle of the huge natural harbour. This walk (one of a series downloadable from ⏣ conservancy.co.uk) offers some wonderful birdwatching and seal-spotting opportunities. Allow 3½ hours and take binoculars, food and drink.

Further east, the village of **Chidham** has its own peninsula ending at Cobnor Point (which occasionally gets submerged at high tide), with views across the water to Bosham, and just offshore a lone stretch of dyke that marks a failed 19th-century land reclamation project. The shoreline walk gives a consistently interesting circuit of five miles, of which a mile and a half are inland link sections along quiet lanes and across fields; there's a car park on the south side of Chidham. The 17th-century pub on the west side of Chidham, the Old House at Home (✆ 01243 572477 ⏣ theoldhouseathome.co.uk), serves sandwiches, soup and heartier pub fare. You can also start from Nutbourne station to the north, which is on the West Coastway Line (Southampton–Brighton), and adds an extra mile. Again, the whole route is on ⏣ conservancy.co.uk.

On the next peninsula to the east, **Bosham** (pronounced 'Bozzum') has a very pretty waterfront with cottages and the yard of the Anchor Bleu pub looking out over waddling ducks and the yacht-filled Chichester Channel. Car-bobbing is big here: avoid parking on the waterfront, unless you really know what the tides are doing, as oblivious visitors are repeatedly foiled by high tides and find their vehicles semi-submerged. You only have to look at the barriers in front of the garden gates here to realise that those signs saying 'this road floods each tide' are serious. Indeed, not messing about with the tide is a long-standing business here: **King Canute**, who had a palace here in the 11th century, famously failed to turn the tide back here when he wanted to demonstrate to his fawning courtiers that even he couldn't command at will. His daughter is thought to have been buried in Holy Trinity Church, in one of two stone-slabbed coffins at the east end of the nave. This is the oldest Christian community in Sussex, one that has certainly existed here since the 7th century. The 11th-century horseshoe-shaped chancel arch is said to be just post

1 High tide laps the village street of Bosham. **2** The enticing stretch of sand at West Wittering Beach. **3** Chichester Harbour is best experienced from the water. **4** An impressive mosaic at Fishbourne Roman Palace. ▶

Norman Conquest, although part of the chancel layout and the tower are Saxon. You'll find a reproduction of part of the *Bayeux Tapestry* depicting Bosham Church (the only church depicted on the tapestry), from where Harold II sailed to Normandy in 1064 to get William's assent to support his claim to the English throne – an overturned promise if there ever was one, as William conquered England two years later. In the churchyard, several sad epitaphs on tombstones act as reminders of man's uneasy alliance with the water.

South of Bosham a **ferry** (✆ 07970 378350 🖫 itchenorferry.co.uk ⊙ roughly every 15 mins: May–Sep daily; Oct–Apr Sat–Sun) takes foot passengers and bicycles across to West Itchenor, a starting point for boat trips.

2 THE MANHOOD PENINSULA: WEST WITTERING TO PAGHAM HARBOUR

Stagecoach buses 52 & 53 (Chichester–Witterings; four per hour Mon–Sat, less frequent Sun) or 51 (Chichester–Selsey; three per hour Mon–Sat, less frequent Sun)

Sussex's southern extremity between the Chichester Channel and Bognor Regis is termed the Manhood peninsula – a name probably derived from 'men's wood' or common land. The flat, fertile farmlands are interrupted by water channels and on the eastern side by Pagham Harbour, making it extremely fiddly to travel west to east around the coast. The villages are mostly modern and suburban-looking, though some parts, such as the western side of Bognor and West Wittering, have quite a show of rather lovely mock-Tudor thatched residences.

West Wittering has by far the best beach in West Sussex, a long, glorious expanse of sand, flanked by that great rarity for Sussex – sand dunes – and a multicoloured row of beach huts. The beach attracts nose-to-tail jams along its approach roads at summer weekends; the signposted **Salterns Way** bike path from Chichester makes a useful way of avoiding the queues and meanders for an agreeable 11 miles around quiet farmland, passing close to **Dell Quay**, the former port for Chichester, and two boating marinas at Birdham. From there it is a short stroll to National Trust-owned **East Head**, a sandy peninsula that has rotated some 90 degrees over a couple of centuries; it gives views over nearby Hayling Island and towards the Isle of Wight. The long beach extends along **Bracklesham Bay**, which has shallow, sandy waters, ideal for families. Famously this is fossil-hunting territory, where it is possible to find fossilised sharks' teeth, shells (including turritella shells, typically an inch or two in length, and oyster shells), ray fish and bits of turtle shell – dating back 45 million years to when this was a tropical sea. The best place to look is immediately east from Bracklesham car park, towards Selsey, towards the end of the shingle. Specimens often wash up on the sand, so you don't need to dig down. The sandy, shallow bay makes for very gentle, family-style bathing, and there's miles of it.

Selsey Bill is the most southerly point in Sussex. No-one could claim it as one of nature's great glories, but the beach westwards is extremely inviting on a summer's day. Poke around the amorphous, mostly modern village of Selsey that spreads around the Bill and you'll find the lifeboat station, the early 19th-century tower mill and a few houses adapted with much ingenuity from railway carriages. These inter-wars plotlands are becoming something of a rarity nationally, as the more temporary structures have been

"You'll find the early 19th-century tower mill and a few houses adapted with much ingenuity from railway carriages."

replaced, but at **Pagham Beach** there's an even richer concentration of splendidly individualistic adapted single-storey dwellings and railway carriages with names like Pagham Halt and Sea Sidings along a grid of unmade roads. Between here and Selsey, 50 Mulberry Harbours were assembled during World War II in preparation for the invasion of Normandy; one of these failed to be raised, and its remains are visible at low tide.

Pagham Harbour, a beautiful, almost landlocked water, is the most easterly and smallest harbour of the Solent and forms part of the eponymous RSPB reserve that includes shingle, saltmarsh, mudflats, farmland and copses. Of international importance for wildlife, it attracts numerous wildfowl and waders in autumn and winter, and summer migrants such as wheatears, sandwich terns, brent geese and curlews. Rare plants such as the childling pink flourish in the shingle ridges along the coast. You can walk virtually the whole way around Pagham Harbour by means of waterside footpaths, and some stretches are suitable for wheelchairs; note that some parts can be wet at any time of year, even at low tide. A self-guided nature trail starts from near the visitor centre south of Sidlesham, on the west side of the water, and a hide nearby looks on to Ferry Field, a part of the reserve to which there is otherwise no public access. From the Bognor Regis side to the east you can start either from a car park at the far end of the shore near the harbour mouth, or from the 13th-century church at the old part of Pagham village, and walk along the inland side of the water along a raised dyke.

¶¶ FOOD & DRINK

Anchor Bleu High St, Bosham PO18 8LS ✆ 01243 573956 ⊗ anchorbleu.co.uk. With a terrific position by the water's edge, this pub is known for local fish and seafood. There's a cosy bar (which can get very full) and a small back terrace with memorable views.

Crab & Lobster Mill Lane, Sidlesham PO20 7NB ✆ 01243 641233 ⊗ crab-lobster.co.uk. Tranquilly placed rural dining pub on the northern side of Pagham Harbour, between the visitor centre and Pagham Church. It offers good, though expensive, locally sourced food (particularly fish and shellfish), stylish bedrooms and a two-bedroom self-catering cottage. If you're wandering in from a walk and just want a pint or one of its well-chosen wines by the glass, that's OK too – there's a pubby little bar and an idyllic back terrace overlooking the reserve.

3 FISHBOURNE ROMAN PALACE & GARDENS

Roman Way, Fishbourne PO19 3QR ✆ 01243 785859 ⊗ sussexpast.co.uk; train to Fishbourne (West Coastway Line, Southampton–Brighton); Stagecoach Coastliner bus 700 (Portsmouth–Chichester; three per hour Mon–Sat, less frequent Sun); Sustrans National Cycle Route 2

Most Roman villas in Britain were fairly modest country houses, but Fishbourne – a couple of miles west of Chichester city centre – is something else: unique in Britain (as far as anyone knows) and built on the scale of an imperial palace. What you see are the excavated floor-level remains of one side of a complex which enclosed a great quadrangle of formal gardens – the other sides extended right across to the present village main street, so most of the site is tantalisingly partly buried under modern housing. A waterside landing stage was probably the main way of arriving in Roman times, when Chichester Harbour was navigable further inland. You can get an idea of the palace's **original harbour setting** by taking Mill Lane, past the duck pond (a former spring in Roman times) – but reeds make it hard to see much.

A **model** of the palace helps you get your bearings and a **film show** cleverly recreates how the palace is thought to have looked. It's also worth seeing what is on – there are daily guided tours, and often demonstrations of Roman crafts, as well as special events and re-enactments some weekends. The **Collections Centre** has handling tours of artefacts (from Chichester and from the palace) on some days; otherwise you can go in and have a look through the windows and perhaps see highly skilled conservators at work.

Fishbourne is absolutely huge. There were more than 100 rooms, making it the largest Roman building yet found north of the Alps: a standard-size British villa would fit into half the garden. In Italy, however, there were similarly palatial villas, often, like Fishbourne, visible from the sea. As many as a hundred people may have lived here, enjoying the luxuries of underfloor heating, baths, fine wines and tableware – it would have positively bustled. Fishbourne is even grander than anything that would normally

"A hundred people may have lived here, enjoying the luxuries of underfloor heating, baths, fine wines and tableware."

have been provided for an imported Roman governor, and was started very early in the Roman period. This has prompted theories that the conquerors had it built as a very public reward for a British ruling family who cooperated with the invasion.

The key figure here – though he did not live to see Fishbourne at its grandest – was probably Togidubnus, the enigmatic local king referred to on the Togidubnus stone found in Chichester and now built into the wall of the Council House (page 38). He may have lived in Rome in his youth and have been brought to power by the Romans: some believe he used his influence to make Fishbourne an early safe haven for the Roman army. But so far there is little direct evidence about him. Finding his tomb would be a major coup.

Fishbourne's **mosaics** are surprisingly varied. The black and white geometric ones date from the time the palace was built and are some of the earliest in Britain; the ones with mythological creatures are later. Some of the designs are mysterious: the so-called shell mosaic appears to be two scallop shells, but Italian workers restoring it in the 1990s referred to it as a peacock. Cupid on a Dolphin, the best preserved and most famous, has a pronounced dip in it, because it was laid over an older rubbish pit which then subsided. Excavations in 1979 found that there had been another mosaic underneath. The borders of the Medusa mosaic were bungled – apparently the creation of an inexperienced craftsman.

FISHBOURNE'S REDISCOVERY

There were a few clues before: a 'Roman urn' mentioned on old maps, a 19th-century bill of sale for a house mentioning 'a curious Roman pavement in the back garden' and the story of a schoolgirl learning about the Romans who went out to dig in the nearby field and (as she had expected) found a mosaic straight away. However, it was workmen laying a water main in 1960 who reported the site. There was huge excitement, along with fear that the farmland could be lost to housing development or roadbuilding. A £50,000 donation bought the field for the Sussex Archaeological Society in 1963, and volunteers excavated the site over nine summers. Many eminent archaeologists started their professional careers here, including Barry Cunliffe, a Cambridge undergraduate when he started directing the work. 'The most memorable time was the last day of the first season,' he said. 'What they found just below the ploughsoil was the Dolphin mosaic. We just stood there on the grass looking down on this mosaic, and saying "it can't be true, this is absolutely amazing!"'

The **museum**, near the entrance desk, has a choice collection of finds. There are fragments of delicately painted wall plaster, a sculpture fragment of a boy's head, possibly Nero, and a life-size reconstruction of part of a room with furniture and painted walls. Some of the tiles bear footprints and pawprints from when they were being made. The **shop** has plenty of replica Roman souvenirs – siege machines, miniature caligulae (Roman soldiers' sandals), coins and so on.

Remarkably the bedding trenches for the Roman **garden**, cut into the local clay, survived in the archaeology. The intricate, wiggly hedging patterns of what was probably the first formal garden to be laid out in Britain have been re-planted, and on the far side you can see an engaging reconstruction of a Roman potting shed, complete with the voice of a grumpy gardener.

The palace was eventually destroyed by fire around AD270–280 – this may have been an accident, or an attack by raiders from the sea. You can see where stone from the ruined building was taken away – some of this may well have ended up in Chichester's city walls – and where later burials were cut through the floor. In one room the mosaic has collapsed back into pre-existing post holes of a storage building or granary dating from the time of the Roman invasion. Within a few hundred years the remains of Fishbourne were hidden beneath fields, and faded from local memory until its dramatic rediscovery in 1960.

4 CHICHESTER

🏠 **4 Canon Lane**

West Coastway Line (Southampton–Brighton); regional bus hub; EV charging at County Hall

Very different in feel from anywhere else in Sussex, Chichester is remarkably orderly and uncomplicated, with its hot-cross-bun layout of circular walls enclosing a simple crisscross of streets – named simply North Street, East Street, South Street and West Street, the whole presided over by the massive presence of the medieval cathedral standing just a few paces away from the Chichester Cross. The settlement originated in Roman times as Noviomagus Reginorum ('new market of proud people'), when the city walls were erected; their medieval successors follow the same line, and much of it can be followed on foot. There are bits and pieces of Roman reminders here and

"Chichester is remarkably orderly and uncomplicated, with its hot-cross-bun layout of circular walls."

there – a corner of Little London car park harbours some fragments of Roman columns from public buildings that stood nearby, and beneath the Council House in North Street is a stone inscription for a temple dedication.

With its impressive legacy of medieval buildings and handsome Georgian houses, Chichester is a hugely satisfying place to walk around. Just about all the interesting features are contained within the town walls. It's very pedestrian-friendly: although it's usually pretty buzzy with shoppers, students and tourists, the pace is leisurely rather than hectic. By contrast, however, walking out of town isn't at all appealing, except along the canal towpath; the busy ring road is daunting and uninviting.

Chichester Tour Guides (✆ 01243 850533 ⬧ chtg.co.uk) offer general-interest and themed **guided walks** (fee payable), led by qualified guides. Their City Highlights tour leaves from the cathedral bell tower on Sundays. It's best to pre-book.

The substantial **town walls** still stand mostly intact, and are rewarding to walk around. Particularly fine sections are reached just beyond the Bishop's Palace Gardens, and around Priory Park.

At the meeting of the four main streets, the **Market Cross** bristles with pinnacles, is capped by a weathervane and has a central column supported by eight flying buttresses. Erected by Bishop Edward Storey in 1501 and built of stone from Caen in France, it served as a shelter for traders who could not afford their own market stall and was in use until the market house was erected in North Street in 1807.

On pedestrianised North Street is the Palladian red-brick **Council House**, where embedded into the wall behind glass beyond the arches is the Neptune and Minerva Stone. Discovered in a neighbouring cellar, it records a dedication of a Roman temple to the gods of the sea and mentions Togidubnus, or Cogidubnus, who may have been associated with Fishbourne Roman Palace (page 34). The Assembly Room in the building dates from 1783; the great violinist Paganini and pianist Liszt played recitals there.

Much of the pleasure in strolling around the city centre is venturing beyond the main four streets. In St Martin's Street, blue doors signify properties belonging to **St Mary's Hospital** (⊘ stmarysalmshouses. org.uk), an almshouse founded nearby in 1158 and moved here in 1252 – the Gothic arched doors of the main hospital building are still in evidence. The chapel is not open except by appointment but if you peer from the car park behind you can see the chapel's vast medieval roof. From here, you can continue into Little London and on to **Priory Park**, with its beautifully placed cricket ground and the remains of a motte in the park's northeast corner – a prominent lump by the cricket pitch. A Coade stone statue of Neptune, formerly positioned over the public water conduit in South Street, lurks by the bowling green. Nearby is the late 13th-century medieval **Guildhall**, originally the chancel of a Franciscan friary and given to the city after Dissolution; it has also served as town hall and courthouse – William Blake was put on trial here for sedition, but acquitted.

"The Guildhall has also served as a courthouse – William Blake was put on trial here for sedition, but acquitted."

To arrange a visit to the Guildhall, ask at the **Novium Museum** (1 Tower St, PO19 1QH ✆ 01243 775888 ⊘ thenovium.org ⊙ Tue–Sat; free entry). Worth a visit in its own right, this pleasing contemporary building houses an excellent collection of artefacts relating to local history, and offers family activities, talks and research facilities. At the bottom you look from a balcony down to the on-site remains of a Roman public bath unearthed in the 1970s, with a slide show projected on the rear wall cleverly evoking the bath as it was; on display are items found in the excavations, such as hairpins, perfume bottles, gaming counters, tweezers and jewellery. The two upstairs galleries house temporary exhibitions, as well as permanent historical and themed displays.

In the southeast quadrant of the city, North Pallant, East Pallant, South Pallant and West Pallant constitute the **Pallants**, at the hub of Georgian Chichester. The name comes from 'palatinate' – the prince concerned being the Archbishop of Canterbury, who owned this area. The houses (including Pallant House Gallery, page 42) are full of period details – including imposing entrances and fine brickwork, as well as boot scrapers installed in the days when sheep and cattle were a common sight on the streets and there was generally more muck around than now. Tucked round in St John's Street and now redundant, the octagonal **Chapel of St John the Evangelist** is a Grade I-listed Georgian proprietary chapel of 1813, one of the few of its period in southern England to survive untouched – it was built at a time of chronic overcrowding of Church of England churches in the city. The chapel was financed by renting and selling pew space, and apart from the insertion of Victorian pews its layout remains intact, with box pews in the gallery. Most unusually, the triple-decker pulpit is in its original position.

There's more art to enjoy east of the Cross at **Oxmarket Contemporary** (St Andrew's Court, off East St, PO19 1YH ℰ 01243 779103 ⊘ oxmarket. org; free entry), a volunteer-run exhibition space in a converted church that has frequently changing exhibitions of paintings, decorative art, sculpture and photography.

Chichester Cathedral
⊘ chichestercathedral.org.uk; free entry (donation expected)

Chichester has the only medieval cathedral in England within sight of the sea. Sailors who just happened to be looking the right way at the right time one day in winter 1861 would have witnessed its spire collapsing entirely, after months of shoring-up operations to rectify the alarming cracks that had appeared over the preceding months, these a result of the removal of a stone screen that was evidently holding the whole thing up. The cathedral had caught fire twice during the 12th century; stone vaulting then replaced the wooden roof, and an elegant extension was added behind the choir. The medieval builders removed the bells to a separate belfry built of Isle of Wight sandstone, although this has stood the test of time less well than the Caen stone of the cathedral. A massive restoration project took place in the mid 1950s

after the foundations proved wobbly in the extreme. More happily, in 2002 peregrine falcons took up occupancy on the spire and have nested there annually from April to June since, swooping from great heights to get their prey; a webcam (⌂ chichesterperegrines.co.uk) captures their comings and goings.

Completed under Bishop Luffa in 1108, the cathedral has been altered in every century since. In the retrochoir you can spot the transition from rounded arch to pointed arch. Particularly fascinating are the monuments and art, ancient and modern. Touring the building anti-clockwise from the entrance, you encounter two exceptionally lifelike stone carvings depicting Lazarus at Bethany, dating from 1125 but rediscovered in 1829, close to an exposed section of 2nd-century mosaic – part of a Roman building discovered in the foundations in 1966 – and Graham Sutherland's painting *Noli Me Tangere* (1961), showing Christ ascending a staircase on his way to the Father (shown as an eye-like aperture in the wall). Next comes John Piper's notable tapestry woven in France in 1966 and depicting the Trinity and the Evangelists, the latter symbolised by beasts; then the vibrantly coloured window by Marc Chagall. In the nave, a glass panel gives a view of a now-subterranean section of Roman mosaic.

Further round is the Arundel Tomb – which inspired a poem by Philip Larkin ('and that faint hint of the absurd – the little dogs under their feet') – of the 13th Earl of Arundel (died 1376) holding hands with his lady, who is turned towards him in a gesture of unmistakable tenderness. Much less celebrated (partly tucked behind display boards), to the left as you enter, in the northwest corner, is the memorial to Matthew Heather Quantock, drowned in a skating accident in 1812 aged 30 – surely the only memorial of its kind in an English cathedral, with its intricately carved skates: 'Gay pastime oft, in man's mysterious doom, has prov'd a prelude to an early tomb…' A marble statue by sculptor Edward Carew commemorates the first person to die in a railway accident, the Rt Hon William Huskisson MP, shown as a Roman senator, in a toga: he died

◄ CHICHESTER: **1** The time-warp cottages and gardens of Vicars Close, with the cathedral spire behind. **2** The Palladian-style Council House is one of the city's many gems of Georgian architecture. **3** Housed in a converted church, Oxmarket Contemporary holds changing exhibitions. **4** Peregrine falcons have nested on the cathedral spire since 2002. **5** Enjoy a trip along the Chichester Canal on the *Kingfisher* boat.

at the opening of the London and Manchester Railway in 1830 when he got out of his railway carriage to greet the Duke of Wellington and failed to notice the *Rocket* approaching on the other track – it ran over his leg and he died a few hours later.

To learn more, you could join a guided tour, which for groups of five or fewer are free, although the usual entry donation is expected. Options include a general overview to the cathedral's history, art and architecture; a visit to the Song School, Cathedral Library and Bishop's Chapel; and an art tour. To ensure an expert guide is available, enquire online in advance.

The **cathedral precincts** make up one of my favourite urban spaces of any place in this book. Beyond the cloisters – built as passageways around the burial ground rather than for any monastic purposes, as the cathedral was never a monastery – and shop and café is **Vicars Close**, built in the 15th century for the Vicars Choral, who officiated at services, and with lavishly flower-filled front gardens. This leads into Canon Lane (also reached through the archway of 16th-century Canon Gate from South Street), which ends by the entrance to the private Bishop's Palace. Here is one of the glories of Chichester that many visitors miss, the tucked-away, surprisingly spacious and blissfully free-access **Bishop's Palace Gardens**, which date in part back to the 12th century and provide the finest picnic spot in the city, with the cathedral peeping up above a pergola walk and Tudor wall. An arboretum spreads across much of the garden, containing many rarities. You can also get access here to the top of the city wall, including a Roman bastion.

Pallant House Gallery
9 North Pallant ✆ 01243 774557 ⌂ pallant.org.uk; free entry to certain exhibitions

Justifying a special visit to Chichester in itself, Pallant House Gallery occupies a Queen Anne house of 1712 – nicknamed Dodo House because of the un-ostrich-like ostriches (the crests of the Peckham family for whom it was built) flanking the main entrance – in the middle of the city-centre area known as the Pallants. In 1982 Pallant House opened its doors as one of the finest modern art galleries in the south, and since then has gone from strength to strength thanks to a major extension in 2006 that quadrupled the exhibition space, enabling exhibitions that have drawn widespread acclaim from the press. The room attendants are all volunteers ('Our volunteers are our lifeblood and we literally couldn't open our doors each day without them,' explained a member of staff), and passionate about art, so it's well worth asking them about their favourite pictures. There's free access to spaces at ground level – including the De'Longhi Print Room, art reference library, café and restaurant, and the garden designed by Christopher Bradley-Hole, Chelsea gold winner, with its outdoor sculpture displays (changing roughly once a year) and a geometrically shaped canopy of London plane trees.

"The volunteers are all passionate about art, so it's well worth asking them about their favourite pictures."

Among the highlights are many works by St Ives artists; a British Pop Art collection including *Swingeing London 67* by Richard Hamilton, taken from a photo of the charge at Chichester Magistrates Court of Mick Jagger and art dealer Robert Fraser after a drugs raid in West Sussex; *The Beatles 1962* by Peter Blake (of the Fab Four before they became famous; pity they never signed their names into the spaces allocated to them on the painting); several works by David Bomberg, a British painter influenced by Picasso, Derain and Modigliani; and Degas' drawing *Femme se Peignant* (c1887–90), which provides an international context to the core of the collection and was previously owned by the unconventional socialite Gladys Deacon, Duchess of Marlborough. Much of the gallery space is devoted to changing exhibitions, so it's never quite the same on successive visits: a place to return to again and again.

Essentially this is a collection of collections assembled by various art lovers with modern British art at its core, such as the founding collection from Chichester's Dean Walter Hussey, including works by Graham Sutherland and John Piper. Another donor was Professor Colin St John ('Sandy') Wilson, who contributed some of the British Pop Art as well as the likes of Lucian Freud and Eduardo Paolozzi. St John Wilson along with his wife M J Long and Rolfe Kentish were the architects of the daring new extension, which was a challenging project given its location in a conservation area and adjoining a Grade I-listed building. It may have raised a few eyebrows locally when it was being erected but I find it admirably fits into a Georgian streetscape without attempting pastiche. The contemporary rooms in the gallery are elegantly simple, with natural, reflected lighting. Also of note are displays made up of two miniature galleries – like doll's houses, except they resemble tiny art galleries with genuine works by the artists themselves, including paintings by Duncan Grant and Vanessa Bell of the Charleston group.

On the staircase of the old house hangs a work from the contemporary installation series – a rolling programme responding to the historic staircase itself or to the permanent collection – variously over the years having featured ceramics, narrative tapestries, large-scale paintings and in one instance tubes of glass relating to the bannisters.

EVENTS

On the north side of the city in Oaklands Park, the distinctive 1960s Modernist structure of **Chichester Festival Theatre** (⊘ cft.org.uk) continues the fine tradition initiated by its first director, Sir Laurence Olivier, and ranks as one of the leading theatre venues in the Southeast. Its festival season runs from April to October, with productions often transferring to London or abroad, and there are touring shows during the winter.

Chichester Cathedral hosts classical-music concerts all year round and, in May or June of even-numbered years, a four-day **Festival of Flowers**.

The eclectic, month-long **Festival of Chichester** (⊘ festivalofchichester.co.uk ⊙ Jun–Jul) features classical music, jazz, rock, pop, jazz, blues and world music as well as theatre, talks, walks, cinema and exhibitions. The Novium Museum (page 38) acts as the box office.

SPECIAL STAYS

George Bell House, 4 Canon Lane Cathedral Cl, PO19 1PX ⊘ 01243 813586 ⊘ chichestercathedral.org.uk. With eight simple but pleasant rooms, this moderately priced guesthouse, owned by the cathedral, is available to guests when not required for visiting clergy. A former archdeaconry, it's in a fine, peaceful location, with free parking and views of the Deanery, Bishop's Palace Garden and cathedral.

FOOD & DRINK

The city centre offers plenty of opportunities for eating, drinking and assembling picnics (particularly idyllic picnic spots are the Bishop's Palace Gardens and Priory Park).

Cloisters Café Chichester Cathedral Cloisters, PO19 1PX ⊘ 01243 211054 ⊘ cloisterskitchengarden.co.uk. Fine cathedral café serving breakfast, lunch and snacks from fair-trade suppliers, with a conservatory-like space and (best of all) a garden. It's well tucked away; lively chatter announces you've found the spot.

Farmers' Market East St, PO19 1HA ⊙ first & third Fri morning of each month. All stallholders are based within 50 miles of Chichester and grow, rear, bake or preserve their own produce.

Little London 35 Little London, PO19 1PL ✆ 01243 774900 ♂ littlelondoncafe.co.uk. Bright and contemporary café in a slim Georgian house with modern prints on the wall, good light meals, sandwiches and afternoon tea.

Pallant Café Pallant House Gallery, PO19 1TJ ✆ 01243 770827 ♂ pallantcafe.co.uk. Offers seasonal lunches and occasional supper events in a stylish, glass-walled interior. The tree-shaded courtyard with sculptures is an idyllic spot to linger on a warmish day. Accessible even if you're not visiting the gallery.

5 Chichester Canal

For details of boat trips (worth booking) ✆ 01243 771363 ♂ chichestercanal.org.uk; train to Chichester, West Coastway Line (Southampton–Brighton)

It is easy to miss Chichester's very own canal, just south of the railway station, which runs four miles from here to a large yacht marina near Birdham, on the Chichester Channel of Chichester Harbour. Opened in 1823 to carry coal to the local gasworks and last used commercially in 1906, this was part of the Portsmouth and Arundel Canal – itself a link in a waterway system forming a route from London and Portsmouth, that was used as a through route up to 1855, including a ship canal from the harbour to Chichester capable of taking vessels up to 85ft long. After it carried its last cargo, it was left to rack and ruin before a band of volunteers formed a society and took it over in 1973.

"After it carried its last cargo, it was left to rack and ruin before a band of volunteers took it over in 1973."

One of the long-standing volunteers told me how things have changed. 'It was chocker with weeds. The basin was cleared first. It took a huge effort by a dedicated group of people. We now have over 130 active volunteers, including marine engineers, crew members, skippers, carpenters and people to mind the shop.' They welcome people who'd like to spend, say, a week volunteering, though. Wildlife is plentiful, with egrets, herons, coots and moorhens. 'We had to stop restoration work once because we spotted a vole. We also have nesting pairs of kingfishers, a pair of swans that nest each year, and roach, rudd, bream, tench, perch and pike.' It's a popular stretch of water for fishing, with day licences available.

Part of their income comes from running very enjoyable scheduled **canal boat trips** on *Kingfisher* four times daily, taking 90 minutes for the round trip; also available are rowing-boat hire and themed cruises including Father Christmas and Easter Bunny trips. They also have the *Richmond* for hire.

Whether going by boat, cycling, pushing a wheelchair or walking, you'll pass Poyntz Bridge (1820), the only swing bridge left and now kept as a curio; it was moved to its present site near the basin from Hunston, further down, where the canal makes an abrupt west turn (it originally ran east from here). Turner painted two pictures of the view from Hunston looking back to Chichester – one is in the basement of the Tate; the other hangs at Petworth House. He used plenty of artistic licence, showing the sun apparently setting in the north, and the cathedral bell tower moved to create a better composition.

SUSSEX'S WESTERNMOST DOWNS

From the Goodwood Estate to the Hampshire border, this is the South Downs at their most enticingly rural, with some very quiet back lanes meandering past remarkably unspoilt villages.

6 UPPARK

Nr South Harting GU31 5QR ✆ 01730 825857; National Trust; Stagecoach bus 54 (Petersfield–Chichester; several daily Mon–Sat)

Acquired by the National Trust in 1954, this remote country house suffered a devastating fire in 1989 which has resulted in an unexpectedly happy twist of events, and caused a bonanza of positive publicity and extra visitors.

Built in Dutch style to a design of William Talman around 1690, its exterior was little changed in 300 years until workmen used a blow torch on the roof to weld lead on what was the penultimate day of a year of roof repairs. It wasn't the ideal house for a fire to be extinguished: alone on a hilltop and far from any water source, meaning water had to be pumped in from a mile away. An immense effort was made to rescue the contents, which were passed from hand to hand, and 27 fire engines were in attendance at the height of the fire, but devastation was comprehensive and a charcoal gunge covered virtually everything. One fortuitous survival was the 300-year-old Flemish tapestries in the Prince Regent's

"An immense effort was made to rescue the contents, which were passed from hand to hand, and 27 fire engines were in attendance."

HARTING DOWNS & A PRE-SEMAPHORE SYSTEM

Just to the east of Uppark, Harting Downs are grazed by sheep and retain the ancient appearance the Downs once had: this is a marvellous place for contemplating the view and browsing the carpet of chalk flora. Beacon Hill, the high point, about a mile's walk along the South Downs Way from a car park on the B2141, is the site of an 18th-century telegraph station, one of a series set up to enable a warning of French invasion to be given by means of opening and closing shutters on the roof. This way it was possible to relay a message from Portsmouth to London in a quarter of an hour.

bedroom, which had been sold by the family to raise death duties and were donated back in a generous gesture after the fire.

Fortunately the fire was covered by Sun Alliance under a policy first taken out in 1753, which paid for complete reconstruction. The National Trust decided not to replace the house as new but as it was the day before the fire, with its patina of age. Craftsmen were employed for all manner of tasks – creating great opportunities for craftspeople and builders (many of whom revived rare old skills) to work here at a time of recession – as Uppark embarked on one of the most ambitious and meticulous restoration tasks of recent years. Marquees were erected to dry textiles and carpets, and the tradition of marking significant events on chimney pots was revived – one announces Margaret Thatcher's resignation ('MT resigned as I was making this pot'). The restoration was expected to take ten years but was completed in six.

Thus Uppark has regained its interior as it was for many years. Much of this is attributable to a marriage in 1825 between 71-year-old Sir Harry Fetherstonhaugh, whose parents furnished it lavishly, and his 20-year-old dairymaid Mary Ann. He lived another 21 years but she hugely outlived him, carrying on residing here with her sister in a Regency timewarp through the Victorian age, which largely passed them by. H G Wells, whose mother was housekeeper for a dozen years and whose room is cosy with brown panelling, remembered them as two old ladies archaically dressed in velvet.

One part of the house to have survived virtually unscathed was the basement, including a line of antique fire buckets which presumably weren't much use in the house's hour of need. The basement includes the kitchens, abandoned in the 1900s in favour of a smaller kitchen, and a butler's room where the butler could check a gauge to see if the rooftop

water tanks needed a top-up. Also down here is a very grand Uppark doll's house, splendidly furnished with Georgian contents right down to the silverware.

The dairy, where Sir Harry's dairymaid worked, is an elegant room with ivy leaf-patterned tiles. At that time there was a Marie Antoinette-ish fashion for the gentry to take part in the butter- and cream-making, and do a few turns of the churn – at a time when romantic male fantasy tended to regard dairymaids as being comely, clean and appetising.

As at Petworth, the landscaping creates the impression of being on the edge of a plateau, with lawns spreading right up to the house – a walk round the front of Uppark before entering helps you to appreciate its situation.

¶¶ FOOD & DRINK

The Three Horseshoes Elsted GU29 0JY ✆ 01730 825746 ⌂ 3hs.co.uk. Around 3½ miles northeast of Uppark and handy for South Downs walks, this is a nicely rustic country pub, with low beams and real ales on draught. The garden has wonderful downland views.

7 STANSTED PARK

Nr Rowlands Castle PO9 6DX ✆ 023 9241 2265 ⌂ stanstedpark.co.uk ⊙ Easter–Sep 13.00–17.00 Sun–Tue; train to Havant, West Coastway Line (four miles by taxi) or Rowlands Castle, Portsmouth Direct Line (two-mile walk)

The longest beech avenue on private land in England approaches this country house. The goose-foot arrangement of three grand vistas cut through the forest gives sightlines southwest to the Isle of Wight and east to Hampshire, with no other buildings in view. It is a quite superlative setting, begun by Capability Brown and completed by James Wyatt; the cricket pitch in front of the house has hosted matches ever since 1740. To get the full picture, walk from Rowlands Castle station and along the mile-long grand central avenue. Fallow and roe deer can be seen in the estate's woodlands, which are largely accessible to the public and are particularly glorious in spring and autumn.

The classical red-brick and Portland stone house is not what it first seems. The original but much remodelled Georgian house was

◀ **1** Uppark House was meticulously restored after a fire in 1989. **2** Laburnum growing over a long archway at West Dean Gardens. **3** Step back in time at the Weald & Downland Living Museum. **4** Experience a taste of opulent Edwardian life at Stansted Park. **5** The yew forest of Kingley Vale is thought to be 2,000 years old.

devastated by fire one day in August 1900, when the owners were eating dinner at home after a day at the races at Goodwood, and numerous paintings and Grinling Gibbons carvings perished in the blaze. It was a similar fate that befell nearby Uppark 89 years later, but in this instance the ruins were demolished and it was built afresh: the new house was created in the appearance of the original mansion, but with all the trappings of modern life too. Thus, although it has very much the feel of an 18th-century house in the proportions and styling of its rooms, this is Edwardian life at its most opulently comfortable, with the latest contrivances – among them electric lighting, garages for motor cars, an electric bell system for calling servants and an electric lift which still works and retains its panelling and bevelled mirrors.

In 1924 the 9th Earl of Bessborough purchased the house after the family seat in Kilkenny, Ireland, was itself burned down during the Troubles. His son, Eric Bessborough, was a minister in the Conservative government under Macmillan and a founder member of the Chichester Festival Theatre; he also set up a foundation so that the public could enjoy the forest, grounds and house in perpetuity. He died in 1993 and his successors live elsewhere on the estate. Today the state rooms on the ground floor are set up as they were in the 10th Earl's day. His favourite room, the library, has scarcely been touched, with the red government despatch boxes in one corner. His love of exotic birds is evident in the feathers kept on his desk and in the fantasy paintings in the stairway hall.

The evocation of life below stairs in the servants' quarters is one of the most fascinating aspects of Stansted Park. Last used in the 1950s and full of all the paraphernalia that would have been there, it vividly evokes the running of a great house, with its Acme mangles for laundry, servants' bells and speaking tubes, the housekeeper's cupboards stacked high with all the linen that would have been in use, a tin bath that all the footmen shared, high-ceilinged kitchen, cheery servants' hall and the butler's accounts books recording expenditure of every item. A former footman came here as a visitor many years later and found his uniform, last worn in the 1930s, still hanging with his name inside.

Christmas events, held in December, offer a chance to see the house a-twinkle with decorations, and there is a summer festival in June or July. The grounds contain a garden centre and a seriously disorienting yew tree maze which has been confusing and bemusing visitors since it was planted in 2011.

🍴 FOOD & DRINK

The Pavilion Tearoom Stansted Park ✆ 023 9241 3432. In the restored fig house in Stansted Park's walled garden, this is a super spot for light lunches, cream teas and cake, full of happy chatter. The menu is prepared freshly every day, with ingredients from local suppliers.

8 KINGLEY VALE

Stagecoach bus 54 (Petersfield–Chichester; several daily Mon–Sat) to East Ashling, then 1½-mile walk

Not exactly on the beaten track, Kingley Vale is for me one of the great Sussex sights. This, western Europe's largest yew forest, spreads across 200 acres over both sides of a downland ridge. It is thought to be 2,000 years old; no-one knows why it's there, though interestingly pollen analysis on Mount Caburn near Lewes indicates that the Downs there were covered with yew forest in prehistoric times. The 30,000 yews here are of all shapes and sizes, but the oldest are in a magical grove on the southeast side: here, massive trees create a dark, tangled canopy – some huge branches have fallen to the ground over the centuries and re-rooted into all sorts of bizarre, serpentine forms. It's a scene reminiscent of some Tolkien or Harry Potter fantasy. Not surprisingly, folklore has sprung up – tales of druids and marauding Viking warrior spirits abound, and it's supposedly a meeting point for witches too. Even on a bright summer's day, the forest exerts its spooky charms.

At the top of the ridge the view opens out gloriously over Chichester Harbour, Chichester itself (with the cathedral spire) and the Isle of Wight (Culver Cliff, on the island's east coast, is prominent). Rising from the turf are the Devil's Humps: two Bronze Age bell barrows standing on flat platforms, believed to be burial mounds for ancient kings. There are 12 other scheduled ancient monuments in the reserve.

The site is maintained by Natural England as a National Nature Reserve, and includes other types of woodland as well as unimproved chalk grassland that harbours 39 of the 58 English species of butterfly (among them chalkhill blue, marbled white and brown argus) and a rich tapestry of flora, including orchids such as twayblade, bee, fragrant and frog. You might also encounter roe or fallow deer, green woodpeckers, marsh tits, blackcaps, buzzards, sparrowhawks and tawny owls.

The one logistical snag about this wonderful place is that to do it justice you really need to climb up from both sides to see all the forest.

If you have time and energy, start from Stoughton, walk up and over to join the nature trail and climb up through the yew grove. I much prefer this direction as the glories of Kingley Vale remain hidden until the later stages. If you just want to skip to the highlights (or want to reach the pub in Stoughton in the middle of your walk), start at the West Stoke car park on Downs Road, signposted from East Ashling, northwest of Chichester, as 'National Nature Reserve'; if travelling by bus, you can walk there from the Horse and Groom bus stop in East Ashling. The track leading north from the car park takes you to the foot of the downs and the entrance to the reserve, from where a clearly marked nature trail makes a circuit of the most spectacular part of the forest and reaches the top of the Downs by the Devil's Humps.

¶¶ FOOD & DRINK

Hare & Hounds Stoughton PO18 9JQ ✆ 023 9263 1433 ⊙ Tue–Sun. There's a mixture of traditional and contemporary at this village dining pub with pleasant outdoor seating areas in a gorgeously rural backwater of a village. It offers Harvey's ale and real farm cider, generous sandwiches, pub standards and handmade pizza nights.

Horse & Groom East Ashling PO18 9AX ✆ 01243 575339 ⊘ horseandgroom.pub ⊙ Wed–Sat & Sun lunch. This delightfully cosy country pub offers upmarket versions of pub classics, and has ten small but classy guest rooms. Nicely in step with walkers and garden explorers, it makes space on its website to list favourite places, including a walk in Kingley Vale and days out near Chichester and Arundel.

9 THE GOODWOOD ESTATE

Goodwood House PO18 0PX ✆ 01243 755000 ⊘ goodwood.com ⊙ Mar–Oct Sun & Mon afternoons; Stagecoach bus 55 (Chichester–Tangmere; twice hourly) or Compass bus 99 (Chichester–Petworth; several daily) to Halnaker, then two-mile walk; EV charging at The Goodwood Hotel

One of the great estates of West Sussex, Goodwood exerts a tremendous presence for miles around. Occupying a wedge of downland running almost into Chichester, the views from the heights range far and wide – but you can feel quite enclosed on its straight, narrow roads between high flint walls. Although Goodwood's business ventures are run on decidedly modern lines, much of the landscape seems little changed since the 17th century.

A visit to the house provides the explanation. In 1697 the 25-year-old Charles Lennox, 1st Duke of Richmond, one of Charles II's illegitimate sons, acquired the house and park as a base for country sports. The nearby village of Charlton was home to one of the earliest and most fashionable hunts, the subject of a Stubbs painting on view in the pillared entrance hall showing an almost unaltered scene: for centuries the estate has been dedicated to sport, along with farming, ensuring the conservation of open country and woodland cover.

Also carefully conserved has been the background of royal lineage. Charles II was quite unabashed about celebrating the continuation of his bloodline, albeit outside his marriage, and loaded the young Charles with titles. Goodwood's collection of portraits focuses on the royal connections; the dark good looks shared by the king and his French mistress, Louise de Kérouaille, seem to have survived through many generations, and the Dukedom of Richmond has passed from father to first-born son (always called Charles) in an almost unbroken chain.

Goodwood House owes its present appearance to the 3rd Duke of Richmond, a scientist, soldier, politician and art lover, who among his other achievements founded Ordnance Survey. His London house burned down in 1791, but the family art collection – including two Canaletto scenes of old Whitehall and the Thames – was rescued. To provide a suitable new setting for it he added two angled wings at Goodwood, lavishly furnished in Regency style, leaving himself heavily in debt. His successors added little during the Victorian period; Edward VII, a regular visitor, did not much care for the striking black and gold Egyptian room, and it was dismantled and painted over. Death duties and dry rot threatened through most of the 20th century, but since the mid-1990s an ambitious restoration project has brought the rooms back to their original splendour. The Egyptian room presented a particular challenge as no pictures of it had survived. Fortuitously, some door furniture had been left forgotten on the back of a locked door, and other items have been imaginatively reconstructed from architectural illustrations of the time. The guided tours (note the restricted opening times) are well worth seeking out.

Goodwood racecourse, a favourite haunt of Edward VII, high up on the Downs, is now best known as the venue of the five-day Glorious Goodwood meeting in late July or early August. Above it, masts mark the hilltop known as **The Trundle**, an impressive Iron Age hillfort with massive ramparts and a view the length of the Sussex Downs, all the way to Beachy Head, with the Isle of Wight also in sight. If you prefer to walk up from the bottom, the village of East Lavant makes a useful starting point. Lord March, the future 11th Duke of Richmond, recalls that when he was a child the public used to watch the racing from The Trundle. The police stopped traffic to allow the race to cross the road, which was spread with sand for the purpose, and it was said that one horse in the 19th century ran right on to Chichester without stopping. Other annual events include the **Festival of Speed** in July, which brings Formula One cars and motorbikes to the park driveways. In September, **Goodwood Revival**, a vintage motorsports festival featuring historic racing cars, with their owners and fans dressed up in period costume, takes place on the Goodwood Motor Circuit, a 1940s racetrack on the former RAF Westhampnett airfield.

Goodwood Home Farm, at the heart of the estate, is a self-sustaining organic farm that rears native breeds for cheese and meat, and exercises considerable clout in requiring vendors at its events to use local produce.

ᵞᵞ FOOD & DRINK

Goodwood Farm Shop Home Farm, Goodwood PO18 0QF ✆ 01243 755153. Stocked with meat, cheese and cream that's produced without pesticides or fertilisers, this organic farm shop also sells Goodwood's own gin, scented with wild juniper, and craft beers, brewed from hops and barley grown on the estate.

10 BOXGROVE & TANGMERE

Stagecoach bus 55 (Chichester–Tangmere; twice hourly) or 500 (Chichester–Littlehampton; twice hourly)

Either side of the A27 west of its junction with the A285, these two places have virtually nothing in common apart from their geographical proximity. In **Boxgrove** village are the substantial ruins of the guest house and other remnants of a **priory** (free access) founded in 1105 by monks from Lessay Abbey in Normandy. Beside it stands the capacious **priory church**, which survived the Dissolution. Its interior is a majestic blend of Norman and Early English styles with soaring arches and vaulted roof painted with flowers and berries. The 16th-century chantry chapel to Lord De La Warr is unique in Sussex for its completeness.

In the churchyard is a grave to Bill Fiske, the Chicago-born pilot who became the first US serviceman to die in World War II. He was stationed at **Tangmere**, a major military airfield that was in use until 1970 and was home to Nos 1 and 43 squadrons; it's now the site of **Tangmere Military**

BOXGROVE MAN: PUTTING THE CLOCK BACK

This part of Sussex doesn't look at all exotic nowadays, but in the 1990s one of the most remarkable archaeological excavations of its time, in a nearby gravel quarry, uncovered an extraordinary snapshot of a long-lost world dating back some half a million years. The setting: a warm period between ice ages, when the land here would have looked more like Africa, and there were early humans roaming alongside lions and hyenas, hunting or scavenging extinct species of elephant, rhinoceros and deer. At the time the fossilised shinbone and two teeth from 'Boxgrove Man' were the earliest known human remains in Britain – their discovery in Sussex prompted a few cynical jibes in the press regarding Sussex's earlier associations with the Piltdown Man hoax.

In this case they were from *Homo heidelbergensis*, an ancestor both of our own species, *Homo sapiens*, and of the Neanderthals. The owner of the shinbone was clearly a tall, well-built individual, more than capable of causing damage with the flint hand axes which were the universal throwing, cutting and scraping tools of the time. The sandy land surface preserved in the depths of the quarry was so little disturbed that archaeologists were able to reconstruct how half a million years ago a flint knapper had sat cross-legged to work on one, leaving a V-shaped pattern of discarded flint flakes. English Heritage bought the site to save it for posterity, but it's hidden away in country lanes, with nothing to see – the finds are still being worked on in London.

Aviation Museum (Tangmere PO20 2ES ✆ 01243 790090 ⬦ tangmere-museum.org.uk ☉ Feb–Nov), one of the leading attractions of its kind. I visited expecting displays of impressive military hardware and, while there is plenty of that in the form of fighter planes outside and in the hangars, it has a huge number of human-interest stories from both world wars (and later) too. It is run by enthusiastic, chatty and extremely helpful volunteer staff (mostly ex-RAF); one visitor remarked 'I only came for a couple of hours but have now been here for seven!'. One of the most striking of many wartime relics is the reassembled wreckage of a Hurricane, shot down in Hove and recovered in 1998 with the body of the pilot Dennis Noble still inside. The more intimate museum displays are packed within the former radio maintenance area, where a model shows the airfield as it was in 1939; little is left outside nowadays, apart from the former control tower, and exhibits and photos tell of such events as Operation Manna, when 6,000 tons of food were dropped by British planes over starving, war-ravaged Holland and the Germans had orders not to fire. There are displays about great agents such as Violette

Szabo (executed January 1945) who received the George Cross, and the poem she had to learn is on display too – it reads innocently enough, and no-one today knows what the coded message was. The range of flight simulators are a hit with children as well as adults, and the scenery below on some of them depicts wartime Tangmere; the most advanced simulator, where the scenery is projected on to a large screen, is suitable for experienced pilots, and is the sort of thing used for training.

11 WEST DEAN, SINGLETON & AROUND

Stagecoach bus 60 (Midhurst–Chichester; twice hourly Mon–Sat, hourly Sun) or Compass bus 99 (Chichester–Petworth; several daily); Centurion Way cycle route

Just below The Trundle, Singleton lies in a downland valley that encompasses the unspoilt flint-built villages of Charlton and East Dean, each with an excellent pub. Just north of Singleton and Charlton, **Levin Down**, a nature reserve owned by the **Sussex Wildlife Trust**, is a prominent hill, where the steep slopes have defied the plough, leaving 70 acres in its pristine state. Chalkland flowers and butterflies proliferate; the last time I walked up, a red kite rose abruptly just yards away. In the 18th century **Charlton** was renowned for its hunt: in 1738 the longest ever hunt ran for ten hours, and one of their number, Tom Johnson, has a memorial in Singleton Church.

Weald & Downland Living Museum

Singleton PO18 0EU ✆ 01243 811348 ⬦ wealddown.co.uk

Back in 1970 this opened as among the very first museums of its kind in Britain, and has been going from strength to strength ever since. The idea had been five years in the making: the vision of Roy Armstrong who after the end of World War II was surveying pre-19th-century buildings in Crawley prior to demolition, and came across a farmhouse built around a rare 14th-century medieval hall structure. He managed to get a preservation order slapped on it, only to find that the order was later reversed and the building pulled down. After witnessing the depressing spectacle of the historic timbers being burnt on a site bonfire, Armstrong recorded 'I have watched funeral pyres of at least two buildings which would have justified preservation had there been anywhere to store the frames.' This sowed the seeds for the concept of an open-air museum on the lines of what already existed in Scandinavia and elsewhere, and in 1965 Armstrong and some other enthusiasts met to discuss how this could be done in the Weald at a time when much of our fragile vernacular building heritage – dwellings, associated farm buildings and places of work – was being destroyed, and the conservation movement was still very young.

The museum was fortunate to be able to lease land from the West Dean estate, giving the museum a superb rural site in a scenic part of the South Downs. The setting really helps: it feels like a real village, with buildings grouped around, and very much part of the landscape. There are now over 40 buildings, among them such fragile evocations of yesteryear as a plumber's workshop, a brick-drying shed, a mid-19th-century village school, a windpump, a medieval shop and a toll cottage.

"In displaying the buildings, the museum has often stripped away later features to get back to the original structure."

In displaying the buildings, the museum has often stripped away later features to get back to the original structure. One example is a medieval house from North Cray in the London borough of Bexley. It was dismantled during road-widening in 1968, and brought here; the 16th- and 17th-century modifications were removed, leaving the original hallhouse structure – with a central hall where a fire would be lit, and smoke would rise up through the roof. The museum also discovered that the external beams were originally painted red, as they are again today. The semi-detached pair known as Whittaker's Cottages, from Ashtead in Surrey, have been fascinatingly presented inside with the bare bones of the building construction revealed in one cottage and the other furnished as it might have looked in the 19th century. Sometimes unexpected twists in the tale appeared when the buildings were dismantled. For instance, a house from Walderton in Sussex that appeared to be 17th-century turned out to be much older: only when it was taken down did they discover the original wattle and found it was of medieval origins. The museum is constantly evolving: recent arrivals include a Saxon hall house, replicated through archaeological evidence of post holes and academic research.

Deeper into the site, the woods are home to a variety of forest activities, including a very spartan-looking charcoal-burner's camp and a rare timber crane; the trees are coppiced for a variety of uses: fencing, besom-making, thatching, charcoal and firewood, as well as for the health of the woodland itself.

A keynote to the museum's character is the presence of the sort of animals you might have expected to see in a rural community some centuries back. The heavy horses perform seasonal tasks such as harrowing, ploughing and cutting crops, and there are Tamworth pigs – chosen as being the closest-looking animals to an old breed that would have been here – chocolate-brown (officially 'red') Sussex cattle and chunky-looking Southdown sheep. When I visited they were training cows in ploughing – within each pair one cow has a name of one syllable, the other of two syllables so that the cows can know they're being addressed – Sol and Saxon.

They make a point of not going down the audio-tour route here; instead, chatty volunteers are on hand to explain the buildings to you, and the guidebook has full descriptions of every building on site. The pod-like modern building known as the Gridshell houses in its basement the artefact store, where a vast array of bits of buildings and items related to crafts and trades have been accumulated, including the contents of a trugmaker's workshop.

Should you like to learn new skills or find out about rural life in the past, or own a historic building and want to know about conserving it, there is no better place to learn. A wide range of courses held here typically include those on traditional rural trades and crafts, early technology workshops like making prehistoric jewellery or tools, countryside skills such as coppice management or learning blacksmith's skills, and historic home life events such as singing Sussex songs or learning about historic clothing. They also run courses in historic building conservation, in which you could learn about timber repairs or lime plasters and renders.

Since 2017, the museum's Court Barn, originally from Lee-on-the-Solent, has been home to the BBC's **The Repair Shop**. The barn is cordoned off from the general public whenever the team are in residence to film a new series, but it's sometimes possible for visitors to take a look at the set on their days off.

The **shop** has locally made crafts including trugs and wellie-boot racks, plus Montezuma's chocolate (made in Birdham, near Chichester). An impressive book selection features a host of titles on vernacular architecture and practical building techniques.

Volunteers are essential to keeping the museum functioning. They are trained up for a variety of tasks such as Tudor brewing and baking, costumes, woodland management, blacksmithing or helping in the shop or car park. It would be possible to come for just a week or so, although most attend on a regular basis.

EVENTS

The Weald & Downland calendar is a lively one, changing every year. Past events have included a Food and Farming Fair, showcasing foods from the southeast; a Heavy Horse Show featuring working horses from the museum and from a loyal band of enthusiasts; a Wood Show; a Rare Breeds Day, a Steam Festival and a Countryside Show. There's an Advent market at the end of November and a tree-dressing celebration in early December, after which the houses may be presented to reflect how Christmas would have been celebrated at various times through the ages. See ⌁ wealddown.co.uk for details.

¶¶ FOOD & DRINK

Cadence Cocking GU29 0HT ✆ 01903 495546 ⌁ cadencecycle.club. One of a small, dynamic rural chain of pitstops spaced out along the South Downs Way, Cadence refuels cyclists and walkers with excellent coffee, toasted sandwiches and treats. The next one is just over five miles east in Upwaltham.

The Fox Goes Free Charlton PO18 0HU ✆ 01243 811461 ⌁ thefoxgoesfree.com. Dining pub with a kitchen that makes everything from scratch. Set in a delightful village, it has a cosy and ancient-feeling interior, characterful guest rooms and a huge back garden looking out to the Downs.

The Star & Garter East Dean PO18 0JG ✆ 01243 811318 ⌁ thestarandgarter.co.uk. This welcoming gastro pub champions local suppliers, particularly of fish, seafood and game. The bar serves local ales, and there are guest rooms, a pleasant garden and live music on Sundays.

Weald & Downland Living Museum Café Singleton PO18 0EU ✆ 01243 811363 ⌁ wealddown.co.uk. Open to all (no museum entry ticket required), this reasonably priced café serves sandwiches, lunch specials and cakes in a bright, modern building overlooking a peaceful mill pond.

West Dean

West Dean PO18 0RX ✆ 01243 818300 ⌁ westdean.ac.uk

The 6,400-acre West Dean estate, which leases land to the Weald & Downland Living Museum, has a grand flint mansion that houses **West Dean College**, an inspiring setting for day and residential courses on arts and crafts. The college opened in 1971 and resulted from a charitable trust set up seven years earlier by Edward James, the former owner of the house, who was variously a painter, poet and patron of surrealism.

He supported Magritte and Dalí and constructed a series of sculptural creations in the heart of the Mexican jungle.

The college website features a booklet of six walks, between 1½ and 4½ miles long, exploring West Dean village, West Dean Estate, West Dean Woods Nature Reserve and The Trundle via country lanes, bridleways and footpaths. One of these includes part of Andy Goldsworthy's Chalk Stones Trail, a five-mile path punctuated with 13 large, roughly carved chalk spheres between West Dean and Cocking Hill on the South Downs Way. Snowball white when Goldsworthy installed them in 2002, the stones have since weathered and merged with the landscape – some cracking, others becoming overgrown.

Restored after devastation in the 1987 storm, **West Dean Gardens** (✆ 01243 818318 ⬦ westdean.ac.uk/gardens) are a visual treat. The formal part beyond West Dean College's sweeping lawns is narrow and linear, spread along a seasonally flowing tributary of the River Lavant, with sudden changes in mood. The planting includes a 300ft-long vine-clad Edwardian pergola; St Roche's Arboretum featuring rhododendrons and azaleas, stunning in spring; and a Spring Garden with subtropical tree ferns, rustic flint bridges and a thatched summerhouse. The Walled Fruit Garden features over 140 heritage varieties of apple and pear, including Victorian favourites, and a splendid round apple store with a thatched roof. The kitchen garden, also walled, has 13 working Victorian glasshouses where orchids, chilli peppers and a cornucopia of fruit including figs, berries, peaches and melons flourish.

As well as art and craft courses, West Dean hosts literary festivals, talks, exhibitions and garden courses. In August the ever-popular Chilli Fiesta features salsa dancing, fiendishly spicy food, Mexican minstrels and puppetry.

12 SLINDON ESTATE

National Trust; Stagecoach bus 500 (Chichester–Littlehampton; twice hourly); South Downs Way

Extending for 3,500 acres, Slindon Estate's woods, fields and downland are laced with 25 miles of footpaths and bridleways. The beechwoods of Slindon Common flank the ambling village of **Slindon**, owned in part by the National Trust, which has a policy of ensuring that local families and workers are given tenancies to keep the village community alive and thriving. Not far from the village pond are St Mary's Church and, roughly opposite, what is surely the only NT-owned railway carriage with a thatched roof, visible from the road just inside the gate of Church House, a private house on Church Hill. Slindon's cricket team continues a venerable tradition stretching back to the 18th century; the first known scorecard of any game dates to a match in 1744 between London and Slindon at the Artillery Ground in Finsbury – one of Slindon's men was Richard Newland (1713–78), the 'father of cricket', and one of the game's great all-rounders; the game has been played here since the 18th century.

On a partly wooded hill north of the village, **Nore Folly** makes a good objective for walks. Built as a sham ruin in the 18th century it serves no purpose except to embellish the landscape.

Just to the south, across the A27, **Denmans Garden** (Fontwell BN18 0SU ✆ 01243 256621 ⌖ denmans.org) packs a lot into four acres. Created by horticulturalist Joyce Robinson in the 1970s and later adapted by landscape designer John Brookes, there's a wild, romantic look to its gravel beds, walled garden and moorhen-populated pond.

13 BIGNOR ROMAN VILLA & AROUND

Bignor RH20 1PH ✆ 01798 869259 ⌖ bignorromanvilla.co.uk ⊙ Mar–Oct; Compass Book-a-Bus 99 Flex (Chichester–Petworth; on demand)

Bignor Roman Villa makes an excellent excursion by bus from Chichester or by bike from Amberley, which is just under five miles away via narrow and quiet country lanes. It's on the edge of the hamlet of Bignor, whose gorgeously preserved old houses include the thatched, 15th-century Yeoman's House (or Old Shop), with its jettied upper storey.

People have been coming to admire the Roman remains for quite some time. In 1811 a ploughman named Joseph Tupper chanced upon some of the finest mosaics yet discovered in this country while ploughing, and a local man named John Hawkins and the antiquary Samuel Lysons spent eight years excavating them. Hawkins put up thatched stone huts to protect the mosaics – these have a charm of their own, and are now listed buildings themselves, even if it's not quite the way archaeologists do things nowadays. People pottered out in horse-driven carriage trips from all over the south-east to see this 'new' wonder. The site is still family-run, by Tupper's descendants.

Although the first building dates from around AD190, most of what's in evidence dates from the 4th century. It underwent a lot of extensions, probably to house separate parts of an extended family, who would have shared the bath suite. This featured a heated changing room (the one with the Medusa mosaic), and cold, warm and hot baths; the slaves would have kept the furnace going.

The mosaics depict scenes from the lives of gladiators and mythical subjects, and in places you can even walk on the still-durable surface of a Roman floor. Bignor's mosaics, underfloor heating and bath suite were the first real evidence of Roman-style living in the British countryside: previously scholars had thought of Britain as a backward frontier zone, with 'civilised' amenities only in the cities.

Since Tupper's fortuitous ploughing exploits, a great number of Roman villas have been discovered all across Sussex. One striking feature many have in common is their view of the Downs – it seems that along with their hot baths the villa owners appreciated a good view. But they were unlikely to have been Romans from Italy. They were probably the descendants of Iron Age landowners who grew rich supplying such markets as the Roman palace at Fishbourne and the new city of Chichester: the villa would have been at the heart of their farming estates.

The villa was strategically positioned close to the London–Chichester Roman road, known as **Stane Street**, which you can still walk nearby on top of the South Downs. From Bignor village, take a lane which climbs for a mile south up the ridge (very steep at the start, but it gets easier). The car park at the top has a modern signpost with Roman names, and you can see the very clear raised bank (*agger*) of the road and sometimes the original flint surface where the local rabbits have nibbled away the turf.

"The villa was strategically positioned close to the London–Chichester Roman road, which you can still walk nearby."

Return on the lanes the same way, or cycle the chalk track of the South Downs Way, following the top of the ridge then down a steep descent back to Amberley.

Burton & Chingford Ponds

North of Bignor, this is a Sussex Wildlife Trust nature reserve whose main feature, Burton Mill Pond, was the hammer pond for a 16th-century iron-smelting site. The water and its surroundings form a rich habitat for birds, including kingfishers, woodpeckers and great crested grebes, and 23 species of dragonfly. The acidic peat and wet woodlands create conditions for southern marsh orchids, tussock sedge and bogbean. There's a circular nature trail from the car park by Burton Mill.

Follow the road southeast from Burton Mill towards the A29, and in a mile you come to **Lord's Piece**, a patch of lowland heath with beautiful views towards the Downs. There are two car parks on the western side; it's not a big area, but feels larger once you stroll around in it. Listen for the rare field crickets – it's one of the very few sites in the country where they're found.

¶¶ FOOD & DRINK

White Horse Sutton RH20 1PS ☏ 01798 869191 ⌂ whitehorseinn-sutton.co.uk. Less than 1½ miles northwest of Bignor, from which it's a pleasant walk along the lane or through fields, this attractively placed village inn is furnished in contemporary style, with interesting bar food, beers and wines, and comfortable accommodation.

THE ROTHER VALLEY & THE NORTH

West Sussex's River Rother (confusingly, there's a different River Rother in East Sussex) rises in Hampshire and flows through Midhurst, joining the Arun near Stopham's historic bridge. Further north the land rises into heathy, wooded and enticingly secretive sandstone hills that aren't geologically part of the South Downs but are of such high landscape quality that they were included in the South Downs National Park. The huge estates of Cowdray near Midhurst and Leconfield at Petworth are very much a feature of country life here.

14 MIDHURST

Stagecoach bus 1 (Worthing–Midhurst; hourly Mon–Sat, less frequent Sun), 60 (Chichester–Midhurst; twice hourly Mon–Sat, hourly Sun), 70 (Guildford–Midhurst; hourly Mon–Sat) or 92 (Petersfield–Midhurst; several daily Mon–Sat)

The market town of Midhurst is the commercial hub of the aristocratic **Cowdray Estate** – centred at Cowdray Park just outside the town – whose lands stretch far across this part of Sussex. The trademark mustard-yellow paint on doors and windows of estate buildings can be seen locally, particularly in Easebourne, the old village that lies just to the northeast. Midhurst is also home to the **South Downs Centre** (North St, GU29 9DH ☏ 01730 814810 ⌂ southdowns.gov.uk ☉ Mon–Fri), the

POLO AT COWDRAY

In Midhurst, the famous Cowdray Park Polo Club (⌂ cowdraypolo.co.uk) is the centre of the horseback sport of polo in Britain, although its origins in this country are Aldershot, where the Royal Hussars first played it in 1869. At Cowdray the lawns spread either side of Cowdray Ruins and Cowdray House, and the public are welcome to come and watch all matches (smart casual dress code); you pay as you enter. Matches are of various durations, played on a 'lawn' measuring 300 by 160yds over seven-minute periods known as chukkas, and can be from four to six chukkas long – an hour to 90 minutes including intervals; every time a goal is scored the play changes end. The polo ponies, as they are known, are put through their paces and move at tremendous speed, necessitating the frequent intervals and changeovers of ponies. Although it's basically a game of scoring goals using sticks to hit the ball for a goal, the rules aren't that easy to grasp – for instance there is a notional 'line of ball' along which a player establishes right of way that an opponent is not allowed to cross if there is any risk of collision, and a player may hook an opponent's stick if he is on the same side of his opponent as the ball – but even if you have little idea what's going on, it does make a thoroughly engrossing spectacle.

The sport was first played here in 1910, when Harold Pearson got things going. He had played polo at Oxford and after his father purchased the estate in 1909 quickly set to having a polo ground laid out at Cowdray House and by the Cowdray Ruins. The sport enjoyed a renaissance of public interest after World War II when crowds flocked to see Prince Philip play – his uncle Lord Mountbatten was a polo enthusiast who encouraged his nephew. A Coronation Cup of six nations drew 15,000 spectators in 1953, and Prince Philip established his own polo club at Windsor. Prince Charles then became an aficionado of the sport and played at Cowdray many times until back problems forced him to retire from polo in 2003. Today some 450 matches are played each season, the highlight being the Veuve Clicquot Gold Cup for the British Open in summer, when some of the world's top players are in action.

headquarters of South Downs National Park, which has an informative visitor centre, shop and a car park with EV charging.

Midhurst's best moments are easily missed. Making for an enjoyable potter around, its villagey **historic centre**, with its Market Square and market house of 1551, and Church Hill, is tucked behind the main street with overhanging jettied houses, tile-hung timber-framed buildings and Georgian façades often hiding older Tudor and Stuart structures. Listen out for the curfew bell that rings from the church tower every evening at 20.00 as ordered by William the Conqueror, and look out for the preserved shopfront of Boots – with its bow windows and black and gold lettering. This was the original site of Midhurst Grammar School, founded in 1672, where H G Wells attended evening classes at the age of 15 while apprenticed at a chemist's shop in town. He taught there a couple of years later; his mother was a housekeeper at Uppark (page 46) at the time. There's also the very pretty **South Pond**, formed in medieval times as a fish breeding ground and later serving as a mill pond for fulling cloth.

The utterly tiny **Midhurst Museum** in Knockhundred Market is free to enter: it's in two bits, one with changing themed exhibitions and the other with all types of artefacts and memorabilia, including Neolithic worked flints, hammered coins, ginger beer bottles and a model of De Bohun Castle, the predecessor to Cowdray.

Midhurst's grandest building, **Cowdray House** (GU29 9DW ⊘ cowdray.co.uk), a Grade I-listed ruin of astonishing proportions, is occasionally the setting for special events. The original lords of the manor here, the Bohun family, had a motte and bailey on St Ann's Hill close to the ruins. They erected a larger house in the 13th century, named 'Coudreye', after the Norman-French word for hazel woods. This was in turn replaced in the 16th century by William Fitzwilliam, a friend of Henry VIII who rather unusually stayed friends with the monarch all his life. Fitzwilliam's Tudor mansion, known as Cowdray, was second only in scale among Tudor mansions to Hampton Court, on which it was modelled.

In the 1770s Capability Brown was engaged to remodel the gardens. But in 1793 a fire devastated Cowdray, and despite locals helping themselves to free building supplies over the ensuing years its shell continued to stand and was much admired by tourists and antiquarians, and painted and sketched by many, including Turner and Constable. It was closed in the late 1980s as it became unsafe, but at the end of the 20th century the people of Midhurst asked Lord Cowdray to do something about restoring it as a tourist attraction before it crumbled away completely.

¶¶ FOOD & DRINK

Cowdray Farm Shop and Café Cowdray Park, Easebourne GU29 0AJ ⊘ 01730 815152 ⊘ cowdray.co.uk. Alongside Cowdray produce including estate-reared meat, artisan cheeses and kefir, this classy farm shop offers fresh bread, veggies and fish from local suppliers. The café has the same ethos. Cowdray steak and chips with a glass of Cowdray Ale, brewed up the road by an estate tenant, Langham, goes down particularly well.

Midhurst Farmers' and Artisan Market Market Sq, GU29 9NJ & Old Library, GU29 9DQ. Held on the first Saturday morning of the month, there's a surprising diversity to the offerings at these two locations, with everything from baked goods to biltong.

The Wheatsheaf Wool Lane GU29 9BX ✆ 01730 813450 ⊘ thewheatsheafmidhurst.co.uk. Dating back to 1621, this characterful local offers draught beer and pub classics such as roast beef sandwiches and ham egg and chips in unpretentious surroundings.

Woolbeding Gardens

✆ 0344 249 1895 ⊘ Apr–Sep Thu–Fri by pre-booking; National Trust; no access by car; minibus every 20 mins from Grange Centre car park, Bepton Rd, Midhurst GU29 9HD

It's well worth making the effort to visit this 26 acres of sheer enchantment and book a visit on one of the two days a week that it opens. Be sure to get a parking ticket at Midhurst for at least three hours – this is not a place to hurry.

The National Trust took over the estate in 1957 but the gardens were only made accessible to the public 54 years later, in 2011. One of the conditions of planning consent was that visitor numbers would be restricted to a couple of hundred a day, and that the public would be shuttled in by minibus instead of being allowed to drive up to the property.

From 1973 the tenancy passed to Sir Simon Sainsbury (great-grandson of the founder of the supermarket chain) and his partner Stewart Grimshaw – who expended great efforts in creating the garden as it is today. Simon died in 2006 but Stewart still lives in the gracious early Georgian mansion (itself not open to the public). The gardens are an exquisite blend of formal and informal, ancient and modern, with surprise views at every turn, with shrubs, lawns and plants embellished with urns, statues and even a Roman sarcophagus. Two installations commemorate the sites of much-loved, much-missed trees: a stainless steel water feature on the site of a cedar tree and a stone folly tower marking the location of what was Europe's largest tulip tree, the timber from which has been recycled into the counter of the visitor reception area. Beneath the main lawns it is wilder, with sprawling oriental plane trees, and below that a curving avenue of gnarled hornbeams.

In the other direction, an old walled garden has been divided by topiary into outdoor rooms with spectacular plantings, and an 18th-century avenue extends 320yds, creating a vista from the house.

The Long Walk (actually more of a Short Stroll) leads past a 'ruined abbey' into a pleasure garden with a long lake spanned by a Chinese Bridge, from where paths weave past canopies of Brazilian giant rhubarb, a River God Grotto, fancifully Gothic summer house, a fibreglass elephant named Edyth who's been embellished with pictures of strawberries, and a thatched Hermit's Hut. All infused with a terrific sense of joy, and the absence of labels and signs enhances the serendipity even further.

15 LODSWORTH TO BLACK DOWN

Stagecoach bus 1 (Midhurst–Worthing; hourly Mon–Sat, less frequent Sun)

This is a supremely rewarding, quiet and verdant corner of West Sussex, extraordinarily remote and unspoilt, with no great visitor attractions but with woodlands to lose yourself in (often literally – this is a complex and confusing landscape), much of it on lands owned by the neighbouring Cowdray and Leconfield estates of Midhurst and Petworth respectively. **Lodsworth** (with its gem of a village shop) and **Lickfold** sit comfortably in a rural scene. **Fernhurst**, further north, is larger, with a large village green that makes one of several good starting points for walks up to **Black Down**, at 919ft the highest point in West or East Sussex, though it's only just south of the Surrey border; reputedly Black Down has the juiciest, tastiest wild bilberries hereabouts because of its altitude. The slopes of the hill are densely wooded or covered with scrub, but at the top the views open up in a few places; most notable is the Temple of the Winds, a viewpoint at the southern end, where the trees frame the distant prospect of the South Downs. The National Trust owns Black Down and Marley Common to its west. The landscapes struck a chord with Alfred Lord Tennyson who in 1867 purchased 60 acres of land and built **Aldworth House** on the slopes of the hill. His study looked straight across the Weald, prompting him to record in a letter to a friend:

You came, and looked and loved the view
Long-known and loved by me,
Green Sussex fading into blue
With one grey glimpse of sea.

A mile west of Fernhurst, a large pond (♥ SU879283; no road access, but public rights of way lead to the spot) marks the site of Fernhurst Furnace (also known as North Park Furnace), said to be the best surviving example of an ironworking site in the Weald. It dates from the

17th and 18th centuries, when it was powered by a water wheel on the pond and used local ore and charcoal.

Driving to the little car park on the dead-end lane in the National Trust-owned **Woolbeding Common** (♀ SU869261) is quite a navigational feat along ever-narrowing lanes (turn off the A272 a mile west of Midhurst, signposted Woolbeding; in a mile keep left at Woolbeding village, then right at the next junction, and a mile later turn right into a dead-end lane signposted Older Hill and with grass growing in the middle in places) rewarded by some of the choicest views in all Sussex from the spine of its ridge over surprisingly wild-feeling heathy expanses against the backdrop of the distant Downs. The paths hereabouts are mightily complicated. The forests nearby contain plenty of evidence of coppicing and of hammer ponds left by the long-defunct Wealden iron industry.

The ever-scenic A272 has some very fine moments west of Midhurst; a couple of miles along it is a turning to **Stedham**, where the churchyard has a hollow yew thought to be 2,500 years old, while against the church are Saxon or pre-Saxon stone tombs, and remnants of Saxon crosses are embedded into the wall near the porch). Continuing on the A272, the scene becomes heathy on the south side: **Iping Common** provides another excellent strolling ground through heathery and intermittently squelchy expanses. It's rich in mosses and liverworts, and the rare heath tiger beetle has been reintroduced in recent years – the only place in Sussex you'll find them.

A little further west on the A272, the interior of St George's Church at **Trotton** reveals a host of outstandingly preserved 14th-century wall paintings, revealed in 1904, including on the west wall a *Last Judgement* depicting figures of good (on the right) and evil (accompanied by the Seven Deadly Sins). Look out in particular for a magnificent brass to Thomas de Camoys (1351–1421) and his wife – one of the finest brasses to survive the Reformation: he led the left wing of Henry V's army at Agincourt.

¶¶ FOOD & DRINK

Langham Brewery Langham Ln, Lodsworth GU28 9BU ☎ 01798 860861
⌂ langhambrewery.co.uk ☺ summer Mon–Sat; winter Thu–Sat. This lively rural spot offers cask-conditioned real ale and tasty handmade pizzas: a winning combination. Brewery tours are available, and the walkers and cyclists on the team can recommend local routes and

excursions. It's around half a mile from the Halfway Bridge bus stop; by taking Stagecoach bus 1 along the A272, you could also visit Pulborough's vineyards (Stopham and Nutbourne) en route.

16 PETWORTH

🏠 The Old Railway Station

Stagecoach bus 1 (Midhurst–Worthing; hourly Mon–Sat, less frequent Sun) or Compass bus 99 (Chichester–Petworth; several daily)

The grand house backs straight on to this handsome small town, rather ignoring it – as do, sadly, many house visitors who are unaware of the treats in store. The traffic is really off-putting and challenging, but you can escape into some very attractive and blissfully quiet back streets and paths. This is an estate town on a grand scale, and those who worked on the Petworth House estate (known as the Leconfield Estate) lived either in the servants' quarters by the house or in estate cottages in the town, where the ubiquitous brown paint appears on front doors of some 400 houses built in the 19th century; note the numbering system, allocated not according to geography but according to when they first appeared on the rent records.

The **Market Square** is at the centre of things and has hosted markets since 1541 and an annual fair in November since 1189. On it stands Leconfield Hall, the town hall, which sports a replica of a bust of William III by Dutch sculptor Honoré Pellé; the extremely precious original is now found in Petworth House. Leading off from there is cobbled **Lombard Street**, the hub of the town's upmarket antiques trade.

Lombard Street re-emerges into the traffic opposite the **Church of St Mary**. Much altered inside and out, it was restored by Charles Barry (of Houses of Parliament fame), and comprises an odd mixture

A GRIM REMINDER

Next to the Court House by Grove Street, a seemingly unexceptional wall encloses a small car-parking bay. The bricks in the wall have been reused from the Petworth House of Correction. You can see re-used bricks carved with the names of prisoners from this locally notorious prison, built in the late 18th century at a time when offences such as theft could lead to transportation to the colonies or hanging. It was a very nasty place to be incarcerated. If you were a vagrant or petty felon, you might have had a term of hard labour and solitary confinement here to deliver 'short sharp shocks'.

of brick and stone, with a blue barrel-vaulted ceiling. A marble statue commemorates George O'Brien, 3rd Earl of Egremont, one of the great artists' patrons, who was instrumental in bringing J M W Turner to Petworth in the 1820s. Rather more architectural fun than the church is Barry's preposterously twiddly iron '**obelisk**' – opposite the church and near the entrance to Lombard Street – of 1851, topped by a street lamp, erected as a thanksgiving to Lord Leconfield who brought the town its gas lighting.

From near the obelisk, Bartons Lane leads down to the edge of town, where you can continue to the right along a scenic tarmacked path known as **Round-the-Hills** that contours round above the top of the Shimmings Valley – a delicious rural outlook. Where it rejoins the town near the Roman Catholic Church, cross over the main road and explore some of the streets built for Petworth's huge servant force. **Egremont Row** in Angel Street was built to a higher specification than was the norm, and the builder was sacked for being so extravagant.

Close by in blissfully tranquil Grove Street is **Percy Terrace**, with its strikingly tall chimneys. Further along at 346 High Street, in **Petworth Cottage Museum** (✆ 01798 342100 ♂ petworthcottagemuseum. co.uk ☉ Apr–Oct 14.00–16.30 Tue–Sat) you can get a good idea how the servants lived. It is the former home of Mrs Mary Cummings who worked at the house and lived here from 1901 to 1930. The cottage has been furnished as it might have looked in her time, with gas lighting, a cooking range and a little cottage garden. Mrs Cummings ended her days in the striking Dutch-gabled building in North Street, an almshouse provided by the Leconfield Estate for elderly tenants.

Petworth Park

There's free access to this vast space in daylight hours, and there are several ways in. From the town side, you can walk down North Street (just below the church) until the estate offices around the Cowyard (so-called because it used to house the park's celebrated cattle): on the far side of this, a tunnel leads through ornamental gates and into the park itself.

---

1 Iping Common offers excellent walking through the heather. **2** Petworth Park is home to the largest herd of fallow deer in Britain. **3** The market town of Midhurst has an attractive historical centre. **4** The vast Grade I-listed ruins of Cowdray House. ▶

Petworth & the Leconfield Estate

❋ OS Explorer map OL33; start: Petworth Pound Street car park ⚲ SU978217; three miles; moderately hilly & with uneven ground in places. **Loos** in Petworth car park. **Refreshments** can be had at the pub in Byworth and various establishments in Petworth.

Within three miles, this route takes you out of central Petworth into the **working estate** for Petworth House: it's an aspect of the town and its hinterland that many visitors never see, but the views over the estate, and the estate village of **Byworth**, are special, and at the end you pass the estate houses in Petworth and the Petworth Cottage Museum. The one section over arable land may be under plough or crops for part of the year.

1 From the car park (pay and display), exit near the loo block, through the Old Bakery Shopping Arcade into Golden Square, and go into the Market Square, past the United Reformed Church and the town hall (on the left) towards the distant church tower. Carry on along cobbled **Lombard Street**, turn right at the end past Charles Barry's splendid **obelisk/lamp standard**, and right into Bartons Lane. Go down to a path junction with a big view ahead over the estate. Go ahead, downhill: you can see the line of the old London Road rising up the spine of the hill, to the right of the hedgerow and up to the wooded summit of Gog and Magog hill.

The path heads down the left of the field to an old stone bridge (it's easiest to arc out to the right and back rather than going straight down). It is not very defined, but keep to the hedgerow on your left uphill. Further up, look behind for a **fine view** of Petworth town and house. After a stile by a gate, the hedgerow ends: continue in the same direction, passing to the left of a small planted enclosure of trees. A red-roofed building comes into view with a power post below and just to the left of it – the stile is found just to the left of the power post.

2 The path carries up a woodland strip known as Lovers' Lane and emerges on a track corner by a sign for **Brinkshole Heath**, an expanse of bracken, birch coppice, holly and pheasant rearing. Go forward (keeping to the right) and follow marker arrows (initially with a field close by to the right). After the field ends you can glimpse Goanah Lodges (also known as **Gog and Magog lodges**) to the right, near the power post. Keep forward at the next two track junctions, then go sharp right 70yds later, heading towards the big stone gateway of the lodges. If you look back here towards Petworth you see a remarkable **vista of Petworth House**. The route then bends left shortly before the lodges and leaves the woodland, descending, with a fine view of the South Downs.

3 Just after some barns on the left, keep forward where the track bends right, and now follow the path down the middle of the field (the path wasn't visible last time I walked this, and the route was obscured by crops, though some passing horseriders assured me it's usually better than this; on previous occasions I've had no problems at this point – just try to keep on a straight bearing), passing to the right of the nearest, lone tree and aiming for the red roofs of Byworth in the mid distance. Cross a stile beside a gate, turn right along the pavement by the A283 for 30yds, then cross the road carefully to take the signposted stile opposite. Walk to the far bottom corner of the field, to find a gate and stile, leading down through a tiny field with gate to a road in the hamlet of **Byworth**. Note the numbers into the 370s – this is still that Petworth estate paint and numbering; the cottages are variously tile-hung, stone and half-timbered.

4 Turn right along the road, then left on a driveway by an old cottage on the left sporting an ancient Hovis sign (where the road bends right; the Black Horse Inn is a few yards further on left along this road). Carry on down to cross a stream (by a stone slab bridge marking the supposed site of a **holy well**), carry on along a fenced path and, on entering a field, turn left along its bottom edge, passing some ponds on your left.

5 At the next path junction go left downhill to cross the stream by a bridge. Turn right at a T-junction of paths (10yds up) on the other side, then through a kissing-gate and diagonally left at the next junction (30yds later), on a path rising towards houses. At the top of the slope, go forward at a crossing of paths, on a path between fences, with houses on your right.

6 Emerge at the edge of Petworth, with **New Grove House** (where Grinling Gibbons stayed) in view to your left. Turn right along the road, past **Percy Terrace** with its tall chimney stacks, Rosemary Lane and the **Petworth Cottage Museum** to reach the town centre.

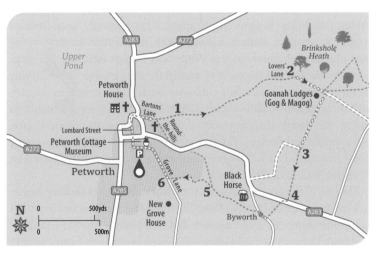

This is landscaping on a hugely ample scale: 700 acres landscaped by Capability Brown in the naturalistic English tradition that improved on nature itself. To achieve his scheme, the main road was rerouted and half of the village of Tillington was demolished. Dotted with specimen trees, the grass gives the illusion of being on a plateau that runs into the distant Downs. The largest herd of fallow deer in Britain roams freely. Then the quite understated classical frontage of the house gives straight on to the parkland – with no formal gardens on that side.

Petworth House
🖉 01798 343929; National Trust

This huge mansion, built by the Dukes of Somerset in the late 17th century, is so abundantly laden with treasures that a single visit barely does it justice. To get an overview, it's well worth catching one of the introductory talks or the Life Below Stairs tours (free, but ticketed) that might take in the bedrooms or – when the bats aren't in residence – the tunnels between the house and the servants' quarters. Its interior is much grander and less restrained than its exterior suggests and contains the finest art collection in any National Trust property. Turner was a guest here, painting and fishing in the lake, and Petworth has many of his works, along with those of others including Van Dyck, Titian, Gainsborough, Bosch and Blake. The original entrance, the **Marble Hall**, was completed in 1692; the driveway that led to it disappeared under Capability Brown's landscaping. This perfectly proportioned room has genuine Roman statuary, with the Grand Staircase rising past murals of Prometheus and Pandora in trompe l'œil style like stage scenery. The **Carved Room** is so named for the virtuoso wood carving by the incomparable Grinling Gibbons – such is its courageous delicacy and three-dimensionality that it almost looks as if it were wrought in metal, the details dripping with musical instruments, cherubs, lace, birds, beads and flowers. Turner's view of the park hangs opposite the point from which it was painted, and rather incongruously below Earl Seymour with his gold pompom shoes.

The hub of the art collection is in the **North Wing Art Gallery**, begun in 1754 and extended in the 1820s. The style of top lighting and paintings hung one above the other against dark-red walls is similar to that of London's Dulwich Picture Gallery, designed by Sir John Soane in 1811 as England's first public art gallery. As a lifelong friend of Turner, Soane may well have been involved in designing the Petworth extension. The north bay of the gallery was designed around John Flaxman's *St Michael overcoming Satan*, where the saint is about to spear the serpentine tail (completed in 1826, the year of Flaxman's death). Look out for the early 15th-century Chaucer manuscript and the depiction of a fête held at Petworth for the poor in 1835, when 6,000 were fed at tables laid in three semi-circles

"Look out for the early 15th-century Chaucer manuscript and the depiction of a fête held at Petworth in 1835."

on the lawn. Quite a few of the ancient classical sculptures were cobbled together from separate bits of statue with heads or torsos missing: hence there's at least one male sporting a female head.

Wander across a back yard to the block containing the fascinating **kitchen and servants' quarters**. That isn't the way the domestic staff would have gone, though: they used steep steps to take a tunnel across to the house, thus keeping them discreetly out of sight as well as necessitating a lot of carting stuff up and down the stairs. Light and airy, the kitchens were cutting-edge in the late Victorian period, and were in use until World War II; the huge gas cookers date from the 1920s. In all they contain about 1,000 brass and copper vessels, now cleaned once a year by volunteers – a gargantuan task that takes two months. Adjacent are the larder, scullery and pastry room.

 ## SPECIAL STAYS

The Old Railway Station Station Rd, GU28 0JF ✆ 01798 342346 ⌂ old-station.co.uk. This former station, closed to passengers since 1955, has a surprisingly opulent, colonial feeling with its shutters and high ceilings. Erected in 1892, it was used by the future Edward VII when he went to the races at Goodwood. It has been sympathetically adapted into a high-class B&B, with two bedrooms in the main building and eight in four historic Pullman carriages alongside the old platform. The former waiting room is now a spacious dining and sitting room. If it's sunny, you might like to take breakfast out on the platform. Not cheap, but highly memorable.

 ## FOOD & DRINK

The Black Horse Inn Byworth GU28 0HL ✆ 01798 342424 ⌂ blackhorsebyworth.co.uk. Just outside Petworth, in an extremely pretty estate village, well out of earshot of the main road, this 17th-century dining pub with rooms has a lovely, relaxing garden. The bar is nicely traditional, with an open fire and beamed ceiling. Expect real ale and good food made from locally sourced ingredients, at prices that aren't over the top.

THE MENS & EBERNOE COMMON

Two very special Sussex Wildlife Trust woodland nature reserves are found close to Petworth. By the A272 northeast of town, **The Mens**, named after an Anglo-Saxon word for common land, comprises a wild, often muddy and decidedly disorienting area of ancient woodland: this is the best surviving unmanaged wood in Sussex, superb for bluebells and fungi, while the Badlands Meadows in the southeast part of the reserve are speckled with wildflowers in summer, including dyer's greenweed and lady's mantle. The Trust occasionally holds fungus-spotting events here in autumn; see ⌀ sussexwildlifetrust.org.uk.

North of Petworth, **Ebernoe Common** is another place for serendipitous strolling. A prized Low Weald woodland, it is remarkably biodiverse, with 14 out of 16 of the native species of bats, including the rare barbastelle and Bechstein's, plus purple emperor butterflies and many lichens and mosses. For centuries, the wood provided grazing for cattle and pigs and was a hive of rural industry, with a pond used in the 16th century to power an iron furnace. The common's preserved moulding shed and kiln belonged to a brickworks dating back to at least 1678, and are now a scheduled ancient monument. A heritage trail threads through the reserve.

INTO THE LOW WEALD AROUND THE UPPER ARUN

North of Amberley, the downland landscape rapidly morphs into the watermeadows around Pulborough. Watermeadows are often confused with any general bog-standard flat field, or any standard boggy field – but there's a key difference. Systems of sluices and water-filled ditches can provide control when the whole lot is deliberately flooded to enrich the farmland with super-fertile river silt. Thus at certain times of year the whole valley is a splashy-looking wetland: it can look at its absolute best in winter. The profusion of bird and plant life makes this a prized pocket of countryside. I first heard about it through the piano music of John Ireland (1875–1962), who lived for many years in Sussex and wrote a hauntingly pastoral *Downland Suite* for orchestra. His *Amberley Wild Brooks* is a gorgeous and undeservedly unknown impressionist piece full of watery ornament. The tract of land after which it is named merges into the meadows of **Pulborough Brooks RSPB Reserve**, of year-round interest for its wildlife.

"The whole valley is a splashy-looking wetland: it can look at its absolute best in winter."

17 LOXWOOD

For a good part of the 19th century you could have travelled by boat from London to Arundel, by way of Weybridge, Guildford and Pulborough and using the 23-mile **Wey and Arun Canal** that linked the rivers Wey and Arun. The canal closed in 1871, and gradually turned into a wilderness, and its glory days were rapidly forgotten. Today the Wey and Arun Canal Trust (weyandarun.co.uk), formed in the early 1970s by a band of enthusiasts, has embarked on a huge programme of restoring it while keeping its rich range of wildlife habitats; weeds have been cleared, bridges and locks rebuilt, and stretches made navigable.

The best vantage point for this impressive industrial relic is from the bridge by The Onslow Arms on the southern edge of Loxwood (there's a large public car park just behind the pub), northwest of Billingshurst. The eastward stretch of the canal (on the pub side of the road) has been restored and boat trips run at weekends and on bank holidays from mid April until October. On the other side of the road you can see a restored lock, and further along is the Devil's Hole, an abandoned oxbow section of canal that was created as an attempt to bypass a slope. Nature soon takes over as you proceed this way, and the canal water eventually disappears. Another notable stretch of this canal is at New Bridge, west of Billingshurst.

They're always on the look-out for volunteers to help the project: all ages, 16 to 75, and all levels of skill are welcome. See the website for details.

18 NUTBOURNE VINEYARDS

Gay St, Pulborough RH20 2HH 01798 815196 nutbournevineyards.com Mon–Sat; Stagecoach bus 1 (Midhurst–Worthing; hourly Mon–Sat, less frequent Sun) to Little Hill, then 1.3-mile walk

There are not many places in Britain where you can stand in a windmill tasting wine from grapes grown yards away and look out to a glorious view. Nutbourne Vineyards is one: the tasting room is in a sail-less tower mill, and the distant view of the South Downs escarpment is one to drink in at leisure. Bridget and Peter Gladwyn admit they weren't looking for a vineyard when they started property-hunting in the locality, but the scenic qualities of this one (which they then enlarged) persuaded them to take up wine production. They have backgrounds in catering. Bridget took a viticulture course at Plumpton College near

TOBY GIBSON/D

JULIAN MORGAN

ED DALLIMORE

Lewes, and had considerable help from the Nyetimber vineyard nearby. Their three boys take a break from their jobs running restaurants and farming livestock to help with the harvest, spraying and digging holes.

You can just turn up and wander around yourself for no charge, and try a free tasting of their excellent wines – these include *Sussex Reserve* ('dry, fragrant, with delicate citrus fruit characteristics'), *Blush* (an 'aromatic, summery rosé'), *Bacchus* ('crisp and fresh with an elderflower bouquet') and sparkling *Nutty Brut*. For pre-arranged groups there are tours at a set price. 'We tell them about growing systems, what happens on the build-up to harvest. We go around the lakes, meet our alpacas.' For the October harvest they get in specialist pickers who know the vines well, and bird-deterring goes big time: 'plastic hawks, anything that floats in the air, glittery things and bird scarers'.

In addition to the Nutbourne and Nyetimber (West Chiltington RH20 2HH ⌀ nyetimber.com), other West Sussex vineyards that offer tours and events include Ashling Park (West Ashling PO18 9DJ ⌀ ashlingpark. co.uk), Highdown (Ferring BN12 6PG ⌀ highdownvineyard.co.uk), Tinwood Estate (Halnaker PO18 0NE ⌀ tinwoodestate.com) and Trotton Estate (Trotton GU31 5DA ⌀ trottonestatevineyards.com).

19 PULBOROUGH BROOKS
Wiggonholt, Pulborough RH20 2EL ⌀ 01798 875851 ⌀ rspb.org.uk; Compass bus 100 (Horsham–Burgess Hill; hourly Mon–Sat)

One of the most accessible parts of the water meadows of the Arun Valley, this large RSPB reserve just south of Pulborough is one of Sussex's great wetlands, but also includes small copses and hedgerow-lined fields; it is home to at least 160 species of birds, butterflies, insects and mammals. The natural wetlands have been carefully managed and nurtured to provide a thriving wildlife haven, by controlling the flooding on the wet grassland, grazing cattle, cutting hay and cleaning out the ditches to maintain the right conditions for wetland birds and plantlife. The woods have partly been coppiced, and rare heathland has been regenerated by removing scrub, bracken and conifers and planting heather seed to provide more habitat for birds such as nightjars.

◀ **1** Stopham Bridge near Pulborough was built in 1423. **2** A nightingale sings at the Pulborough Brooks RSPB reserve. **3** Sample wine while sitting in a windmill at Nutbourne Vineyard. **4** Stretches of the Wey and Arun Canal have been made navigable – in all seasons!

You can hire binoculars at the visitor centre, where chatty volunteers are on hand to explain what to look for. They're at pains for visitors not to feel out of their depth; one explained to me 'it gives me a real buzz to see kids full of enthusiasm having spotted an adder or a dragonfly'. Introductory talks and walks are held year round. In winter there are huge numbers of wintering ducks, geese and swans here. Summer is particularly good for butterflies and dragonflies, and in the evening you may hear owls and nightjars, while spring sees wading birds breeding here. The walk around the reserve is a scenic pleasure in itself, with watery views extending towards Pulborough village, and fallow deer often in evidence. Strategically placed hides make excellent vantage points and the café is good value.

20 HARDHAM

Train to Pulborough (Arun Valley Line, Three Bridges–West Coastway), then 1½-mile walk

This tiny village off the A29 has Roman origins as a road station on the Roman route known as Stane Street; Roman bricks and tiles from a nearby camp have been re-used in the building of the **Church of St Botolph**. Thought to be of Saxon origins – some of its round-arched windows may date from then – this remarkable building has the earliest near-complete set of medieval wall paintings of any English church. They were created around 1100, and although they have faded it is still possible to pick out the details, including the *Torments of Hell* on the west wall, the *Nativity* on the south wall and the *Flight into Egypt* on the north wall. Clearest of all is the Picasso-esque depiction of Adam and Eve on the west wall of the chancel. The fact that up to 1866 the whole lot had been covered over with plaster for many years has probably kept them looking relatively fresh.

"This remarkable building has the earliest near-complete set of medieval wall paintings of any English church."

Beside the A283 west from Pulborough and spanning the River Arun, **Stopham Bridge** is perhaps Sussex's most venerable span, built in stone in 1423 to replace an earlier wooden structure. Its central arch was raised in 1822 to allow boats to pass beneath. The bridge is closed to traffic, which now crosses the modern adjacent bridge; there is a spot where you can park and walk across. Further north, a house called Brinkwells (not open to the public) near **Fittleworth** was where Sir Edward Elgar took refuge from 1917 to 1921 and wrote his piano quintet, string quartet, violin sonata and part of his cello concerto.

THE LOWER ARUN VALLEY

The Arun wiggles its way sluggishly through one of the largest surviving systems of watermeadows in Sussex between **Amberley** and **Arundel**. Arundel Castle is what most tourists come to look at, and formidably impressive it is too, but many miss what lies close by – including some treasured bird reserves, and one of the most absorbing ways of finding out about the industrial past in the form of the Amberley Museum. A well-presented museum in the Old School at **Storrington** (⊘ storringtonmuseum.org ⊙ Wed & Sat–Sun; free entry) covers local history.

South of Arundel is less special, but you might like to venture out to the beach south of **Climping** for one of those rare stretches of undeveloped Sussex coast; it's between Littlehampton and Middleton-on-Sea (the latter being on the easternmost arm of Bognor Regis). The beach, backed by low dunes, is a refreshing place for a stroll, with the hamlet of **Atherington** being the best starting point, and it's pretty nice for a swim if you don't mind the pebbles. You get a good idea how a lot of the undeveloped Sussex seaside must have looked before the 20th century.

21 PARHAM HOUSE & GARDENS

Storrington, nr Pulborough RH20 4HR ⊘ 01903 742021 ⊘ parhaminsussex.co.uk ⊙ Easter Sun–early Oct Wed–Fri, Sun & public holidays; Compass bus 100 (Horsham–Burgess Hill; hourly Mon–Sat) to Cootham, then one-mile walk

As you approach through the deer park via the main driveway, what is immediately apparent is the setting of this Elizabethan mansion beneath the South Downs. The house in its full glory only appears at the last minute; it dates from 1577 and has always been a family home, although the family do not live in the part of the house that you see. The panelled, plaster-ceilinged Great Hall has changed little over the years, and the smaller rooms contain choice examples of needlework, paintings and furniture. At the top of the house the Long Gallery has a fascinating array of curios and an exhibition about the Pearson family and the wartime evacuees.

The **walled garden** can be visited separately. From the driveway you can just get a glimpse of it over the walls, which give not only privacy but also protection against the salt-laden winds blowing up from the sea. The natural soil is almost entirely sand here, but centuries of careful composting and manuring have created a fertile paradise inside. The garden layout dates from the 1920s, but the planting was transformed from the 1980s. A series of interlocking pictures, woven into each other with a tapestry-like effect, the garden has opulent mixed borders planted in a 'wild and woolly' style in the English Romantic tradition and which supply the cut flowers for decorating the house. The Wendy House, a child-scale residence set into a brick wall, was built in one corner in the 1920s for the Pearsons' three daughters, and has two storeys, a fireplace and a wooden parquet floor.

Parham's varied calendar of **events** include a Sussex Day fair in mid June, a steam rally in July and a programme of day **courses** linked to Parham themes such as garden photography.

Even when the house and gardens are closed, simply strolling through the **estate** is hugely enjoyable. The deer park and woodlands shelter over 300 deer, herons (nesting in the northwest part of the estate), woodland birds, and many rare insects and lichens. This is very much a landscape evolved over many generations by the owners (currently the Barnards) and estate team at Parham. Some of the ancient oaks in the park date back 600 years. The 1987 storm devastated much of the estate, bringing down many trees in its wake – some 80,000 trees and saplings came down, and 30-odd years on you can still see the damage to many of those which survived. Fortuitously this turned out to be the making of the estate as an important wildlife sanctuary. From that time on they have deliberately allowed any fallen or cut wood from ageing or damaged trees to decay and a new ecosystem has grown up.

Some years back I spoke to Richard Edwards, then the Parham Estate Manager, who had vivid memories of the storm. 'You could hear the wind coming up like an express train roaring, and a barn next door collapsed and we didn't hear it. It took us three days to cut our way out of the park. You couldn't see the drive – it was all covered with trees. In the end we hired a helicopter to assess the damage. We had to bring in contractors from Scotland and Yorkshire and the Gurkhas to clear the trees. When we replanted we could leave wider spaces between the plantations to make sunny corridors for butterflies, so there were some good effects.'

HIGH FLIERS

Southdown Gliding Club Cootham RH20 4HP ✆ 01903 742137
🖱 southdowngliding.co.uk

Just across the main road from the Parham estate, the Southdown Gliding Club offers gliding instruction. Beginners can have a trial lesson in which you're towed up and then the engine is switched off and the controls are handed over to you until the instructor takes care of the landing. It's a strange, marvellous sensation of being over the landscape, at a normal maximum speed of around 50 knots; vertigo, curiously, is rarely a problem. The situation by the South Downs assists gliding considerably, allowing the aircraft to 'hill-soar'. This is historic gliding terrain: it was from Amberley Mount on 27 June 1909 that the world's first recorded soaring flight by glider was made, in a glider made by a French artist José Weiss who was living in Amberley; the pilot was just 17.

Each year between February and May herons return to the heronry on the northwest side of the estate to breed. The trees are also, rather unusually, the home for greylag geese, who nest well out of foxes' reach; woodland birds include nuthatches, tree creepers, nightjars and all three species of woodpecker. Winter sees cormorants and mandarin ducks on the estate. At Parham they're also rather proud of being one of a very few release sites for **field crickets**, which are bred at London Zoo and have taken to the well-drained, sandy soil and south-facing slopes. You might hear these now very rare insects during late afternoon or early evening in May and June when they 'sing' at the entrance to their barrows to attract a mate.

Near the house entrance is an 18th-century **dovecote,** where several hundred pigeons and doves kept for their eggs, meat and feathers nested. Close by, a door set into a grassy slope marks the entrance to the **ice house** – ice from the lake when it froze in winter was brought here by a chain of estate workers. The underground chamber, insulated by the earth around it, was cool enough to keep ice cold all summer; it would have been full of grit, leaves and worse though, so was not put directly into food and drinks. It's now a protected habitat for bats.

On the downland side of the house, the church is thought to date from Tudor times but was rebuilt in the 1800s and furnished with box pews made of yew wood. The family pew has a private fireplace and the 14th-century lead font is a rarity for being inscribed with lettering. Beyond lies an idyllic **cricket pitch**, used by the local team; in former days the estate mustered enough workers to form a team themselves.

There has been a **fallow deer herd** since 1628: unusually, they are rather darker coloured than you may see elsewhere. There are over 300 of them, with seven does to each buck. Fawns are born in June and hidden in clumps of grass by their mothers for two or three days until they are strong enough to walk. Never approach one (if the fawn smells of human the mother will reject it), and keep a safe distance from rutting bucks in October, when you may hear them clashing antlers. The estate has to manage the herd to keep the numbers down, balanced between does and bucks, and generally healthy; there's a humane cull by shooting each year in February and September. If this were not done, the condition of the herd would deteriorate and more bucks would be injured through rutting. The most oft-shot beast is beside the house in the form of an iron 'target stag' on wheels which came from Lady Emma Barnard's family home in Ireland. It would have been pulled by ropes and used for shooting practice.

22 AMBERLEY
Arun Valley Line (Three Bridges–West Coastway)

Ranged around a grid of quiet streets and a few miles upriver from Arundel is this improbably perfect-looking village where thatch predominates on the rooftops and the stone walls are set off by a parade of carefully tended cottage gardens (with an Open Gardens event in June on even-numbered years). It always astonishes me that it's not better known. The Old Bake House, Old Postings and Old Brew House hint at a more industrious past, but thankfully the village is still very much a living community, with two good pubs, lots of local organisations, a school, a village shop stacked with Sussex produce and an excellent tearoom. Probably founded by Bishop de Luffa (founder of Chichester Cathedral), **St Michael's Church** has vestiges of a wall painting but is more striking for its Norman work, with a huge chancel arch bearing palm-tree ornamentation, and a rare iron hour-glass stand above the pulpit. Close by the church in a former United Reformed Chapel is **Amberley Village Pottery** (⊘ amberleypottery.co.uk ☉ Thu–Sun), with a showroom at the back.

Beyond the church a dead-end lane slopes down to the marshy dragonfly-populated flats of the watermeadows known as **Amberley**

Wildbrooks ('wild' deriving from 'weald'), a Sussex Wildlife Trust reserve where the formidable curtain wall of **Amberley Castle**, now a very upmarket hotel, towers over a scene vaguely suggestive of some little lost paradise somewhere in rural France. A single track, Wey South Path (very muddy in winter, beware), crosses the Wildbrooks, which was nearly drained and converted into conventional farmland some years back, to much (thankfully successful) local protest. There aren't a

"Amberley Castle towers over a scene vaguely suggestive of some little lost paradise somewhere in rural France."

great many public footpaths hereabouts, so it's well worth the docile wander along this track a couple of miles to **Greatham Bridge**, a series of wonky arches dating from the 16th century and an idyllic picnic spot on the river banks, with fleets of Bewick's swans patrolling the Arun. Above the village, the Downs are virtually treeless, and the view along the South Downs Way is quite terrific, with **Amberley Mount** making a rewarding objective.

Close by Greatham Bridge, **Greatham Church**, a simple Norman building, has been restored but is remarkably untouched overall: no road leads to it, just a grassy track, and it's lit by oil lamps and served by a harmonium.

Amberley Museum & Heritage Centre

Amberley Station, BN18 9LT ✆ 01798 831370 ⌂ amberleymuseum.co.uk ☺ Feb–Oct Wed–Sun; Nov Wed & Sat–Sun

This has to be one of the most serendipitous museums I've seen. Close to the South Downs Way and right next to the railway station, it's variously a huge industrial relic, a nature reserve, a community of craftspeople and a collection of all sorts representing industry in the southeast over the centuries. The museum – amply deserving at least most of a day to visit – occupies a chalk pit where chalk was quarried from the 1840s to the 1960s and burnt here in the kilns to make lime for mortar and for agricultural fertiliser – then the biggest operation of its kind anywhere in the country, and run for most of that period by Pepper & Son. Thanks to massive volunteer efforts it opened to the public in 1979. The kilns and site railway now form part of the site.

Much of the pleasure of being here is just nosing around the huge array of all things industrial, much of it organised into a series of display buildings, and full of curios of various periods to chance upon – a phone box with a stamp machine integrated into it, a brickyard drying shed, an ancient AA box and a sawmill, among many others. Above all it gives the impression of being a real industrial site, and a lot of it is work in progress, with all manner of restorations taking place. Among its contents are some great rarities, including a working steam crane, which on occasions is put through its paces to lift uncut logs and load them ready for sawing.

Of the museums-within-the-museum, some are tiny, like the bagmender's shed, others seriously time-consuming, such as the Electricity Hall with its wondrous selection of antique appliances, the transplanted Southdown Bus Garage with its vintage buses and advertising boards promising trips to Michelham Priory or Bodiam Castle, and the BT Connected Earth Telecommunications Hall comprising 'the most complete collection of telephone instruments and overhead line insulators in the country'. Vintage buses and narrow-gauge trains take foot-weary visitors round the site.

"Weekends are often the liveliest times to visit, with numerous special events, many centred around transport themes."

The chatty staff help make this a day not to rush. They are true aficionados: one maintains the extraordinary collection of wirelesses, while others make a living working on the site, repairing bicycles, woodturning, making pots, working as a wheelwright, creating traditional besoms from silver-birch twigs or heather, or operating the print works where they'll show you the hot metal process, explain the vintage presses and print you out a certificate or sell you a print. Weekends are often the liveliest times to visit, with numerous special events, many centred around transport themes – vintage cars, motorcycles, buses and so on.

The site has an unexpected physical beauty, with its once gleaming white chalk cliffs now atmospherically overgrown with all sorts of species. Wild orchids are here in abundance, and there are 129 types of fungi, 24 species of butterfly and peregrine falcons nesting in a secret spot on the cliff. You can follow a trail up to the top of the White Pit for a view over the South Downs. The museum depends on voluntary effort and has an army of some 400 volunteers who spend their days on all sorts of restoration and other tasks.

¶¶ FOOD & DRINK

Amberley Village Tea Room The Square, BN18 9SR ☏ 01798 839196 ⊙ Thu–Sun.
Thoroughly cheerful village-centre tea room with plenty of rustic character, a front courtyard
and a woodburner for chillier months. Locally sourced or fair-trade products including Jackie
and Laura's homemade cakes, clotted cream scones with local jam, specially roasted coffee
and loose-leaf tea are served in or on items made in the village pottery.

The Bridge Inn Houghton Bridge BN18 9LR ☏ 01798 8316419 ⌂ bridgeinnamberley.
com ⊙ Wed–Sun. Close to the bridge, railway station and museum, this unpretentious pub
serves real ale and hearty, reasonably priced food, and hosts live music once a month or so.

Riverside South Downs Houghton Bridge BN18 9LP ☏ 01798 831066
⌂ riversidesouthdowns.com. Café with a terrace right by the river, and a mountain bike and
e-bike hire shop.

The Sportsman Inn Rackham Rd BN18 9NR ☏ 01798 831787 ⌂ thesportsmansussex.co.uk
⊙ Wed–Sun. This rural dining pub with rooms has a raised deck, from where you can enjoy
magnificent views of Amberley Wildbrooks while tucking into above-average pub standards
such as burgers and scampi. The bar has Harvey's, Dark Star and other Sussex ales on tap.

23 ARUNDEL

Arun Valley Line (Three Bridges–West Coastway); Compass bus 85 (Chichester–Arundel;
several daily Mon–Fri)

With its castle and cathedral crowning an abrupt rise in the Downs, this
most captivating of small towns has a French look to it from a distance.
The castle deserves plenty of time in itself, but there's much pleasure
to be had from a walk up the main street, and into the handsome side
streets – such as Maltravers and Tarrant streets – along the river and
through Arundel Park (free access), the wider estate of the castle itself.
A day here passes very pleasantly, with a potter around the town's shops,
a visit to the castle and Wetlands Centre, a walk around the river and a
swim in the scenically sited Arundel Lido.

The **railway station** is slightly out of things, but less than ten minutes'
walk to the centre; it does involve crossing the unpleasant A27 by traffic
lights and then wandering along a suburban road, but soon gets better.
For **parking**, the best bet is to turn off the A27 at the easternmost of the
two roundabouts, then turn right as soon as you cross the river – there's
lots of free parking along Mill Road (right along to the WWT Arundel
Wetland Centre and beyond, and you can get into Arundel Park from
here), which saves you parking in town. Note that at summer weekends
it can get extremely busy and even Mill Road fills up with parked cars.

At the top of the town, vertical, spiky and flamboyant, the 19th-century **Roman Catholic Cathedral** designed by Joseph Hansom (of hansom cab fame) sets off the skyline alongside the castle in a recreation of the French Gothic style of the 1400s. The dedication is to St Philip Howard, the 20th Earl of Arundel (1557–95), who is portrayed in a 1986 stained-glass window with his wife and dog, and whose remains are here too. He was once a favourite of Elizabeth I, fell from her favour after rediscovering his Catholic faith and died after being kept in the Tower of London for 11 years along with his faithful dog.

"Vertical, spiky and flamboyant, the 19th-century Roman Catholic Cathedral sets off the skyline alongside the castle."

Along Mill Road, Arundel continues with its Little France look: a shady avenue invites picnics, and off it is a tea garden by a very prettily kept putting green. Near the river is the **Arundel Lido** (✆ 01903 884772 ⚭ arundel-lido.com ☉ Apr–Sep), where the castle provides a choice backdrop for swimmers, sunbathers and paddlers. Lidos are something of an endangered species, and this one – opened as the Fitzalan Pool in 1960 following a donation of land by the Duke of Norfolk to celebrate the 21st birthday of his eldest daughter – nearly became history after closure by the council in 1999. A group of dedicated locals recognised its very special qualities and set up the charitable Arundel and Downland Community Leisure Trust to rescue it. The paddling pool was the first stage of the rescue act, and then the main pool was reduced in size to 25m (with a 5m splash pool at one end) and heated. The crowds of people here on warm summer days testify to its lasting popularity.

Run by volunteers, the **Arundel Museum** (Mill Rd, BN18 9PA ⚭ arundelmuseum.org) has an absorbing, well-presented collection about the town's past, from prehistoric to modern times. Items range from palaeolithic hand axes found near Slindon, chunks of mosaic and floor tiles from a nearby Roman villa, models of ships that used to

1 The formidable Arundel Castle sprawls across half a hillside. **2** Arundel town hosts an arts festival in August. **3** Get close to wildlife on a boat trip at the Arundel Wetland Centre. **4** Amberley Museum and Heritage Centre includes vintage buses at the transplanted Southdown Bus Garage. **5** The Elizabethan Long Gallery in Parham runs the entire length of the building. ▶

THE DRONE AWAKENS

CHARLIE WARING

DARREN COOL IMAGES/WWT

NEIL WRAIGHT/D

JONATHAN WILSON

Arundel, the Arun & Arundel Park

✻ OS Explorer map OL10; start: Mill Rd car park, Arundel town centre ♀ SU021071 (large car park backing on to the river, next to the museum); full walk seven miles, short walk 3½ miles; riverside paths, plus downland; steep climb through forest on seven-mile walk; one gentler climb on the shorter walk. Note that there's also free parking along Mill Rd, although this can be very full at peak times. **Loos** in Mill Road car park. By **train**: Arundel: exit on to A27, turn left along pavement, cross road near roundabout & continue towards town centre; just over the river bridge, turn right, past museum & turn right into Mill Rd car park. **Refreshments** in Arundel, at Swanbourne Lake & at Black Rabbit.

A more bucolic walk in rural England would be hard to imagine: this supremely varied route has a bit of everything. I've presented it as a short and long version. Both routes begin with taking in a calming, reedy stretch along the Arun. The short route diverts near the **WWT Arundel Wetland Centre** for a wander along **Swanbourne Lake** (where rowing boats are for hire), while the longer version ventures further up this increasingly remote-feeling valley – either along the river or away from it – then through mixed woodlands clinging on to downland slopes beneath the Arundel Castle estate, and on to **Arundel Park**. Here, vintage views unfold as you climb and then descend to the valley floor, where our two routes merge. Past Hiorne Tower, you enter into the top of Arundel, where the grandeur of the Roman Catholic Cathedral and Castle present a captivating townscape.

At South Stoke, the **suspension bridge** was rebuilt in 2009 after the original bridge had suffered storm damage. The council intended to replace it with a bog-standard span but an Amberley villager had connections with the Gurkhas and persuaded them to organise a group of soldiers to set up a camp and rebuild it. One villager described it to me: 'It ended with a fantastic party with Indian food and Gurkha families and locals, and the Gurkhas performing their kukri knife dance. The Gurkhas loved the project, which was a wonderful training job.' The bridge is now officially renamed the Gurkha Suspension Bridge. I've put in a couple of variants to avoid midsummer stinging nettles.

1 Go to the back of Mill Road car park to find the path by Waterside Café, and turn left on it, almost immediately alongside the river. Carry on for a mile.

2 Where a tributary appears on the left at a sluice, you have a choice of routes:

For the short walk via Swanbourne Lake: turn left (there are paths either side of this tributary; the one on the near side has lovely views of the castle and the tributary but can be a bit nettly in high summer; to avoid the nettles, cross over at the sluice and find the path leading left on the other side. Both paths lead to a footbridge beneath the road bridge.) Turn right on to the road and take the path almost immediately on the left, along the left side of Swanbourne Lake. (For the east side of the lake, carry on the road a few yards, then left at Swanbourne Lodge – tea rooms and boat hire here.) Beyond the end of the lake, the two paths that led either side of it eventually merge. Carry on up to a meeting of tracks with a dry valley stretching ahead. Turn sharp left on the rising track and join the directions at point **4**.

For the full walk via South Stoke: carry on along the riverside path, eventually reaching the lane near the **Black Rabbit** pub. Here you have a choice: either carry on along the river, through the pub car park, then through trees to resume the route along the river, and follow it 1½ miles to the second bridge (at South Stoke), then leave the river, turning left along the lane, past the church, then right after South Stoke Farm, on the bridleway. Or if you feel you've walked long enough by the river (but beware, a section of this can be a bit nettly in summer), fork left on the rising lane, which is cut spectacularly deep through the bedrock. At the T-junction, turn left towards South Stoke but after 50yds turn right on the signposted bridleway. The nettles might pose a problem for a few hundred yards, but then it gets much easier. At the road at South Stoke, turn left, then right, just above **South Stoke Farm**. Both options: beyond the end of the strangely ecclesiastical-looking South Stoke Farm, turn left on the signposted bridleway, rising gently. This takes you along a field edge and eventually into mixed woodland. ▶

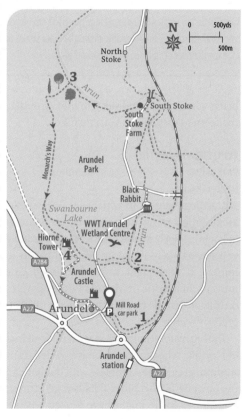

Arundel, the Arun & Arundel Park (continued)

3 ◄ Nearly a mile from South Stoke you reach the Arundel Park estate wall on your left, with a gate and noticeboard about Arundel Park. Go through this gate, and follow the waymarked path, initially to the left along the wall, then steeply up. Later on the views open out across the Arun valley, and you fork left at a marker post, soon into woods again. Finally leave the wooded area and carry on across open grassland (no path visible), aiming for the right side of a copse, where you join a track. Shortly before a gate ahead across the track, descend diagonally right past a waymarked stile and down a beautiful grassy valley with **Hiorne Tower** in view ahead and the sea in the background. Drop to a crossing of tracks (if you want to see Swanbourne Lake, detour a few minutes down to the left here) and take the track that rises up the other side of the valley, leading left.

4 Just after a gate, turn right up steps and cross the grass, keeping to the left of Hiorne Tower. Turn left on the estate road, past a lodge, then left on the public road into Arundel, passing the cathedral and the castle. Then drop down the main street, forking left near the war memorial to reach the river bridge near Mill Road car park.

bring wine, cheese and salt fish into Arundel, and a printing press from the town's West Sussex Gazette office.

Arundel Castle

BN18 9AB ✆ 01903 882173 ✇ arundelcastle.org ☉ Apr–Oct Tue–Sun (Aug daily) & public holidays

A startling sight from whichever way you approach it, Arundel Castle looks almost too good to be true. Its battlemented form sprawls across half a hillside above the little town in a grand gesture of feudalism. What you see is largely Victorian, but that hardly detracts from its emotional impact. It is thought to have inspired Gormenghast, the sprawling universe of a castle in Mervyn Peake's novels, and has been used for the setting of various films including the 1990s comic drama *The Madness of King George*.

The big restoration work was carried out in the 1870s–90s by the Dukes of Norfolk, whose ancestors have owned it since 1138. All is improbably smooth, grey stone, complete with battlements and turrets. If you ignore the obvious 19th-century details it gives a very good impression of how a medieval castle might have looked when new. And in any case, the Victorian revamp is very much part of its character.

Few other houses have such a long continuous occupation. It was founded on Christmas Day in 1067 by Roger de Montgomery, Earl of Arundel, one of William the Conqueror's associates. In the 16th century it passed to the Howards of Norfolk, who were Royalists in the Civil War and temporarily lost it to Cromwell in 1643. In that conflict the defences were destroyed, and the castle lay in ruins. Several rebuilds followed, including an extravagant revamp by Thomas Howard, the 8th Duke, and apartments, art and furnishings added by the 13th Duke.

Within the structure is the mechanism for the portcullis and the original medieval keep, giving a tremendous view over the coastal plain (when it was built, the sea would have been much closer). In contrast to the austerity of the oldest part, the residential portion of the castle has almost too much for the eye to take in. It all conjures up a great sense of dynastic continuity, with family portraits and photos from various centuries up to the present. The cavernous Great Hall accommodates an entertaining array of seemingly unrelated bits and pieces – a sedan chair, lion-skin rug, portraits of cardinals, a sleigh, and German silver figures of an orchestra with nodding heads. Another room has three Canalettos, while the spare rooms still used for guests boast high Victorian comfort with baskets of logs, armchairs by the fire, great deep baths, and Turners and Constables displayed on the walls. Electric light was installed in the 1890s – all the switches and lamps are of Gothic design and are quite a feature in themselves.

The Dukes of Norfolk never renounced their Catholic allegiance; several were executed for treason and had land confiscated, yet they have remained second in the nobility ladder. One of their number presented a whole series of tasty female relatives to Henry VIII, including Anne Boleyn, her sister Mary and Catherine Howard; eventually even Henry lost patience and that Norfolk ended up being executed for plotting.

The extensive **grounds** include a walled garden that incorporates five gardens, including the Collector Earl's Garden with its Oberon's Palace fountain.

Accessed through the castle grounds, the family's **Fitzalan Chapel** is Catholic yet backs on to the Church of England parish church, with which it connects – a unique arrangement arising from the Dissolution: a metal grille and glass screen separate the two parts of the building. In 1977 it was opened for a combined service for the Week of Prayer for Christian Unity, the first time the whole building had been used for a combined act of worship since 1544; it has only been opened half a dozen times since. Among the family tombs within is an extraordinary cadaver sculpture of a decomposing corpse, depicted beneath the effigy of the 7th Earl who died in 1435.

WWT Arundel Wetland Centre

Mill Rd, Arundel BN18 9PB ✎ 01903 883355 ⊘ wwt.org.uk; train to Arundel (Arun Valley Line), then 1.3-mile walk

Opened in 1976 on a marshy wetland of old watercress beds and tucked away by the river, under the shelter of the castle and its wooded slopes, this is one of nine Wildfowl and Wetlands Trust (WWT) sites across the country. It's a wondrous little world unto itself, a place to slow down, look, listen and thoroughly immerse yourself in the wildlife of this important reserve for wild birds and other wetland species, and allow birds to feed out of your hand. You do get a feeling of being part of the wider landscape though, with the castle and Downs in view and the occasional train trundling across in mid-distance.

Electric boat tours lasting 20 minutes are available between 11.00 and 15.00 for a small fee: these silent craft can get close to any wildlife that happens to be around, and pass near *"It's a wondrous little* enough to the reeds for them to tickle you *world unto itself, a place* as you glide by. With so much that is easily *to slow down, look, listen* spotted and binoculars available for hire, *and immerse yourself* these short trips suit beginners as much as *in the wildlife."* aficionados. Disabled access is excellent, with wheelchair-accessible paths and boats. The centre also hosts special events including art workshops and Discover Birds weekends, and offers opportunities for volunteers; see the website for details.

The Water's Edge Café at the entrance gives a fine panorama of the wildlife lagoon known as Arun Riverlife – a habitat for lapwings, little egrets, water voles and kingfishers. Before heading off on the boardwalks through the reserve, you can peruse the board in the reception area indicating recent sightings, and pick up a guide listing seasonal wild species, a checklist of the living collection and an overview of the grounds. Among the hides is a thatched camera obscura built by landscape artist Chris Drury, rather like a miniature Sydney Opera House made out of reeds. The birds live in naturalised areas and include

DORMICE IN THE WETLAND CENTRE

The WWT Arundel Wetland Centre's ground manager Paul Stevens told me about an unexpected new arrival in the form of the rare, internationally protected hazel or common dormouse, which first appeared in 2005. 'Before I started here, one of the ground staff was strimming the bank and found a hibernating mouse that didn't wake up. When we got someone to look at it, it had disappeared, but the fact it didn't wake up seemed to point towards a dormouse. It wasn't until I came here in 2008 that we started surveying for dormice and we had immediate success: within a month of putting up survey tubes we found two dormice making their haven there. Finding dormice in the reserve was unexpected as their usual habitat is associated with coppiced woodland. They have been found on different habitats, but to find them on a wetland was fantastic!'

How many are there, and can you see them? 'It's very difficult to gauge how many,' said Paul, 'we've seen at least seven individuals. They're very hard to see, sleeping six months of the year and being nocturnal, but they're all over the site.' Only registered handlers like Paul are legally permitted to touch this rare species.

the only harlequin ducks on display in the UK. Less glamorous are the corrugated sheets around the place which serve as grass-snake habitats. Each snake's markings are different, and each one they've found here is named after a staff member.

Most children are likely to be very happy here, with two play areas and numerous child-focused activities. Pat Warren, who showed me round, said the children particularly love feeding ducks at the Hand Feeding Bay and pond dipping (☉ weekends Apr–Oct & daily during school holidays). The latter is a fascinating way of seeing a microscopic world open up – children take samples of pond water and the results are flashed up on a screen via a microscope; when I looked in, one small girl was very proud to have found a caddisfly larva and a water boatman.

Spring brings out the most eye-catching plumage, while late spring and early summer are the peak time for young birds, and further into summer the wetland wild flowers are at their best. During August birdlife quietens down, but dragonflies and butterflies are prolific. Autumn and winter bring migrant birds, and you have a better chance of seeing kingfishers in winter, when you might also witness wildfowl sliding on the ice.

The reserve is constantly evolving. In 2005 they began a successful programme to increase the numbers of water voles in the valley; these were becoming very rare, and six years later a hectare of wet grassland was developed as a habitat for breeding lapwings every spring. The Sir Peter Scott Centenary Hide plays recordings to attract hordes of migrating sand martins in autumn. In winter the robust reedbeds are host to a starling murmuration that peaks at 2,000 each winter.

SHOPPING

There is plenty of scope for browsing in Arundel, with several antiques shops. The **Old Print Works** in Tarrant Street houses a number of interesting retailers, including a milliner and a vintage-style fashion boutique. There are a couple of bookshops – **Kim's** (10 High St; second hand and antiquarian) and **The Book Ferret** (34 High St; eclectic range of new books). The town also has some great independent food shops, including a chocolatier, a fishmonger, and a fantastic deli/wine merchant, **Pallant of Arundel** (17 High St ⏁ pallantofarundel. co.uk) on the site of the 1905 grocer Denton's Stores. The many local offerings here include Nutbourne and Nyetimber wines, smoked salmon, free-range eggs, cakes, preserves and chutneys.

EVENTS

Arundel's big moment is the **Arundel Festival of the Arts** in late August, with more than a week of arts-related events culminating in outdoor performances of Shakespeare in the castle grounds.

At Arundel Castle, there's a **Tulip Festival** in April and May, with a blaze of 30,000-odd tulips in bloom, and an **Allium Extravaganza** during May and June. In July there's a **jousting and medieval tournament** with an international team of armour-clad knights on specially trained horses, and competitors in hand-to-hand combat, medieval style.

FOOD & DRINK

Black Rabbit Mill Rd, BN18 9PA ✆ 01903 882638 ⏁ theblackrabbitarundel.co.uk. Popular country pub, festooned with dried hops, in a lovely riverside location. Serves real ale and classic fare. Proudly dog-friendly.

The Brewhouse Project Lyminster Rd, BN17 7QQ ✆ 01903 889997 ⏁ brewhouseproject. co.uk. Out of town, but handy for the A27 and worth seeking out, this barn-like hipster set-up is the tap room for Arundel Brewery. To complement its beers, it serves excellent sandwiches and moreish nibbles.

Motte & Bailey 49 High St, BN18 9AG ✆ 01903 883813 ⏁ motteandbaileycafe.com. Appealing independent café in a Georgian building on Arundel's handsome High Street. It serves generous cooked breakfasts, egg dishes and sandwiches at fair prices.

The Parson's Table Castle Mews, BN18 9DG ✆ 01903 883477 🖅 theparsonstable.co.uk
🕑 Tue–Sat. This high-flying contemporary restaurant works wonders with local, seasonal
ingredients. Menus change daily and may feature brill with artichoke, apple and hazelnuts,
partridge breast with quince or roasted cauliflower with sunflower hummus and cavolo nero.

24 BURPHAM

Train to Arundel (Arun Valley Line), then 2½-mile walk

A real backwater of a village, Burpham (pronounced Burfam) is on the
sleepy side of the Arun. St Mary's Church has some notable Norman
work in the form of its mid-12th-century arches, one displaying
zigzag decoration, the other carved with grotesque humanoid and
ape-like heads.

Behind **The George** (✆ 01903 883131 🖅 georgeatburpham.co.uk),
a popular dining pub, an apparently bland recreation field edged by a
bank which drops steeply on all sides provides a clue to the village name:
burh (or *burgh*), denoting a fortified Anglo-Saxon settlement, and *ham*,
or a homestead. For this is a **burgh**, or
fortified settlement – one of 30 established
by Alfred the Great in his kingdom of
Wessex as he embarked on the first spate
of town-building in this country since the
departure of the Romans, when trading
effectively collapsed. The burghs were

"For this is a burgh, or fortified settlement – one of 30 established by Alfred the Great in his kingdom of Wessex."

protected against Danish incursions, and included some re-occupied
Roman towns such as Winchester and Chichester, and others such as
Lewes – which may have had Roman origins or may have been Alfred's
innovation; some of these became administrative centres with their own
coin mints. Burpham was never an important town though. At its peak
it was a fortified village, and as Arundel eclipsed it, Burpham dwindled
into obscurity, leaving the fortified site around the flat expanse known
as the Wall Field (or the War Field) in strikingly good condition.

25 CLIMPING & WEST BEACHES

Train to Littlehampton (West Coastway Line), then one-mile walk

Climping Beach and West Beach, between Middleton-on-Sea
(effectively the easternmost part of Bognor Regis) and Littlehampton,
are on a rare section of undeveloped coast, popular with families. All
pebbles at high tide but with a strand of dark sand at low tide, they are

INTO HAMPSHIRE

It says Sussex on the cover of this book, but the South Downs National Park doesn't stop at the county border. To the west, it continues almost as far as the cathedral city of Winchester. Here are a few pointers to my favourite spots in the westernmost part of the national park. You could visit them on a circular tour, starting from Winchester and proceeding clockwise.

Upper Itchen Valley Alluring back-lane cycling along National Cycle Network 23, through some delectably watery landscapes and unspoilt villages such as Avington, Tichborne and Cheriton.

Hinton Ampner A country house meticulously rebuilt after a fire in 1960 and now owned by the National Trust. It's the grounds here that really impress, with glorious downland views, an arcing Philadelphus Walk and cascades of foliage in the shady Dell.

The Church in the Woods A tiny tin church in the middle of Bramdean Woods (♀ SU631292). Guaranteed to get you rubbing your eyes in disbelief.

Chawton Jane Austen's house, complete with the little writing desk where she penned some of her greatest literary works.

Selborne The home of the 18th-century naturalist Gilbert White. After visiting his house you can wander up the Zigzag Path he and his brother constructed, and into his favourite strolling ground – the fields behind the church known as the Long Lythe and Short Lythe.

The Harrow, Steep Gorgeously unchanged rural pub where they've been serving pea and ham soup for as long as anyone can remember.

Butser Hill The whopper of all South Downs at 886ft, with the Isle of Wight in view from the top.

Butser Ancient Farm An admirable experimental archaeology project, with reconstructions evoking life in Roman and prehistoric times.

Meon Valley On the clear trout-populated waters of the Meon, West Meon is a visual treat, while East Meon's church has an astonishing Norman font. Rising above the valley, Old Winchester Hill abounds in butterflies and orchids, with a huge view from the grassy ramparts of its Iron Age hillfort.

reached from Littlehampton at the end of a dead-end road with old flint walls concealing a car park, toilets and not much else, which is just how its fans like it. The pebbly bays between groynes feel almost like private rooms. There are saltmarsh meadows to the west.

It does get massively busy on warm days here, and tailbacks along the small approach road can be tediously long. A handy car-free way of getting here is to take a train to Littlehampton: leave the town on the river side, cross over the bridge, from where you get a view of the town's various boatyards, and follow the road (initially called Rope Walk) parallel to the river for a short mile to the beaches. Just inland from the estuary mouth here are the overgrown remains of a fort dating from 1854, and thought to have been refortified in World War II.

⫬ FOOD & DRINK

East Beach Café The Promenade, Littlehampton BN17 5GB ✆ 01903 731903 ⬙ eastbeachcafe.co.uk ◷ summer brunch & lunch daily; winter brunch & lunch Thu–Sun; all year dinner Fri–Sat. Right on the beach, Thomas Heatherwick's strikingly curvaceous architectural creation has floor-to-ceiling sea-facing windows that are flung open whenever the weather allows. The kitchen cooks breakfast classics and simple, well-prepared fish dishes.

West Beach Café Rope Walk, Littlehampton BN17 5DL ✆ 01903 946872 ◷ Wed–Sun. This colourful little café with a contemporary beach-shack vibe serves light meals such as fish-finger sandwiches, toasties, coffee and ice cream.

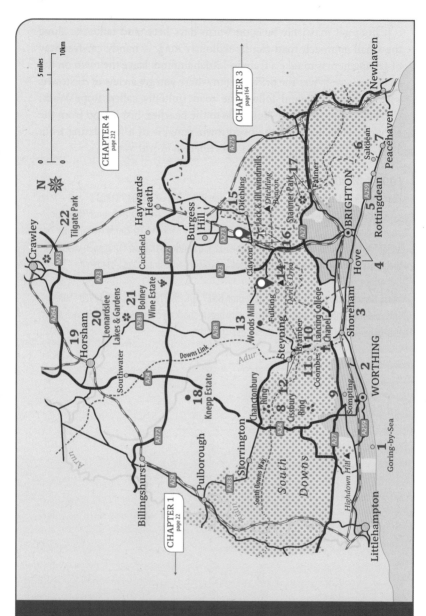

BRIGHTON & ITS HINTERLAND

2
BRIGHTON & ITS HINTERLAND

The most densely populated strip of coast in the southeast is a proverbial mixed bag, and it's not somewhere in which I could promise a sense of place wherever you go. But Brighton and Hove, as they are jointly called, celebrate being different with great aplomb, and I find there's much pleasure picking one's way through their less likely looking further reaches as well as the more trumpeted aspects of one of the country's most rewarding seaside resorts. Connoisseurs of local museums should beat a path to Worthing, Hove and Brighton, which together have a notable trio. Worthing's Museum and Art Gallery stands out for archaeology and costume; Hove's Museum of Creativity offers clips from the very early silent films of the Hove Pioneers (and a great café); and Brighton's Museum and Art Gallery, as you'd expect, is wonderfully eclectic. For complete unexpected quirkiness, Shoreham takes some beating with its Art Deco airport, Norman church architecture, maritime/local history museum and jaw-dropping assemblage of houseboats.

Inland are some of the most visited parts of the South Downs: Ditchling Beacon and Devil's Dyke get the crowds, but I prefer to walk over to the Chattri War Memorial, Cissbury's prehistoric ramparts and flint mines or Jack and Jill Windmills, or to savour the immediate sense of tranquillity found in those innumerable folds in the landscape. Ditchling's imaginatively revamped museum explores a variety of changing art-related themes; the village was home to a notable colony of craftspeople in the early 20th century. Steyning is a town with plenty of Slow attributes, and is handily placed for walks up to Chanctonbury Ring, one of those rare features on the Downs that are identifiable from a distance. Further north, the Low Weald has some notable moments, with the headquarters of the Sussex Wildlife Trust at Woods Mill and the Downs Link cycle route, which heads north to Surrey. In the far north of the area covered by this chapter, **Horsham** has some lovely streetscapes around its church, and **Tilgate Park** is a rewarding strolling ground on the peripheries of Crawley.

GETTING AROUND

The Brighton and Hove conurbation isn't fun to drive around, even less to park in (especially central Brighton), but it has the highest concentration of public EV charging points in Sussex. Public transport is good, and parts are cycle-friendly.

TRAINS

Arriving by train still conjures up a sense of occasion: Brighton station opened in 1841, but what distinguishes it dates from 1882 when the huge, curvaceous shed was added, 597ft long, with a handsome roof of glass and iron spanning two and a half arches.

Served by trains from points north, east and west, this is a great destination for rail travellers. **Brighton Main Line** whisks you down from London Victoria, London Bridge or London St Pancras in one to 1½ hours via East Croydon, Gatwick Airport and Haywards Heath, with services from Victoria also stopping at Clapham Junction. The **East Coastway Line** (Hastings–Brighton via Eastbourne and Lewes) is extremely scenic the whole way, slicing spectacularly through the South Downs in the section east of Lewes before arriving over a grand viaduct looking over Brighton. Sit on the south side of the train for the best views. The **West Coastway Line** provides direct services from Southampton and Portsmouth; while the journey can seem interminable with its frequent stops at coastal towns and suburbs, there's pleasant countryside in between, plus glimpses of Arundel, Lancing College Chapel and Shoreham Airport. Fishbourne, Chichester and Shoreham-by-Sea are useful stops for Slow tourists.

BUSES

It isn't easy to work out the intricacies of the Brighton & Hove Bus network, even when armed with a map and smartphone app (from *⊘* buses.co.uk). As well as covering the city and suburbs, it extends west to Steyning, north to Tunbridge Wells and east to Rottingdean, Seaford and Eastbourne, with additional services from Compass Travel (*⊘* compass-travel.co.uk), Metrobus (*⊘* metrobus.co.uk) and Stagecoach

(🖉 stagecoachbus.com) covering Worthing and points further afield. Buses are marked with their destination, leaving intermediary stops obscure to the uninitiated, but it's worth persevering, since services tend to be frequent and affordable, and some run well into the night.

The main interchanges – Old Steine (near the Royal Pavilion), Clock Tower, Churchill Square and Brighton Station – are all very central. For the best-value fares, it's easiest to use a contactless card to tap on and off; you're charged each time you board a bus, up to a daily or weekly cap. Alternatively, you can buy tickets through the app, ready to activate when you board. Endearingly, the buses are named after well-loved local figures, such as the comedians Max Miller and Arthur Askey, and the inveterate Lewes conservationist and champion of cyclists' causes Elisabeth Howard.

Local buses make car-free excursions to the **South Downs** perfectly feasible. Three Brighton & Hove Breeze buses travel from the city centre into the national park, each departing roughly once per hour: bus 77 to **Devil's Dyke** (◷ Apr–Oct daily; Sep–Mar Sat–Sun & bank holidays); bus 78 to **Stanmer Park** (◷ daily); and bus 79 to **Ditchling Beacon** (◷ Sat–Sun & bank holidays). The bus to Stanmer Park is handier than the train, which only gets you to Falmer, almost half a mile from the park entrance. The downland walk from Devil's Dyke to Ditchling Beacon or vice versa, with a bus at either end, is a classic Brighton outing.

CYCLING

The city of **Brighton and Hove** has a cycle path along the seafront, much of it a painted zone on the pavement, on to which pedestrians inadvertently stray. It's part of the mighty Sustrans Route 2. There are also cycle paths alongside the **A23** northwards and the **A27** to Lewes – useful, but not much fun. A free map (🖉 brightonandhovecyclemap. co.uk) shows the routes. For off-roading, the **South Downs Way** has magnificent stretches – I particularly savour the ride from Lewes to Shoreham via the South Downs Way, leaving it at Beeding Hill (just southeast of Upper Beeding) and swooping down the traffic-free lane to the edge of Shoreham, from where you can get the train back. The South Downs south of Steyning have some blissfully quiet and easily ridden tracks over the chalky plateau, connecting Chanctonbury Ring and Cissbury Ring – the slowly changing views making some of it not vintage territory for walking, perhaps, but it works very well on a mountain or hybrid bike. Busy north–south A roads rather break up the possibilities for quiet ambles around the lanes, although the Ditchling/Plumpton vicinity has some lovely, unproblematic cycling.

The Downs Link bridleway

From Shoreham to St Martha's Hill near Guildford, the Downs Link shared-use path (Regional Route 79) is a particularly enjoyable 37-mile ride through the low Weald along old railway routes. You can of course walk along it, but it works much better on a bike. The route slices across Sussex centre from the sea and South Downs to the North Downs Way on the Surrey Hills, with various places for refreshment on the way.

At the Shoreham end it follows the east bank of the Adur, crossing it a mile southeast of Bramber – where you head through some uneventful residential areas before resuming on the railway route, skirting the western fringes of Henfield and Partridge Green. Beyond Southwater and Christ's Hospital you pass the atmospheric site of Baynards station, with its defunct platform still in place.

BIKE HIRE

Beryl BTN Bikes ⊘ beryl.cc. Brighton's self-service bike and e-bike hire scheme.
Brighton Beach Bikes King's Road Arches, Brighton BN1 1NB ⊘ 01273 601863 ⊘ brightonbeachbikes.co.uk. Bikes, tandems and sea-swimming kit.
Cannonball E-Bikes Julian Rd, Hove BN3 1TH ⊘ 07576 306575 ⊘ cannonballbikes.co.uk.
Rents out a fleet of mountain e-bikes and organises guided e-bike tours of the Downs and coast.

WORTHING & THE WEST

Although they haven't the visitor pulling power of Brighton and Hove, these mostly western pockets of the conurbation offer some surprisingly rewarding offerings.

1 GORING-BY-SEA

Train to Goring-by-Sea, West Coastway Line (Southampton–Brighton); Compass bus 8 (Angmering–Worthing; hourly Mon–Sat); Stagecoach Coastliner 700 (Wick–Brighton; five hourly Mon–Sat, less frequent Sun)

Built-up Goring-by-Sea has one jaw-dropping surprise. The quite unassuming 1960s hangar-like **Church of the English Martyrs** (Goring Way, Goring BN12 4UE ✆ 01903 506890 ⬦ english-martyrs. co.uk ⊙ Apr–Oct 10.00–1300 Mon, 10.00–1600 Tue–Fri) a short walk southeast of the railway station reveals nothing until you enter to see a faithful two-thirds size recreation of the Sistine Chapel ceiling painting, created in painstaking detail by professional signwriter and parishioner Gary Bevans from 1987 until 1993, and covering the full 3,500 sq feet. The ceiling is 30ft lower than Michelangelo's original, so as well as saving you a trip to the Vatican and an awful lot of queuing, it's quite a bit easier to see the details in their full (acrylic) glory.

Gary got the idea after a pilgrimage to Rome in 1986 and applied to the Bishop of Arundel and Brighton for permission to transform the church. The congregation was initially incredulous but after he painted one panel they saw the quality. He replaced the fibreboard ceiling with marine ply, and over five and a half years the whole project took shape. Every Sunday the congregation saw a little bit more of the masterwork had been completed. It was the ultimate labour of love by a man who'd never trained at art college.

During the day there's usually someone to tell you the story of how it came together. On my visit a man named Adrian showed me a jigsaw model of the Sistine Chapel, with removable roof, for comparison, and pointed out Gary's other paintings, including a *Last Supper* (with his own little witty adaptations to show people connected with the current church) and an icon in the side chapel.

Not to be confused with the rather more famous Goring Gap in the Thames Valley, Sussex's **Goring Gap**, half a mile south of Goring-by-Sea railway station, takes a bit of seeking out, following residential roads down to Marine Drive. One of 22 gaps between settlements conserved by local authority policy in West Sussex, this little chunk of coast on the west side of Worthing has repeatedly been threatened by new housing projects, but at the time of writing, most of it remains green.

You can't see much sprawl inland either, so there's the illusion of the distant Downs merging into an untampered coastal plain. The Gap itself is a broad agricultural strip fringed by a spacious seafront lawn, part of Goring Greensward, so it gives a good idea of how the whole Sussex coast looked before it was built over. The usual shingle beach with groynes is what you expect in these parts; modern development is screened by a long line of trees known as the Plantation on the east side, while to the north the Ilex Way, an avenue of 400 holm oaks planted in the 1840s along a carriage road for Goring Hall, extends from St Mary's Church in Goring to Ferring.

North of Ferring and sandwiched between main roads and suburban fringes, **Highdown Hill** is another isolated tract of rural Sussex and is owned by the National Trust: rising 261ft, it gives a view over the built-up stretch of coast, extending in clear conditions eastwards to Beachy Head and westwards to the Isle of Wight. Lumps of an Iron Age hillfort are in evidence. The OS Explorer map marks the Miller's Tomb just to the east – this belongs to John Olliver, an 18th-century miller turned smuggler who used to set his sails at a certain angle to signal to other gang members whether the coast was clear of customs men.

2 WORTHING

West Coastway Line (Southampton–Brighton); regular Compass and Stagecoach buses from Angmering, Arundel, Brighton, Crawley, Littlehampton, Midhurst and Shoreham

Worthing hit the big time when fashionable visitors came from Brighton in Regency days, and its success was pretty much ensured in 1798 with the arrival of the convalescent Princess Amelia, youngest daughter of George III. In August 1895 Oscar Wilde stayed with his family here and rapidly penned the comedy *The Importance of Being Earnest*, naming one of its main characters Jack Worthing. The handbag joke, incidentally, has a piece of railway snobbery that is probably lost on modern audiences – when Jack attempts to justify his being found as a baby in a handbag ('A *handbag*?') at Victoria station it was on the Brighton line, which was considered the 'posh' side as opposed to the distinctly less salubrious London, Chatham and Dover Railway section of the station.

Worthing isn't really a prime seaside resort nowadays, and there's not a lot there compared with the likes of Brighton, but its pescatarian dining scene is blossoming and it does other seasidey things extremely well. Some of its places of entertainment are of considerable style: the **Connaught** (doubling as a theatre and cinema) and the pier are elegantly Art Deco affairs, the latter with a theatre at its near end, while also on the seafront the **Dome** is one of the country's oldest cinemas, opened in 1911 and full of period detail inside.

Worthing Museum and Art Gallery (Union Pl, BN11 1LG ✐ 01903 206206 ⚭ wtm.uk/museum ⊙ Wed–Sat; free entry), a five-minute walk from the station, has the third-largest costume collection in the country (focusing on 19th- and 20th-century apparel) and fascinating sections on toys and the history of the town, as well as a sculpture garden. It also has one of the best public displays of archaeology in Sussex: as well as an early ferry boat from Hardham, dated to 1030–1220, notable treasures include the Patching Hoard of 1997, which includes 23 gold Roman coins unearthed by a metal detectorist, happily in Worthing after it was initially supposed they would end up in the British Museum. Virtually next to the museum and opposite the main street from the Connaught, **Ambrose Place** is as sweet and perfect an example of white, balconied Regency seaside architecture as you'll find anywhere in Brighton or Hove; note the leafy private gardens across the street.

⑪ FOOD & DRINK

Crab Shack Marine Pde, BN11 3PN ✐ 01903 215070 ⚭ crabshackworthing.co.uk ⊙ Tue–Sun. Rustic restaurant with a beach-bar vibe, serving up simple but excellent fish and seafood at indoor and outdoor tables.

The Fish Factory 51 Brighton Rd BN11 3EE ✐ 01903 207123 ⚭ protorestaurantgroup. com ⊙ Wed–Sun. Freshest seafood, including whitebait, calamari and chowder, along with top-notch fish and chips (very generous servings).

Perch on the Pier Worthing Pier, BN11 3PX ⚭ perchonthepier.com ⊙ noon–21.00 Mon–Fri, 09.00–2100 Sat–Sun. This pavilion-style venue at the end of Worthing's Art Deco pier is a stylish spot for a casual meal, with wraparound sea views.

Tern Worthing Pier, BN11 3PX ⚭ ternrestaurant.co.uk ⊙ Thu–Sun. It's well worth pushing the boat out for lunch or dinner at this high-flying restaurant, which offers imaginative and beautifully presented British tasting menus.

3 SHOREHAM

Train to Shoreham-by-Sea (West Coastway Line, Southampton–Brighton); regular B&H and Stagecoach buses from Arundel, Brighton, Littlehampton, Steyning, Rottingdean and Worthing

Although it's perhaps not enticing at first sight, there are good reasons to linger in this long-established port between Brighton and Worthing. New Shoreham – the 'new' denoting the Norman settlement that succeeded

the Saxon village at Old Shoreham further north as the Adur silted up – enjoyed cross-Channel trade with Normandy in early times, and in the 20th century was the prime arrival point in Britain for sherry and port from Iberia. In the early 1900s Shoreham Beach had its own film industry, where the clarity of the light prompted filmmakers to set up in town in 1914. Productions included a film of *The Mayor of Casterbridge* made while Thomas Hardy was still alive (the team consulted with the author at his Dorset home), with outdoor scenes filmed in Steyning. Shoreham became the centre of the silent-movie industry in Britain but fire destroyed many of the studio buildings in 1923; the rest were later demolished.

The town has enough old buildings surviving for an absorbing walkabout, with beach-cobble-fronted houses along Church Street leading to **St Mary de Haura Church**. Built in 1103 on a grand scale, it is one of Sussex's most impressive Norman churches: ruins in the churchyard of what was the nave indicate its former size. The Norman work is seen in the lower part of the tower and transepts, while the choir and upper part of the tower display transitional elements. Facing the waterfront, **Marlipins Museum** (⊙ May–Oct, Thu–Sat) partly occupies a 12th-century building with a striking façade chequered alternately with flint and Caen limestone. Within is a wide array of material on local and maritime history, with ship models, archaeology and fossils. You can peer into a deep hole thought to have been a medieval loo, where a 14th-century cooking pot and cat skeleton were discovered during excavations in 2002.

The best views of town are from the glass-sided footbridge/cycle bridge over the Adur, worth crossing in any case for Shoreham's big surprise – one of the most eye-opening assemblages of **houseboats** in the country. Stretching along the river immediately upstream from the footbridge, they line a track called Riverside. Originating from 1945 as housing for those who had lived in railway carriages and shacks in what was called 'Bungalow Town' on Shoreham Beach, these are now desirably bohemian homes. They are made from a strange list of retired craft, among them a coal barge, an ammunition lighter, a minesweeper, a 1905

◄ **1** Worthing's pier has an Art Deco pavilion at its entrance. **2** Shoreham Airport – the country's oldest licensed airfield – is another Art Deco gem. **3** Goring's Church of the English Martyrs displays an astonishing recreation of the Sistine Chapel's ceiling painting.

passenger steamer and a 1941 torpedo boat, and have been variously adapted with DIY improvements and sunny gardens filled with potted plants and frequented by contented cats and dogs. *Verda*, built in 1929 as the Portsmouth–Gosport ferry, has been ingeniously extended by the addition of a coach split lengthwise and added to either side; this in turn links to *Venture*, a World War II motor gunboat, adorned by a dissected mustard-coloured Reliant Robin. Elsewhere you might spot a garden gate made of cricket bats and a windchime made out of the inside of a piano. The catalogue of dwellings (and their accoutrements) slowly evolves; sad remains of former residences may be visible in the mudflats. While you're on this side of the river you might like to venture past the swish contemporary seaside villas of Shoreham Beach to the end of the

"Elsewhere you might spot a garden gate made of cricket bats and a windchime made out of the inside of a piano."

peninsula, where the remains of **Shoreham Fort** stand at the land's end looking towards the chimney of defunct Shoreham power station. Built in the 1850s to repel a possible French invasion, the fort was installed with six 68-pounder guns and a barrack block. There's free access to the site, which is sometimes host to special events.

Further upriver is **Old Shoreham**, where the restored Saxon and Norman Church of St Nicolas is the major landmark; it has striking 12th-century stone carving at the crossing. Just across the road and hidden from view is Shoreham's much-loved wooden **tollbridge**, originating from 1781 and largely rebuilt in 1916 but eclipsed by the opening of a new bypass in 1970. Demoted to use as a bridleway, it deteriorated and was deemed unsafe in 1997; its future looked very bleak indeed with a huge sum of money required to avoid it rotting into history. Local campaigners kickstarted a bid to save the bridge, and happily the Old Shoreham Community Trust helped raise the money in partnership with West Sussex County Council. The bridge was faithfully restored and reopened in 2008. The Shoreham to Guildford **Downs Link** cycle and walking route goes straight past it.

You can cross over the tollbridge to the west bank and turn left (or walk up through fields from the houseboats) to **Shoreham Airport** (⌀ flybrighton.com), one of the Art Deco treasures of Sussex and the oldest licensed airfield in the country. Officially opened in 1911 and also known as Brighton City Airport, it gained its terminal building in 1936 and still evokes the days of early aviation – the departure board in the elegant main building refers to private flights, although not so long ago there were scheduled services to France. A curious relic of its wartime days can be glimpsed on the north side of the airfield, where a camouflaged brick-built training dome is one of only five remaining: it was used for teaching aircraft recognition by means of projecting images on to the inside of the dome and changing the lighting to simulate different times of day. The Royal Air Forces Association (RAFA) held an annual military and historic airshow here until 2015 when, tragically, a vintage Hawker Hurricane jet crashed, killing 11 people. Adjacent to the terminal building, the **visitor centre** (⊙ 10.00–15.00 Mon–Fri, noon–15.00 Sat–Sun) has a fascinating stash of aviation memorabilia, including models of some of the earliest craft, among them the Valkyrie monoplane which in 1911 made the world's first registered freight flight, delivering a box of lightbulbs from here to Hove Lawns. **Airport tours** take in the terminal building, main hangar and runways (✐ 01273 467351; advance booking required). The good-value café in the terminal building and the terrace outside make vantage points for watching planes landing.

 SHOPPING

Locals claim Shoreham's **farmers' market** (East St, second Saturday of the month) is the best in Sussex. **La Poissonnerie** (Fisherman's Wharf, Brighton Rd, BN43 6RN) sells fish straight off the boats.

4 BRIGHTON & HOVE

🏠 **Hotel du Vin** & ⛺ **Experience Freedom**
Train to Brighton or Hove (Brighton Main Line, London–Brighton; West Coastway Line, Southampton–Brighton; East Coastway Line, Hastings–Brighton); regional bus hub

Exuberant, quirky and even outrageous, Brighton is the liveliest seaside resort in Britain. Outwardly it gives the impression of anything but Slow, so instead of trying to cover each and every aspect, I have focussed on a selection of attributes that show off Brighton-ness to best effect. And of course Hove-ness: the two places merge to form the city of Brighton and Hove – Hove lying to the west of Brighton – and it needs local knowledge to determine where one ends and the next begins.

Let's start with **Richard Russell**. He was a successful Lewes doctor and an astute businessman who in 1750 published a paper entitled

Glandular Diseases, or a Dissertation on the Use of Sea-Water in the Affections of the Glands; it was written in Latin, so may not have been great bedtime reading. He trained at Leiden and studied the European concept of spas; he was one of a group of doctors who had the idea of using seawater instead of a spa water. To this end he prescribed seawater cures for his patients and encouraged wealthy people to visit Brighthelmstone, as it was called then, and to where he himself moved in 1753. The idea was to bathe in the sea, inhale the sea air, partake of treatments such as a pill made of crabs' eyes, cuttlefish bones and woodlice, and imbibe pints of seawater.

His prescription indicated the length of time the patient needed to spend in the water. Patients were wheeled out to the sea in bathing machines – actually little cabins on wheels, towed by horses – and immersion was effected with the aid of 'dippers' who engaged in the task of submerging the body completely; the victim would emerge spluttering from the ordeal by dunking. Attending to the needs of the thalassotherapy-seekers gave the fishing community an important new source of income.

Russell is sometimes heralded as the inventor of the seaside resort, but the trend of going to Brighthelmstone to recuperate dates from the 1730s. It was wealthy local people who recommended Brighton to their friends, who with Russell and other locals helped make Brighton a success. From 1783, the Prince of Wales, the future George IV, came because the resort was popular with his uncles and friends, and developed a lodging house into the Royal Pavilion. He revelled in the Brighton social scene, and was much caricatured by the political cartoonists of the day.

"The little town was transformed by commodious squares and elegant crescents. Many of the Regency buildings survive today."

From the 1790s the town's population boomed. A contributing factor to this was the army who were periodically in residence from the 1790s to 1815; it was believed that a Napoleonic invasion might be attempted in the shallow bay on which stood Brighton. Officers often brought their families with them and soon the little town was transformed by commodious squares and elegant crescents. Many of the Regency buildings survive today, making this one of Britain's most rewarding examples of **seaside architecture**. Somewhat less celebrated are its highly distinguished 19th-century places of worship; not all of them are open outside services – it is a pity, for instance, that the Middle Street Synagogue, reputed as one of the finest in Europe, is rarely open – but you can usually look into the spectacular trio of **Anglo-Catholic churches**: St Michael's and All Angels, St Paul's and St Bartholomew's.

Brighton revived after a very quiet, recession-hit period in the 1830s; Queen Victoria didn't really care for it, due to the lack of privacy at the Royal Pavilion, remarking 'there were far too many of the wrong sort of people, and they were all staring at me'. From 1841 onwards the railways brought the masses, and Brighton's fortunes soared. Along the seafront various contrivances were devised to extract money from pleasure-seekers. Seaside amusement arcades, a concept imported from America, sprang up. Brighton's fame spread; other seaside resorts named Brighton were built as far away as New York and Melbourne.

The city has long had a seamier side; even the Brighton Museum celebrates the resort's role as a venue for a dirty weekend. This famously was the place a couple could get 'a Brighton quickie' divorce. The husband would hire a private detective to observe him signing into a hotel, with a hired 'mistress' acting the part, as 'Mr and Mrs Smith'. A chambermaid would ever so accidentally open the door to see the couple, and the deed was done.

Graham Greene in his novel *Brighton Rock* depicted the Brighton underworld with its teenage gangland leader Pinkie and his innocent waitress girlfriend Rose, and John Boulting's 1947 film noir of the novel marvellously used the Brighton backdrop; the 2011 remake was filmed in Brighton and Eastbourne. The bank holiday weekend clashes on the seafront between mods and rockers started in 1964 and inspired the film *Quadrophenia*.

Brighton has long been a place of sexual liberation and, around the 1970s at a time when homophobia was rife, gay people felt relatively comfortable visiting for a weekend of pleasure. Now, as the undisputed LGBTQIA+ capital of Britain, Brighton hosts each August the biggest Pride festival in the country, and there's plenty in the way of gay pubs and clubs, and gay-friendly accommodation. Much of the action revolves around Kemptown and St James's Street, and the spending power of the pink pound partly accounts for the city's eclectic shopping and eating out.

Another key to Brighton's distinctiveness is its high proportion of young people, thanks in part to the existence of its two universities –

the University of Brighton and the University of Sussex. Although their main campuses are out of town at Falmer, the students tend to come into Brighton itself for nightlife and so on, and quite a few like it so much they end up living here.

THE SEAFRONT

The city's long-held status as lotus-eating capital of Sussex has imbued the whole seaside scene with a terrific atmosphere. The beach is clean, spacious and (on calm days) great for lounging and open-water swimming, assuming you're equipped to cope with pebbles: there are reputedly 614 billion of them heaped above the sandy seabed, which is only exposed when the tide is very low. Few coastal resorts have such architectural set pieces along their seafront as do Brighton and its neighbour, Hove. The first element is the cream-stucco frontages, which date from Regency times: the finest include Brunswick Square at the Hove end, Regency Square near the old West Pier and Lewes Crescent in Kemptown in the far east.

At first glance, the seafront looks handsomely uniform, with stucco buildings on one side, and the esplanade with its trademark aquamarine and white lampposts on the other: but a walk from end to end reveals that the seafront changes in character from one moment to the next. The pivotal point, and best place from which to admire the seafront, from Shoreham power station's chimney in the west to the Marina in the east, is **Brighton Palace Pier** (reverting to its original name of Palace Pier in 2016 after a 16-year campaign to change back from Brighton Pier, though they opted to keep the 'Brighton' part of the name), an exuberant example of late Victoriana, exactly a third of a mile long, completed in 1899. The far end has a funfair, continuing a tradition of rides on the pier stretching back to 1938. Though it has evolved with the years – the clock tower and entrance pavilion are post-war additions – the balustrades, two entrance kiosks and basic structure are original. In fact the kiosks originate from Brighton's very first pier, which this structure replaced: it was called the Chain Pier, built in 1823 like a suspension bridge, and primarily intended as an embarkation point for packet boats. It doubled as a promenading ground and was among the very first seaside piers in the world. In the mid 19th century an early version of the booze cruise would depart from here, as visitors took the boat out to foreign waters and enjoyed tax-free alcohol. The pier acts as a roosting ground

LONDON TO BRIGHTON VETERAN CAR RUN

⏃ veterancarrun.com

The longest-running car event in the world (emphatically a car run and not a race), this simply has to be seen to be believed, with up to 600 beautifully preserved and miraculously still working pre-1905 vehicles brought in from various parts of the globe given a run by their owners in front of an admiring audience of up to a million. It starts at sunrise from London's Hyde Park on a Sunday morning in early November: you'd have to be very keen to get there for the beginning. Fortunately, Sussex has it easier – the run stops by in Crawley, and carries on through Cuckfield and Burgess Hill to end up at the seafront in Brighton, on Madeira Drive. Not all of the entrants make it, but most get there eventually – giving a tremendous free show of the vehicles along the seafront until late afternoon. The car run goes back to 1896 – at a time when petrol would have been bought at a chemist's shop – to celebrate a change in the law whereby drivers could dispense with the red-flag-bearing attendant who walked in front, and zoom along at a brisk maximum of 14mph. The effervescent 1953 comedy film *Genevieve* is about two rival motorists who complete the run in their 1904 vehicles, a Darracq nicknamed *Genevieve* and a Spyker (both now retired to museums in Holland), then race back to London for a bet, to the exasperation of their womenfolk: 'I don't know what it is about these silly old cars. The moment people get in them they start behaving like idiots!'

At other times of year, Brighton hosts numerous other vehicle rallies, which also end up on Madeira Drive – including for Land Rovers and vintage motor bikes.

for starlings in winter; they turn up here from Scandinavia. Though in decline nationally, the numbers here are healthy in the extreme: on winter evenings, the birds form huge murmurations, clouds that change shape as they move around.

East of Brighton Palace Pier

Just across the road from the pier on the east side, **Sea Life Brighton** (⏃ 01273 647708 ⏃ visitsealife.com) is one of the worldwide chain of 55 aquaria that feature all manner of marine life and do a lot in the way of conservation and education. Architecturally this is the most significant aquarium in the country (and the oldest one anywhere still in operation), retaining many of its original Victorian tanks within the main crypt-like aisled hall, with its almost ecclesiastical Gothic vaulted ceiling. It was a wonder of the age, and still very much catches the eye; the granite columns have colourfully painted capitals carved with depictions of sea life. The largest in the world when opened in 1872 at a cost of £130,000, the building was the creation of Eugenius Birch, better known for designing seaside piers, including Brighton's sadly defunct West Pier. His Aquarium in Brighton was deliberately given subterranean qualities to convey an impression of life under the ocean. After a new entrance with stone kiosks and a sun terrace was added in the 1920s, it suffered a chequered history. It was requisitioned in World War II, hosted (in its ballroom) the very first Rhythm and Blues venue in Britain, and in the 1970s operated as a rather tacky Dolphinarium.

Since 1991, the aquarium has had a new lease of life as part of the well-run Sea Life chain. In recent years, its successes include helping restore tsunami-damaged coral reefs, breeding endangered cardinal fish and trialling ways to make aquaria more welcoming towards neurodivergent visitors. Beyond its vaulted Victorian hall, you head through a simulated Amazonian rainforest environment, followed by the main tank which you can view from above in the Auditorium (the former ballroom) via glass-bottom boat tours (extra admission payable) as well as from the walk-through glass tunnel, where sharks, giant turtles and other species glide overhead. Feeding times for the turtles are 11.00 and 14.00 daily; sharks are fed on Tuedays, Thursdays, Saturdays and Sundays at 14.00.

Beneath the esplanade is one of Brighton's unsung (and endangered) treasures, the extraordinary two-tiered **Madeira Terrace**, a covered promenade of 1889–97 along Madeira Drive, all cast iron and open fronted, providing a shady, sheltered walk and dating from the days when a tan was definitely to be avoided; it runs beneath the sea wall for half a mile. Alas, it's been closed since 2013, pending restoration.

Running along the entire extent of Madeira Drive, **Volk's Electric Railway** (⊘ volkselectricrailway.co.uk) has been in operation since 1883 – the world's oldest electrically operated commercial railway (there was an earlier industrial electric railway outside Berlin, so the claims that it was the very first electric railway aren't quite valid); it now runs from the Brighton Sea Life Centre to Black Rock, near the marina. The track is narrow gauge and carriages are engagingly scaled down. This was the creation of Magnus Volk, an electrical engineer whose house was the first in Brighton to be installed with electric lighting, and who as a result won the contract to install electric incandescent lighting in the Royal Pavilion. At first the railway ran just a quarter of a mile from the Aquarium to the Chain Pier (which was adjacent to where the Brighton

Palace Pier now stands), but later was extended westwards. The public loved it, but it was at the mercy of the elements: accordingly, it was raised on to a wooden viaduct for its entire length in 1886. In 1894 Volk turned his attention to another seafront mode of transport that would enable people to travel on to Rottingdean. The snag was that the cliffs formed too much of a barrier, so he opted for a route through the sea itself, and created the *Pioneer*, an astonishing contraption comprising a large tram-like

"The railway was at the mercy of the elements: accordingly, it was raised on to a wooden viaduct for its entire length."

cabin raised on tall supports that ran with its wheels on tracks in the chalk bedrock beneath the sea: 'A Sea Voyage on Wheels' proclaimed the poster of what became dubbed the 'Daddy Longlegs'. Volk's grand scheme opened in 1896 but operated for only a week until a huge storm damaged it; repairs were made and services resumed, but the project faltered through technical problems and this unique passenger service closed a few years later; in 1910 the remains of the passenger car were carted off for scrap.

Close to the Volk's halfway point is one of Brighton's coolest modern developments: a striking, low-key cluster of cafés, small business units and beach sports centres (pages 121 and 133), including the shimmering Sea Lanes lido. They're fringed by flourishing rewilding projects and a new boardwalk that leads past Brighton's **naturist beach**, screened by a slight rise in the shingle.

Ensconced beneath the cliffs to the east, **Brighton Marina** is an unlikely grid of apartment blocks, retail units and moorings that doesn't feel like Britain at all. It reminds me of the set of *The Truman Show*, the 1998 film about the man who doesn't realise he's the subject of a reality TV show and has his every move watched by millions of Americans. A Walk of Fame remembers Brighton celebs, past and present, in Hollywood Boulevard style, with plaques set in the boardwalk. There's a multi-screen cinema, a bleak car park and a big branch of Asda, and it's geared to driving into rather than approaching on foot. However, its yachts and fishing boats add a splash of colour to the blandness, and eastwards Peacehaven Heights look wonderfully wild. The best reason to come is to stroll or cycle along the Undercliff Walk, a three-mile path from the marina to Saltdean, wedged between the cliffs and – depending on the day – the glittering or roaring sea.

Developed by Thomas Kemp in the early 19th century, the eastern district of **Kemptown** didn't take off quickly and was eclipsed in success by Brighton's more central developments. Kemp overreached himself by trying to build carcasses of houses, and much of it remained uninhabited till the 1850s, by which time the façades were somewhat out of fashion. Kemp engaged Charles Busby and Amon Wilds as architects to develop countryside into 250 houses. His plan includes the majestic curves of Lewes Crescent, representing seaside architecture at its very grandest.

If you can find them open, two Kemptown churches deserve seeking out: **St John the Baptist Catholic Church** in Bristol Road, built in the 1830s and with a particularly fine show of memorials, and **St George's Church** in St George's Road, a high-quality Regency Greek Revival-style preaching box opened in 1826.

West of Brighton Palace Pier: the i360 & Hove's seafront

The shore-level promenade immediately west of the pier beneath the esplanade represents the liveliest part of the seafront with a range of little businesses set up in the arches beneath street level, and a magnificent 1888 merry-go-round, fully restored and with its real fairground organ operating. Among the busy bars and clubs of the **Artists' Quarter**, there are booths advertising tarot, clairvoyant and palmist services, and a place filled with **antique slot machines**. Brighton's fishing industry still sells fish and shellfish nearby – one of the great little institutions is **The Brighton Smokehouse** under the arches (page 134); just across the path is the minute smokehouse where fish are smoked in the traditional way. Next to it, the tiny, volunteer-run **Brighton Fishing Museum** (free entry) chronicles Brighton's fishing community from the early days; the largest exhibit is a 27ft clinker-built punt boat of a type typical to Sussex, while an adjacent room has a few poignant relics from the sadly defunct West Pier and a display about the story of the seafront.

BRIGHTON & HOVE: **1** The 531ft i360 tower looks over the beach and the pier. **2** The aquarium has a strikingly Gothic vaulted ceiling. **3** Brunswick Square in Hove is a wonderful example of seaside Regency architecture. **4** The North Laine shopping district features a maze of narrow streets. ▶

All you can now see of the **West Pier**, directly opposite Regency Square, is an island of skeletal iron. This was Britain's only Grade I-listed pier, last in use in 1972 (and immortalised in the 1969 musical film *Oh! What a Lovely War*) and very splendid, but neglected. Just when things looked rosy for its restoration it mysteriously burned down in 2003. It has now lost its listed status.

The ex-pier's landward end is now dominated by the 531ft-tall **Brighton i360** (⊘ brightoni360.co.uk). Opened in 2016, this unique structure is Britain's tallest and thinnest moving viewing tower – built by the same architectural team that constructed the London Eye: the thinking behind the i360 was to create a vertical pier, replacing the walk above the water that the West Pier provided with a walk above the air. By means of cable-car technology, a large doughnut-like glass pod silently and smoothly conveys up to 200 passengers high above the city as it gently glides up the steel pole, getting a terrific view normally reserved for the seagulls, westwards as far as the Isle of Wight and eastwards towards the Seven Sisters and Beachy Head, with the South Downs to the north. To the south you see, well, just the sea, punctuated by the distant turbines of the **Rampion Offshore Wind Farm**. Though pricey, it makes for a memorable 20 minutes, and it's good to see Sussex drinks on offer at the bar to enhance the experience further – Harvey's beer, Nyetimber wine, Brighton Gin and Folkington's fruit juice. The slender tower's appearance, it must be said, has divided opinion – it's rather more city corporate style (with airport-like security and a sleek, steely look to it all) than vintage Sussex by the sea, sitting somewhat incongruously among the Brighton-style aquamarine and white lampposts and railings. But it's certainly got people talking – controversial architecture is nothing new in Brighton – and the chief executive told me there's been a lot of interest elsewhere for similar schemes in the future. And at least the faithful replication of Eugenius Birch's two entrance kiosks to the West Pier as the i360's ticket booth and tea room should appeal to traditionalists.

> *"A large doughnut-like glass pod silently and smoothly conveys up to 200 passengers high above the city."*

Close to the foot of the i360, the **Rampion Offshore Wind Farm Visitor Centre** (76–81 Kings Road Arches, BN1 2FN ⊘ rampionoffshore. com ☉ Tue–Sun) houses permanent displays telling the history and significance of this remarkable addition to the coast – the first offshore power station in southeast England. Construction began in 2015, took around three years, and cost £1.3 billion. Covering 28 sq miles and stretching from Brighton to East Worthing, Rampion (named after the county flower of Sussex) is capable of powering half the houses in Sussex. The centre has details of several boat operators based in Brighton and Eastbourne that offer trips out to gaze up at the mighty, whirling turbines, which stretch 459ft into the sky.

This part of the seafront is sadly let down by the **Brighton Centre** and the **Odeon**, both spectacular examples of concrete brutalism; the former is where the political party conferences are often held. It was in 1984 that Patrick Magee, a member of the IRA, planted a bomb at the adjacent **Grand Hotel**, intending to kill the then prime minister Margaret Thatcher and her cabinet; the bomb caused huge damage, and killed five, including the MP Sir Anthony Berry, and severely wounded others. The building was massively damaged, but not irreparably so, and its flamboyantly Victorian interior was restored much to what it had been.

Just inland, the very top of **Sussex Heights**, at 334ft and with 24 floors the tallest residential block in all Sussex, has been home to a nesting pair of **peregrine falcons** since 1998; the nesting box subsequently provided for them is visible from the street on the north side, and often one peregrine may be seen perched outside, or its piercing high call may be heard. The peregrine is the fastest known living creature, and has been recorded swooping down at around 150mph. One wonders how many passers-by below are aware of the aerial mayhem caused by this

SEAFRONT SPORTS

As well as swimming, the Brighton and Hove beachfront is full of scope for activities, with windsurfing, wakeboarding and SUP training on Hove Lagoon, basketball, a pétanque piste, self-service bike hire and marker posts for joggers. Three of the most popular spots are east of Brighton Palace Pier: Jumble Rumble (⊘ brighton. junglerumble.co.uk), a colourful and hugely popular minigolf course; Yellowave (⊘ yellowave.co.uk), a beach volleyball centre; and Sea Lanes (⊘ sealanesbrighton. co.uk), an outdoor pool right on the beach, with solar heating to keep the temperature manageable. The Seafront Office (141 King's Road Arches, BN1 2FN ⊘ 01273 292716) has all-terrain beach wheelchairs available to hire for up to two hours at a time. Brighton is also the main place in Sussex for surfboard hire.

rare bird (with a UK population of 1,500 pairs) when a couple of pigeon feathers drift down into the street as a peregrine snaffles a tasty meal. You can see the birds on the webcam at sussexheights.co.uk.

The Hove end is really worth walking around thanks to its magnificent examples of seaside Regency architecture. The **Brunswick** district was completed by 1828 and inhabited by local moneyed classes and visitors. Things were made more attractive by the fact that in Hove there wasn't a tax on coal. It was built as a new suburb, with views of the Downs behind imposing architectural set pieces in the forms of Brunswick Square, and a little further west, Adelaide Crescent (completed in the 1850s). Brunswick was successful in attracting people as soon as it was built and developed rapidly. Brunswick Square has its own little festival in summer, and 13 Brunswick Square, **The Regency Town House** (01273 206306 rth.org.uk; advance booking essential), is occasionally open for tours; the strikingly deep cream hue to the stucco in Brunswick was revived in recent years by an astute planning officer's enforcement of an ancient covenant. This square leads into **Palmeira Square**, begun as Palmeira Crescent in the 1830s by Decimus Burton, who also with his father James developed St Leonards, on the west side of Hastings. The style here is more pared down than Brunswick Square, and leans towards the Italianate. The **Montpelier** district extends inland and has some exuberant canopied terraces that were all the rage in the early Victorian period.

Further on, **Hove Lawns** is a long-established place for kite-flying, jogging and picnics, while Hove Lagoon is always busy with watersports enthusiasts (pages 121 and 133).

THE LANES & NORTH LAINE

Inland, North, West and East streets enclose the old town, including the knot of twittens known as **The Lanes**. This is prime territory for eclectic shopping and eating, though the days when it had interesting junk shops are long gone, eclipsed by more upmarket art, jewellery, clothing and perfume retailers.

East of The Lanes, the **Old Steine** (pronounced Steen, and sometimes spelt Steyne) was originally a damp expanse once given over to grazing and sloping towards the sea where nets would be dried out on the beach, and where capstans were used to haul boats up (one capstan survives, near the Fishing Museum). It was considered the 'centre' of town in the early resort days, when it became the strolling ground, a place to see and be seen – Brighton's own passeggiata area – with shops selling lace and bonbons to tourists. A model in the Brighton Museum and Art Gallery hints at its former charm. Although a lot of the Regency buildings have survived, it's too much a whirl of traffic to walk through for pleasure now.

Often confused with The Lanes (which are closer to the sea), **North Laine** and the streets to the east were developed from the 1850s on what had been agricultural strips from medieval times in an area of market gardening: the roads today mark the lines of the agricultural strips (or the access tracks between them), making a striking fossilised pattern of what has otherwise long vanished. Portsea in Portsmouth and parts of Worthing developed on similar lines.

Brighton's answer to Camden Lock market in London, North Laine is an enjoyable, funkily anarchic shopping, eating and entertainment district. Its spine is a set of narrow streets, one leading into another – Bond Street, Gardner Street, Kensington Gardens and Sydney Street – with the action spilling over into adjoining areas including Jubilee Square, where Brighton's handsome library stands. On Infinity Foods in North Road a plaque honours Ken Fines (1923–2008), the Borough Planning Officer responsible for saving the whole caboodle from the bulldozer, when a flyover was proposed from Preston Circus to Church Street, and making it a Conservation Area in 1976; Fines also named this quarter North Laine and is very much the local hero.

Though well known to locals, this chunk of the city is easily missed: to find it from the railway station, turn right under the canopy of the station, then immediately sharp left down Trafalgar Street, which heads down through a steep subway-like road tunnel adjacent to the bowels of the station frontage. Soon after you will see Sydney Street leading off to the right, marking the northern extent of the main North Laine axis.

In the above-mentioned railway station netherworld on Trafalgar Street and housed in the former Bass Charrington beer store, the Tardis-like **Brighton Toy and Model Museum** (✆ 01273 749494 ⌨ brightontoymuseum.co.uk ⊙ Tue–Sat) reveals a nostalgia-inducing stash of over 10,000 items. The owner Chris Littledale told me 'it all started with my obsession with model trains, going back to when I was a child – I've been collecting ever since; there were so many things I had to find a home for.' All the trains are his, but he has had numerous loans and donations of vintage teddies, dolls, puppets, toy castles, toy theatre, model soldiers and the like. He showed me his prize pieces, a display of German model trains; they stand by a station bookstall from the 1920s in pristine condition, complete with minuscule copies of *Punch* and *Ideal Home* and a train indicator next to it. A vintage model railway layout is the centrepiece, depicting an entire town, with a bowling match in progress; in it there are toy cars, taxis and a bridge (the only known example in existence). Some very interesting bits and pieces are for sale in the foyer, including old bits of Hornby train sets and the like – from about £5 upwards.

"A vintage model railway layout is the centrepiece, depicting an entire town, with a bowling match in progress."

It's worth strolling to Ann Street for **St Bartholomew's Church** (1872–74, by the otherwise unknown architect Edmund Scott), barn-like, brick and vast, with no spire or tower, or side aisles, and with a nave taller than Westminster Abbey's. Inside it is reminiscent of Westminster Cathedral with its bare brickwork, adorned with a quartet of onion-domed confessionals, and rich decoration in the form of Byzantine-style mosaics and Arts and Crafts metalwork. This is a notable place to see very high-quality late 19th-century and early 20th-century interior work by nationally recognised designers.

Down in the city centre, West Street meets North Street at the conspicuous **clock tower**, erected to celebrate Queen Victoria's golden jubilee in 1887 and doubling as an elaborate signpost pointing to Hove, The Sea, The Station and Kemptown. It's appealingly OTT, with mosaics of Victoria, Albert and the Prince and Princess of Wales, while female figures denoting the four seasons sit at each corner. This is otherwise not Brighton's most gloriously architectural corner, though in West Street, **St Paul's Church** is an exceptional early Victorian church by R C Carpenter with a spectacular and individualistic spire rising to octagonal bell-stage and a simple interior with stained glass by Augustus Pugin.

THE ROYAL PAVILION

BN1 1FN ℰ 0300 029 0900 ⬠ brightonmuseums.org.uk

Most memorably entered through the magnificent arch of the William IV Gate on the north side of the grounds, the Royal Pavilion is a quite startling sight, flamboyantly over-the-top and bristling with domes and minarets. As an Indian fantasy, it's actually something you'd never encounter in India, and within it is more Chinese-inspired, the most complete example of the *chinoiserie* style anywhere, beautifully restored and furnished much as it was in the heyday of the Prince Regent, the future George IV. After the relatively pale and restrained entrance hall, guests would be conducted through the salmon-pink and blue Long Gallery to the astonishing Banqueting Room, with its huge crystal and mirrored chandeliers, held in the jaws of dragons, glittering above a table laid out for a feast. They would be invited to inspect the Great Kitchen, where food was prepared in a high-ceilinged room supported by columns with palm-leaf capitals, and entertained afterwards in the hot, scented atmosphere of the Music Room with its great dome lined with 26,000 hand-gilded cockle shells.

By the 1750s, Russell's sea cure was drawing numbers of wealthy people to the town, among them the Duke of Cumberland. In 1783 his nephew, the 21-year-old George, who became Prince Regent in 1811 during George III's decline into insanity and king in 1820, was recommended to try the Russell treatment to ease his swelling neck glands. So he went to stay with his uncle there. Whatever he thought of the sea water, the prince greatly took to Brighton's social life, the theatre and the races, in defiance of his frugal father. He very soon opted to rent a plain Georgian lodging house on the fashionable strolling ground of the Old Steine, which improbably evolved into one of the most engagingly eccentric royal palaces in the world. Its transformation began in the form of the Marine Pavilion designed by Henry Holland in 1787, with a rotunda added. Shortly the prince's devotion to riding and racing horses managed spectacularly to upstage this, as he had an Indian-style stable building constructed nearby during 1803–08. John Nash was engaged in 1815 to adapt the pavilion in similar style. By 1823 it was complete. As was the prince's wish, it was very public, right in the middle of things: when concerts were held inside, the prince often would have the windows opened so that the promenaders outside could hear.

"The prince greatly took to Brighton's social life, the theatre and the races, in defiance of his frugal father."

Some observed at the time that it was 'far too handsome for Brighton', and predicted that it would be a ruin in 50 years. And indeed things were not always rosy for the Pavilion. Almost from the start, the innovative iron frame of the added-on structures began to decay in the wet and salt air, and leaks led to extensive dry rot. Queen Victoria, who came to the throne in 1837, found the Pavilion too small for her burgeoning young family and regretted its lack of sea views: in 1850 it was sold to the town of Brighton, but not before the Crown Estate had stripped out all the furniture, wallpapers and other decorative features, right down to the hearths and the wires for the bell pulls. Refurbishment was carried out – and the lavish ceilings of the Music Room, Banqueting Room and Saloon were restored to how they had been, but other rooms that had been stripped bare were decorated in all manner of ways. Then in World War I it was used as a hospital for some 4,000 convalescent Indian soldiers. When they came round and found themselves in this place, some might have thought they were hallucinating, but one described it as paradise: 'It is as if one were in the next world'. In gratitude the Indian government donated the gate at the south entrance to the gardens. Following 1918, a huge project to restore the Pavilion's Regency authenticity was carried out through much of the 20th century, with Buckingham Palace returning many of the original furnishings and decorations. An arson attack in the Music Room in 1975 was a major setback, and just when it was finally repaired, the Great Storm of 1987 sent an architectural stone ball crashing through the dome, embedding itself in the floor and damaging the costly new hand-knotted replica carpet. Some attribute the Music Room's misfortunes to bad *feng shui*; apparently its décor's combination of dragons and snakes would produce reactions of superstitious horror in China.

Meticulous restoration has once again left the Royal Pavilion looking quite remarkably good: even for those jaded by country-house visits, it simply has to be seen to be believed. Three years of work went into recreating the glories of the saloon as it might have looked when freshly decorated for George IV in 1823, compete with shimmering walls and opulent crimson and gold silk drapes. Scraps of carpet found in

BON APPETIT?

One of the greatest banquets ever prepared at the Royal Pavilion was for the Grand Duke Nicholas of Russia, in 1817. Among more than 100 dishes were 'the head of a great sturgeon in champagne', 'a terrine of larks', 'a pyramid of lobsters with fried parsley', and 'the Royal Pavilion rendered in pastry'. Since no more than 30 guests ever dined here at one time, the servants that night must have been very well fed.

Buckingham Palace were the clues to how the floor once looked – a large central sunflower motif with 20 serpents and 274 lotus leaves around it – and now a magnificent Axminster carpet perfectly recreates the original. Upstairs, there's yet more chinoiserie in the suite of bedrooms, a display on restoration work, and a gallery of viciously satirical contemporary cartoons of the Prince Regent. The café, Royal Pavilion Tea By Sugardough, serves elegant light lunches and teas on a pleasant terrace overlooking the gardens.

The **gardens** surrounding the Pavilion are presented as they would have been in Regency times: a naturalistic effect with trees and shrubs arranged around snaking paths through shaggy grass, cut to the length it would have been scythed by hand; adorned with antique gas lamps, this space has become a favourite sitting place within central Brighton, not that it's that big. Most weekends there are events here, often with a band playing.

"The gardens surrounding the Pavilion are presented as they would have been in Regency times: a naturalistic effect."

The Indian-style former Royal Stables and its adjacent Riding House now house the **Brighton Dome**, **Corn Exchange** and **Studio Theatre**, Brighton's principal concert hall and performing arts venue.

So that George could get from the Pavilion to his horses in the stables without being seen at the height of his unpopularity, when he wanted to remain hidden from the public gaze, he had a **tunnel** constructed beneath the gardens in 1821. A special Basement and Tunnel Tour gives access; book ahead through the Royal Pavilion.

BRIGHTON MUSEUM & ART GALLERY

Royal Pavilion Gardens, BN1 1FN ✆ 0300 029 0900 ⬦ brightonmuseums.org.uk
⊙ Tue–Sun & bank holidays

Entertainingly eclectic, the Brighton Museum and Art Gallery's permanent collection features splendid displays of art and costume (including George IV's breeches and shirt). The furniture gallery's most eye-catching pieces include very fine Art Deco and Art Nouveau furniture and two sofas with a difference, one in the form of Mae West's lips (by Dalí, c1938) and another in the form of a gigantic baseball glove (inspired by the baseball player Joe Di Maggio). Images of Brighton looks at a range of aspects of the resort, including its gay scene and the seamier, dirty-weekend side, and has models of the Old Steine as it was in 1804, and of Brighton's two vanished piers: the West Pier and the Chain Pier. Henry Willett, one of the founders of the museum, was an ardent collector, and his extraordinary assemblage of ceramics depicting social history themes makes up the display of Mr Willett's Popular Pottery – which he grouped into 23 subjects such as pastimes, statesmen and music. The display of Brighton Life includes oral histories from Brightonians and the frontage of 'the only cork factory on the South Coast', an antiquated shop that existed for exactly a century in Gardner Street in North Laine before its closure in 1983.

INLAND: WESTWARD & INTO HOVE

Between Seven Dials (to the north), Dyke Road (east), Western Road (south) and Boundary Passage (west), the **Montpelier** and **Clifton Hill** areas constitute one of Brighton's most rewarding strolling territories, and one missed by many visitors – a hilly residential district of white-stucco Victorian terraces, all immensely characterful with unexpected twists and vistas. In all it has 351 listed buildings, among the most striking being Montpelier Crescent of 1843–47 by Amon Wilds and sporting the trademark 'ammonite capitals' (a visual pun on Wilds's Christian name; at the top of the columns are representations of ammonite fossils), the bow-windowed frontages of Temple Gardens, the Arts and Crafts houses of Windlesham Road, and the streetscapes of Clifton Road and Powis Villas.

In the southeastern corner of this vicinity, a few steps away from the busy environs of Churchill Square, **St Nicholas' Church** was the old parish church for Brighthelmstone, very much safely up the slope and on the edge of things; although the church was comprehensively rebuilt in the 1850s it still has a rustic feel to its hilly churchyard, and gives you the impression you're on the Downs (as technically you are). Tombstones here mark some of the great Brighton characters including the famous 'dipper' Martha Gunn, and the immensely long-lived Phoebe Hessel (1713–1821) who had dressed up as a soldier so she could be with her lover; they both served in the West Indies and Gibraltar. Just below the church is the collegiate-looking Wykeham Terrace, used at one time as a refuge for repentant fallen women and prostitutes: it's a very attractive Gothic confection in grey and white, with castellations and a tower.

Only open on Saturdays but definitely worth seeking out, its red brick contrasting strikingly with the white stucco of the area's domestic architecture, the Grade I-listed **St Michael and All Angels Church**,

Victoria Road, is one of the greatest Victorian churches anywhere. Designed by G F Bodley and built in 1860–61, it was later enlarged with cathedral-like proportions to designs by William Burges, who memorably embellished Cardiff Castle among others. The stained glass in this Anglo-Catholic incense-filled church is the finest of this period in Sussex, with examples by William Morris, Edward Burne-Jones, Philip Webb, Peter Paul Marshall, Charles Kempe and Ford Madox Brown: the man on duty who lends out binoculars to visitors told me 'from the east window in the south aisle which forms the original church, if you make a clockwise tour of the building you've got a complete history of Victorian stained glass.' He pointed out the window for which Dante Gabriel Rossetti's wife was the model and urged me not to miss the Lady's Chapel with its stained glass of the *Flight into Egypt* by Burne-Jones and the *Three Marys at the Sepulchre* by Morris. He also showed me the particularly quaint carved misericords – which feature a grasshopper atop a snail, and one frog shaving another (yes, really).

Further inland, the **Booth Museum of Natural History** (194 Dyke Rd, BN1 5AA ✆ 0300 029 0900 ⌂ brightonmuseums.org.uk ⊙ noon–17.00 Tue–Wed, 10.00–17.00 Sat–Sun; free entry) dates from 1874 when Edward Booth presented his collection of stuffed-bird dioramas to the public. Since then, galleries of insects, fossils and ecology have been added, making this one of the most notable displays of its kind. Jeremy Adams, one of the curators (now retired), explained to me that in the

MATHEMATICAL TILES

The shiny black bricks you see here and there in Regency Brighton aren't bricks at all, but so-called mathematical tiles – thin clay veneers that were all the rage in this corner of Sussex in the late 18th and early 19th centuries. Royal Crescent, in Kemptown, is the longest frontage of mathematical tiles anywhere. The tiles appear in other colours too (and sometimes have been painted over). Lewes has the shiny black variety, as well as brick-coloured versions that take some spotting, and were tapped on over timber frontages to make the houses look more trendy. You can spot them throughout Lewes' High Street: look out for bow-windowed frontages where the tiles aren't quite flush and the building corners are covered over with wooden boards; the mathematical variety is slightly shorter than normal bricks.

The term 'mathematical' appears to be a piece of Georgian pretension, alluding to an age of discovery when all things scientific were deemed very cool.

VISITBRIGHTON.COM/ADAM BRONKHORST

JAZMINE MILES-LONG/ROYAL PAVILION & MUSEUMS

LAGOON WATERSPORTS

SIMON DACK/ROYAL PAVILION & MUSEUMS

ALL SAINTS CHURCH

1850s Booth was one of the pioneers of the concept of dioramas or ecological displays that illustrate the whole ecology of birds rather than just exhibiting birds by themselves. Of its hundreds of such exhibits, about 300 date from Booth's time. 'The Booth Museum is known as the birthplace of dioramas, and the Smithsonian copied the concept from us. Booth's aim was to have one of every British bird – a male, a female, a juvenile and any plumage variation. He didn't quite make the full list but made a very good start.'

Hove, mainly Victorian in character, was traditionally rather more sedate and relaxed than Brighton, but the nuances are fading and the transition between Brighton and (as it's jocularly known) Hove Actually is hard for all but locals to discern.

Sussex County Cricket Club has used Hove as its main ground since 1872, and the likes of Ranjitsinhji, John Snow, Tony Greig and Imran Khan have all played here. It's on a very appreciable slope leaning seawards and surrounded by blocks of flats, and the pavilion side-on to the playing area. The southern end is known with wonderful simplicity as the Sea End.

Hove Museum of Creativity (19 New Church Rd, BN3 4AB ✆ 0300 029 0900 ⟐ brightonmuseums.org.uk ☺ Thu–Mon; free entry) occupies a grandiose villa. Outside is the supremely ornate Jaipur Gate, carved from teak and sent by the Maharajah of Jaipur to London for the Colonial and Indian Exhibition in 1886, and installed here 40 years later. Inside the museum is an eclectic collection of art, changing exhibits, a Wizard's Attic of toys and an excellent display about early Hove and environs. Perhaps best of all is the room about the early pre-Hollywood movie industry in Hove that was pioneered by James Williamson and George Albert Smith. The two were members of the Hove Camera Club, and began making films in the late 1890s. You can sit in a seven-seater cinema in the museum and watch a medley of their efforts – comic or melodramatic miniatures with titles such as *Mary Jane's Mishap – or Don't Fool with the Paraffin*, and *Our New Errand Boy*, some of it not that far removed from music hall acts, but

◄ BRIGHTON & HOVE: **1** The flamboyant Royal Pavilion was a palace for King George IV. **2** Brighton is an excellent place for watersports, including wakeboarding. **3** Taxidermy in progress at the Booth Museum. **4** The Brighton Museum and Art Gallery has an eclectic mix of displays. **5** Marvel at Hove's All Saints Church while enjoying a concert.

sometimes with a touch of special-effects wizardry that must have been astounding to early audiences. Note the everyday streets of Hove that served as a backdrop, and the children and pets of the film-makers that inevitably end up in the action. The mini show also includes some shots of everyday life along the Brighton seafront in various decades of the 20th century, and a magic lantern narration relating tales of woe and awe.

On its western edge, Hove merges with Portslade, where the **Foredown Tower** (Foredown Rd, BN41 2EW ✐ 01273 415625), a learning centre in a former water tower, houses an operational camera obscura with views of the South Downs.

🎭 ENTERTAINMENT

Pleasure-seeking is what Brighton is all about, with dozens of pubs hosting band nights and cabaret venues popping up in the city centre's green spaces in summer. Here are some suggestions for starters:

The Actors 4 Prince's St, BN2 1RD ⊘ actors.pub. Wonderfully intimate and atmospheric cabaret and fringe-theatre venue at the Marlborough pub. Dating back to 1794, it has over the years served as a ballroom, gambling hall and LGBTQ performance space.

All Saints Hove The Drive BN3 3QE ⊘ allsaintshove.org ⊙ Jun–Oct 13.00 Thu. Weekly lunchtime concerts of jazz and classical music. An excellent opportunity to bask in the architectural glories of All Saints.

Artists' Open Houses City-wide ⊘ aoh.org.uk ⊙ May & Nov–Dec Sat–Sun. One of the UK's original and best art trails. Local artists' homes and studios become shared gallery spaces where you can view paintings, sculpture, ceramics, jewellery and textiles, chat to the makers over drinks and cake, and buy from them direct.

Brighton Dome Church St, BN1 1UE ⊘ brightondome.org. The city's principal music, dance and comedy venue, with a star-studded calendar of performances.

Brighton Festival & Brighton Fringe City-wide ⊘ brightonfestival.org, brightonfringe. org ⊙ May. One of Britain's leading art festivals, featuring a healthy mix of new and old, conventional and avant garde, with an international flavour. Main events take place in the evenings; there are also daytime parades, recitals, talks and fringe shows.

Brighton Little Theatre 9 Clarence Gdns, BN1 2EG ⊘ brightonlittletheatre.com. Amateur theatre which has been going since 1940 and puts on ten or so productions each year.

Brighton Unitarian Church New Rd, BN1 1UF ⊘ brightonunitarian.org.uk ⊙ 12.30 Fri. Classical lunchtime recitals at an elegantly neoclassical church near the Royal Pavilion.

Duke of York's Preston Rd, BN1 4NA ◌ picturehouses.com. The oldest purpose-built cinema in the UK, and a Grade II-listed building, this Edwardian picture palace opened in 1910 and is part of the excellent Picturehouse chain. Going here is always an occasion. It has a smaller and more intimate sister cinema in North Laine, Duke's at Komedia.

Komedia 44 Gardner St, BN1 1UN ◌ komedia.co.uk/brighton. A North Laine institution, this is Brighton's top venue for comedy and cabaret, with an arthouse cinema (Duke's at Komedia) attached.

The Old Market Upper Market St, BN3 1AS ◌ theoldmarket.com. Versatile performance venue in an elegant Regency building, originally a fresh produce market, close to Western Road in Hove. Hosts music, theatre and comedy.

Theatre Royal New Rd ◌ theatreroyalbrighton.com. Just across from the Royal Pavilion, this beautifully preserved theatre has a Georgian core. The gorgeous adjacent theatre bar (with its main entrance on the street) called The Colonnade is full of theatrical memorabilia.

TOURS

For a comprehensive selection of tours, including tours led by Blue Badge guides, themed walks and bike rides, visit ◌ visitbrighton.com/things-to-do.

Ghost Walk of the Lanes ✆ 01273 328297 ◌ ghostwalkbrighton.co.uk ◌ Feb–Dec 19.30 Wed–Sat. Creepy ambles with tales of apparitions and chilling happenings, commencing outside the Druid's Head pub on Brighton Place.

WATER ACTIVITIES

Brighton Watersports 185 Kings Road Arches BN1 1NB ✆ 01273 323160 ◌ thebrightonwatersports.co.uk. Based on the seafront near Middle Street, this outfit hires out kayaking, paddleboarding, sailing, windsurfing and surfing equipment, and offers lessons and group sessions.

Lagoon Watersports Hove Lagoon, Kingsway BN3 4LX ✆ 01273 424842 ◌ lagoon.co.uk. Various water sports including windsurfing (page 134), wakeboarding, kayaking and SUP.

Ross Boat Trips Pontoon 4, Brighton Marina ✆ 07958 246414 ◌ rossboats.co.uk. Offers 45-minute boat trips along the Brighton seafront as well as fishing trips.

SPECIAL STAYS

Experience Freedom East Brighton Park, BN2 5TS ✆ 01273 626546 ◌ experiencefreedom.com ◌ glamping all year, camping Apr–Sep. Perched on Brighton's eastern edge, where it meets the Downs, this family-friendly campsite is unbeatably good value. As well as pitches for tents and vans, if offers pods (well-insulated huts, with private or shared bathrooms and kitchens) for far less than a hotel room.

WINDSURFING FOR BEGINNERS

Standing on water attached to a board and a flimsy-looking sail may look like a recipe for extreme dampness, but the experts reassure me that total novices can be windsurfing within half an hour, though becoming an expert obviously takes longer. Lagoon Watersports offers a group and private tuition, from taster sessions to RYA courses, on Hove Lagoon, a former Victorian boating lake.

The shallowness of the water and the sheltered conditions make this one of just a handful of places in Sussex to learn windsurfing (other possibilities include Ardingly Reservoir, Princes Park Lake in Eastbourne, Northpoint Water near Rye and, at low tide, in the Solent at West Wittering). To windsurf on the lagoon, you don't need to be a strong swimmer or super-fit, but it's a pretty thorough workout that seemingly uses every muscle in your body. The age range is eight upwards and they have had active members well into their seventies.

Hotel du Vin 2 Ship St, BN1 1AD ✆ 01273 855221 ⌂ hotelduvin.com. In a brilliant location, between the seafront and The Lanes, Brighton's Hotel du Vin has quirky rooms that ooze style, but don't break the bank. The menu is as expertly curated as the wine list, with vegans particularly well catered for. For a twin-centre trip, this 19th-century mock-Tudor hotel combines very well with its elegant 18th century counterpart in the characterful spa town of Tunbridge Wells, which is close to the Sussex-Kent border, with the glories of the High Weald AONB on the doorstep.

FOOD & DRINK

Brighton and Hove has an abundance of places to eat and drink – particularly coffee shops, pubs and mid-range international restaurants – with vegetarians, vegans and pescatarians exceptionally well-catered for. While every neighbourhood has its highlights, The Lanes is the hub. The most interesting places prepare and serve seasonal local ingredients in a contemporary style.

Restaurants & takeaways

Bankers 116A Western Rd, BN1 2AB ⌂ bankers-restaurant.co.uk. Amid stiff competition for the best fish and chips in Brighton, Bankers wins out for its strong sustainability credentials.
Brighton Smokehouse 197 Kings Rd Arches, BN1 1NB. Seafront institution, selling sandwiches stuffed with crab, fish fingers and its signature smoked mackerel.
Food for Friends 17 Prince Albert St, BN1 1HF ⌂ foodforfriends.com. Long-established vegetarian and vegan restaurant in The Lanes, preparing delicious plant-based dishes such as beer-battered banana blossom or tomato and aubergine rigatoni.
Kindling 69 East St, BN1 1HQ ⌂ kindlingrestaurant.com. Modern restaurant that takes ethical sourcing seriously. Best known for its charcoal-grilled lunches and evening tasting menus.

Plateau 1 Bartholemews, BN1 1HG ⟨⟩ plateaubrighton.co.uk. Cosy and imaginative bistro in The Lanes, specialising in small plates prepared from Sussex produce and natural wine (prepared without pesticides, herbicides or chemical additives).

Pubs
The Basketmakers Arms 12 Gloucester Rd, BN1 4AD ⟨⟩ thebasketmakers.pub. Amenable Fuller's local, tucked away in North Laine, with exceptionally well-kept beer and decent pub grub. The walls feature a genuinely antique collection of tins, advertisements and posters.
The Bristol Bar Paston Place BN2 1HA ⟨⟩ thebristolbar.co.uk. One of the few traditional Brighton pubs with a sea view, this Kemptown favourite is worth seeking out for its calm, welcoming atmosphere.
The Cricketers Black Lion St, BN1 1ND ⟨⟩ cricketersbrighton.co.uk. Together with its neighbour The Black Lion, this is one of the most historic pubs in The Lanes. Lively atmosphere amid a Victorian vibe.
The Evening Star 55 Surrey St, BN1 3PB ⟨⟩ eveningstarpub.co.uk. Cosy real-ale drinkers' favourite, near the railway station, with a comprehensive collection of cask-conditioned beer from independent breweries.

Food shops & markets
The Cheese Hut 1 Basin Rd South, BN1 1WF ⟨⟩ thecheesehut.co.uk. Independent shop specialising in Sussex cheeses, in a light industrial unit near Hove Lagoon.
Foodies Festival Preston Park, BN1 6SD ⟨⟩ foodiesfestival.com ⊙ Jun. Major open-air event, featuring stalls, tastings, music and celebrity appearances.
Hisbe 20 York Pl, BN1 4GU ⟨⟩ hisbe.co.uk. Ethical food shop (the name is short for How It Should Be) selling affordable fresh produce and groceries with minimal single-use packaging.
Infinity Foods 25 North Rd, BN1 1YA ⟨⟩ infinityfoodsretail.coop. North Laine sustainability champion, selling wholefoods, vegan specialities and very good bread.
The Open Market Marshalls Row, BN1 4JU ⟨⟩ brightonopenmarket.co.uk. Permanent bakeries and cafés and an ever-changing range of stalls in the busy London Road neighbourhood. Vegan market on the first Saturday of the month.

EAST OF BRIGHTON

The coast road eastwards morphs abruptly from a city street fringed by the grand terraces of Kemptown to the green expanses between the white manorial pile of the ultra-exclusive Roedean girls' school and the slope beneath Rottingdean's smock mill. Beyond Rottingdean's old village centre, suburbia spreads through Saltdean, with its landmark lido, and Peacehaven, before dropping down to Newhaven.

5 ROTTINGDEAN

B&H bus 2 (Steyning–Rottingdean), 12 (Brighton–Eastbourne), 14 (Brighton–Newhaven), 27 (Westdene–Saltdean); several per hour

For many years this refuge from bustling Brighton enticed artists and writers to settle. The old centre is still appealingly villagey, with gracious old houses around its green, pond and the Rudyard Kipling flint-walled rose garden – despite the heavy, slow-moving traffic that nudges its way between the coast and the A27. In earlier times, from the 17th century, the place was notorious for smuggling – wool from Downland sheep was taken out in fishing boats and wine, spices, tea and so on were brought in from France. The smugglers built a system of tunnels beneath Rottingdean, wide enough for a man and a donkey, deep beneath the village.

The pre-Raphaelite designer and artist Edward Burne-Jones moved here in 1880 and joined together three properties to form North End House, by the green. He is buried in the nave of St Margaret's Church, in which he designed a notable set of stained-glass windows. In 1897 his nephew Rudyard Kipling arrived from Torquay with his wife, two children and a third on the way, to take up residency at The Elms. He was thus among an extended family that included his favourite aunt, Georgie (the wife of Burne-Jones) and his cousin Stanley Baldwin, the future prime minister, a frequent visitor to his in-laws, who lived in a nearby house called The Dene.

Kipling made numerous family excursions by car into the Sussex countryside, which had a profound effect on him, and recorded that the cousins took their families in farm carts 'into the safe clean heart of the motherly Downs for jam-smeared picnics'. During his time here he penned his *Just So Stories* and the village's smuggling links were encapsulated in his poem *A Smuggler's Song* ('Watch the wall my darling, while the Gentlemen go by'). Eventually Kipling tired of the sightseers from Brighton, who would arrive by double-decker bus and could peer over his garden wall, and he left in 1902 for the Wealden seclusion of Bateman's near Burwash (page 277).

Another artist, William Nicholson, visited to create a woodcut portrait of Kipling and was so taken with the village that he moved into the former vicarage, renaming it The Grange; it is now the volunteer-run **Grange Museum and Art Gallery** (✆ 01273 301004 ✆ rottingdeanheritage.org. uk ⊙ 10.00–16.00 Wed–Sat, 13.00–16.00 Sun; free entry), with works by Sussex artists, and rooms dedicated to Kipling and Burne-Jones as well as local history. On the west side of the village, the tar-black Rottingdean smock windmill (1802) – also known as Beacon Mill – stands just above the coast on a grassy miniature South Down, surveying a satisfying panorama.

6 SALTDEAN

B&H bus 12 (Brighton–Eastbourne), 14 (Brighton–Newhaven), 27 (Westdene–Saltdean); frequent services

During the 1930s Brighton began to expand eastward, and Saltdean promoted itself as the 'Coming Resort'. Although it's no longer an obvious choice for a holiday, it contains two magnificent examples of Art Deco in the form of the Saltdean Lido and Ocean Hotel. The Lido is the greatest example of its kind to survive. Built in 1935–38, this was perhaps inspired by the De La Warr Pavilion in Bexhill (page 296). Designed by R W H Jones, Jones's creation included a fountain, boating lake, paddling pool, three-tier diving board and an upper-storey café with curved metal windows, very much in the spirit of contemporary airport design. After long periods of neglect, when it faced possible demolition, it has at last been restored using a multi-million-pound grant from the Heritage Lottery Fund.

More Art Deco awaits in the form of the Ocean Hotel (also by Jones, and now flats), which was once home to Butlins. Look out too for a group of modernist houses just above the lido.

Beneath the cliffs is the shared-use concrete Undercliff Walk to Rottingdean and Brighton, an enjoyable level traffic-free route for strollers, runners and cyclists. There's also a beach, with lifeguards during summer and a small café.

7 PEACEHAVEN

B&H bus 12 (Brighton–Eastbourne), 14 (Brighton–Newhaven); frequent services

Conceived in 1914 as a garden city by the sea, Peacehaven, east of Saltdean, never quite lived up to the aspirations of its pioneer, Charles Neville. 'A seaside home for £350' exclaimed a poster in 1929: 'Have your own seaside home on the South Coast – it will pay for itself. Live on the glorious South Downs for HEALTH AND HAPPINESS. Every site commands views over Sea and Downs.'

People who had never ventured to the south coast before came to look at this utopia, named New Anzac-on-Sea in homage to the Australia and New Zealand Army Corps. Later renamed Peacehaven and marketed to British servicemen returning from the war, it grew into a neat suburb of bungalows with a distinctly un-British feel – it could almost be somewhere in the US or Australia.

East of the globe-topped obelisk that marks the point where the Greenwich Meridian leaves Britain's south coast, there's access to the foot of the sheer, chalky cliffs, a celebrated spot for fossils including giant ammonites, some of which measure more than 6ft across. Just beyond Peacehaven's eastern edge, the Peacehaven Heights clifftop path leads to the remnants of a **World War II radar station** that provided information to Newhaven Fort and the Emergency Coast Batteries at Brighton and Newhaven. In their midst is the grassy mound of a **Bronze Age bowl barrow**, some 2,000–3,000 years old. Excavations here uncovered hunter-gatherers' tools dating back to the Mesolithic period (8000–4000BC). A path leading inland on the Peacehaven side rises past the remains of a pair of **anti-aircraft gun bases**. You can combine this with a wander along the foot of the cliffs, reached by an access track west of the Meridian marker and by a spectacular staircase at the far east of town.

AWAY FROM THE COAST

Head northward from the coastal towns and you are soon into some very accessible and unspoilt country, especially away from the main roads. Sompting and Lancing lie close to the nastily busy A27, which heads eastwards past the campuses for the universities of Brighton and Sussex.

8 CISSBURY RING
Stagecoach bus 1 (Midhurst–Worthing; hourly, less frequent on Sun) to Findon

This is easily the most impressive of Sussex's 27 Iron Age hillforts. Actually the term is something of a misnomer: probably not all of them were defensive and some span more than the Iron Age. Viewed from Google Earth, Cissbury is one of the most prominent features of the South Downs, with still-massive ramparts that take a good 20 minutes to walk around even at a brisk pace. There's a free car park at its foot, at the end of a dead-end road leading up from Findon on the A24; but to make more of a walk of it, you could start beneath the car park at Chanctonbury Ring (page 147), itself within strolling distance of Steyning and bus connections: from Chanctonbury there are plenty of easy bridleways crossing the arable plateau of the Downs, making it excellent mountain-biking terrain though it's a bit too intensively farmed to rank as one of the great walks in the area.

HOW TO SPOT A WORKED FLINT

Present in great supply on England's chalklands, flint was the prized material of the pre-metal age. Extremely hard yet easily shaped, with the capacity to cut, bore or scrape, it was employed for a great range of purposes, including scrapers, knives, arrowheads and axes for felling trees.

The South Downs is one of the most renowned sources of prehistoric flintwork, and if you know what you're looking for, it's possible to spot flakes that were worked by prehistoric people thousands of years ago. By the flint mines in Cissbury there's quite a large concentration (though bear in mind that as it's a Scheduled Monument you can't dig here or take anything away – just look on the surface where the heritage-oblivious rabbits have unwittingly unearthed items). You'll mostly find waste flakes, not tools: they were chipped off when the flint knapper was making some object, typically using an antler pick or a stone for the fine work.

TOP HINTS FOR SPOTTING A WORKED FLINT ARE:

Colour: look for white flints. When a flint is newly broken, the broken part is black; over many centuries it gets a patina from the surrounding subsoil, which here is the white chalk (in other places you might be looking for grey, bluish, brown or – confusingly – black flints).
Shape: ignore the chunky bits, and look for thin slices.
Platform and face: there will be a flat 'platform' where the flint was struck, at right angles to the smooth (originally inside) face. Beneath the platform on the smooth face (which was the side of the flint joined to the larger bit of flint before it was struck) there's a little bulbous lump called a 'bulb of percussion'. This face will have a series of ripples that appeared like shock waves when the flint was struck. Sometimes you may even find evidence that the flint was 'retouched' along one edge to make it usable as a tool – for example as a 'scraper' for removing bark from a branch or flesh from a hide.
Scars: on the back, or dorsal, side there may be long bevelled facets where other bits of flint were knocked off.

As a hillfort, the site dates from about 350BC: it surveys the coast from Beachy Head near Eastbourne to the east to Culver Cliff on the Isle of Wight to the west. In its day the ramparts would have been built up with a timber stockade; this protected the community, who lived in thatched roundhouses, and their livestock.

If you turn right along the ramparts you reach one of the largest of the ten known **Neolithic flint mines** in England. There's no sign announcing this, but it's an obviously disturbed, bumpy patch within the ramparts, where people mined for flint between about 4500BC and 2300BC. Using antlers for picks, they dug down through a series of shafts, all of which have been filled in, but the bushy hollows give the game away. It's a mystery why these folk went to such efforts to mine flint, when there was plenty of the stuff lying around on the surface – particularly good quality along parts of the coast. It's possible that there was some ritual attached to the perilous task of crawling into a hole and mining flint, or perhaps the mined flint had a certain prestige value assuming you knew someone had gone to all that effort. Archaeologists have found something that looks like graffiti etched into walls of some shafts, and rather more sinisterly some skeletons – one of a woman – who might have been performing some rite of passage; they were buried with some partly worked flint axes.

9 SOMPTING

Compass bus 7 (Lancing–Worthing; hourly Mon–Sat)

One very striking oddity lies in Sompting, between Worthing and Lancing: **St Mary the Blessed Virgin Church**, north of the A27, has a tower unlike any other in Sussex, but of a style commonly seen in the Rhineland of Germany. Rising 100ft, it is of a type known as a **Rhenish helm**, with a four-sided, shingled, pyramidal cap. Its origins are clearly Saxon, and it dates from around 1000, although the timber within it has been radio-carbon-dated to the 14th century. Elsewhere are numerous Norman features, including the chancel and the characteristic rounded arches in the north transept. As Rhenish helms go, this is the oldest to be found anywhere in the country.

10 LANCING COLLEGE CHAPEL

Lancing College, BN15 0RW ✐ 01273 452213 ⌂ lancingcollege.co.uk ☉ 10.00–16.00 Mon–Sat, noon–16.00 Sun; Lancing railway station, West Coastway Line (Southampton–Brighton), then 2½-mile walk

More ecclesiastical wonders await within this, the largest school chapel in the world, visible for miles for anyone travelling along the South Downs Way, the Brighton to Worthing railway or the A27. Begun in 1868 to the design of R H Carpenter and William Slater, it is built of Sussex sandstone. The chapel is a spectacular Gothic revival edifice, lofty and ethereal, with its vaulted stone roof rising 90ft and giving it cathedral-like proportions. Clear windows bathe the interior in natural light and illuminate tapestries designed at the William Morris workshops and richly carved stall canopies originally from Eton Chapel. At the west end, the rose window contains 30,000 pieces of blown glass and was the largest stained-glass window since medieval times.

Lancing College has a strong musical tradition: its past pupils include the great tenor Peter Pears, whose lifelong partner Benjamin Britten composed the *St Nicolas Cantata* for its centenary in 1948. An enduring favourite of choral societies, this work was conceived so that it could be performed by amateurs, with the addition of a professional tenor and string quartet to lead the other strings in the orchestra. Public concerts and services take place during the school year.

11 COOMBES

Tucked under a fold of the Downs and north of the A27 and Lancing College, the tiny hamlet of Coombes gets very busy in spring, when **Church Farm** (BN15 0RS ✆ 01273 452028 ⊘ coombes.co.uk ⊙ Mar–Apr; three miles from Lancing railway station) opens for the lambing and calving season, with hundreds of visitors each year. It is a long tradition, stretching back to 1979, when this became the very first farm tour in the country, and gives a privileged insight into life and work on a Sussex farm. You are taken on a tractor and trailer right up to the top of the Downs, looking far over the Weald; you'll hear about what you're looking at, how the farm is run, and how dew ponds are important and how they are formed.

Five generations of Passmores have farmed these 1,000 acres since 1901, the original family bringing their cattle from Devon. They had dairy cows until the 1950s, and in the following two decades turned to intensive farming in a period where food production was paramount. They now farm sheep and beef cattle and have arable fields with wheat for bread flour, animal feed, cakes and biscuits, and barley for animal feed and brewing beer.

Jenny Passmore told me that her father, Dick, received an MBE in 1992 for his farming and education efforts in the field of conservation. 'The conservation areas begun in the 1950s are always called "Dad's follies" – people didn't do conservation then. He was progressive, and deliberately left areas for birdlife, planted trees and left what we call the "bank of flowers" – this we graze sensitively to keep the scrub down. We get scabious, cowslips, orchids, poppies, clover and lots of butterflies like chalkhill blues.'

The South Downs is one of Britain's **Environmentally Sensitive Areas** (ESAs), in which farmers get subsidies in return for adopting agricultural practices that enhance landscape, wildlife habitats and areas of historic value. 'In 1987, the first year of the ESA, we joined the scheme – we're not allowed to use spray or fertiliser on the grassland, but manage it with sheep and cattle grazing and we 'top' the stinging nestles and thistles. We do use sprays and fertilisers on arable fields, where we grow wheat and barley; without doing this the crops wouldn't grow, as the Downs are so flinty and poor that we just wouldn't get a crop otherwise. Also if there's a disease in the area, we spray against it.'

'We have 800 ewes (Welsh mules) and rams (Charollais). We sometimes go to Breconshire, in Wales, in October, to buy replacements, near my brother's farm in the Llanthony valley. Welsh mules are a good breed that produces good twins and meat; the wool is a by-product – the price is half the cost of the shearing. My son Andrew has a shearing certificate, and Plumpton College students come here to learn.' The Passmores have 80 pedigree Sussex cattle: chocolate brown, but officially described as red. 'They're good, hardy animals, they rear their own calves, which stay with us till October. They produce a nice marbled beef – we used to have Limousin and Charolais cattle, which were leaner, but tastes have changed.'

Jenny says she loves the diversity of farming. 'The seasons and animals are always changing. In winter the animals stay out – the cows until Christmas and the sheep till the end of February. We end up with 1,200–1,400 lambs. We sell most of them and buy in replacements

1 A walkway follows the cliffs below Saltdean. **2** Looking across the duck pond in Rottingdean, towards Kipling's house. **3** The vast Iron Age hillfort of Cissbury Ring. **4** Lancing is home to the largest school chapel in the world. **5** The statue of St Cuthman at Steyning's St Andrew's Church. ▶

SS

NICOLA PULHAM /D

CLICKOS /D

LILY TROTT /D

PHILIP BIRD /D

SHEEP ON THE DOWNS

Traditionally the Southdown breed were, as the name implies, the sheep of the South Downs. Sheep have probably grazed the Downs since Neolithic times, although the early beasts would have looked very different. Gilbert White in *The Natural History and Antiquities of Selborne* (1773) describes sheep on the west of the Adur valley as horned with smooth, white faces and white legs 'but as soon as one passes over the river heading eastwards the animals become hornless, have black faces and speckled legs. Shepherds tell you this has been the case since time immemorial'. The speckled type became the norm of Southdown sheep through careful selective breeding by one John Ellman of Glynde, who saw the scope for producing a hardy strain of sheep that could flourish on downland vegetation. Other farmers paid huge sums for the services of Ellman's ram, and he and other landowners founded the Sussex County Agricultural Society. In the 19th century, Southdown sheep became big business, with the annual wool fair at Lewes bringing in up to 30,000 of them; they were exported worldwide, allegedly as far as the Andes in Peru.

A sharp demise followed, intensified by the need in World War II to give over some areas to tank training. Southdowns are now quite a rarity – in 1798 around 150,000 grazed the Downs between Shoreham and Eastbourne; by the 1950s this number was down to 25,000 on the Downs between Brighton and Eastbourne; today barely a tenth of that number is found across the entire country, and the Southdown has been declared a Rare Breed. The old Southdowns' fatty meat has fallen out of favour, though one farmer told me you need that fat to make the most of the special taste. Instead a breed of sheep known as mules are ubiquitous across much of Britain – they produce saleable meat and a ewe reliably has two or three lambs.

Despite a recent upturn in knitting as a hobby, the prices sheep farmers get for their wool are derisory, meaning that meat production is always the reason for having sheep nowadays.

On some of the Downs, hardy sheep breeds – such as Herdwicks from the Lake District – have periodically been introduced to keep down the amount of invasive scrub that threatens grassland species. The Sussex Wildlife Trust has been instrumental in operating grazing schemes, centred on Southerham Farm, by the Trust's reserve on Malling Down near Lewes, where it manages a flock of sheep, including many rare breeds.

because you can't cross daughter and father. The beauty about lambing and calving is that everything's new. We calve and lamb at the same time. It's tiring but fun.'

The Passmores run **coarse fishing** here throughout the year on two ponds – Passies Pond and Match Lake – for carp, roach, tench, chub, rudd, bream and perch, with instruction and equipment available.

Church Farm also hosts the **Glastonwick Beer Festival**, on the first weekend of June, with music, poetry reading and other entertainment in addition to 80 real ales and numerous real ciders.

Coombes Church

Accessed through a field just above Church Farm, Coombes Church is seemingly oblivious to the passing of the ages: no electricity, no heavy-handed Victorian restorations, just a beautifully simple, untampered-with medieval building, with remains of 12th-century wall paintings uncovered in 1949 which include Christ in Majesty over the chancel arch, the inside of which bears some well-preserved geometric abstract decoration. The bell could well be as early as 1100 and is thought to be the oldest in Sussex. The pews seat around 60, but over a hundred might squeeze in for the service on Christmas Day morning, followed by coffee in Church Farm's barn. On Rogation Sunday in May, the congregation processes around the fields in a blessing ceremony with readings and singing.

You can cycle here from Shoreham-by-Sea railway station, following the traffic-free, entirely level Downs Link until it joins the South Downs Way, then turning south along the lane to Coombes.

Shoreham Cement Works

Quite possibly the least beautiful thing in all Sussex, this abandoned factory gouged into the Downs beside the A283 between Upper Beeding and the cloverleaf flyover junction with the A27 is a spectacular blot on the landscape – fenced off, forbidding and compelling in its sheer ugliness. The quarrying started here in 1851 and continued for 140 years. Several redevelopment ideas have been proposed – possibly transforming the site into housing or a leisure park – and at the time of writing, a lengthy consultation is underway. Watch this space, or rather this gigantic hole.

12 STEYNING & BRAMBER

B&H bus 2 (Rottingdean–Steyning; three per hour Mon–Sat, less frequent Sun)

Just west of the Adur, these two join together. **Bramber Castle** (free access) comprises merely the toothlike ruin of a gatehouse and chunks of curtain wall, in what is a favourite picnic ground for local families. Built as a motte and bailey, Bramber dates from the castle-building days of the Normans following the Conquest. Remnants of the outline of the foundations of the guardhouse and living quarters can be discerned next to it, but architecturally this is perhaps not one of the great castle moments of Sussex. At its base, the church built to serve the castle took a battering in the Civil War but still functions. Towards the river **St Mary's House** (*⊘* stmarysbramber.co.uk *⊙* May–Sep 14.00–18.00 Thu & Sun) is a conspicuously historic half-timbered 15th-century house, originally a hospital for pilgrims. Its panelled interior features 16th-century parquetry overmantels, and the gardens contain rose beds, herbaceous borders, pools and topiary. Its Victorian music room, resplendent with stained glass and Gothic detailing, stages numerous concerts and recitals.

Steyning is a handsome small town, in medieval times a prosperous port but doomed by the silting up of the river. Its High Street looks thriving enough nowadays, though, with proper food shops, as well as a bookshop doubling as the box office for professional chamber concerts and recitals organised by the Steyning Music Society. An impressive array of old buildings survive from its heady days, especially in Church Street, which is quite a treat for the eyes with its exceptionally well preserved jettied timber-frame houses and imposing brick façades. Near the library an absorbing stash of informatively captioned local history is on show in the free **museum**.

> *"Church Street is quite a treat for the eyes with its exceptionally well-preserved jettied timber-frame houses."*

Opposite, **St Andrew's Church** was built by Norman monks from Fécamp in the 11th to early 12th centuries: within its lofty interior, massive dog-toothed arches and Norman windows survive from the early days. In the porch is a little-sung ancient curio in the form of a stone slab inscribed with primitive, possibly pre-Christian markings; for centuries this was placed face down and served as a step into the churchyard. No-one knows what it was, but it's possibly an idol from a pagan cult adhered to by locals until the arrival of St Cuthman in the 8th century. He was carrying his mother in a wheelbarrow, as one does, only for the strings around his shoulders to break here at Steyning, where he was persuaded to stay, and eventually built the church and converted locals. In a typical gesture of defiance of old ways, the stone seems to have been placed at the entrance so that Christian worshippers would effectively be disdainfully stamping out the pagans. The stone, which may give Steyning its name, meaning 'people of the stone', was only rediscovered in 1938. In the churchyard a modern sculpture of St Cuthman shows him doing his stuff with the evil stone – his foot rests on top of it. In spite of his endeavours, he was ousted as favoured saint here when French monks rededicated the church to St Andrew in the 12th century.

Chanctonbury Ring

Steyning (and a car park further west, just beneath the Downs and signposted off the A283) is a useful starting point for walks up on to the Downs, notably taking in Chanctonbury Ring, a prominent clump of beeches that is one of the most identifiable features on the escarpment. The Great Storm of 1987 wrecked it, and it is a fragment of how it previously looked, but is slowly regenerating itself. It occupies the site of a Romano-British temple on the location of an earlier hillfort, and excavations after the storm revealed archaeology beneath where the trees had been. The dew pond at the top is a beautiful spot for a picnic, and the chalky tracks over the intensively farmed rolling plateau make for easy wandering right over to Cissbury.

ᵠ FOOD & DRINK

The Cobblestone Tea House Cobblestone Walk, 74 High St, BN44 3RD ✆ 01903 366171 ◉ cobblestoneteahouse.com. Brimming with historic appeal, this pretty café serves full English and vegan breakfasts, jacket potatoes, scones and all the tea shop treats you'd expect.

Victoria's Sponge 116 High St, BN44 3RD ✆ 01903 814517. Cosy, friendly village café with delicious handmade cakes (including vegan and gluten-free) and smoothies.

DEW PONDS

With the lack of surface water for cattle and sheep to drink on the permeable chalk, dew ponds are very much a characteristic of the South Downs landscape, and may originate from Saxon or even prehistoric times. These small ponds, high up and sometimes marked by a few trees, are manmade: layers of straw and clay form an impermeable lining on the chalk or lime base, with a top layer of rubble as a protection from beasts' hoofs. Contrary to what was formerly thought by some, the act of animals walking around the dew pond actually helps reseal the bottom of the pond and prevents cracking and the growth of pond weed. As a farmer explained to me, 'If the animals are healthy, then the pond is healthy.'

Devil's Dyke

❄ OS Explorer map OL11; start: either Poynings village centre ♀ TQ262120 (off the A281, southwest of Henfield, with roadside parking near the Royal Oak pub) or Devil's Dyke ♀ TQ258110 (bus 77 at weekends from central Brighton; pay & display car park); three miles; one steep ascent from the base of the Downs to the top. There are **loos** by the Devil's Dyke pub, right at the top of the escarpment. Another, more appealing **pub** is usefully placed on the route: the Royal Oak in Poynings.

You get a lot of scenery in the three miles of this outstanding downland walk. This version is my favourite of numerous variants: much better, in my opinion, to start at the bottom of the South Downs – as I've done here – and walk up, then earn the view far over the Weald to the Surrey Hills. You soon leave the crowds behind as you dip down into the longest downland dry valley, and past a wooded lake for the finale. I've suggested an **alternative start** – useful for bus travellers – from Devil's Dyke itself, though it does rather give the game away and reduces the element of surprise. I've picked the path that makes a less steep ascent than the alternatives and looks out across the Weald in its early stages.

1 With the Royal Oak on your right, follow the road for 30yds, then just after Dyke Lane House turn left into Dyke Lane (signposted as a bridleway). At the Devil's Dyke National Trust sign, just inside the woods, fork right uphill, then 20yds later fork right again on a roughly level path (the steps up to the left also lead up to the Devil's Dyke pub but are very steep and there are fewer views). The path runs close to the field edge then eventually rises slightly, still in the woods. Where a path crosses keep forward along the level (avoiding the path to the left that rises steeply).

2 The path eventually emerges into a field corner then immediately goes left through a gate, back into the woods. Follow the bridleway, which rises steadily, eventually getting big views as you emerge on to open downland. At the top go forward at a four-way signpost, following the bridleway a further 20yds, then turn left along the top (Brighton briefly comes into view away to the right) to the Devil's Dyke pub.

13 WOODS MILL

Shoreham Rd, BN5 9SD, off the A2037 a mile south of Henfield ⬧ sussexwildlifetrust.org.uk; Compass bus 100 (Horsham–Burgess Hill; hourly Mon–Sat)

The headquarters of the Sussex Wildlife Trust, Woods Mill is where you can find out more about the Trust's reserves, activities and courses. Free to access all year round, the reserve around the 18th-century watermill

3 Standing with the view behind you, take the public road to the right of the Devil's Dyke pub, past the bus stop, then find the waymarked path on the left just after the bus-turning circle, through a kissing gate and through some trees, where you can see the valley ahead that you're about to drop into. Turn right at the next junction after 50yds, through a gate, then left on the path that leads down into the floor of the dry valley (this is Devil's Dyke). There's a chunk of brickwork on the valley floor, presumably part of the long-defunct cable car that once came this way (there's a bit more visible on the top of the slope to the right). Carry on along the bottom of the valley for half a mile.

4 At a fence by a National Trust sign for Devil's Dyke (facing the other way), take the right-hand gate by the bridleway signpost. This track leads through woods, dropping gently (soon ignore a rising path to the right). A long, thin lake appears among the trees to the left; soon take the left fork of paths inside the edge of the wood, still close to and above the lake. Emerge into a field and carry on alongside the lake, crossing it at the end by a mini-dam on the left, then turn right in the next field, along the right edge towards Poynings. Go over a stile by a gate and through a yard on to the road; turn left to reach the Royal Oak.

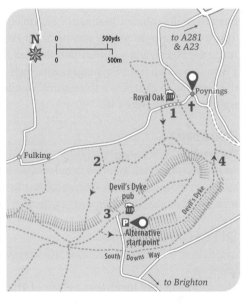

is used heavily for educational purposes, but is a beautiful and richly diverse place in its own right, with a wheelchair-friendly trail of just under a mile lacing its way through coppice woodland, past a dipping pond frequented by water boatmen and dragonflies, across meadow land and around a reedy lake. Mike Russell of the Trust told me 'I'm very keen on stopping and listening. Woods Mill is one of the best places for nightingales – there are four types here. This is the essence of slowing down; as dusk comes, everything else goes quiet. The reserve demonstrates the richness of the ordinary.'

14 DEVIL'S DYKE

B&H Breeze bus 77 (Brighton–Devil's Dyke; Mar–Sep daily; Sep–Mar hourly Sat–Sun & public holidays)

Kite fliers will be very happy here on the escarpment, looking out across the Weald. The ramparts of an Iron Age hillfort crown the top of the slope at this most satisfying of viewpoints. Sadly a good many visitors miss the Devil's Dyke itself – a deeply incised dry valley owned by the National Trust and formed during the last Ice Age. So named because of a legend that the devil gouged it out in a fit of pique, it has a few visible remains of the concrete footings of Britain's first cable car, built in 1894. This wasn't the only novelty way up: from Poynings a funicular railway made the ascent, and a railway line climbed its way up from Hove. The 1½-mile walk up from Poynings is extremely satisfying, but in my view the best way to experience this natural wonder is to follow the circular walk featured on page 148.

¶¶ FOOD & DRINK

The Royal Oak The St, Poynings BN45 7AQ ✐ 01273 843147 ⊘ theroyaloakpoynings.com. Set at the foot of the South Downs and handy for walkers, this family-friendly country inn has Harvey's ales on tap and serves satisfying pub food. The garden tables quickly fill up on warm sunny days, particularly when there's a barbecue on the go.

15 DITCHLING

Compass buses 167 (Lewes–Burgess Hill) and 168 (Burgess Hill–Wivelsfield Green); limited service

The conspicuously handsome village of Ditchling, a mile or so away from the foot of the scarp slope and due north of central Brighton (which feels miles further away than it is), drew a notable circle of artists and calligraphers in the first half of the 20th century – most famously the typographic designers Edward Johnston and Eric Gill – whose sans serif fonts Johnston Sans and Gill Sans are so familiar today. It was Johnston's lettering that was adopted by London Transport for all its Underground typography back in 1915, with a small restyling made in 1985.

GILL, JOHNSTON & 'LONDON'S HANDWRITING'

Eric Gill was one of ten children and was brought up in Sussex. He was a leading artistic light of the day, living with his wife next door to William Morris's daughter in Hammersmith, acquainted with Roger Fry – who brought post modernism into Britain – and a close friend of Vanessa Bell and Virginia Woolf. He was appointed to create the *Stations of the Cross* at Westminster Cathedral as well as statues of *Ariel* and *Prospero* outside Broadcasting House. While in London he also met Edward Johnston and admired his calligraphy; Gill took Johnson in hand and gained him commissions.

Gill converted to Catholicism and moved to Ditchling (first to a house called Sopers – look out for the plaque). He adhered to the idea of 'distributism' – communism with a Christian perspective – and then established a community of craftspeople and artists based outside the village at Ditchling Common. His Guild only admitted men and Catholics, but others worked alongside him; Johnston was among them, but never joined the Guild. Gill's personal life was, to put it bluntly, unsavoury in the extreme (including an incestuous relationship with his daughters), and sometimes overshadows his undoubted pedigree as an artist and lettering designer.

Gill Sans is a household name among all those who use a computer. And Johnston's unmistakable, timelessly stylish sans serif lettering for the London Underground became known as 'the handwriting for London'. It was based on the proportions of Roman capitals, and its design was originally to be a joint project between Gill and Johnston, but Gill was unable to proceed on it because of other work commitments. Transport for London still owns the copyright of the font.

The regenerated **Ditchling Museum of Art + Craft** (Lodge Hill Lane BN6 8SP ⌂ ditchlingmuseumartcraft.org.uk ☺ Wed–Mon) showcases the work of Gill, Johnston and other leading lights in Ditchling's Arts and Crafts movement. It was founded in 1985 by two septuagenarian sisters, Hilary and Joanna Bourne, as a labour of love: they filled a former school with all sorts of memorabilia and donations they had collected over the years. It fell into poor repair, but a substantial Heritage Lottery Fund grant proved its salvation. The village's pride in its artistic heritage clearly helped: locals formed an association to buy the adjacent green when it was threatened by developers, and leased a long-disused 18th-century cart lodge for a peppercorn rent to the museum. This now forms the entrance building – part of an admirably imaginative conversion that won a RIBA (Royal Institute of British Architects) award and opened in 2013.

Apart from such permanent exhibits as Johnston's desk, the Bournes' artefacts and the 200-year-old printing press that was brought by fellow artist Hilary Pepler and placed at the back of Gill's house, the displays change regularly. There's a comprehensive programme of talks and workshops, so this is very much a place for repeat visits.

"Ditchling Beacon is a favourite viewpoint capped by discernible ramparts of an Iron Age hillfort."

The annual London-to-Brighton Bike Ride – Britain's biggest event of its kind – saves its toughest moment for near the end with the ascent of **Ditchling Beacon** (814ft), south of the village – a favourite viewpoint capped by discernible ramparts of an Iron Age hillfort. The site was donated to the National Trust in memory of a 21-year-old pilot shot down in the Battle of Britain: a finer memorial is hard to imagine. Brighton & Hove bus 79 runs up here from central Brighton on Saturdays, Sundays and public holidays.

¶¶ FOOD & DRINK

The Bull 2 High St, BN6 8TA ✆ 01273 843147 ⬙ thebullditchling.com. Hugely popular at weekends, this dining pub with rooms retains the convivial feel of a historic coaching inn. The menu features upmarket pub classics and a roaring fire in the bar adds to the atmosphere in winter.

The Green Welly 1 High St, BN6 8SY ✆ 01273 841010 ⬙ thegreenwellycafe.co.uk ◷ Tue–Sun. Family-friendly café serving breakfast, lunch, pastries, cakes and speciality coffee, with a pleasant yard at the back.

The Nutmeg Tree 6 West St, BN6 8TS ✆ 01273 842708 ⬙ thenutmegtree.co.uk. Tea room and garden with a vintage feel, serving light lunches, triangle-cut sandwiches and other retro treats.

The Rows & Vine Ridgeview Wine Estate, Ditchling Common BN6 8TP ✆ 01444 242040 ⬙ ridgeview.co.uk ◷ Thu–Mon. North of Ditchling, this Certified B Corp winery's sparkling wines have soared to prominence in recent years. Founded by the Roberts family in 1995, the enterprise has won dozens of medals and trophies, and offers tastings and tours. The stylish Rows & Vine restaurant offers small plates created from local South Downs ingredients, and has glorious vineyard views.

---

1 Devil's Dyke offers stunning views across the Weald. **2** Knepp Estate gives the privileged chance to spot white storks. **3** The Ditchling Museum of Art + Craft pays tribute to leading 20th-century artists from the area. **4** Leonardslee Gardens are awash with colour when the rhododendrons and azaleas bloom. ▶

South Downs Heritage Centre Hassocks BN6 9LY ☎ 01273 845232 ⟨ tatesofsussex.
co.uk. Sharing a site with a garden centre west of Ditchling, this craft centre and museum of
gardening and rural culture has a foodhall and café selling Sussex produce.
The White Horse 16 West St, BN6 8TS ☎ 01273 842006 ⟨ whitehorseditchling.com. More
modest than The Bull, this dining pub with rooms has a garden and a kids' menu, making it
popular with families.

16 CLAYTON & JACK & JILL WINDMILLS

Metrobus 270, 271, 272, 273 from Ardingly, Brighton, Cuckfield, East Grinstead, Handcross,
Hassocks, Haywards Heath and Wakehurst Place (hourly Mon–Sat, less frequent on Sun)

Just beneath the downs at **Clayton**, the pre-Conquest **Church of
St John** has one of the finest series of wall paintings in Sussex,
depicting the *Fall of Satan*, the *New Jerusalem* and other scenes, painted
in the 11th century. Across the A273, **Clayton railway tunnel** has a
spectacular castle-like portal – which you can just see by peeping over
from the road. The tunnel witnessed what was at the time the worst-
ever train collision in Britain in 1861 when three northbound trains
crashed into each other after the first had stopped because of a red
flag being waved by a signalman; the mayhem resulted in 176
people being injured and 23 deaths. Charles Dickens was very likely
prompted by this event to write his short supernatural story of 1866
The Signal-Man.

Above, on the Downs and most easily reached from the dead-end
road leading up from the A273 just south of Clayton, two windmills
known as **Jack and Jill** (⟨ jillwindmill.org.uk) preside over the scene
as they did when last in full use in 1906. Jack is a brick tower mill, in
private ownership, but Jill, a wooden post mill, is open most Sunday
afternoons between May and September. Jack resulted in the invention
of the rotating gun turret for naval ships by Captain Cowper Coles:
his daughter and naval-officer son-in-law lived in the windmill, the
technology of which germinated the idea.

West of Clayton, **Wolstonbury Hill** is a rare separate peak in the
South Downs. Capped by prehistoric earthworks, it is often bypassed
by walkers because it is not on the South Downs Way, and although it
is sandwiched between the A23 and A273 you can neither see nor hear
the roads from the top. The National Trail officer for the South Downs
Way, Andy Gattiker, told me that it is a favourite spot of his: 'Its subtle
detachment makes it special and gives it a 360-degree view you don't get

from other viewpoints. You can see the undersides of the scarp, both to the east and to the west.'

17 FALMER & STANMER PARK

Train to Falmer (East Coastway Line, Brighton–Hastings) then ½-mile walk; B&H Bus 25 & 23 (Brighton–Universities; several per hour); B&H Breeze bus 78 (Brighton–Stanmer Park; one per hour)

The village of **Falmer** is uncomfortably squidged between the roaring A27 dual carriageway and its feeder roads, with Brighton and Hove Albion's sleekly curvaceous Amex football stadium towering close by, but retains a serene old centre gathered around a pond on the south side of the main road. Either side of the main road and railway are the two universities – Brighton and Sussex. The **University of Sussex**, on the north side and reached from Falmer station by pedestrian tunnel, has the rare distinction of including a 1960s

"It has several inspiring themed areas including dry-climate planting and a bee-friendly garden."

building of Grade I-listed status. Designed by Sir Basil Spence, the campus occupies a sloping site, with a lantern-shaped Meeting House and curving arches echoing the shapes of the Downs. Its architectural merits might win over the most cynical anti-modernist, though its pitiful over-abundance of steps won't endear it to wheelchair users.

Adjacent, just to the west, **Stanmer Park** is a municipally owned country estate around Stanmer House, a Grade I-listed Palladian mansion built in the 1720s. Its public footpaths, activity trails and off-road family cycle routes crisscross 500 acres of grass, farmland and woodland. Easy access from Brighton and elsewhere can make the park busy at weekends, but it's easy enough to find comparative solitude by walking or mountain-biking from here up to Ditchling Beacon and other points on the South Downs Way.

Within the park, **One Garden Brighton** (Stanmer Park, BN1 9SE ✆ 01273 892034 ✆ onegardenbrighton.com), a large walled garden that once belonged to Stanmer House, is now managed as a public garden and horticultural training centre by Plumpton College. Reimagined by landscape architect Dominic Cole, best known for his work on The Eden Project, it has several beautiful and inspiring themed areas including dry-climate planting, a bee-friendly garden and a rain garden designed to retain rainwater. One Market, a shop selling plants, local produce

Jack & Jill windmills, the Chattri & Ditchling Beacon

❀ OS Explorer map OL11; start: either Jack & Jill car park ♥ TQ303135 (off the A273, two miles southeast of Hassocks – turn off ½ mile south of A273/B2112 junction; free parking), or Ditchling Beacon National Trust car park (at the top of the road signed to Ditchling from the A27; B&H bus 79, Brighton–Ditchling Beacon, Sat–Sun & public holidays only, several per day; join the route at point **4**); five miles. Moderate, undulating, with one well-graded longer ascent. **Loos**: none. **Refreshments**: often an ice-cream van in Ditchling Beacon car park.

T his five-mile route gets you really deep into the Downs scenery that feels miles from anywhere, into the secretive folds, ancient-looking dry valleys and rolling cornfields speckled with poppies and skylarks singing above, then Brighton suddenly appears as a reminder of how close it is, before the finale along the much more frequented South Downs Way, with those endless views over the Weald, the Surrey hills and Black Down. On the way you pass **Ditchling Beacon** and can take a detour to the Chattri War Memorial.

The **Chattri War Memorial** was erected to honour 'the memory of all the Indian soldiers who gave their lives for their King-Emperor' on the site of the funeral pyre of the 53 Sikh and Hindu soldiers who fought for Britain on the Western Front during World War I and died after being brought to Brighton for hospital treatment. In its downland setting looking over Brighton,

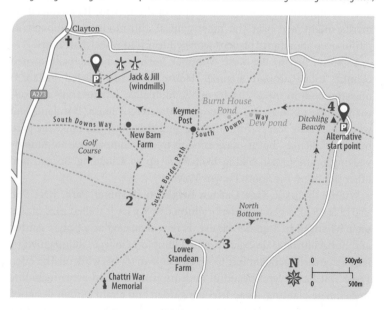

the Chattri – 'umbrella' in Punjabi, Urdu and Hindi – was created of Sicilian marble by a Mumbai designer, its canopy supported by eight columns. In June a memorial service takes place here, with a sizeable turnout from local dignitaries, Indian soldiers in spectacular formal dress and the British Legion. The detour to the Chattri adds an extra mile but is very easy walking.

1 Turn left out of main entrance to Jack and Jill car park, on a lane which soon becomes an unmade track (the sail-less Jack tower mill is glimpsed to the left); ignore the first bridleway signposted to the left, and soon after fork right on the South Downs Way. This passes through **New Barn Farm**; just after keep forward at a crossing of tracks (the South Downs Way goes off to the right), skirting a golf course away to your right.

2 Turn left at the T-junction by a signpost. The track soon bends right through a gate, then left through another gate, following a fence on the right. At a cross-junction at the next gate on the right, ahead is the continuation, but first go right for the **Chattri War Memorial**, following the track for just over half a mile, through a gate and then left to the Chattri. Return to the above-mentioned junction and continue right. The track wiggles downhill, past a brick barn on the right and some pig sties. Another path joins coming down steeply from the left. Take the next left fork (the right fork is just about to pass a pond on the right and then goes through **Lower Standean Farm**), rising and then dropping slightly to the valley floor. Carry on to the left up the valley floor.

3 After 150yds along the valley floor look for a small (not very prominent) gate in the right-hand fence (if you reach a field gate across the track with a dry valley ahead you have overshot by about 100yds), and maintain the same direction, with the fence on the left. Eventually you go through a gate and enter open downland, following the valley of **North Bottom** (you might see traffic on the Ditchling Beacon road up to the right, including perhaps the odd double-decker bus from Brighton) up to the top, where through a gate in the left-hand fence you pick up a signposted track between fences. After half a mile you reach the top of the escarpment at the huge view northwards over the Weald: this is the South Downs Way – detour a few yards to the right to **Ditchling Beacon**. This is the perfect spot to contemplate the view which you'll have most of the way back.

4 Take in the views east from Ditchling Beacon, which extend past the Amex Stadium (Brighton and Hove Albion's ground) towards Seaford Head and the Downs beyond Lewes, then retrace along the South Downs Way (if you've started from the car park here, go through the gate at the back of the car park, by the National Trust sign for Ditchling Beacon, to pick up the South Downs Way). ▶

> ## Jack & Jill windmills, the Chattri & Ditchling Beacon (continued)
>
> ◀ Follow this for two miles, passing a **dew pond** by a couple of characteristically wind-blown trees on the left after a mile and **Burnt House Pond** on the right soon after, then the **Keymer Post** (a signpost) on the right. Eventually the South Downs Way is signposted off to the left (the point reached earlier if you started from Jack and Jill windmills). Just beyond this turn right at the bridleway signpost (you can see Ditchling windmill in the mid distance) and follow this short track round Jack Windmill to emerge in the car park by Jill Windmill.

and Plumpton Estate wine, is open daily, and the garden hosts farmers' markets, gardening courses, craft workshops and other events.

Stanmer Park is also home to **Earthship Brighton** (⊘ lowcarbon. co.uk), a passive solar earth-sheltered building that was England's first Earthship. Completed in 2006 and built from natural and upcycled materials, it blends attractively into the landscape. It's used as an eco-building education centre, with staff offering tours once a month.

18 KNEPP ESTATE
Dial Post, nr Horsham RH13 8NQ ✆ 01403 713230 ⊘ knepp.co.uk; Metrobus 23 (Worthing–Crawley; hourly) to Steyning Rd; nine miles from Horsham railway station (Arun Valley and Sutton & Mole Valley lines)

The rural landscapes of southern England have been farmed for so long that it's hard to imagine how they looked and felt before cultivation and animal husbandry took over. When, in the early 2000s, Charles Burrell and Isabella Tree made the decision to transform their loss-making arable and dairy farm into something entirely different, 'rewilding' was not yet a buzzword. Knepp Wildland became England's first major lowland rewilding project, comprising 3,460 acres of what is now flourishing, wildlife-rich land.

The crucial first steps set the tone: the team restored the landscape park around Knepp's castellated mansion by removing fences, smashing up land drains, allowing thorny scrub and saplings to colonise the field, and introducing free-roaming Old English longhorn cattle, Exmoor ponies, Tamworth pigs and red and fallow deer. Left largely to their own devices, these hardy creatures sculpted the landscape into a mosaic of water meadows, wood pasture and scrubland in a similar fashion to the wild cattle, horses and boar that lived here thousands of years ago. It's now an English Eden, a breeding hotspot for a host of rare species including turtle doves, barbastelle bats, grass snakes, purple emperor butterflies, moths, ravens and nightingales. White storks, carefully reintroduced in 2018, produced England's first wild stork chicks in 600 years. These dramatic birds, nesting at the top of oak trees, are now a big feature of Knepp's rewilded landscape. Beavers were added to the mix in 2020.

Wild Range meat, butchered on-site, and produce from an organic market garden, established in 2022, keep Knepp's contemporary eateries and farm shop well supplied.

Visitors can dip in by exploring some of the estate's 16 miles of public footpaths, which lead to viewing platforms and hides, and eating at the Wilding Kitchen (see below). To appreciate the season's happenings, from birds singing and butterflies hatching to stags rutting, book a guided safari, either by vehicle or on foot. Tours of the rewilded Walled Garden include tips on making your own plot nature-friendly, and there are in-depth rewilding workshops, too. For a fuller immersion (literally, if you choose to check out the wild swimming pond), it's possible to spend a few nights here (⊘ May–Oct): camping in a meadow with a shared cooking hut and pizza oven, or snuggling down in one of Knepp's delightful and highly sought-after woodland shepherd's huts, bell tents, yurts and treehouses.

￤￤ FOOD & DRINK

Wilding Kitchen Worthing Rd, Knepp ✐ 01403 713230 ⊘ knepp.co.uk/wilding-kitchen ⊘ café 09.00–16.00 daily; restaurant noon–16.00 Wed–Sun. Knepp's chefs are Bradley Adams, who specialises in sustainable food, and Ned Burrell, who was born and brought up here. Together, they create menus using organic produce reared or harvested on the estate – think pasta primavera with salads of herbs and flowers, potato terrine with wild garlic aioli, platters of charcuterie, or old English longhorn steak. The setting is a wildlife-friendly, water-neutral restored Sussex barn powered by renewable energy, with a large garden courtyard for outside eating in warm weather.

19 HORSHAM

Arun Valley Line (Three Bridges–West Coastway) and Sutton & Mole Valley Line (London–Horsham); Stagecoach bus 17 (Brighton–Horsham; hourly Mon–Sat); Compass bus 100 (Burgess Hill–Horsham; hourly Mon–Sat)

Not far from the Surrey border, this amiable town has ancient origins but expanded hugely after the advent of the railway in 1848. It focuses on a crisscross of shopping streets, with the Carfax at its centre home to summer bandstand concerts and markets on Thursdays and Saturdays. Horsham's best moments are on its southern peripheries, where **The Causeway** is a broad, quiet, villagey street lined with a wonderful parade of Wealden buildings, and leading towards the church. **Horsham Museum and Art Gallery** (9 Causeway RH12 1HE ℰ 01403 254959 ℰ horshammuseum.org ☺ Tue–Sat; free entry) has a cottagey feel and plenty of well-presented goodies, including Victorian shops, an 1868 Horsham fire engine and a display about the radically minded poet Percy Bysshe Shelley, born nearby in Warnham in 1792.

20 LEONARDSLEE LAKES & GARDENS

Lower Beeding, nr Horsham RH13 6PP ℰ 08718 733389 ℰ leonardsleegardens.co.uk; Stagecoach bus 17 (Brighton–Horsham; hourly Mon–Sat)

From May to June and from October to November, this glorious ornamental garden is awash with colour: in spring, its signature rhododendrons and azaleas burst into bloom, and in autumn, its deciduous woodlands positively glow. While these are the most vivid months, it's enjoyable all year round, with lakes that softly reflect the ethereal beauty of their surroundings in summer and a celebrated rock garden that's austerely haunting in winter.

"From May to June and from October to November, this glorious ornamental garden is awash with colour."

A classic late-Victorian collector's garden, Leonardslee was created in the 1890s and 1900s by the British plantsman Sir Edmund Loder, a rhododendron specialist and zoology enthusiast. Its hickory, nyssa and gingko trees, among other exotic specimens, occupy a naturally sloping plot with an excitingly three-dimensional feel. Painstakingly restored after a period of neglect in the 2010s, the borders and groves protect rare and endangered species. Leading local botanical artists are creating a Leonardslee florilegium to document these; they give talks about the project from time to time.

Around 240 acres in extent, Leonardslee harbours several surprises, including the UK's first commercial Pinotage vineyard, sculptures of human figures by the South African contemporary artist Anton Smit, and a friendly mob of wallabies, who live here happily alongside wildlife such as deer, foxes, badgers, weasels and stoats. There's also a delightfully detailed indoor model village depicting an Edwardian estate, complete with gardeners trimming the hedges, chemists distilling medicines and ladies shopping for frocks. Special events punctuate the year; the winter illuminations are particularly magical. Leonardslee House, the Victorian Italianate mansion at the heart of the estate, has a Michelin-starred restaurant, Interlude, and ten pricey but spacious and tastefully presented guest bedrooms – just the thing if you fancy splurging. It's also conveniently close to Botanica, the zero-waste bistro at South Lodge (⊘ exclusive.co.uk/south-lodge), a country house hotel that's open to non-residents.

21 BOLNEY WINE ESTATE

Bolney, nr Haywards Heath RH17 5NB ⊘ 01444 711722 ⊘ bolneywineestate.com;
Metrobus 273 (Brighton–Crawley; several daily, less frequent Sun) then 0.8-mile walk;
EV charging

Founded in 1972 in a sheltered, south-facing spot with a mild climate and sandstone soil, this pioneering English winery has produced a string of award-winning sparkling wines over the years. Still innovating, it's making great strides towards sustainability by making good use of renewable energy and water recycling and providing space for Brighton Energy Cooperative to install community-owned, solar-linked electric vehicle charge points. Bolney also makes its own gin.

Knowledgeable winery guides run daily tours and tastings that pair the estate's wines with different cheeses. The more in-depth tours include a spot of lunch in the Eighteen Acre Café, which prepares delicious mezze boards from seasonal ingredients, served in an airy contemporary building with glorious vineyard views. Bolney also hosts events such as live-music sessions, craft workshops, gourmet experiences and Wine and Spirit Education Trust courses.

22 TILGATE PARK

Crawley RH10 5PQ ⊘ crawley.gov.uk/tilgatepark; two miles from Three Bridges railway
station (Brighton Main Line, London–Brighton)

On the southeast fringes of the postwar new town of Crawley, this old estate is a country park that's much valued by nearby residents. The main downside is the traffic noise from the M23 on the southern peripheries. Nothing remains of the Tudoresque Victorian mansion that was built by John Nix there, but elsewhere there's much to enjoy, including a play area, outdoor gym and a small zoo, **Tilgate Nature Centre**, featuring over 100 species including owls, meerkats and reindeer. From the main car park by the **Go Ape** forest adventure park you can head out to **Tilgate Lake** – the largest of several lakes – then south towards the **pinetum** planted by Nix and his descendants and the **walled garden** on the west side of the estate.

Adventures in Britain

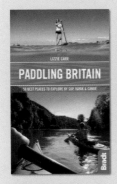

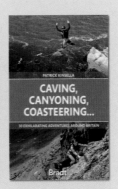

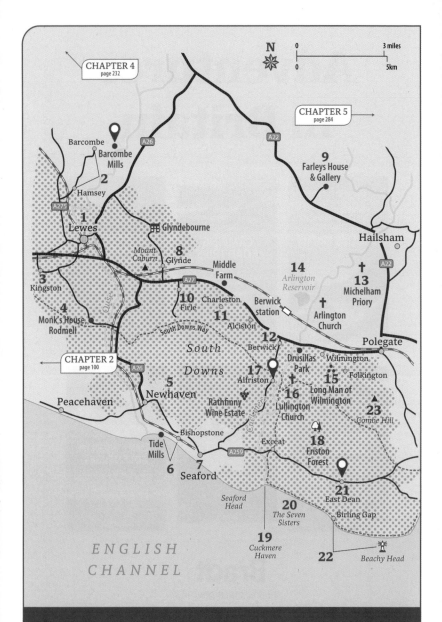

CHAPTER 4
page 232

CHAPTER 5
page 284

Barcombe

2 Barcombe Mills

Hamsey

A26

A275

1 Lewes

3 Kingston

Glyndebourne

Mount Caburn

8 Glynde

Middle Farm

A27

10 Firle

Charleston

11 Alciston

4 Monk's House Rodmell

Ouse

South Downs Way

South Downs

12 Berwick

17 Alfriston

5 Newhaven

Rathfinny Wine Estate

Peacehaven

Bishopstone

Tide Mills

6

7 Seaford

CHAPTER 2
page 100

A26

9 Farleys House & Gallery

Hailsham

14 Arlington Reservoir

13 Michelham Priory

A22

Berwick station

Arlington Church

Polegate

Drusillas Park

Wilmington

15 Folkington

16 Lullington Church

Long Man of Wilmington

23 Combe Hill

Exceat

18 Friston Forest

20 The Seven Sisters

19 Cuckmere Haven

Seaford Head

A259

21 East Dean

Birling Gap

22 Beachy Head

ENGLISH CHANNEL

LEWES DOWNS TO BEACHY HEAD

3
LEWES DOWNS TO BEACHY HEAD

Sussex's most sublime stretch of coast is within this small chunk of the South Downs, comprising the cliffs between Seaford and Eastbourne. But it's a relatively brief affair; if there's one place above all that needs to be savoured slowly, this is it – browsing a rock pool at Cuckmere Haven, munching a sandwich and spotting Bronze Age flints on turf clifftops, or drinking in the view of the wavy profile of the Seven Sisters from Seaford Head. Westwards, a huge shingle beach lines the low-lying coast all the way to Newhaven, a clean and inviting sweep of shore that makes one of the best swimming spots hereabouts.

Inland, the Downs have some really quiet moments: even though this is one of the most thoroughly thumbed parts of the national park, there is plenty for escapists. The noisy but useful A27 disappears from view and earshot as you ascend into the world of skylarks either side of the Cuckmere Valley near Alfriston; the South Downs Way encounters a primeval moment above the enigmatic Long Man of Wilmington, Britain's tallest chalk hill figure above the head of Deep Dean, a secretive dry valley unaltered by modern agriculture, its slopes too steep for the plough.

Lewes, the largest town in the South Downs National Park, gets a trickle of tourists but apart from the spectacular exception of bonfire night in November is never particularly overrun. Sloping, neighbourly, enticing, nonconformist, ancient, distinctive – it suggests plenty of adjectives. It is my own town, and if I had to single out a favourite landmark view I would say it is the prospect down School Hill, past Harvey's Brewery with its periodic malty aroma wafting over passing shoppers, to the Downs above. Art and music are big in the vicinity: many musicians working at **Glyndebourne Opera House** are based in town or around, and opera-goers often stay over and discover the town's many pleasures. Lewes also makes an obvious base for those on the trail of Virginia Woolf, who lived nearby at Monk's House in Rodmell, and her bohemian sister Vanessa Bell and her entourage at Charleston near the estate village of Firle. Anyone keen on the Charleston set should also beat a path to Farleys House and Gallery at Muddles Green for an entertaining and erudite tour of the former house of surrealist painter Roland Penrose and the photographer Lee Miller, where Picasso once visited.

GETTING AROUND

For some ideas of how to make the most of visiting the area around Lewes on foot or by bike, bus or train, I have created a leaflet funded by the South Downs National Park titled *Car-Free Days Out from Lewes*, downloadable from ⬧ bit.ly/car-free-lewes. It includes trips to Seaford (then Seaford Head, Exceat, Tide Mills and Bishopstone); over Mount Caburn to Glynde, Firle, Charleston, Berwick Church and Alfriston; and down the Ouse Valley to Monk's House via the South Downs Way and River Ouse.

TRAINS

Your options by rail aren't bad at all. Lewes, the hub, is on the Brighton Main Line and East Coastway Line, with frequent services to Brighton, Eastbourne, Hastings, Seaford and London Victoria.

Lewes to Seaford: This strange little branch line keeps going by virtue of the ferry at Newhaven. **Southease** is a tiny, rural halt slap bang on the South Downs Way, so it is ideal for walkers or cyclists. Heading westwards across the Ouse, you can follow the riverbank towards Virginia Woolf's house at Rodmell, or climb the SDW up onto the Downs above Kingston and Iford. Eastwards, the SDW leads up to Itford Hill, Beddingham Hill and Firle Beacon, from where you can drop down to Firle, Firle Place and Charleston for a very full day's walking and cultural sightseeing. **Newhaven Town** and **Newhaven Harbour** stations, less than half a mile apart, are on the other side of the harbour from the fort (a 20-minute walk, grotty at the start but better once you're off the main road). Their unappetising location, which is gradually being spruced up by a regeneration programme, offers a strangely fascinating stroll to Tide Mills and Seaford Bay. **Bishopstone**, which is even closer to the beach, lies east of Tide Mills and west of **Seaford**. From here, the end of the line, it's an easy stroll into town or along the beach to Seaford Head with its views of the Seven Sisters.

Lewes to Eastbourne: Just one stop after Lewes is **Glynde**, a classic little Victorian country station right in the middle of the village. From here, you could wander up Mount Caburn and back down to Lewes, or southwest to Firle. The next stop, at the north end of the scattered village of **Berwick**, links up nicely with the buses that tour the Cuckmere Valley (see below). **Polegate** is useful for cyclists, as the station is close to the Cuckoo Trail and to the tranquil, marshy farmlands of the Pevensey Levels (page 287).

BUSES

Brighton & Hove bus 12 runs along the A259, the coast road between Brighton and Eastbourne, remarkably frequently (every ten minutes; every 30 minutes on Sunday), calling at **Newhaven** and **Seaford**. It's particularly useful for point-to-point coastal walks, such as from **Cuckmere Haven** along the Seven Sisters to **East Dean**. For Cuckmere

KEEPING THE CUCKMERE VALLEY ON THE BUS MAP

Thanks to an inspired community effort, the Cuckmere Valley retains a useful bus network, **Cuckmere Buses** (⏏ cuckmerebuses.org.uk), entirely run by volunteers and funded by fares and grants. The story starts in 1976 when the Sussex Women's Institute lobbied parliament and effected a change in the law so that minibuses could be driven with a normal car licence provided it was voluntary. At that time the Southdown Bus company was withdrawing most of its rural services, and a door-to-door survey by local WIs revealed widespread support for a community-run alternative. Today Cuckmere Buses runs a fleet of minibuses, some as shopping services, others used by visitors, all of it to a timetable. Most routes only operate on certain days of the week but, with a little planning, you can build outings around them, visiting attractions such as Michelham Priory, Drusillas and Charleston, or going on country walks. Richard Goldsmith, the publicity officer, says the most popular option is to walk from Alfriston to Cuckmere Haven and Exceat, then take the Cuckmere Valley Ramblerbus back. The network has been awarded the Buses for Pleasure award for improving car-free access to the countryside and the Queen's Award for Voluntary Services. What drives drivers to volunteer? 'It's a service to the community, and the drivers enjoy meeting people and it keeps them active,' says Richard.

Haven and the Seven Sisters Country Park, get off at **Exceat** – not really a village, just a pub, activity hub and visitor centre at a wiggle on the A259 before it rises eastwards. Brighton & Hove bus 13X follows a similar route to the 12, but loops south to **Beachy Head**; it runs daily in summer, and on Sundays for the rest of the year.

Compass Travel runs a basic network of rural buses, and, on certain days of the week, Cuckmere Buses link the **Cuckmere Valley** to nearby towns and attractions (page 167). A particularly useful circular service, the Cuckmere Valley Ramblerbus, runs hourly on Saturdays, Sundays and public holidays in British Summer Time, stopping at Berwick, Drusillas, Alfriston, High and Over, Seaford, Exceat, Friston Forest, Litlington and Wilmington. There are also Cuckmere Bus Bloomsbury Route and Art Shuttle services, connecting cultural highlights such as Eastbourne's Towner Gallery, Alfriston, Charleston, Glyndebourne and Lewes.

CYCLING

For cyclists, the picture is mixed but improving: the roads southwards down the Ouse Valley from Lewes to Newhaven are not recommended, but a new bike route through this region, the **Egrets Way** (⊘ egretsway.org.uk), is in development. Elsewhere, there are decent alternatives, notably the new bike path along the A27 between Lewes and Polegate, and the network of quiet lanes in the vicinity of Glynde, Ripe, Selmeston and Laughton, and north of Lewes towards the High Weald.

Off-road possibilities are abundant and by no means confined to the South Downs: you can take the **Cuckoo Trail** (page 206) between Eastbourne and Heathfield, much of it along a former rail trackbed and easily reached from Polegate station; or the **Old Coach Road**, an unsurfaced track beneath the Downs from West Firle to Alfriston. The **South Downs Way**, though popular, is rarely congested; for an energetic day's off-roading, the section from Lewes to Eastbourne is recommended.

 TOURIST INFORMATION

Lewes 187 High St BN7 2DE ⊘ 01273 483448 ⊘ visitlewes.co.uk
Seaford 37 Church St BN25 1HG ⊘ 01323 897426

Dedicated cycle paths from Lewes include: routes to Ringmer (giving access to the lane network beyond Ringmer); and through the industrial estate to join the A27 cycle path to Polegate, which gives options of visiting Firle, Charleston and Berwick Church, with access to stations and Glynde, Berwick and Polegate itself. I've produced a free cycle map *Cycle Lewes*, which is available from the Lewes Tourist Information Centre or online (⊘ visitlewes.co.uk/cycling).

BIKE HIRE

Cuckmere Cycle Company East Dean Rd, Exceat BN25 4AD ⊘ 07943 954458 ⊘ cuckmerecycle.co

Cycle Shack 53 Cliffe High St, Lewes ⊘ 01273 668816 ⊘ lewescycleshack.co.uk

LEWES & THE LOWER OUSE VALLEY

The National Park spreads just north of Lewes, where the land rises. Southwards the Ouse meanders towards the sea, and in winter the valley is often speckled with partially flooded fields. Quarrying has left some striking cliff edges above the valley; on the east side of Lewes, peregrine falcons can often be seen above the sheer chalky drops. The unclassified road heading from Lewes Prison down to Newhaven bypasses a string of villages, notably Rodmell. Southease is an unexpected haven of tranquillity with its sloping triangular green below the church, while a rare bottle-shaped brick kiln – the only one in Sussex – marks the entrance to one-street Piddinghoe, the easiest access point for the riverside path.

1 LEWES

Brighton Main Line (London–Eastbourne & Hastings) & East Coastway Line (Brighton–Hastings); regional bus hub

Ensconced on the River Ouse as it flows between the South Downs, Lewes has a character unlike any other town in the southeast. It's strikingly hilly and squashed together by its setting, with a Norman castle crowning an imposing hillock and the South Downs dominating the view as you look down its main street. Its array of historic buildings is remarkable for both quantity and variety – along the main High Street and down School Hill, across the river into Cliffe, and down the hillside to the south to the Southover district, with its supremely handsome shop-less High Street.

The main axis runs along a shelving ridge for about a mile, lined for the most part with notable buildings – variously tile-hung, brick, weatherboarded, with mathematical tiles (page 129), stone-fronted and flint-cobbled. Leading from this are the narrow lanes known in this part of Sussex as **twittens**; some date back to Saxon times and all of them are worth exploring. **Pipe Passage** (named after the manufacture of clay pipes in a tiny, now partly collapsed kiln behind the Freemasons' hall), by the site of what was once the West Gate, leads along the former sentry walk above a high chunk of town wall; the sail-less windmill here was briefly leased by Virginia Woolf. Across the High Street, cobbled **Keere Street** drops steeply southwards – at the bottom another section of town wall faces Grange Gardens and Southover High Street lies just beyond.

Lewes has kept itself happily free from the cloned town-centre look, thanks in part to its preponderance of independent shops, selling everything from artisan jewellery and vintage counterpanes to local beer. Edward Reeves, reputedly the world's oldest high-street photographers, has been at 159 High Street since 1858 and still has some Victorian equipment and glass slides in the studio at the back.

The town has long had a tradition of nonconformity – comedian Mark Steel described its essential character as 'stroppy' – and on 5 November (or the day before if 5 November falls on a Sunday) celebrates **Bonfire**, the hugest and most clamorous Guy Fawkes Night in the country. If you visit Lewes in the weeks preceding, you'll see 'bonfire boys' wearing hand-knitted hooped jumpers and selling bonfire programmes or generally at large in the town centre. The event features races with tar barrels, laying wreaths at the war memorial, a mammoth procession with bonfire society members of all ages in elaborate, hand-made costumes, marching bands, effigies and satirical tableaux stuffed with fireworks and destined to be exploded, and bonfire boys dropping lit 'rookies' (commercial bird-scarers) that detonate with ear-shattering noise. Bonfire societies from various parts of Sussex – who have their celebrations on other weeks (page 276) – join in the main procession, apart from the Cliffe Bonfire Society, who for historical reasons march separately. After that, the Lewes societies – Waterloo, Commercial Square, Cliffe, Southover, South Street and Borough – march off with burning torches to their various bonfire sites for their own displays. The organisers always stress that this is an event for the town and not really for outsiders; nothing is timed to precision, and although no-one will be turned away, the event is not actively promoted. Nevertheless huge crowds flock to the town and hotels get booked for the event years ahead.

Quite what Lewes Bonfire is all about is open to a lot of debate. Its origins are undoubtedly anti-Catholic, including commemorating the burning of 17 Protestant martyrs outside Lewes Town Hall in the 1550s and the installation of William of Orange as a Protestant monarch. The Cliffe Bonfire Society put up banners proclaiming 'no popery' in Cliffe High Street and ceremonially burn an effigy of the Pope who was installed at the time of the Gunpowder Plot. That said, there are Catholic members in the bonfire societies, so it doesn't do to try to read too much into it, and I reckon it is essentially a community celebration of the old adage 'a Sussex man won't be druv'. Other similar celebrations took place in other southern English towns but died out or were suppressed; in Lewes the organisation into formalised bonfire societies in the 19th century probably saved the day.

Lewes Castle & its precincts
⊘ sussexpast.co.uk

The castle crowns a steep-sided artificial mound within a dry moat. William de Warenne, the brother-in-law of William the Conqueror, built the first castle on nearby Brack Mount (page 173) to show in no uncertain terms who was in charge. This was soon replaced by a simple motte and bailey on this main mound, to be rebuilt stronger and larger around 1100, with angled towers added in the first half of the 13th century.

Castle Gate, the little cobbled street that leads to it from the High Street, is spanned by two contrasting arches – the imposing Barbican, complete with portcullis slot, was built in the early 14th century primarily for show; beyond it the simpler, rounded arch is Norman. You can wander up this street for free and peer into the castle precincts, but of course the views are much more revealing from within (you pay at Barbican House, opposite). Lewes Castle is owned by Sussex Past, the commercial arm of the Sussex Archaeological Society.

The **castle grounds** were partly beautified into a pleasure garden by Thomas Friend, who acquired the site in 1726, and by his successors, and Lewes Castle's gardens became an early tourist attraction. At the bottom, the gun garden has some quaintly irrelevant bits and pieces:

a Crimean-era Russian cannon, a huge, rusty 300-year-old anchor from Newhaven and some ancient stocks. A path climbs up, giving access to the rooms over the Barbican itself, where you get the chance to try building a wall with a replicated medieval crane, and children (or adventurous adults) can try on medieval costumes. Further up the path reaches a higher garden and from the very top plaques help to pick out the landmarks, which extend over the rooftops and long, narrow medieval backyards as far as the sea at Newhaven.

Your ticket into the castle also gets you into the **Barbican House Museum**, with displays of archaeology and local interest, and a painstakingly created model showing the town as it was in the 1880s. Some 100 locals made this remarkable artefact in the 1980s using old photos and architectural plans as source material. Commentary backed up by spotlighting and projected images (◷ every 30 minutes, on the hour and half hour) gives an excellent introduction to the town. The museum shop includes a good selection of local history and archaeology books, with a secondhand section too.

"Some 100 locals made this remarkable artefact in the 1980s using old photos and architectural plans."

Further up Castle Gate you are still in the castle precincts. On the right a grassy space marks the site of the former tilting yard (a practice ground for jousting and the like), which since at least the 18th century has been a **bowling green** – Britain's oldest. It's not exactly a level playing field, and the participants, often out there at weekends, never wear whites. The great Thomas Paine (page 179) was himself a member, and when curiosity got the better of me I asked a friendly member if I could make a guest appearance one Sunday morning. Pete showed me the selection of woods in the tiny pavilion. These are much smaller than modern woods but no two are exactly the same size or weight and most have been patched up over many years of use; some are 18th-century, which makes one wonder which ones Paine might have played with. Pete picked two reasonably similar-sized ones that would suit a beginner, and helpfully pointed out the lumps, bumps and 'valleys' on the green. I still lost massively, but managed to avoid steering my woods into the flowerbed, which alongside various other bowling misdemeanours attracts a fine of a princely 5p.

At the end of the bowling green by railings and a descriptive plaque, benches provide a look-out point towards the **site of the Battle of**

Lewes, which took place in 1264 on the Downs just above the town's modern fringes. This was effectively the first triumph in establishing parliamentary democracy: Simon de Montfort gathered an army of barons and Londoners and defeated Henry III, forcing him to sign the Mise of Lewes, which resulted in the very first meeting of parliament at Westminster the following year.

The castle precincts are one of only two such sites in Britain to feature two castle mounds, Lincoln being the other. You can see the second lump, **Brack Mount**, looking over the Lewes Arms, although there's no public access. An occupant of adjacent Brack Mount House in the interwar years was novelist Alice Dudeney, whose diary was kept under wraps for many decades as so many local people still living were acerbically described. It's a fascinating picture of the town at that time, and though Mrs Dudeney was a bit of a snob her diary has proved more enduring than her mostly forgotten novels.

Southover

In the Southover district on the south side of the historic centre of Lewes, **Grange Gardens** is a public park which makes a gorgeous retreat in summer. An ancient mulberry tree on a zimmerframe arrangement of wooden props casts shade over picnickers. A lot of stone from Lewes Priory (page 175) ended up here, some of it in the form of Southover Grange, the Cotswoldian-looking house now owned by the council and which was the boyhood home of the diarist John Evelyn, and later home of an extraordinary woman called Violet Gordon Woodhouse, the first great woman harpsichordist, who in the early 20th century revived the harpsichord for Baroque music such as Bach and Handel. She was charismatic and all sorts of people, male and female, fell for her: here she lived in a *ménage à cinq* with her husband and three other men. More stone arches and bits of column and other carved masonry were used to create a garden wall. This screens a wonderfully colourful garden where bedding plants are installed for a few weeks and then ripped out; it's a bit of an indulgence but very much cherished by Lewesians – the council once proposed cutting costs by planting something more herbaceous and permanent but were met with howls of protest. A tiny kiosk operates from a hatch and serves, tea, coffee, homemade cake and other snacks.

Focused on the lives and legacy of the Bloomsbury Group, **Charleston in Lewes** (Southover Rd, BN7 1AB ⊘ charleston.org.uk; café) presents

art exhibitions and runs gallery activities and workshops. Occupying a former council office building, it's an offshoot of Charleston near Firle (page 202), the cultural centre associated with the much-mythologised Charleston Farmhouse where, in the early 20th century, Vanessa Bell and Duncan Gray lived, worked and entertained a fluid entourage of upper-class artists, writers and thinkers.

Southover High Street is an architectural treat for its entire length, with all manner of villas and ancient town houses along it including the very London-like Priory Crescent. A gateway on one side of the crescent is a relic of **Lewes Priory**, a Cluniac house founded by William de Warenne and his wife Gundrada between 1078 and 1082. Longer than Chichester Cathedral, and set in a walled precinct approaching the size of a medieval town, its great church was blown up during the Dissolution. The remains stood until the 1840s when the London-to-Brighton railway was built right through them; in response, incensed local antiquarians formed the Sussex Archaeological Society, one of the earliest bodies to protect ancient buildings, including Lewes Castle and Anne of Cleves House. The substantial remains of the monks' living quarters have been restored by the Lewes Priory Trust and now form Priory Park, an absorbing and always-open free sight rivalling many paid-for heritage sites. It's best reached by taking Cockshut Lane, off Southover High Street, and turning left just after the railway bridge. Clever reconstruction drawings on 11 panels around a trail help to make sense

"The most prominent structure at Priory Park is one of the largest surviving medieval loo blocks in Britain."

of the stonework. The most prominent structure is one of the largest surviving medieval loo blocks in Britain, with individual cubicles for dozens of monks to sit simultaneously, perched high over what was once a running stream. Nearby is a recreation of a small monastic herb garden and a little further on is a curious grassy mound (yes, another one), not thought to be as ancient as the two at the castle. It overlooks Lewes' football stadium, quaintly named the Dripping Pan, a rectangular basin

◄ LEWES: **1** The Norman castle gets the prime view in town. **2** The 15th-century Anne of Cleves House. **3** Cobbled together with bits of stone from the priory, an archway leads to the colourful beds of Grange Gardens. **4** The town holds the biggest Guy Fawkes Night celebrations in the country.

dating from the time of the Priory, and probably used to stock fish; quite possibly the mound is the dug-out spoil from this feature.

A fine example of a tile-hung, timber-framed 15th-century Wealden hall house is the **Anne of Cleves House** ($\oslash$ sussexpast.co.uk), a venerable old place which has somehow survived the centuries remarkably intact. It was given by Henry VIII to Anne of Cleves as part of her divorce settlement, but she probably never actually set eyes on the building; it has been in the care of the Sussex Archaeological Society since the 19th century. As well as a creaky upstairs room with a barn-like roof and period furniture, the building contains a prized collection of Wealden-made iron artefacts, including firebacks and bootscrapers, and an ancient octagonal table of 'Sussex marble'. Allegedly the knights who murdered Thomas Becket in 1170 rested their weapons on the table and it twice hurled the whole lot off. The Lewes Room is a fine stash of local interest, with a 1785 fire engine and two very well-known paintings: of Lewes Bonfire as it was in the 19th century, with masked men in smuggler outfits and a No Popery banner, and of the Lewes Avalanche in 1836. The latter depicts the worst avalanche in British history, in which nine people perished after a 15ft ridge of snow formed on the cliff above South Street and then tumbled down. The pub standing on the site is named the Snowdrop – not after the flower but after the natural disaster. The secluded courtyard, with a lawn, topiary and rose beds, makes an inviting place for sitting out.

Unobvious Lewes

The High Street and castle are what visitors see, but it's all too easy to miss out on the less conspicuous pleasures of the town. Lewes is full of surprise **vistas**, several of them preserved for posterity by the campaigning efforts of its residents. One of the best is from the far side of the **Paddock**, a hilly recreation ground which occupies a dry valley just below the castle precincts: walk up to one of the strategic benches for the view of the castle and town that features on numerous greetings cards – the whole thing could easily have been ruined in the 1970s by the insertion of a proposed, totally monstrous relief road right through the middle of the Paddock. Adjoining this little park is the actual horse-inhabited paddock itself, and beyond that **Baxter's Field**, with its backdrop of the castle and Malling Down; when it came up for sale in 2003, locals wasted no time in organising a trust and buying it as a

THE LEWES POUND

During the freefall of the pound sterling in late 2008, one monetary unit in Britain soared, though not in terms of conventional exchange rates. The Lewes pound (⚲ thelewespound.org), launched in September that year, was intended to boost the fortunes of local shops, and was inspired by a similar scheme in Totnes, Devon. It's really a token: you swap the conventional sterling for the Lewesian variant at the Farmers' Market or at other outlets (or ask for them in your change) and then spend them at participating retailers.

Within only weeks of its launch, collectors round the world were trying to get their hands on them, and they were going for as much as £40 on eBay. The Lewes pound organisers offered to sell Lewes pounds for 99p for a while on eBay in order to stop this happening. In the end it probably didn't matter much, as it put the town on the map and everyone was talking about this new 'currency'.

In such a nonconformist town you'd hardly expect the Queen to be put on the banknote (even if it were legal to do so). So as quasi-monarch, local hero Thomas Paine (page 179) has his wise head depicted on the currency. No-one's going to argue with that, not in Lewes. At the time of writing, some 100 local businesses take the Lewes pound. So what's it really for? Patrick Crawford, one of the people who run the scheme, told me 'It's about social inclusion, about supporting Lewes traders, and about keeping money circulating in Lewes. The grand scheme is that the circle helps to help local suppliers and local employment. And people get to hear about Lewes. If we can encourage people to visit Lewes and to visit local shops because of the Lewes pound this benefits Lewes.'

I'd add that although it's hard to quantify the benefits, it's something that Lewesians are rather proud of too, though admittedly I tend to keep a few in my wallet to show to incredulous outsiders and don't often get round to spending them.

It's issued in denominations of £1, £5, £10 and, bizarrely, £21 – 'because we can,' explained Patrick, 'and because it symbolises the fact that 5% of the money we issue goes into a fund that is used for local projects, including energy-saving schemes, giving advice on growing your own food and promoting seasonal recipes through Lewes' Friday food market.'

public space for posterity. Lewes can count itself extremely fortunate to have rural views of this calibre – a rarity in the middle of a town.

Another prize viewpoint is up **Chapel Hill**: walk down the High Street over the bridge and into Cliffe. At the very end a somewhat Cornish-looking street called Chapel Hill, with slate-hung cottages, rises abruptly on to the Downs (for a longer walk you can carry on up to the golf course, turning right at the club house and follow the path that eventually climbs up to Mount Caburn). Soon you look down on the whole town from a path raised above the road; immediately beneath, the chalk cliff-face drops nearly vertically to the river. The spiral feature formed in the reedbeds on the far bank is a heart-shaped creation by landscape artist Chris Drury on the **Railway Land nature reserve**, itself accessed from the High Street – take Railway Lane on the west side of the bridge, by The Riverside shopping mall; beyond an old level crossing gate you enter the reserve, which leads out on to the water meadows of the Ouse valley. Yet again, Lewesians came to the rescue when a few decades back a supermarket wanted to plonk itself here on this wasteland of former rail yards, so instead the town gained a nature reserve and retains another chunk of rurality minutes away from the town centre. A rich wildlife habitat, it is now used for ecological, educational and community projects.

That same community spirit of standing up for what you believe in is also exemplified in the form of the **Pells Pool** (Brook St, BN7 2BA ∂ pellspool.org.uk), the oldest open-air swimming pool in the country – near the river, in the part of town known as the Pells, conspicuous for its L-shaped, canal-like millpond amidst the trees a few yards from the swimming pool. Opened in 1860, the pool is almost Olympic-sized; fed by spring water, it can be distinctly bracing but has none of the smack of chlorine associated with indoor pools. In the 1990s the council wanted to close it and turn the space into a nice, neat and completely unwanted car park, but Lewes wouldn't stand for it of course, and the inevitable action group formed itself; a photo appeared in *The Guardian*, people pledged money and time, and a trust took over. It's now a cherished spot on those hot summer afternoons, when half the town seems there, yet the pool's so large that the water doesn't feel too crowded.

For one of several ways to sample Lewes life behind the scenes, visit during **Artwave** in late August to early September when artists – and there are a lot of them in Lewes – open their houses for free to show the artworks for sale within.

Harvey's Brewery

Known reverently by locals as Lewes Cathedral, this brick and mock-Tudor-cum-Gothic pile is the only Victorian brewery of its kind surviving in the southeast. The Harvey's brewing tradition spans two centuries, and has been on this site since 1838, with the present structure

LOCAL HERO THOMAS PAINE

A mural in Lewes' market tower, near the Town Hall and adjacent to the Crown Inn, depicts famous Lewes resident Tom Paine (1737–1809), who once worked as a Customs Officer here and lived at Bull House in the upper High Street, opposite the Tom Paine Printing Press Gallery. Born in Thetford in Norfolk, was a controversial republican thinker who went on to inspire both the American and the French revolutions and write *The Rights of Man*. He became a French citizen after the revolution but was thrown into prison and only narrowly escaped the guillotine himself when he opposed the execution of the King.

He also invented the term 'United States of America'; bad luck after all his heroic deeds that he died in poverty and obscurity in New York. His name was originally spelt 'Pain' but someone misread his signature, which ended with a squiggly flourish and thought it was 'Paine', so the e stuck.

dating from the 1860s. Harvey's is one of those companies that everyone in Lewes seems to revere: the brewers donate money to local causes, they use local hops from suppliers who would otherwise have gone out of business, they take pride in using English malt only, and put on a terrific series of seasonal ales – each one highly distinctive – including Copperwheat for the balmy harvest days of September, Bonfire Boy for November, a light mild called Knots of May for late spring, a Porter brewed to an 1859 recipe for March, a dark, sweet Old to warm you through winter, and a lethally strong Christmas Ale that's almost like a barley wine in character.

Their Sussex Best Bitter is a masterpiece: the head brewer Miles Jenner, who lives in the Georgian brewers' house that adjoins (and obviously predates) the brewery, told me that one of the hardest things to brew is a less strong ale: this one's only 4%. You could use the same recipe and come up with a totally different tasting beer. The liquor – that's what they call the water that's drilled by artesian well right beneath the brewery – is one of the elements; another is the yeast that gives it that distinctive, almost metallic aftertaste. Harvey's nearly lost it in the flood of 2000, when the Ouse burst its banks and the water came almost up to the ceiling. It was very touch and go, and Shepherd Neame (in Kent) would have helped them out by giving them some of their own brewer's yeast, but then Harvey's might have never quite tasted the same again.

Should you be so lucky to get on a brewery tour – the bad news is that the waiting list is usually two or three years – you'll find a marvellously untouched factory where even the paint colour is original, and the manager's office almost Dickensian.

To sample the wonderful ale, pop into **Harvey's Brewery Shop** on Cliffe High Street, where they sell Best and one or two others straight from the barrel, along with bottles of most of their seasonal products, beer glasses, aprons, bags and other Lewes-oriented souvenir, plus some very classy wines. The brewery tap is just across Cliffe High Street: the **John Harvey Tavern**, where they keep several Harvey varieties in perfect condition. Other pubs in town where the Harvey's is consistently excellent include the Lewes Arms, tucked behind the castle, The Rights of Man, next to the law courts on the High Street, and The Dorset, on Malling Street in Cliffe.

In 2007, Greene King, who used to own the Lewes Arms, tried to remove Harvey's from the beers it served and faced an extraordinarily hostile campaign from locals – ending with picketing, petitions, interviews on Radio 4's *Today* programme, and finally, a totally humiliating climbdown by the pub retailer, who has since sold it on to Fuller's (who stock Harvey's on condition that the one Harvey's pub in London sell Fuller's; a very neat solution). Another indication of the passion Lewesians feel about Harvey's is an incident in the 1990s when one night someone set fire to empty cardboard boxes outside the Harvey's Brewery Shop and the shop burned down, destroying most of the brewery's archives in the process: no-one found the culprit, but the 'Cliffe Ars(e)onist' was duly burned in effigy at that year's Lewes Bonfire celebrations.

SHOPPING

Several **antiques centres** are dotted around the High Street, the two largest being Cliffe Antiques Centre in Cliffe and the Fleamarket in Market Street. Gorringes **auctioneers** hold weekly Monday auctions in its premises at 15 North Street (viewing on Mondays, Fridays and Saturday mornings) and periodic sales of more select antiques such as paintings, books and fine furniture. Wallis & Wallis have regular auctions of toys and militaria at West Street.

Lewes is stuffed full of **galleries and craft shops** with the most rewarding browsing grounds being along the main street, in the Hop Gallery (in the old Star Brewery building by Fisher Street and opposite the Lewes Arms) and in the Needlemakers (a former hypodermic-needle factory, imaginatively converted, between Market Street and Fisher Street).

At 151 High Street, opposite Bull House (where Thomas Paine lived), is perhaps Lewes' most extraordinary shop, the **Tom Paine Printing Press Gallery**, run by artist and Paine enthusiast Peter Chasseaud. Its cluttered interior evokes a scene from 200 years back: hand-printed bills proclaiming 'The Riot Act has been read', 'Lewes – centre of the cosmos' and various quotes from Benjamin Franklin ('Beer is living proof that God loves us and wants us to be happy') and Paine. Peter runs this non-profit-making enterprise more or less as a hobby, to make a connection between Paine, his radical ideas and printing (his main method of communication), and printing all manner of painstakingly laid-out pamphlets and posters using the same technology as in Paine's day. I spotted a replica of the first pamphlet Paine wrote, originally printed by William Lee – a replica of Lee's press is on display.

¶¶ FOOD & DRINK

Lewes **farmers' market** takes place on the first and third Saturday mornings of the month in Friars Walk car park, and there's a very good smaller food market on Friday mornings in the 18th century Market Tower on Market Street. Fresh fish and organic meat are on sale in the **Riverside**, an old converted building by the bridge in the middle of town. Opposite Riverside, a short walk from Harvey's Brewery, is the **brewery shop**.

Depot Pinwell Rd, BN7 2JS ⟨⟩ lewesdepot.org. Open for breakfast, lunch, dinner and drinks, the restaurant at Lewes' excellent independent cinema has courtyard tables and a light, airy interior. Stylish but reasonably priced, it champions local suppliers. Expect dishes such as cinnamon French toast, smoked haddock fish fingers and artichoke risotto.

The Gardener's Arms 46 Cliffe High St, BN7 2AN. A locals' favourite, right on the Bonfire Night parade route, this pub offers interesting beer and cider. No food.

John Harvey Tavern Bear Yard, Cliffe High St, BN7 2AN ⟨⟩ johnharveytavern.co.uk. The brewery tap, a short stroll from Harvey's, serves good-value food and seasonal ales fresh from the makers.

Lewes Arms 1 Mount Pl, BN7 1YH ⟨⟩ lewesarms.co.uk. This is the place to meet after an archaeology lecture, stoolball match or LOS Musical Theatre rehearsal, so it's nearly always full of convivial chat. It serves Fullers and Harvey's real ales and very reasonably priced main courses, and has a tiny terrace abutting Brack Mount. It hosts wacky events such as a very adult panto in March, the world pea-throwing championships (record = 127ft) and dwyle-flunking (involving a lot of splashing about as participants attempt to lob a dishcloth soaked in stale beer at each other).

The Rights of Man 179 High St, BN7 1YE ⟨⟩ rightsofmanlewes.com. This Harvey's pub is one of the best bets in town for pub food, including excellent Sunday roasts. There's a secretive roof garden for fine days.

Swan Inn 30A Southover High St, BN7 1HU ⟨⟩ theswaninnlewes.co.uk. Near Anne of Cleves House, with Lewes' largest beer garden, this pub has classic Sussex character and consistently satisfying food.

2 HAMSEY & BARCOMBE

Train to Lewes, Brighton Main Line (London–Eastbourne and Hastings) and East Coastway Line (Brighton–Hastings), then three-mile walk

The footbridge known as Willey's Bridge near the Pells marks the start of walks upriver on the **Sussex Ouse Valley Way** and out of town: it immediately becomes rural. A recommended wander is as far as **Hamsey**, where you turn right along the road to the remote, beautifully primitive, electricity-less medieval church – it is usually locked but the key is available from a nearby house in the village. The ancient pews here are staggeringly uncomfortable; presumably the shallowness of the seat was intended to stop the congregation nodding off during services.

The Sussex Ouse Valley Way carries on northwards – through fields rather than along the Ouse itself – to **Barcombe Mills**, where mills stood from the 11th century up to 1939, when the last one burned down. Nothing remains of the mills, only the millponds, and an ancient board listing tolls for the bridge. Here for many years ivory buttons were manufactured – not from elephant ivory but 'vegetable ivory' from the nuts from palm trees – and fashioned into shape.

"Barcombe has seen intensive archaeological action with a notable concentration of Roman sites being revealed."

In recent years Barcombe has seen intensive archaeological action with a notable concentration of **Roman sites** being revealed: near Barcombe Church a substantial Romano-British villa was excavated along with a mysteriously huge bathhouse more akin to what would be found on Hadrian's Wall than beside a run-of-the-mill Roman villa. I had the privilege of being there on the very day when the digger removed the plough soil: I stood on the spoil heap and looked down – all the mosaic floors had disappeared but the entire outline of the corridored, winged villa with its room layout was apparent through the soil coloration. A fine section of Roman road was excavated, and since then an entire Roman fortified settlement has appeared on a geophysics survey of the fields of Bridge Farm near Barcombe Mills, giving potential for excavations for many years to come. For information on the site, including any planned site tours, open days and opportunities for volunteering on the excavations see ⬦ culverproject.co.uk. More recently, Barcombe has started working towards becoming the UK's first net-zero village by transitioning from fossil fuels to low-carbon domestic heating technology.

You can carry on further along the river to **Isfield**, where from the Victorian station the volunteer-run **Lavender Line** (⊘ lavender-line. co.uk) runs steam and diesel locos along a mile or so of the former Lewes–Uckfield line. A long-running campaign (⊘ railfuture.org.uk/ Uckfield+Lewes) aims to reinstate this line into the national rail network.

⊺⊺ FOOD & DRINK

The Anchor Inn Anchor Ln, Barcombe BN8 5EA ⊘ 01273 400014 ⊘ anchorinnandboating. com. Idyllically placed by the River Ouse, this is a pleasant spot for a drink. You can also hire boats here.

The Laughing Fish Station Rd, Isfield TN22 5XB ⊘ 01825 750349 ⊘ laughingfishisfield. com. Hearty pub food and half a dozen real ales, including local tipples Burning Sky and Long Man.

Lavenders Isfield Station TN22 5XB ⊘ lavender-line.co.uk. The bargain-price Lavender Line station buffet has walls hung with old photos of the railway in its heyday and makes a nice stop-off for a mug of coffee and the likes of beans on toast.

3 KINGSTON

Train to Lewes, Brighton Main Line (London–Eastbourne and Hastings) and East Coastway Line (Brighton–Hastings), then two-mile walk

This is a spreading village with an old centre, set beneath the Downs southwest of Lewes. The prominent Y shape of chalk tracks on the escarpment includes the **Juggs Road**, an ancient route supposedly so called because womenfolk used to carry baskets or 'juggs' of fish along it from the coast to Lewes. The pub in Kingston is called the Juggs, and has a cosy main room with a huge open fireplace. If you want the feeling of your feet taking you cross-country from Lewes to Brighton, there's no better way to go. From the Swan Inn in Southover, the Juggs Road begins as a small road, crosses a very high bridge over the A27, then peters out into a track along the spine of Kingston Ridge – a mini South Down.

Along here you'll find the picture-perfect six-sailed weatherboarded **Ashcombe Windmill**. Not all is what it seems: it is an exact copy of what stood there until 1916 and was known as Old Six-Sweeps, with the replacement completed 99 years after the original's demise. On 28 March of that year it collapsed in a mighty blizzard, and many of the bits and pieces were rapidly carted away. Lewes's foundry owner John Every took an interest in the fallen mill, and removed the unique triple

Barcombe Mills & the Ouse

✹ OS Explorer map OL11. Two possibilities: start at the free car park at Barcombe Mills, on road signposted to Barcombe off the A26, three miles north of Lewes (♥ TQ434146), five miles; or two separate walks of 2½ miles each. Both options are on the level, along a stony track, through fields and along a riverside path. **Loos**: no public facilities on route. **Refreshments**: Laughing Fish & Lavender Line station buffet at Isfield; Anchor Inn. **Buses**: best to start from Isfield, served by buses from Lewes.

A perennial favourite stroll in the Low Weald countryside, taking in the atmospheric site of Barcombe Mills (page 182) and with a waterside pub on the way, and opportunities to hire out a rowing boat or ride on a heritage railway. It starts along a mile-long stretch of the trackbed of the former Lewes–Uckfield line, now open to walkers and cyclists as a permissive path. You can either return from the Anchor Inn or carry on along a classic green track called Blunt's Lane to Isfield (bus 29 to Lewes and Tunbridge Wells), where you can take a ride on the Lavender Line.

The return is vintage-quality riverside, with the Ouse showing it as a much more beautiful river this side of Lewes than its gracelessly canalised persona further south. The route is obvious pretty much all the way, although a couple of points might cause brief confusion.

On the way you pass several wartime **pillboxes**, reminders that this valley was heavily defended in World War II.

The walk can also be started in Isfield, which has plenty of roadside parking as well as buses. You could also walk as far as the Anchor from here and turn right along the road to cut out the southern section to Barcombe Mills.

1 Start at the turning with the no entry sign and marked 'weak bridge'. (If starting from the car park, stand with the road behind you and take the entrance away to the left, a short path leads to this point).

Follow this small road, over a series of bridges, spanning the river and **millpool of Barcombe Mills**, and passing a well-weathered noticeboard displaying the list of **bridge tolls**. Beyond these, turn left at a junction (on the right is the entrance to Barcombe House) and carry on the track to emerge on the public road, along which turn right.

Soon on the left you'll see the **former Barcombe Mills railway station**, which saw its last train in 1969. Turn right here (signposted 'Anchor Lane'), on the track of the old railway line, and continue for a mile, crossing a railway bridge and keeping forward where the main track narrows to path width.

Reach the road, where there are rails still embedded in the road surface. ▶

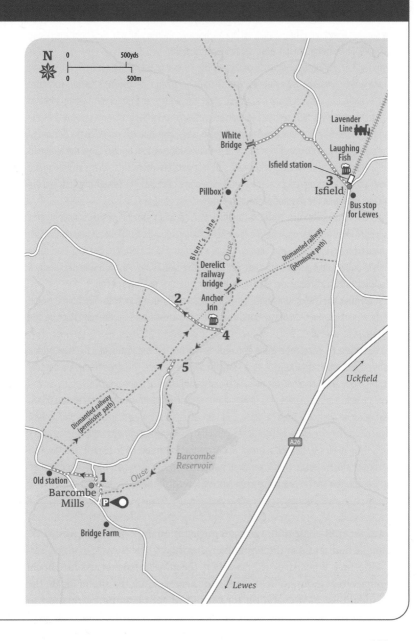

N

0   500yds

0   500m

White Bridge

Lavender Line

Laughing Fish

Isfield station

3 Isfield

Bus stop for Lewes

Pillbox

Blunt's Lane

Ouse

Dismantled railway (permissive path)

Derelict railway bridge

2

Anchor Inn

4

5

Uckfield

A26

Dismantled railway (permissive path)

Barcombe Reservoir

Old station

1

Ouse

Barcombe Mills

P

Bridge Farm

Lewes

Barcombe Mills & the Ouse (continued)

◀ For the short version of the walk via the Anchor Inn (omitting Isfield), turn right and skip to point **4**. **For Isfield** turn left, past two fields on the right.

2 Turn right at a bridleway signpost, and go to the far end of the triangular field, carrying on along a broad, wonderfully timeless grassy track or 'green lane' (**Blunt's Lane**). This later enters another grassy triangle – carry on, soon into a field, and go forward along a line of oak trees, past a wartime pillbox and then keep along the right side of more oak trees. As the land dips, the track becomes well marked again, and drops through a gate to the bottom of the slope. Carry on diagonally on the field path towards a distant bridge. Cross the bridge (if not continuing to Isfield, turn right over a stile immediately afterwards), then carry along the lane into Isfield, turning right at the T-junction along a road, past the **Laughing Fish** and old railway station to the bus stop at the next junction.

3 From Isfield village centre, with the Laughing Fish on your right, follow the road along past Culpeper Close and then just before the Isfield village sign take the next turning on the left, a hard track signposted as a bridleway. Ignore a later turn to the left. Just before a footbridge (White Bridge) take a stile on the left. Follow the riverside all the way. You later pass under a **derelict railway bridge** and then reach a footbridge near the **Anchor Inn**.

If returning to Isfield, turn right along the road, over the hump and old rails set in the road surface marking the old railway track, then after the second field on the right, pick up the directions at point **2**.

4 **To continue to Barcombe Mills** Opposite the Anchor Inn and just before the river bridge turn right through the car park on a footpath along the river. This goes through a gate by sluices, and carries on along the river, later along a tributary of the main river.

5 Emerge from a group of trees near some millstones (a newish house is seen away to your right), and continue along the concrete track, and turn left just after a barn and over a bridge. Turn right on the far side of the bridge, again along the river. It is straightforward all the way back from here. You'll see the embankment of **Barcombe Reservoir** up to the left, and there's a particularly lovely section with the river on both sides. You eventually pass a pillbox and emerge on the lane near the car park, where you turn left to reach the Barcombe Mills car park.

canister mill-shaft to the private museum, mainly of Sussex ironwork, that he had set up at the Phoenix ironworks.

The first I heard of it was when the present owner asked a local archaeology group to field-walk and then excavate the site to locate the foundations, in preparation for his bid to get planning permission to rebuild the mill on the same spot. For a few days the ploughed field was full of archaeologists and soon they found the brick and concrete footings. While field-walking we picked up all sorts of bits of mill – my most spectacular find was a huge chunk of millstone I prised out of a hedgerow with a rake.

Happily this building (instead of the very much less wonderful County Hall in Lewes) now dominates the view from the top of the downs above Kingston, thus nicely bucking the trend for the decline of windmills over the past hundred years in the Sussex landscape.

To continue the walk to Brighton from the windmill, follow the chalky Juggs Road up to the South Downs Way, turn right and keep on, past Brighton Racecourse and descend through Kemptown.

4 MONK'S HOUSE, RODMELL
☖ YHA South Downs
Rodmell BN7 3HF ✆ 01323 474760; National Trust; pre-booking required; train to Southease, East Coastway Line (Lewes–Seaford branch); Compass bus 123 (Lewes–Newhaven; several daily Mon–Sat)

A parade of vernacular architecture awaits at the village of Rodmell, four miles south of Lewes: the Old Rectory with its handsome flint frontage; Deep Thatch Cottage, a long weatherboarded structure beneath a massive thatched roof; and the Monk's House, the 'unpretending house, long and low, a house of many doors' described by Virginia Woolf in her diary in 1919. She and her husband Leonard came here that year and it became their country base while visiting her sister Vanessa Bell and entourage at Charleston. The lean-to greenhouse became 'Leonard's Crystal Palace'; his writing desk retains letters, pens, bundles of magazines and albums of 78s. In the orchard at the end of the garden is Virginia's summer house that she used as her 'writing hut', with a bottle of green ink laid out at the ready on her desk. Leonard increasingly lavished his attention on the garden, where Virginia found sanctuary. In fact green is very much the theme of the interior. Virginia Woolf had a passion for the colour, which gives the house something of an underwater feeling.

In 1941, driven into depression during the dark years of the war, she committed suicide in the Ouse. It's quite a long walk along the flat track to the river; the last things she saw must have been Lewes Castle away to the left, and Mount Caburn in front of her, with the Woolfs' former house of Asham not far ahead. She filled her pockets with heavy stones and plunged in. You can trace Virginia's last steps by following the stony track just left of Rodmell's car park (where the road bends left beyond Monk's House) to the river.

🧳 SPECIAL STAYS

YHA South Downs Itford Farm, Southease BN8 6JS ✆ 0345 371 9574 ⌂ yha.org.uk/hostel/yha-south-downs. There's a shortage of proper hostels on the South Downs Way, so this rural pitstop is hugely popular with walkers and cyclists. Conveniently close to Southease railway station, it has shared rooms, private rooms and a communal kitchen, plus, for a close-to-nature experience, a campsite with tent pitches, timber glamping huts and canvas bell tents. The café and bar offers filling basics such as baps, pizzas and an all-you-can-eat breakfast.

🍴 FOOD & DRINK

Abergavenny Arms Rodmell BN7 3EZ ✆ 01273 472416 ⌂ abergavennyarms.com. Usefully placed for the Ouse Valley and five minutes' walk from Monk's House, this roomy village pub has Harvey's ales on tap and offers stone-baked pizzas and other decent-value food.

5 NEWHAVEN

East Coastway Line (Lewes–Seaford branch); B&H bus 12 (Brighton–Eastbourne) and 14 (Brighton–Newhaven); frequent services

Best known as a cross-Channel port, with ferries to Dieppe in Normandy, Newhaven is not a pretty place at all, but there's appreciable atmosphere, with a distinctively salty whiff among the fishing jetties, marina and harbour all adding up to an infectious sense of place. Waves of government-funded regeneration and development are injecting fresh energy into the town, and, with property cheaper here than in the likes of Brighton and Lewes, there's already been a mild influx of artists, students and young families. For cyclists, the Egrets Way provides an alluring off-road route along the River Ouse, although be aware that a section half a mile or so north of Southease bridge is rugged and unsurfaced, and seasonally muddy.

A swing bridge intermittently brings traffic to a halt on the main road that rings the town far too close to its old centre. From there the road along the west side of the harbour area leads out to West Beach, sandy and alluring at low tide. Earmarked for development, it may soon

---

1 The rebuilt Ashcombe Windmill by Kingston Ridge. **2** Kittiwakes nest on the cliffs at Seaford Head. **3** Sea kale grows among the shingle of Tide Mills. **4** Monk's House in Rodmell was home to Virginia Woolf. **5** There's some picturesque walking near Barcombe Mills. ▶

MATTHEW J THOMAS/S

MELANIE HOBSON/S

NIGEL SAWYER/A

SS

CHRISTOPHER CANNON/S

A WEIRD WANDER FROM NEWHAVEN

Just yards from the ferry is Newhaven Harbour station – though still open, ferry passengers are discouraged from using it. It stands desolate and little used, but for connoisseurs of surreal walks it makes a memorable little excursion along the coast 6½ miles to Seaford Head, with stations at Bishopstone and Seaford to get you back. From the station, walk off the platform past a huge rusty anchor, turn right on the road and right again following signs for the Vanguard Way. All very industrial so far, but oddly photogenic in the right light, and things soon start getting more rural. As you go over a footbridge and edge along Mill Creek, the scenery starts to improve by the minute as atmospheric urban dereliction gives way to watery solitude: later on are the crumbling flint walls and mill pond of the once vast Tide Mills and the cheerily painted beach huts towards Seaford Head. It's tempting to head on right to the end, past the Martello tower, to Splash Point, for a tremendous view beneath the chalky heights.

have a new restaurant, playground and outdoor gym. To the west of the breakwater, built in 1890 to prevent the build-up of shingle that had previously hindered the flow of the Ouse (creating a 'new haven' in the process), a large, rather wild shingle beach is backed by the crumbling cliffs of **Peacehaven Heights**.

Newhaven had a military role for many years. During World War I it became the port through which troops and supplies were sent to Europe, and during the latter half of that war the town was designated a Special Military Area. In World War II, the ill-fated Dieppe raid of 1942 was launched from here, in which large numbers of Canadian military personnel stationed in town perished or were taken prisoner.

Above the harbour and dating from 1859, **Newhaven Fort** (BN9 9DS ✆ 01273 517622 ⌖ newhavenfort.org.uk) is the largest fortification ever erected in Sussex, and was very much working up to 1945. It houses an excellent museum evoking the two world wars, with much more to look at than at first meets the eye as you enter the courtyard. Undergoing further restoration at the time of writing, it will reopen in early 2025.

6 TIDE MILLS & BISHOPSTONE

East Coastway Line (Lewes–Seaford branch) to Bishopstone; B&H bus 12 (Brighton–Eastbourne; frequent)

Though it doesn't look an obvious place to stop off, the concrete track from a small car park south of the A259 between Newhaven and

Seaford leads to a bracing beach with added interest – an eerie place of shingle and ruined flint walls that seems at first sight like an abandoned monastery. These are the remains of the once-immense **Tide Mills**, which dominated the corn trade hereabouts from the 1760s until they closed in 1883. People carried on living here until the workers' village was demolished in World War II – the ruins were used by Canadian troops to practise street fighting. Further out on the shingle are the remains of a World War I seaplane base and a 1930s hospital for children with disabilities, now colonised by a range of seashore plants such as sea kale and yellow horned-poppy. The derelict military railway running along the shore here was used for testing the first armoured train in 1874.

You can walk to Tide Mills in about 15 minutes from Bishopstone station: just exit the end of the platform signed to the beach. In the other direction, you can walk inland from the station to Bishopstone Church. Just after you pass under the railway bridge, on the landward side of the bridge on the left look out for a small, ugly derelict **concrete hut** just below the level of the road – this is a rare World War II survival, containing remains of a pump that in the event of an enemy invasion would have unleashed a vast quantity of petrol, which when ignited would have presented the enemy with a wall of fire. At least that's the theory; whether it would have actually worked is open to debate. Carry on along the road, cross the A259 to take a path opposite the bus shelter – this leads in about 15–20 minutes to the church, which is in a surprisingly tucked-away rural location. The church has Saxon origins, evidenced in the form of a Saxon sundial above the porch, and was enlarged around 1200.

Immediately north of Tide Mills is the **Ouse Estuary Nature Reserve**, a landscaped country park area that's home to the internationally protected great crested newt. A pleasant cycle path runs through it, connecting Newhaven to Seaford.

7 SEAFORD

East Coastway Line (Lewes–Seaford branch); B&H bus 12 (Brighton–Eastbourne; frequent)

Once a thriving medieval port, Seaford – the next major place east along the coast from Newhaven – has long since seen its harbour silted up; its oldest streets are now inland around the church. Its special qualities lie along the shore, one of the most inviting beaches despite the shingle, yet one that never gets seriously crowded. The beach runs for several miles, and with almost no commercial development, it couldn't be more different to Brighton. In summer you'll see toddlers paddling, cross-Channel ferries coming and going, and sub-aqua divers waddling over the beach. Towards evening, fishermen set up camp and barbecues begin to sizzle.

Forty-seven surviving **Martello towers**, erected during Napoleonic times to counter the threat of invasion by France, are dotted along the coast from Sussex to Suffolk (there were originally 103 of them), but Seaford's, the most westerly, is one of the very few to open its doors to the public. On the section of beach immediately south of the town centre, it's home to the **Seaford Museum** (BN25 1JH 01323 898222 seafordmuseum. co.uk 14.00–16.00 Wed, 11.00–16.00 Sat, Sun & bank holidays), one of the most absorbing local-history collections in Sussex and, very unusually, it retains its rooftop cannon. It is far larger inside than seems possible from outside, and it's easy to get immersed for an hour or two with its eclectic stash of kitchen bygones, historic shop contents, historic radios, and model of Seaford station as it was in 1922; look out for a cheque for £471.62 carved in concrete and presented to the Inland Revenue in 1975 after a dispute about tax from Louis Scharer of Seaford, in the days when processed cheques were returned to the drawer – in this case the cheque had to be sent back to Mr Scharer by taxi. The name Martello, incidentally, is seemingly a mistake: the towers are modelled from Mortella Point Tower in Corsica, which was attacked by the British in 1793 and 1794, and its rounded form impressed as a formidable defence.

"It is far larger inside than seems possible from outside, and it's easy to get immersed for an hour or two."

Seaford Head – an 830-hectare nature reserve managed by the Sussex Wildlife Trust – rises abruptly at the east end of the seafront, taking you up into another world. As you look along the base of the crumbling chalk cliffs from Splash Point at the end of the esplanade, a pong of kittiwake droppings will greet you during the nesting season – Sussex's prime colony of these seabirds occupies these cliffs. This easily missed shoreline viewpoint gives one of the most startling cliff views along this stretch of coast, looking up to the precarious chalky heights. The climb up along the cliff from here leads you past perhaps Sussex's most scenically placed golf course, where green-winged orchids flower in May. Beyond, Cuckmere Haven and the Seven Sisters appear: one of the great coastal scenes of southern England. Further east are the group of former coastguards' cottages that provide the foreground for the most photographed version of that view. Close by, steps lead down to a fascinating, potentially ankle-turning rocky foreshore. If you want the view without the climb, find the obscurely located South Hill Barn car park, reached via a maze of residential roads on Seaford's eastern edge.

¶| FOOD & DRINK

Holy Cow 14 Sutton Rd, BN25 1RU ⌀ holycowicecream.co.uk. Shop serving locally made ice cream in mouthwatering flavours including lemon, blood orange and poppy seed.
Pomegranate 45A Broad St, BN25 1NG. Friendly café with a relaxed vintage style and an appetising menu of cooked breakfasts and light lunches such as rarebit with smoked haddock quiche and mixed salad, prepared in the open kitchen. Delicious cakes, too.

FROM THE OUSE TO THE CUCKMERE

The South Downs' knack of looking far larger than they really are is seen to spectacular effect here, with the steep grassy escarpment rising abruptly from the bewitching one-street villages of Firle, Alciston and Berwick, where grazing sheep look absurdly oversize on the slopes. The Old Coach Road – an unmade track for walkers, cyclists and horse riders – makes an unproblematic way to see the Downs from beneath and to link the places, or to combine high and low levels by travelling the other direction on the South Downs Way.

If you want to make a car-free day of it, Glynde and Berwick stations are useful, as are Compass bus 125, Cuckmere Buses (page 167) and the A27 cycle path.

Steep, dead-end roads, known as 'bostals' in South-Downs-speak (also spelt bostalls or borstalls), climb up the Downs from Firle to a point between Beddingham Hill and Firle Beacon and from a crossroads near Alciston to what's known locally as Bo Peep (after a long-abandoned chalk pit of the same name). From either of these little car parks there's marvellous elevated walking, with the sea in view, and it's all preposterously easy: you could wander along the South Downs Way in slippers. In fact, I've accompanied a wheelchair-bound friend up here for her first-ever sample of the Downs at high level.

8 GLYNDE

East Coastway Line (Brighton–Hastings); Compass bus 125 and Cuckmere Buses Bloomsbury Route 25 (Lewes–Eastbourne; limited service)

Every front door here is painted in blue: the whole village is still owned by the Glynde estate that built it. It's not conventionally chocolate-box stuff, but a real rural community of somewhat stark terraces evoking a pit village in the middle of the Sussex countryside a few miles' walk east of Lewes. After the railway was built in 1846, mining began in chalk pits nearby, to produce lime from three kilns set up in Glynde itself. It hasn't quite lost that working-class atmosphere: it's a place where the cricket team thrives and everyone knows each other. They maintain a healthy rivalry with that distinctively smarter estate village, Firle, a short distance away across the A27. It's not every day you find a village with its own tearoom, forge, paraglider school, railway station, stately home and – just a mile up the road – its own opera house.

Glynde Forge, in the village centre, marvellously evokes the pre-motor age. Bearing the date of 1907 by its quaint horseshoe-shaped doorway, this was meticulously copied from another smithy (now a garage) in the Kent village of Penshurst after the estate manager at Glynde happened to see it and decided it was what Glynde needed. Thomas Gontar creates a range of sculptural iron objects in this retro-style place of work. He is always happy to chat to anyone who pops in to have a look round, and it's usually open at weekends as well as on weekdays, though there's seldom anything set out for sale. Hanging over a pair of brick-built hearths there's a fascinating array of horse bits, stirrups, a wartime stirrup pump, a shoe stretcher, weather-vane templates, some gas torches, latch bars, bits of spectacularly rusty bikes and a framed photo of his predecessor.

The country house at the heart of the estate, **Glynde Place** (Glynde BN8 6SX ✆ 01273 858224 ⬙ glyndeplace.co.uk ☉ May–Jun Wed, Thu & Sun, plus Aug bank holiday), seems rather un-grand from the front. Plonked next to a Palladian-style temple-like church, it looks more the part from the back, with imposing Tudor flint gables and brick chimneys, and a sweeping view across meadows and towards Firle Beacon. Guided tours explain the history of the inter-related Morleys, Trevors and Brands in what is very much a family home, with the ubiquitous set of Old Masters brought back from the Grand Tour. The tea room has a cobbled courtyard shaded by fruit trees, and the estate occasionally hosts concerts, including the Love Supreme Jazz Festival in July.

PARAGLIDING ON THE DOWNS

When the thermals are doing the right things you'll often see swarms of multicoloured paragliders hovering over Mount Caburn and around Firle Beacon. Glynde has two places where you can learn and teaching takes place all year; you just need warm windproof clothes and supportive boots.

It looks simple enough from a distance, as paragliders drift along around each other at 15mph. But nothing is ever as easy as it looks, is it?

Tim Cox teaches beginners and experts at **Fly Sussex Paragliding**. His enthusiasm for the sport is certainly infectious, and after chatting with him for a while I was sorely tempted to try something I'd always thought of as merely suicidal. 'There's nothing like free flight. Have you ever had a dream about flying? You step off a hill – and instead of falling you fly.'

I ask him to rate the best places for flying in the world. In fourth place are the Atlas Mountains in Morocco, third Tenerife, second the Alps, and first, yes, the South Downs. 'Because of the way the South Downs are formed it's probably one of the best and safest places in world to paraglide, and over the years this area has become the epicentre of paragliding. The South Downs are superb, with ridges you can pootle along even in winter. We teach complete beginners to fly – so you can turn up here

and in a day would be doing your first solo flight. We take you out to one of our flight sites, we teach you how to take off and land at very low levels, just a few inches up, and we do some gentle flights down some inclines; when you feel confident we creep you up a little bit, then when you can satisfactorily fly the glider and land it we'll get you up a few metres – once you've done that we'll get you up quite high.'

Tim says you don't need to be super-fit. 'As you get more experienced you can do cross-country flights – like today someone went from Brighton to here (25km). You can steer the glider, any way you want to go. I've got from Devil's Dyke to Pevensey and on to Polegate.'

I signalled my apprehension. Tim said 'It's a bit like learning to ski – if you go hell for leather on a black run on day two, you'll hurt yourself; if you choose nice weather to fly in and have good equipment and proper tuition, it's safer than cycling.'

It's a steep learning curve and you can become a competent private pilot after about ten days of instruction. 'People are usually amazed at their progress – on day one they can't quite believe what they've done. If you're reasonably fit and can climb a flight of stairs, then you can fly. The oldest person we had last year was an 82-year-old who went off to India, and last time I heard she was 12,000ft up in the Himalayas.'

PARAGLIDING SCHOOLS

Airworks Laughton BN8 6BN ✆ 01273 434002 ⊘ airworks.co.uk. Meets at the car park in Glynde.

Fly Sussex Paragliding Mill Ln, Beddingham BN8 6JZ ✆ 01273 858170 ⊘ flysussex.com

Mount Caburn

Just above Glynde village you'll see the lumpy outlier of the South Downs known rather pompously as Mount Caburn, a 15-minute walk up the path opposite the Little Cottage Tearooms on Ranscombe Lane. Topped by an ancient hillfort and with a sweeping view of the Downs and sea, it's full of mystery – in Neolithic times there was a huge yew forest here, and Iron Age occupants dug a series of 164 pits and for some reason put deposits in them – dog bones, boar's tusks, potins (Iron Age coins), weaving combs and deliberately broken tools and weapons. The pits may have been used for grain storage, followed by ceremonies involving the burial of special symbolic objects. We would expect there to have been a population nearby, though there is little sign of habitation on Caburn itself. I've helped on an archaeological dig up here for a couple of seasons and discovered that it can get beastly cold even in July – so I doubt anyone lived here year-round.

Archaeologists are still trying to work out what it's about, and whether it was indeed reoccupied in Norman times as an outpost of Lewes Castle, forming a look-out to scan the vulnerable coastal approach. During the very late Iron Age and Roman period Caburn seems to have lost significance and become an agricultural site. It's a hopeless place to defend, as you keep losing sight of people if you wander around the top – hillforts aren't all thought to be primarily defensive anyway. The hill dominates the landscape to the south and east but is less prominent from the north, suggesting it was a focus for that part of the landscape, which would have been more watery than it is today.

Glyndebourne Opera House

Nr Lewes BN8 5UU ✆ 01273 812321 ⬙ glyndebourne.com; Glynde station then 1.6-mile walk or coach shuttle from Lewes station before and after performances

North of Glynde, beyond Glynde Place, is Glyndebourne, a 15th-century manor with a theatre in the grounds, home to Britain's top country-house opera company. It's a major local employer – one reason Lewes is full of rather accomplished musicians. It all started in the 1920s when Glyndebourne's owner, John Christie, began to stage concerts and amateur opera excerpts in the Organ Room for friends and family. Through this he met his wife, Audrey Mildmay, a professional singer, and the idea of an opera season developed. In 1934 they opened the first theatre, built on the former kitchen garden; its

1990s successor, sublime both acoustically and aesthetically, is a fitting venue for one of the great opera festivals in the world. The summer festival (May to August) features long intervals when opera-lovers dressed in evening finery set up lavish picnics in the grounds; tickets are horribly hard to come by. In October, there's a shorter season where tickets aren't quite so pricey and you might just strike lucky. The first time I went to Glyndebourne, to see a wonderful production of *Così fan tutte*,

> *"The summer festival features long intervals when opera-lovers dressed in evening finery set up lavish picnics."*

my group walked over the Downs from Lewes in dinner garb, cagoule, walking boots, brollies, the lot – carrying our posh picnic in rucksacks. It poured relentlessly all day; the only others braving the outdoor picnic at the interval apart from our party were an elderly couple who'd arrived by helicopter and were being served by someone who seemed to be their butler. And on another occasion the very first words I heard someone say as we made our way in were 'And how are your pheasants this year, Jeremy?' Actually it's not at all universally snooty; in Lewes I'm very much aware what a remarkable range of people have been to Glyndebourne and the huge affection in which it is held by the community. But it's all a world apart from Glynde – both places have the same first six letters, but there the similarity ends.

¶¶ FOOD & DRINK

Little Cottage Tea Rooms Glynde BN8 6RP ☎ 01273 858215 ⌂ littlecottagetearooms. co.uk. Directly opposite the path up to Mount Caburn from the centre of Glynde, and offering cream teas, light lunches and cake, this is everything a vintage tea shop should be.

9 FARLEYS HOUSE & GALLERY
⌂ Old Whyly

Muddles Green BN8 6HW ☎ 01825 872856 ⌂ farleyshouseandgallery.co.uk ☉ tours Apr–Oct Thu, Fri & Sun; B&H Regency Route bus 28 (Brighton–Eastbourne; three per hour Mon–Sat, less frequent Sun)

It's an almost startling experience to pass from the very ordinary-looking farmyard off Muddles Green's village street into a garden filled with sculpture and then to what is probably the most surprising farmhouse you will ever see. Home from 1949 to British surrealist painter and art promoter Roland Penrose and his American wife, photographer

Lee Miller, Farleys has been kept largely as it was by their son Antony Penrose, one of the family members who conduct tours in person.

A brick-floored corridor leads to a well-appointed 1950s kitchen, where a tile painted by Picasso is cemented into the wall rather off-centre above the AGA stove, and two of his lithographs hang over the table where Lee Miller, an accomplished cook, used to set her guests to peeling potatoes. In the dining room the great fireplace alcove is joyously decorated in golden yellow and shows the nearby Long Man of Wilmington chalk carving (page 208) as a sun god. Works by Roland Penrose range from a Magritte-like image of his wife-to-be to a blackly humorous representation of himself in old age as a dried-up toad with hip pain, his world reduced to a cube supported by London taxis.

"In the dining room the great fireplace alcove is joyously decorated in golden yellow."

Seen along with Charleston (page 202), Farleys encapsulates the influences on British modern art through most of the 20th century. Penrose himself was a key figure, bringing Picasso's *Guernica* on tour to Britain in 1938, and co-founding the Institute of Contemporary Arts. But where Charleston presents an art-centred domestic world apparently remote from politics, the malign effect of World War II is palpable at Farleys House and Gallery. Lee Miller worked with surrealist photographer Man Ray in Paris, and became a photojournalist with the US army in 1944. She was long haunted by her experiences covering the liberation of Buchenwald and Dachau concentration camps, which revived a personal childhood trauma, and never quite recovered the sunny personality indicated by her pre-war portraits. Life at Farleys House and Gallery and developing a new interest in imaginative cooking provided some respite, and the couple hosted many giants of the modern movement: Miller photographed Picasso by the village sign and greeting the farm bull. Antony Penrose's children's book *The Boy Who Bit Picasso* recalls his childhood friendship with the artist, while cleverly introducing the concepts of modern art to youngsters, as does his follow-up story *Miro's Magic Animals*.

▐▌ SPECIAL STAYS

Old Whyly London Rd, East Hoathly BN8 6EL ✆ 01825 840216 ⌂ oldwhyly.co.uk.
Approached via a drive lined with venerable oaks, this is a superior and elegant B&B (with

dinner and Glyndebourne picnic hampers available on request) in a fine country house, squared off in Georgian times but with medieval parts too. Rooms are restrained, well proportioned and light, with thoughtfully chosen antiques and paintings. The gardens are quintessentially English, with lawns, herbaceous borders and a pergola, plus a heated swimming pool and a tennis court.

¶¶ FOOD & DRINK

Six Bells The Street, Chiddingly BN8 6HE ☏ 01825 872227. Unpretentious and welcoming village pub with good-value food, open fires and weekend live music, little changed since Lee Miller photographed willowy *Vogue* models there in the 1950s. Very popular with weekend bikers, and with the author of this book.

10 FIRLE

Compass bus 125 & Cuckmere Buses Bloomsbury Route 25 (Lewes–Eastbourne; limited service)

Turn south off the busy A27 along Firle Bostal, east of Lewes, and you're suddenly transported back a century. The Firle Estate owns pretty much everything in **West Firle** (known locally as plain Firle), and the village street is a classic, with estate cottages fronted with flint, some selling produce from makeshift stalls in front; poke around a bit and you'll also find a microbrewery and a workshop buying and selling shepherds' huts. In summer, village cricket matches provide a bucolic scene, all very perfect even for those without the slightest interest in the game. Round the

"The village street is a classic, with estate cottages fronted with flint, some selling produce from makeshift stalls."

corner, **St Peter's Church** has Gage family monuments and some highly striking modern coloured stained-glass by John Piper, one of the foremost painters and stained-glass designers of the 20th century; the graves of Duncan Grant, Quentin Bell and Vanessa Bell are in the churchyard.

Southwest of the village, Firle Bostal leads you steeply up to a car park on the South Downs Way. To the left it leads to the trig point at **Firle Beacon**, where a prominent grassy lump that is a Neolithic long barrow surveys a scene over Seaford, Newhaven and the English Channel to the south and far over the Weald in the other direction, towards the heights of Ashdown Forest. Closer at hand, just beneath the scarp, is the estate folly of Firle Tower and Arlington Reservoir, which appears as a strangely regular-looking lake.

Firle Place

Firle BN8 6LP ℘ 01273 858307 ♦ firle.com ☉ summer afternoons Sun–Thu

If you've seen Autumn de Wilde's 2020 film adaptation of Jane Austen's *Emma*, Firle Place will probably look familiar, as it was used as the setting. It could hardly be less conspicuous in the wider landscape: you see nothing as you come up the sweeping arc of the carriageway, until the last moment when it appears, snuggled beneath the Downs, with gardens rising beyond.

Its owners, the Gages, have been here for half a millennium. The house was begun in 1530 by Sir John Gage whose roles included being the Constable of the Tower of London, where he presided over executions of Catherine Howard and Lady Jane Grey, and over the imprisonment of the young Princess Elizabeth (later Elizabeth I). His son supervised the burning of the Lewes Martyrs in the 1550s, so can't have been too popular in Lewes. Far less nasty folk came later – most famously the horticulturalist Sir Thomas Gage who acquired Reine Claude plum trees from

"His son supervised the burning of the Lewes Martyrs in the 1550s, so can't have been too popular in Lewes."

monks in France only to completely lose track of what they were called by the time they arrived, so they were called 'greengages' instead.

In the 18th century, to the Tudor core of the house was added a crisp-looking stone façade of Caen stone, originally brought over from Normandy to England for the building of Lewes Priory just up the road. When the Priory was dissolved in Henry VIII's time, it was robbed of much of its building material, some of which ended up here.

The 18th-century remodelling extended to the inside: all is light, airiness and space, with a cream and gold drawing room and some wonderfully intricate plasterwork. It's clearly very much still lived in, with board games, art books and a Dansette record player in evidence along with family portraits by the likes of Gainsborough. The Long Gallery has gorgeous views over the park. The collection of Sèvres porcelain is said to be of national importance.

◄ **1** Mount Caburn offers sweeping views of the Downs. **2** The timeless interior of Glynde Forge. **3** One of many art offerings at Farleys, the home of Roland Penrose and Lee Miller. **4** Murals by members of the Charleston circle in Berwick's Church of St Michael and All Angels show the life of Christ against a backdrop of the South Downs.

Middle Farm

Near Firle BN8 6LJ ✆ 01323 811411 ⏚ middlefarm.com; bus to Charleston (Compass 125, Cuckmere 25 or 39, limited service) then one-mile walk

Right beside the A27 near Firle, this has fair claim to be Britain's very first farm shop, opened in 1960. It's also home to the National Collection of Cider and Perry, with the largest choice of ciders and perries anywhere in the country. As well as the bottled varieties, they have an astonishing array of cider barrels ranged in order of taste – dry at the left end, medium in the middle and sweet to the right, and you can sample them before you buy. They stock their own cider and apple juice too, and you can also bring your own apples in and they'll juice them for you. The residual pomace is fed to animals, including geese, which are fattened up for sale for Christmas.

Visitors can also meet the animals at the 'open farm' and watch the Jersey cows being milked, see the rare-breed chickens, ducks, goats, llamas and harvest mice, and follow the nature trail.

⫟ FOOD & DRINK

Firle Place Tea Room Firle Pl, BN8 6LP ✆ 01323 818771 ⏚ firle.com ☉ summer afternoons Sun–Tue. Accessible even if you're not visiting the house, this eco-conscious tea room offers light lunches, locally made cakes and posh teas, including a blowout with Rathfinny bubbly.

The **Ram Inn** The Street, Firle BN8 6NS ✆ 01273 858222 ⏚ raminn.co.uk. Handily placed, with plenty of outdoor space in a front courtyard and a rear beer garden, Firle's village pub focuses on dining. Upstairs, there are five characterful guest rooms.

11 CHARLESTON

Near Firle BN8 6LL ✆ 01323 811265 ⏚ charleston.org.uk ☉ Apr–Oct Wed– Sun & bank holidays; advance booking advised; Compass bus 125, Cuckmere Buses Bloomsbury Route 25, Cuckmere Sussex Art Shuttle Bus 39 (Lewes–Eastbourne; limited service)

A modest pebbledashed farmhouse set just below the South Downs and signposted off the A27 around six miles east of Lewes, Charleston was for more than 60 years the cherished retreat of the circle of artists, writers and intellectuals known as the **Bloomsbury Group**, who have remained enduring objects of fascination as much for their unorthodox relationships as for their creative talent. The first arrivals, in 1916, were Virginia Woolf's artist sister Vanessa Bell, her lifelong painting partner and occasional lover Duncan Grant, and Grant's then male lover, writer

David Garnett – Vanessa's husband Clive Bell joined them at weekends. Virginia and Leonard Woolf had a series of homes hereabouts, ending up at Monk's House (page 187). Grant and Garnett, as conscientious objectors, had been directed to do farm work, which they found nearby.

Amid this Bohemian enclave, a regular guest was economist and Treasury adviser John Maynard Keynes: after World War I he wrote his denunciation of the Versailles Treaty, *The Economic Consequences of the Peace*, here. Following his marriage to a Russian ballet dancer – a move which shocked the Bloomsbury Set considerably more than their free-thinking lifestyles might have suggested – he leased Tilton House, a few fields away.

Bell and Grant's art was influenced by French Post-Impressionists like Cézanne and Matisse at a time when the British had scarcely even heard of the Impressionists. One story goes that in 1918 Keynes left a freshly acquired Cézanne temporarily in the hedge after he was dropped off at the end of the road with too much luggage. The artists developed highly individual styles completely at variance with the modernist minimalism which became fashionable during the interwar period, adorning walls and furniture with bright, splashy designs and pictures, and creating endearingly homespun details like beaded lampshades based on pottery colanders and woollen fringes to cover radiators. But as they never owned the house, the décor was done cheaply and not intended to last.

"One story goes that in 1918 Keynes left a freshly acquired Cézanne temporarily in the hedge."

After Duncan Grant's death in 1978 the fragile interiors could easily have been obliterated, but the Charleston Trust raised more than a million pounds to buy the house and commence restoration. This was immensely complex: in the dining room, restorers – including Angelica Garnett, Bell and Grant's daughter, who had created some of the original works – found eight layers of wallpaper ravaged by damp. The Trust's huge achievement is to have re-captured the lived-in appearance and atmosphere of Charleston as it was in the 1950s.

The colourful, densely packed cottage-style garden has also been restored, and the site shop sells pottery, textiles and furniture inspired by Bloomsbury designs. More of Grant and Bell's work can be seen at the Church of St Michael and All Angels in nearby Berwick (page 204), which they were commissioned to decorate with wall paintings in 1941.

A visit nicely ties in with a side trip to Charleston in Lewes (page 173).

12 BERWICK

East Coastway Line (Brighton–Hastings) to Berwick, 1½ miles from Berwick Church; Compass bus 125 & Cuckmere Buses 25, 26 & 47 (from Lewes, Seaford & Eastbourne, limited service)

One of the string of delightfully unspoilt villages alongside dead-end lanes running towards the Downs – only Berwick has a difference. During World War II Vanessa Bell and Duncan Grant put their own very individual stamp on the otherwise typical rural **Church of St Michael and All Angels**, illustrating the life of Christ against a background of the South Downs as they looked during the war. The decision by the Bishop of Chichester to allow these pacifist, radical, free-thinking bohemians to transform the building in the heart of war-torn Sussex certainly raised a few eyebrows but nowadays brings great numbers of appreciative visitors. The Bloomsbury Set used themselves, their friends, their children and local people as models. If you've just been to

"However unusual now, the idea of a church covered in wall paintings echoes medieval times."

Charleston, the almost outrageously multi-coloured pulpit decorations will be instantly recognisable. However unusual now, the idea of a church covered in wall paintings echoes medieval times, though the details –

including a soldier, airman and sailor – are clearly 20th century: look out for their hair styles, for instance. Their model for Christ (over the chancel arch) was the artist Edward Le Bas, who gallantly let himself be secured to an easel at Charleston in a crucified position and was fortified with brandy during the ordeal. Sussex cameos are everywhere in the pictures, among them the South Downs, shepherds' crooks (of the type made for many years at Pyecombe, near Clayton), a Sussex trug full of fresh produce and the pond at Charleston.

A short walk or bike ride, taking the road towards the Downs, then turning right on the chalk track known as The Old Coach Road, then right again at the wooden bench on a grassy triangle, brings you to **Alciston**. Around the Grade I-listed church cluster the village's medieval remains, including a ruined dovecote. The massive tithe barn here is at 170ft one of the longest in the country and would have been used for storing parishioners' compulsory contributions of a tenth (or tithe) of their produce to the church authorities. The roof is reputed to contain 50,000 tiles. If you retrace your steps to The Old Coach Road, you can continue to Firle (page 199).

¶¶ FOOD & DRINK

Cricketers' Arms Berwick BN26 6SP ✆ 01323 870469 ⬦ cricketersberwick.co.uk. An attractively placed brick and flint house with a cottagey garden crammed with flowers, handily close to the A27, but far enough away for the road noise to be muffled. Inside, there are half-panelled walls, low ceilings and cricket bats hanging up. The bar serves well-kept Harvey's Best and seasonal beers and there's an extensive menu.

Sussex Ox Milton Street BN26 5RL ✆ 01323 870840 ⬦ thesussexox.co.uk. In the hamlet of Milton Street near Berwick and Wilmington, this civilised dining pub uses ingredients from its own organic farm, including potatoes, beef and lamb. There's a decent wine list and beer from the very local Long Man brewery.

CUCKMERE VALLEY: FROM HAILSHAM TO THE SEA

The Cuckmere meanders its way from the Weald past a succession of historic and scenic goodies, with ample scope for exploring on foot, by bike or by bus. South of the unassuming town of Hailsham the A27 intrudes, but then the river cuts beneath the Downs to reach its finale between Seaford Head and the Seven Sisters at Cuckmere Haven.

13 MICHELHAM PRIORY

Upper Dicker BN27 3QS ✆ 01323 844224 ⬦ sussexpast.co.uk ⊙ Feb–Dec; Cuckmere Bus 48 (Eastbourne–Deanland Wood Park; limited service)

Founded as an Augustinian monastery in 1229 and now run by Sussex Past (the Sussex Archaeological Society's commercial arm), Michelham Priory bears virtually no resemblance to a religious house these days: dissolution in 1537 was followed by the demolition of the church, whose outline is marked by stones in the lawn, but part of the range was adapted into the house that stands today. It later became a farm and declined into near-ruination, and in 1927, soon after a restoration programme was begun, the Tudor wing of the house was destroyed by fire just days before a ball was to be held.

Inside, the entrance hall – a vaulted undercroft – sets an ecclesiastical note and a model of the priory in its heyday gives the historical context. Elsewhere, domesticity prevails, though there's a spectacularly strange moment upstairs when part of the great Gothic west window of the former refectory is revealed with crudely hacked-off tracery. Very little survived of the days when the Child family ran their farm here,

CUCKOO TRAIL

This hugely popular path for walkers, cyclists and horseriders runs for 14 largely traffic-free miles between Heathfield to Shinewater Park in Eastbourne, mostly (apart from the odd, well signposted diversion through quiet streets) along a defunct railway. Named after the Sussex legend that the first cuckoo of spring was always heard at Heathfield Fair, the line saw its last train in 1968.

The trail slopes downhill very gently from north to south, but is easy in either direction. Part of the National Cycle Network and opened in 1990, it's ornamented with carved benches and chunky sculptures made from recycled materials. I always think it feels like an optimistic vision of the future, where people commute around on two wheels instead of four. Don't expect scenery, by the way: it's largely between hedgerows and viewless.

For those arriving by train, Polegate station on the Brighton–Hastings East Coastway Line is ideally placed. For a map of the ten-mile Sustrans section, visit ⊘ sustrans.org.uk/ncn/map/route/cuckoo-trail.

although there are some displays of items that have been brought in from elsewhere, and the place is engagingly bitty in character. Contents include recreations of a Victorian kitchen and a World War II evacuee child's bedroom, evoking the days when a dozen children from Rotherhithe were brought to live in the priory in what must have been a character-forming episode in their lives.

Perhaps Michelham's most enduring trait is the exquisite atmosphere of the site itself, surrounded by what was once England's longest water-filled **moat** (sadly the moat is silting up, requiring millions of pounds to take it back to its former glory) and entered through a huge medieval **gatehouse** that almost looks like somewhere in rural France. The lavishly landscaped **grounds** feature a gorgeously secluded kitchen garden enclosed by hedges of box and yew. Look out for medieval and other history-themed weekends and country fairs when Michelham particularly comes to life.

Just outside the grounds, Michelham's **watermill** was first used to grind flour in the 1430s, or perhaps even earlier, and is still impressively intact, but not open to the public.

Elsewhere on site are a café, a play area, a periodically working blacksmith's forge – which is adjacent to a little rope museum that commemorates an aspect of the industrial history of nearby Hailsham – and the Elizabethan Great Barn, an agricultural storage barn dating from 1597–1601, and now used for wedding ceremonies, receptions and other functions (it's sometimes possible to peek inside).

¶¶ FOOD & DRINK

Upper Dicker Village Shop Upper Dicker BN27 3QE ✆ 01323 844352 ⊘ upperdicker. com. Just north of Michelham Priory, this cottagey emporium is a wonderfully homespun local institution, informal and jolly, with a miscellany of furniture. The caff serves soups, sandwiches and the like, and is famous for its hearty build-your-own brunches. The shop, going strong since the 1840s, has a good range of local produce.

14 ARLINGTON RESERVOIR

Train to Berwick (East Coastway Line, Brighton–Hastings) then half-mile walk

Look down from the South Downs and you might spot this near-circular body of water. It's ringed by a footpath that's nice for a cobweb-removing stroll, but hardly worth crossing the county for; one wishes it was a bit more raggedy-edged. The 1960s constructors unwittingly ignored the archaeology: it's now known that various Roman roads converge here. As there are other Roman remains in the locality, it's likely the reservoir was built on the site of a Roman town.

On its eastern side, Arlington's **Church of St Pancras** overlooks various grassy lumps hinting that the village was once larger. The church, possibly linked to St Pancras Priory in Lewes, is evocatively ancient: it's unknown when it was founded, but churches dedicated to St Pancras are often very early. The exterior has some recycled Roman ceramics incorporated into the small Saxon window by the porch. Inside, beneath a roof

"The church, possibly linked to St Pancras Priory in Lewes, is evocatively ancient: it's unknown when it was founded."

with 15th-century kingposts and trusses, a show of 14th-century wall paintings includes depictions of St Christopher on the nave north wall and St George on the south wall. Arlington churchwardens' accounts for 1455–79 have miraculously survived and are said to be the earliest ones left in Sussex; they're now kept in the British Museum. There's also some 1624 graffiti on a holy water piscina in the porch.

And while on the subject of Roman leftovers, the strikingly rectangular grid of roads just to the west of here around **Ripe**, **Chalvington** and **Laughton** has very early origins. The historian Ivan Margary, an authority on Roman roads, believed the area was 'centuriated' – divided into rectangular blocks using Roman measurements, and given as plots to retiring soldiers (a sort of Roman Peacehaven). Archaeological finds suggest there was certainly Roman activity; this was a huge grain-growing area, exporting via Pevensey. However the latest thinking is that the Roman road/track system was itself based on earlier straight drove roads which could date back to the Bronze Age.

15 LONG MAN OF WILMINGTON

Compass bus 125 & Cuckmere Buses Bloomsbury Route 25 (Lewes–Eastbourne; limited service), then one-mile walk

No-one has the faintest idea what this colossal man is doing here, carved into the chalk escarpment of the Downs, how old he is or what he's carrying in each hand – or if he's actually standing in a doorway. From the A27, carry on along the main street of Wilmington, past the Giant's Rest pub, through the village and past the church.

You can glimpse the Long Man from the A27, but to see it at close range, make for the free car park at the southern end of the village of Wilmington, where there's an information panel. Beyond, a footpath leads to the base of the figure. It's also possible to take a path up across the steep escarpment. Note how little sense you can make of it all upside down, with all the clever tricks of perspective in operation.

Measuring 235ft from foot to head, the Long Man is the largest hill carving in Britain, an iconic image much used to symbolise the South Downs. He has been variously explained as a fertility symbol, though he has a conspicuous lack of manly attributes (some argue because he in fact has his back to us); a surveyor of ley lines (holding two staffs); a religious image from the Bronze or Iron ages; a Roman figure, similar to many depicted on Roman coins; an Anglo-Saxon representation of Odin with two spears, as on the 7th-century Finglesham buckle, and a medieval Christian image of the Good Shepherd associated with Wilmington Priory. Or he could be even earlier.

"Measuring 235ft from foot to head, the Long Man is the largest hill carving in Britain, an iconic image."

What we do know is that in the 19th century the carving was re-laid in bricks and its shape got somewhat distorted; it's now outlined with white-painted concrete blocks. Perhaps the greatest mystery is that there are no written records of the figure existing at all before 1710. Recent archaeological work suggests it isn't as ancient as frequently supposed: it could well date from the Tudor period, when post-Reformation landowners taking over monastic sites like nearby Wilmington Priory sometimes literally put their own mark on the land with such pagan-looking figures.

In 1700 the Wilmington estate passed to Spencer Compton, Speaker of Parliament, who adopted the title Baron Wilmington, and the Long Man first appears on a map he commissioned in 1710. There's a good view of the figure from the Priory, and Compton's map-maker/surveyor would have had the skills to lay it out. It's feasible that at a time of heightened interest in ancient monuments, Compton decided to add a new one with secular, even pagan, associations, to 'his' landscape.

But all that doesn't preclude the possibility that there has been a Long Man in one form or another for much longer than that, as it has certainly been tampered with over time. Some are sure it is Neolithic and functioned as a solstice indicator.

St Mary and St Peter Church, at the south end of Wilmington's unspoilt single street, has what is thought to be the oldest tree in Sussex – a huge yew, gigantically propped up but still very much alive. A certificate in the porch dates it as 1,600 years old and requests 'Please do all you can to prolong the life of this venerable member of your local community.' Inside, a very beloved medieval window depicting bees and butterflies around the figure of St Peter was sadly destroyed by fire in 2002, but has been replaced by a painted glass window created by Paul San Casciani in 2004. He partially recreated the original, with the addition of a phoenix symbolising its return from the ashes; surviving bits of the original window have been incorporated into the bottom of the new one.

LONG MAN BREWERY

Church Farm, Litlington BN26 5RA ⊘ longmanbrewery.com

Established in 2012 and named after Wilmington's famed chalk hill figure, this excellent, multi-award-winning venture uses barley grown on the farm and across the Cuckmere Valley at Rathfinny vineyard. Brewery tours are available, starting and ending in the shop and tasting room in a restored flint-walled building on Church Farm. The farmyard is also home to Cadence (⊘ cadencecycle.club), a shipping container converted into a buzzing café kiosk, which refuels cyclists and walkers with delicious coffee and toasties.

⑪ FOOD & DRINK

Long Man Inn Wilmington BN26 5SQ ✆ 01323 870207 ⌂ longmaninn.co.uk. Just off the A27, this Edwardian pub is very congenially set up for dining and drinking. Offering local ales and ciders and a good range of bar food, it can get very busy at weekends and on curry, quiz and music nights. There are four cosy guest rooms upstairs.

FOLKINGTON

Compass bus 125 (Lewes–Eastbourne; limited service), then 1.2-mile walk

The Wealdway, here a quite lovely section of byway from opposite the church at Wilmington, leads up onto the lower slopes of the South Downs, getting choice views of the Low Weald and close-ups of the escarpment; you can alternatively join the Wealdway by turning left under the Long Man and following the well-marked track at the foot of the downland escarpment. About 15–20 minutes' delectable walking leads up to the tiny village of Folkington, as tucked away as could be at the top end of a lane and partly shrouded by trees. Folkington's well cared for Church of St Peter is a charmingly simple downland church with box pews, with lancet windows indicating 13th-century origins. In the churchyard is the grave of cookery writer Elizabeth David (1913–92), whose recipe books endeared the qualities of Mediterranean (among other) cuisine to the British public. Her gravestone is appropriately decorated with carvings of fresh produce and a cooking pot. From here you can carry along the track as it winds southwards towards Jevington, and return on the South Downs Way to the top of Wilmington Hill, above the Long Man and over the summit Hunter's Burgh for a steep final descent (a total circuit of about 5½ miles). It's five-star scenery – the South Downs don't come much more sublime than this.

16 LULLINGTON CHURCH (CHURCH OF THE GOOD SHEPHERD)

Blink and you'll miss the turning for this isolated, improbably minute 13th-century place of worship: a small signposted path leads past it from

---

1 A ship's figurehead in the form of a red lion outside the Star Inn bears witness to Alfriston's smuggling past. **2** Lullington's Church of the Good Shepherd is one of England's smallest churches. **3** Michelham Priory became a house after dissolution in the 16th century. **4** The mysterious Long Man of Wilmington is Britain's largest hill carving. ▶

the road between Wilmington and Litlington (about 400yds after the road begins to drop if you're coming from Wilmington). Alternatively you can reach it by walking up from Alfriston, crossing the footbridge to the left of the church, carrying straight on over a road, and continuing on for another quarter mile.

In the league for church superlatives it's a contender for England's smallest, at about 13 sq feet. Before it was almost entirely destroyed by fire (probably in the time of Cromwell), it was a much more normal size; all that remains is a fragment of the chancel. There's a harmonium, and no electricity. It has 20-odd chairs but a congregation of a dozen would make it feel positively crowded. During its Harvest Festival half the congregation has to sit out in the churchyard.

17 ALFRISTON

Train to Berwick (East Coastway Line, Brighton–Hastings), then 2.4-mile walk; Compass and Cuckmere Buses (several routes from Berwick Station, Charleston, Eastbourne, Exceat, Lewes, Seaford, Wilmington; limited services)

This, the largest of the Cuckmere Valley villages, lies between the A27 and Seaford, at a point where three branches of the South Downs Way meet. With three ancient pubs, delightful shops and tea rooms, and a village store bursting with nostalgic character, its very handsome main street is one of the most hospitable in the county.

Apart, perhaps, from the deluge of vehicles and visitors that arrive throughout the year, it has no jarring note. Virtually all of it is 18th century or earlier. A memento of Alfriston's smuggling days is incorporated into the façade of the 16th-century **Star Inn**: a ship's figurehead in the form of a red lion, pilfered from a wreck off the Sussex coast by the notorious Alfriston gang member Stanton Collins (page 221) in the early 1800s.

Right in the middle of things stands an ancient **market cross**, weathered into what's now not much more than a stone pillar, vulnerable to errant lorries; one once smashed into the Smugglers pub and caused an almighty mess.

On **The Tye**, or village green, stands Alfriston's village sign, unveiled in 2000 by local resident and erstwhile Chancellor of the Exchequer the late Lord Healey. Nearby, there's a collecting box made out of an unexploded 1940s mine. Set on a rise on the south side of the green, well away from the road, is the **Church of St Andrew**, the 'cathedral of the Downs', which dates from 1360 and hosts a lively programme of musical events. Inside, it is unusually spacious and beautifully light. There can't be many other churches that have actually gained a musicians' gallery in living memory; this was added in 1995 to provide extra space.

Pretty much contemporary with the church is the adjacent **Alfriston Clergy House** (✆ 01323 871961 ⊙ Easter–Oct; National Trust) with small diamond-leaded windows beneath a massive thatched roof. In 1896 the newly formed National Trust paid just a tenner to rescue this ancient timber-framed Wealden yeoman's house of around 1350 from a state of spectacular decay; it was the Trust's very first purchase anywhere, though it didn't open its doors to the public for another 81 years. Clearly the Trust recognised the house's rarity value. Inside you can see a *"In 1896 the National Trust paid just a tenner to rescue this ancient timber-framed Wealden yeoman's house."* photograph of its alarming condition in 1893, and happily it has been painstakingly restored. The main hall is very much as it was 650 years ago: there's no chimney, just a central fireplace from which the smoke drifts surprisingly unchokingly up through the high ceiling. Its floor is made of rammed chalk mixed with milk, a traditional and surprisingly durable surface: when the modern craftsmen first had a go at it, this didn't quite come off, and then they realised they were using pasteurised milk, and only the unpasteurised version solidified properly. The cottage garden has old rose varieties, lilies, clematis and poppies giving directly on to a wilder landscape of river reeds, while raised vegetable beds are edged with lavender.

The northeast corner of the green leads to the White Bridge, a footbridge over the Cuckmere that lies on the South Downs Way and is the starting point for the **Kissing Gate Walk**, a gentle stroll that goes up one side of the river towards Litlington and returns on the other bank.

Rathfinny Wine Estate

Alfriston BN26 5TU ✆ 01323 870022 ⊗ rathfinnyestate.com

With a higher concentration of vineyards than any other part of the UK, including heavyweights such as Bolney, Nyetimber and Ridgeview, Sussex has truly become a wine region to be reckoned with. The flinty, chalky soil, sunny climate and relatively frost-free south-facing slopes are ideal for vines. The road between Alfriston and Seaford offers glimpses

Alfriston, the Cuckmere Valley & Lullington Heath

✤ OS Explorer map OL25; start: Alfriston village centre, by the Star Inn (main car park; reached by Cuckmere Ramblerbus at weekends from Berwick station & bus 125 from Lewes)
♥ TQ521033; seven miles; hilly, with one steady ascent. **Loos**: in Alfriston. **Refreshments**: full range in Alfriston; Litlington Tea Gardens, Plough & Harrow and Cadence in Litlington.

The area bounded by Alfriston and Litlington to the west, Westdean to the south, Jevington to the east and Folkington (pronounced Foe-ington) and Wilmington to the north has abundant possibilities for walks. For all-round views the seven-mile route mapped here is one of my favourites and is well signposted throughout, taking in the **Cuckmere Valley**, the heights of **Lullington Heath** and the tiny church of **Lullington**.

1 From Alfriston's Market Cross, follow the High Street south past The George Inn, and go left on the path signposted to the Alfriston Clergy House. You'll see the church across the Tye (village green to the right), but continue ahead between flint walls to the left of the Gun Room café, then cross the footbridge over the Cuckmere. On the other side, turn right downstream (signposted South Downs Way to Exceat) to follow the Cuckmere south to Litlington.

2 After half a mile you pass through a pair of kissing gates. Then when level with Litlington away to the left, you go through a kissing gate into a semi-wooded, reedy expanse. About 150yds later, turn left shortly before the next footbridge, into Litlington; the **Plough and Harrow** (to the right) makes a useful pub stop. You might also like to peep inside **Litlington Tea Gardens** (to the left), one of England's oldest tea gardens; this dates from the 1870s when visitors arrived by horse and carriage on their day out. A few remnants of those days survive, and although it's obviously evolved with the times it retains a fetching assemblage of ageless sheds and summerhouses around tables and chairs set out on two terraces, one gravel and the other grassy. At the north end of the village, near the church, is Church Farm, home to the Long Man Brewery and Cadence coffee bar (page 209).

Back at the Plough and Harrow, head south along the village street then turn left along Clapham Lane, past the village hall and immediately right on the **South Downs Way**. This rises up through three fields, and then eventually drops into a valley. Visible away to the right is the **Hindover White Horse** carved into the hillside beneath High and Over (page 218).

3 At the bottom cross a stile and turn left on a track at a South Downs Way signpost inside woodland, skirting the grounds of **Charleston Manor** (to the right), at the end of which bear left (where the South Downs Way continues ahead up steps) along the idyllically peaceful valley of **Charleston Bottom** for more than a mile. You later enter a semi-wooded area by a gate; after five minutes' walking, keep forward, ignoring tracks to the left and right.

4 At a track junction where there are two gates ahead, do not go through the gates but go sharp left uphill on a track that immediately bends right through the forest. As you emerge into the open, go over the first track crossing, between concrete bollards and past a weather station. Down to the right is **Lullington Heath National Nature Reserve**, where the cohabitation of species suited variously to chalk grassland and acid soils throws up some unusual botanical neighbours such as heather and salad burnet.

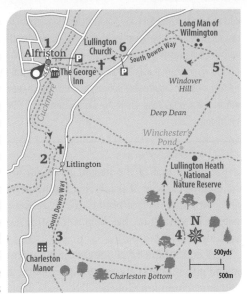

At the next track junction, where the view opens out to the left, take the track ahead (to the left of the nature reserve sign, which itself is by the entrance to the 18th-century dew pond known as **Winchester's Pond**, a dragonfly haunt). Carry straight on through a gate, gently uphill and (after the next gate) alongside a fence on the left.

5 Just before you reach a point above the head of Deep Dean valley down to your left, the South Downs Way joins from the right. A delectable view now opens on the left, over **Deep Dean** – a good indication of how much of the Downs must have looked before modern agricultural methods. With the sea in the background, this panorama for me epitomises the South Downs.

Go through a gate; the South Downs Way leads all the way back to Alfriston, but I prefer beyond the gate to turn right, along the fence, and immediately bending left along it, directly above the steep escarpment. You'll see the **Long Man of Wilmington** (page 208) from above – not the familiar view, and it makes little sense, but shows how ingenious its creators were in dealing with foreshortening and working on an extremely steep site. Beyond it, **Wilmington Priory** is in view at the near end of Wilmington village.

Soon, you rejoin the South Downs Way, which bends to the left, down to the left of a covered reservoir. ▶

Alfriston, the Cuckmere Valley & Lullington Heath (continued)

6 ◀ At the road, either take the South Downs Way opposite (it's quicker to cut a corner by crossing the stile on the left after 50yds and then crossing the field directly towards Alfriston church, finally crossing through a hedgerow belt and turning right at a T-junction of paths), or if you want to see the almost comically tiny **Lullington Church** turn left along the road and then right on a path after 300yds, past the church (up to the right). Carry on down the path, across another road, along the path opposite and slightly to the right and to the river at Alfriston.

---

of Rathfinny, one of the newest additions and the largest vineyard in the county, capable of producing a million bottles of sparkling wine a year. Now that its first bottles are on sale, a new chapter in England's history of viticulture has begun, creating tangible excitement in the Cuckmere Valley.

Mark and Sarah Driver bought the 600-acre estate in 2010, a year after he had given up his City career and embarked on a two-year viticulture course at Plumpton College. Two years later, the first vines had been planted, and local tradespeople engaged to take on a multitude of tasks.

Their first relatively modest harvest was in 2014 – just 5,500 bottles, explained their winemaker Jonathan Médard. Jonathan hails from Épernay, at the heart of the French champagne country, and has worked in vineyards in California. 'After harvesting the grapes, the first step is to create a still wine. Yeasts are added to the juice in stainless still tanks, and they convert the natural sugars into alcohol and carbon dioxide (CO_2). This is our "base wine". Then, we add sugar and yeasts while transferring this wine into bottles to initiate a second fermentation. The CO_2 released during this fermentation is trapped in the bottle, creating the fizz. After consuming all the sugars, the yeasts die and will eventually break down. This is called autolysis: it releases flavour compounds in the wine and we get the flavour profile we're looking for. At this stage in the process, our wine has been ageing in the bottle for one year and it's already tasting very nice, but after three years the wine will have even more complexity. This is precisely where we want to go.'

One very special aspect of Rathfinny is its bewitching setting, tucked into the Downs, with the Cuckmere meanders and the sea in the distance. The estate, which is B Corp certified, offers seasonal tours. There's also a Cellar Door shop, which is open all year (plus a posh modern British restaurant and a pared-back B&B, both rather pricey for what they offer). There are waymarked walking trails to explore, linked to the valley's public footpaths from High and Over, Bo Peep or Alfriston.

Drusillas Park

Near Berwick BN26 5QS ℘ 01323 874100 ⊘ drusillas.co.uk; train to Berwick (East Coastway Line, Brighton–Hastings) then 1.2-mile walk; Compass and Cuckmere Buses (several routes from nearby towns and villages; limited services)

It would be hard to find any child or indeed accompanying adult who wasn't fascinated by something at this particularly intimate-scale zoo and playground. Mice live in a Mouse House like a doll's house, tiny monkeys look as curious about the visitors as the visitors are about them and children can go through a tunnel to look at the meerkats through a clear dome right inside their enclosure, and greet the ring-tailed lemurs. Elsewhere there are otters, capybaras, sloths, red pandas, macaques and penguins, a mini railway and some very innovative play areas. Drusillas has an accent on learning too – at key holiday times there's a rogues' gallery of confiscated illegally traded objects like crocodile bags and snakeskin shoes – and they carefully place labels at child level.

"Children can go through a tunnel to look at the meerkats through a clear dome right inside their enclosure."

As a family attraction Drusillas is cherished by many locals, quite a few of whom have season tickets. Perhaps the most enriching Slow experience of all is to become **Keeper for a Day**, where with expert supervision you get to help out with the cleaning and feeding. It's very hands on, mucking out straw for pigs, scattering feed for the meerkats and chucking sprats for the penguins. Not surprisingly such a close-up encounter of the animal kind is hugely popular and the slots get booked up months ahead.

Visitors are welcome to bring their own picnics, but Drusillas also has several family-friendly cafés – a far cry from its earliest incarnation, when it was a simple thatched tea room named after the founder's wife. On the way out, you see the 1920s original and can just about imagine its old mock-Tudor chintziness. Look out too for (or perhaps avoid) the seriously purse-emptying menagerie of toy animals that awaits in the gift shop.

High & Over

The road south from Alfriston climbs up past the viewpoint known as High and Over – which sometimes gets garbled into 'Hindover'. A very special view over the Cuckmere's meanders extends from here. Just below where you stand is the **Hindover White Horse**, seen to its best effect from across the valley near Lullington. The horse was carved in 1838 by the Pagden brothers – James Pagden of Alfriston was also a Sussex county cricketer and beekeeper who pioneered a method of artificial swarming. He made rather more of bees than he did of cricket: though his playing career spanned 23 years, he played only two first-class matches, one in 1835 for the MCC, and one in 1858 for Sussex; his four innings featured not out = 1, highest score = 1, total runs = 1, and he didn't bowl a ball. His former house is in the main street in Alfriston. He was the author of the snappily titled *£70 a year, How I Make it by MY BEES and How a Cottager or Others May Soon do the Same*.

¶¶ FOOD & DRINK

Alfriston Village Store Waterloo Sq, BN26 5UE. Open daily, this well-stocked grocer, deli and general store sells fresh bread, pasties, sandwiches, cheese and local produce: useful fuel for walkers and cyclists.

Badgers Tea House North St, BN26 5UG ℰ 01323 871336 ♦ badgersteahouse.com. Sip tea from bone china and tuck into a light lunch or home-baked cakes and scones in this delightful 500-year-old cottage (which was a bakery from the early 18th century until 1933, so they're continuing a fine tradition). The tranquil, pretty walled garden at the back has an awning for shelter and shade.

The George Inn High St, BN26 5SY ℰ 01323 870319 ♦ thegeorge-alfriston.com. Supremely pleasant old village inn, with oak beams, log fires and a beer garden. Though largely a dining pub, with an interesting menu using local produce, you'll often see locals gathered round the bar for a drink and a chat. There are guest rooms upstairs.

Ye Olde Smugglers Inne Waterloo Sq, BN26 5UE ℰ 01323 870241. Refreshingly unprecious 14th-century village local right by the worn stump of the market cross. Pub nosh, decent local beer and cider including Harvey's, Long Man and Sea Cider; garden; rooms upstairs. Note the vintage, utterly lovely Cyclists' Touring Club sign outside.

18 FRISTON FOREST

B&H bus 12 (Brighton–Eastbourne; frequent service) then half-mile walk; Cuckmere Buses (several routes from nearby towns and villages; limited services)

You can wander where you like (subject to closure during felling operations) along the paths and rides of this forest, one of the few substantially tree-covered expanses of the East Sussex South Downs. Trees were planted here from 1926 over an underground reservoir constructed a few years earlier to serve Eastbourne on the understanding that planting a forest on top would keep the groundwater clean. That measure turned out to be quite unnecessary, but the forest has become a prized amenity, and is now managed for leisure use. This is a calming, sheltered place that is lovely to wander into when the weather is unruly, and it also makes a satisfyingly contrasting inland leg to the circular walk along the Seven Sisters. It isn't bland plantation-style uniformity by any means, with a nice mix of beech, Scots pine and Corsican pine on the whole, and fritillary butterflies, adders, roe deer and badgers.

"The forest is a calming, sheltered place that is lovely to wander into when the weather is unruly."

Useful starting points are from Seven Sisters Country Park on the southwest corner and from car parks on the Friston–Jevington road to the east. Colour-coded **walking trails** lace the forest. With enough serious ups and downs, **mountain bikers** are kept very happy here: 'If you can find your way to the downhill track, the descent is a real buzz, with jumps and drops on the way down' pronounces an online guide for off-roaders.

Surrounded by the forest, the remote-feeling village of **Westdean** seems to be a complete retreat from the modern world. It's primarily a former estate, so many of the buildings are converted barns and the like, and a striking ancient dovecote has been restored. The Church of All Saints is partly Norman and is the oldest church in the valley; next to it stands a rectory dating from around 1280, possibly built by monks from Wilmington Priory, and is one of the longest continually inhabited houses in Britain. A 9th-century chronicler recorded Alfred the Great's palace to have been situated here. There's no parking in the village, so walk up the signposted route from Exceat car park near the Seven Sisters Visitor Centre. On the east side of the forest, **Jevington Church** contains a stone carving (dating from around AD950) of Christ stabbing a beast, depicting the triumph of Good over Evil.

19 CUCKMERE HAVEN

B&H bus 12 (Brighton–Eastbourne; frequent service) or Cuckmere Buses (several routes from Berwick, Charleston, Eastbourne, Lewes, Seaford, Wilmington; limited services) to Exceat

Cuckmere Haven, east of Seaford and at the western end of the Seven Sisters, is the only estuary in Sussex to be undeveloped. Its gorgeous curves – the meandering course of the River Cuckmere complemented by its grassy banks and the soft hillsides all around – have inspired countless artists and photographers, notably the painter Eric Ravilious.

During World War II, a mock town with the valley lit up was created here, to dupe enemy bombers into thinking this was Newhaven, on which they set their coordinates. This resulted in them dropping bombs east of central London. Other wartime relics that have survived include pillboxes and concrete 'dragons' teeth' tank traps in the form of concrete blocks just inland from the shingle beach. At the Seven Sisters end of the tank traps is the D-shaped foundation of an anti-aircraft battery. One of the pillboxes is now a bat hibernaculum, while another is an unusual cylindrical type and was restored. One visitor, whom staff at the country park met not so long ago, had been on duty here (when in the Home Guard aged 14) in one of the pillboxes with a World War I veteran. Together they formed a force of two, ensconced with a thermos flask and waiting for the enemy, with the master plan: 'When the Boche arrive, we'll set the guns up and fire every bullet we've got down the valley, then run like hell and hide in the forest'.

Since it's globally famous and easy to reach by bus or car via the main south-coast road, a steady stream of visitors arrives, especially in summer, to stroll along the river, potter on the beach, or linger over drinks or lunch. There are bikes to hire and an activity centre for those wishing to have a go at kayaking or SUP on the Cuckmere's invitingly smooth waters.

¶¶ FOOD & DRINK

Cuckmere Inn Exceat BN25 4AB ⌂ vintageinn.co.uk. Though a chain pub, this is a reliable choice for an outdoor beer or hearty lunch – and you can't argue with the location, right beside Exceat bridge, with views across the protected estuary.

Saltmarsh Farmhouse Café Exceat BN25 4AD ⌂ saltmarshfarmhouse.co.uk. Charming little café serving cooked breakfasts and light lunches such as porridge, smashed avo with eggs or shakshuka in a pretty courtyard. There are five delightful guest rooms upstairs.

A SMUGGLERS' COAST

The cliffs hereabouts have a heady history of illicit money-making in centuries past. Locals made a good income plundering the contents of wrecked shipping driven against the cliffs: these folk included the Seaford Shags, a very rough lot who might well have finished off any survivors before helping themselves to the swag. Cuckmere Haven was long the hub of smuggling activities for duty-free or illegal goods. Typically cargoes of brandy and gin were brought close to the shore in barrels known as 'half-ankers' and then retrieved at low tide. The preventive officers had the desperate job of trying to stop the trade, and were hopelessly outnumbered and often vulnerable to bribery. The notoriously violent Alfriston Gang wrought havoc in the area, using the Cuckmere River to bring goods into the village for distribution inland. Things ended for the gang in the 1830s when its leader, Stanton Collins, was transported to Australia for sheep rustling.

Seven Sisters Visitor Centre Exceat BN25 4AD ⬙ sevensisters.org.uk. This beautifully presented national park information centre has a shop selling local beer and cider, and a café counter for coffee, sandwiches and snacks.

20 THE SEVEN SISTERS

⬙ sevensisters.org.uk. Access to the clifftop via the South Downs Way from Birling Gap or from near Cuckmere Haven; B&H bus 12 (Brighton–Eastbourne; frequent service)

One of the glorious things about this highly cherished stretch of completely unspoilt coast is how it never quite looks the same from one day to the next, thanks to natural lighting effects. In spring sunshine it can seem surreally bright, and the cliffs can take on a pinkish hue at sunset, while under sea fog the full septet partially disappears into an ominous grey nothing. The clifftop walk is five-star stuff, as are the views from Seaford Head (page 192) and along the foot of the cliffs from Cuckmere Haven. As one of the undoubted glories of the British coast, it is no surprise that great numbers come to walk here.

The 'Sisters' are a wavy series of 500ft cliff-edge summits, with dry valleys in between. Once this chalky landscape extended across to France, until some 8,500 years ago when the English Channel broke through, leaving a sheer wall of chalk. Sea erosion is constantly chopping the coast back quite a lot more (though no-one knows exactly how much) and intermittently much larger chunks fall away. Unlike the not very White Cliffs of Dover, the unprotected Sisters and neighbouring Beachy Head really are white – a result of constant eroding back by wave

ROCK POOLING BENEATH THE SEVEN SISTERS

Robin, a ranger at the Seven Sisters Country Park, pointed me in the direction of the joys of low-tide rock pooling and encountering a constantly changing microcosm. 'Find a good-size rock pool and you'll typically see crabs, bearded rock things that use their bearded bits as sensory organs. You might find strawberry sea anemones (which look like strawberries) or red and green-blobbed beadlet anemones, which grow big – they're global warming indicators. Devil's crabs – or velvet swimming crabs – are so called because they have red eyes – they're the most vicious things you'll find, and might swim across a rock pool and chase you off. My favourite are porcelain crabs – these live on the underside of rocks, are very hairy and are the size of a little fingernail;

they're slow and elusive; most people miss them completely. I also like seaweed – several types are edible and a lot of them beautiful. I've made very tasty sugar kelp crisps and carrageen mousse from the stuff.'

A few tips: watch the tides, and be extra careful on the slippery rocks; summer is particularly good as there is greater diversity of rock-pool life. If you have a bucket for looking at what you find, make sure there is water in it. Never prise anything off a rock, such as a limpet, and replace any stones you've turned over. Access points to the shore are Cuckmere Haven, Birling Gap and at the east side of Seaford Head. Periodically there are guided rock-pooling events in the Seven Sisters Country Park.

action and through fissures in the bedrock. After a cliff fall, the debris protects the cliff edge until it's eroded or washed away – during which time caves form, then fissures form through the rocks and the caves collapse. You can often see evidence of recent rockfalls on the shore beneath the patently crumbling cliffs.

Why they are called Sisters isn't that clear, but it may be a name dreamt up by sailors, who tended to give female names to quite a lot of things. There are indeed seven, though some reckon seven and a half, and as the sea is eroding back extra ones will develop: we'll eventually have eight.

There are nine different habitats here, including chalk grassland, vegetated shingle, saltmarsh, scrub and intertidal zone (or foreshore). Most unusually for this part of the world, the estuary has a lagoon. Viper's bugloss, blue and pink and growing to spectacular heights, is

◄ 1 The curves of the River Cuckmere have long inspired artists. 2 The striking chalk cliffs of the Seven Sisters. 3 Enjoy a clifftop walk along Beachy Head. 4 Peaceful Friston Forest offers a satisfying contrast to the wild coast.

Beachy Head & the Seven Sisters: variations on a theme

❋ OS Explorer OL25; start: East Dean ♀ TV556977; three or eight miles; fairly energetic, over downland & through forest. **Loos**: at Birling Gap & Exceat. **Refreshments**: Tiger Inn & the tea room and deli at East Dean, Cuckmere Inn and cafés at Exceat.

Plenty of permutations exist here, from easy saunters lasting half an hour to more demanding explorations taking most of the day. Getting lost is not a problem, except in Friston Forest, where you'll certainly need to follow an OS map. You have to pay to use car parks at Alfriston, Birling Gap and Exceat, but you can park free a bit further east at East Dean. Bus access is excellent, with great views: the 12 along the A259 and the 13X Beachy Head loop are quite outstanding.

The map here and the directions below show a long (eight-mile) walk taking in all the Sisters and a short (three-mile) circular walk that starts the same way then cuts off at Crowlink, giving a walk along the eastern Sisters. Both start from the free car park in East Dean.

1 Turn right out of the car park to leave it on the village side, and emerge on the village green by the Tiger Inn; go up the green and turn right on the road in front of the Thai Terre restaurant and delicatessen. After 50yds, where the road bends right, turn left on a concrete track, past a National Trust sign for Farrer Hall, through a gate. Walk up the field to the top, then through a gate and Friston churchyard, at the far end of which emerge by the road junction.

2 **For the three-mile walk**, turn left along the road to Crowlink, past the small car park and then down the track past Crowlink House itself. There used to be coastguard cottages here, like at Seaford Head and Birling Gap, but these were demolished because of erosion. A very wet and windy excavation near the cliff edge in 2015 unearthed walls and a fireplace, as well as bullets, buttons and clay pipes – the bullets dating to World War II when the Canadian army used the remains of the building for target practice. From there, drop across the grassy slopes by any route towards the clifftops and turn left along the top of the Seven Sisters. Pick up the walk again at point **5**.

For the eight-mile walk, cross over the main road by the pond and take the signposted woodland path opposite on the far side of the grass triangle, immediately bearing right, dropping and soon crossing a field towards a stile and gate in the bottom corner. Go over a road, up steps and take the obvious path ahead across another field. Turn left on the metalled road (or follow the path immediately parallel on its right side), and left again as the route skirts two sides of a rectangle around **Friston Place**. Then when the driveway joins from the left from Friston Place itself, turn right up a track (signposted Westdean, blue waymarker) leading

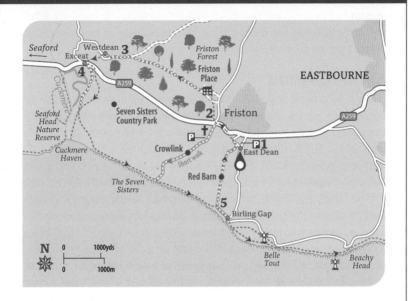

through the forest. Keep forward in a straight line all the way, ignoring all side turns; you later go along a field edge then re-enter the forest. Finally, as the track drops, keep forward as the left fork goes through a barrier, and descend through another barrier, past a cottage.

3 Enter Westdean village. Follow the road to the left around the village (though you may like to look at the church and medieval rectory to the right first), then by Pond Cottage and a phone box turn left on a track, up a flight of steps (signposted Cuckmere Haven). At the top, cross the steps over the wall and drop down to the car park and buildings at Exceat.

4 Cross (with great care) the A259 and carry on along the Cuckmere valley to the sea – either along the concrete track or closer to the river. Where the concrete track bends left at a signpost, carry on through the gate and along the left-hand fence (signposted to the beach). Shortly before the beach, a steep path leads up to the left on to the **Seven Sisters**, but first carry on a short distance and explore the beach at **Cuckmere Haven** ahead. After visiting Cuckmere Haven, climb the aforementioned path and follow it near the cliff edge of the Seven Sisters for two miles. A prominent red-roofed barn (the **Red Barn**) later comes into view inland.

5 Just above the hamlet of Birling Gap by the last Sister, turn inland over a stile, rising up over the open grassland (there's no defined path on the ground) and past the Red Barn (which ▶

Beachy Head & the Seven Sisters: variations on a theme (continued)

◀ comes back into view), keeping alongside the dwarf woodland on the right. Some 400yds later, find a signposted path dropping to the right into East Dean. At the first houses, go through a gate and follow the road into the village centre by the green.

CLIFFTOP ALTERNATIVES

Instead of following the circular routes I have described here you might prefer to follow the clifftops all the way and to return by bus. For the **main clifftop walk along the South Downs Way** (8½ miles), start in Eastbourne, and walk up to Beachy Head, then along the cliffs westward, past Belle Tout lighthouse, and down to Birling Gap. This part of the walk is really much better in this direction, as otherwise it's an uphill slog west to east up to Beachy Head. Then carry on from the track behind the loo block at Birling Gap, past a line of houses and along all of the Seven Sisters. From the last Sister you have a choice of either dropping down to the Cuckmere Valley near the beach at Cuckmere Haven and following the obvious concrete track to Exceat, or taking the down-and-up route of the South Downs Way. At Exceat is the South Downs National Park Visitor Centre, with loos, a snack counter and a café; from there frequent buses run to Eastbourne, Seaford or Brighton. An **extension to Seaford rail station** can be made by taking the waterside path along the straight cut of the Cuckmere to Exceat Bridge, and then heading back to the coast on the west side of Cuckmere Haven. Then climb up Seaford Head, and follow the cliff edge (looking behind for the most famous view of all along the length of the Seven Sisters), and drop down into Seaford.

a common sight on the clifftop turf, alongside chalk milkwort, bastard toadflax and round-headed rampion, and the downland supports a range of butterflies, including five species of blue and the marbled white. This is very good birdwatching territory, especially for spring and autumn migrants, waders and winter ducks.

21 EAST DEAN

B&H bus 12 (Brighton–Eastbourne; frequent service) then half-mile walk

With its free car park and idyllic village green, East Dean (just off the A259 east of Friston) makes the perfect point to start a walk on to the Seven Sisters or Belle Tout, and there's access to Crowlink for a shorter stroll over two or three Sisters. Fronting on to the green are the Tiger Inn and a useful coffee shop, the Hiker's Rest.

Above the village, a walk up the grassy field known as Hobbs Eares leads to Friston's **Church of St Simon and St Jude**, with its Saxon tower. Its ingenious centrally pivoted tapsel gate – a design seemingly unique to Sussex – is designed both to keep cattle out and to make it easier for coffin bearers to get through. The first such gate is thought to have been made by one John Tapsel of Mountfield, near Battle; other examples are found in Pyecombe (near Clayton), Kingston-near-Lewes, East Dean and Coombes (near Shoreham-by-Sea). In the churchyard, a simple (presumably 20th-century) grave marks an unknown body, marked starkly 'Washed ashore', close to four World War II graves to similarly anonymous naval sailors. Inside the church are Tudor monuments to the local Selwyn family, and a memorial to the composer Frank Bridge, a teacher of Benjamin Britten, who died in Eastbourne in 1941; look too for graffiti in the porch, scratched by medieval pilgrims. **Friston Pond**, just above the church and by the A259, was the first pond in the country to be designated an ancient monument.

Fields in this valley are unusual for East Sussex in that they have flint walls. These were created by a landowner as a local employment scheme after the Napoleonic wars.

¶¶ FOOD & DRINK

East Dean's village hall hosts a **farmers' market** on Wed mornings.

Deli on the Green Upper St, East Dean BN20 0BY ⏱ deli-onthegreen.com. Well-stocked deli and coffee bar with a few café tables, gazing across East Dean's perfect, cottage-lined village green.

Hiker's Rest Tea Room East Dean BN20 0DR ✆ 01323 423733. Opposite the Tiger Inn, this is a casual spot for light refreshments, with a gift shop selling local produce, art and crafts.

The Tiger Inn East Dean BN20 0DA ✆ 01323 423209 ⏱ beachyhead.org.uk. This highly photogenic pub is a focal point of the village green, decked with flowers in summer and with a row of inviting tables outside. Inside, it's ancient feeling, with a stove in an inglenook, well-used old wooden furniture and a stuffed tiger's head. The bar serves decent food and local real ales such as Long Man. Upstairs, there are five pleasant guest bedrooms.

22 BIRLING GAP & BEACHY HEAD

B&H bus 13X (Brighton–Eastbourne)

The wind-battered hamlet of **Birling Gap** marks the point at the eastern end of the Seven Sisters, south of East Dean. Steps lead down to the shore by the row of coastguard cottages; like the rest of the hamlet they are threatened with collapse as the cliffs become undermined by weathering. The decision has been made – not without local controversy – not to bolster them up with hugely costly and unsightly sea defences. The beach is a wild, rugged place, good for rock-pool browsing and with sublime views of the cliffs from below; the submerged jagged flinty rocks make beach shoes a good idea if you are swimming.

"The beach is a wild, rugged place, good for rock-pool browsing and with sublime views of the cliffs from below."

Eastwards from here, it is a short stroll past **Belle Tout**, the former lighthouse that perches near the edge of the cliffs: it was built in 1832 and decommissioned 70 years later. In 1999 it was famously moved back on rails from the cliff edge by a few yards, an operation that was seen on TV across the world. Now a very superior and characterful B&B ($\mathcal{O}$ belletout.co.uk), the lighthouse was used for target practice by Canadians in World War II, which didn't do it a great deal of good; it was restored as a home in the 1950s, hence its strange hotchpotch of ages and styles. In the 1980s the BBC filmed the miniseries of Fay Weldon's novel *The Life and Loves of a She-Devil* there. Beneath it on the inland side, a striking **prehistoric earthwork** runs near the foot of the hill. It's very little understood, and more of it has fallen into the sea, but we know it enclosed an early Bronze Age (Beaker) settlement and would have been one of the largest prehistoric enclosures in the country. In the 1980s a cliff fall exposed a shaft about 3ft across in the chalk, with footholds, running right down through the cliff and into the bedrock (its base is now on the foreshore and being investigated for survival of environmental material in the waterlogged fill). Pottery found within it dated the shaft to the Bronze Age. This feature would have been at the centre of the Belle Tout settlement and possibly used for rituals; it would have been a daunting test climbing up or down.

Continuing eastwards, the South Downs Way touches on a bend in the road where you can look down to the vertigo-inducing view of Beachy Head Lighthouse, at sea level beneath **Beachy Head**, which at 530ft is the tallest sheer chalk cliff in Britain. In exceptionally clear conditions the view can extend as far as Dungeness in Kent to the east and westwards to Culver Cliff on the Isle of Wight. The lighthouse itself was built of some 3,500 granite blocks imported from Cornwall, which were cut to size and lowered from the clifftop. It was painted with its distinctive red and white stripes in the 1950s. Trinity House declared it redundant, but a big campaign to raise the £27,000 for repainting the much-admired landmark was successful and in 2013 a team of five, including two abseilers, spent three weeks doing the honours with the paint pots.

At the time of writing, a new arts, education and cultural centre, **Black Robin Farm**, was in the pipeline. Run by Eastbourne's Towner art gallery and situated around 1½ miles north of Beachy Head, it will exhibit art inspired by the chalk landscapes of the South Downs.

TELLING TALES

Writers' imaginations have long been fired by the landscapes and atmospheres of this supremely varied county: the novels written in or about Sussex, or both, are equally varied. In Lewes, the precocious Daisy Ashford, aged nine, produced the unconsciously comic *The Young Visiters* [sic] in 1892, beginning with the words 'Mr Salteena was an elderly man of forty-two'. H G Wells went to school in Midhurst and set the opening scene of *The Invisible Man* (1897) in the village of Iping; Kipling made his final home at Bateman's, in the Weald, which inspired the historical fantasy stories of *Puck of Pook's Hill* (1906). Meanwhile, in Hastings, socialist Robert Tressell was enduring the life of desperate working poverty he portrayed in *The Ragged-Trousered Philanthropists* (1914) – this became hugely influential in the Labour movement, although he did not live to see it.

A cluster of novelists settled in Rye in the early 20th century: among them master stylist Henry James, his friend E F Benson, who wrote the delicate social comedies of the *Mapp and Lucia* series (1920–31), and Radclyffe Hall, pioneering lesbian author of *The Well of Loneliness* (1928).

Between the wars, the proceeds of *Mrs Dalloway* (1925) paid for indoor plumbing at Virginia Woolf's country home at Rodmell, while from the safety of Hampstead, Stella Gibbons satirised the rural Gothic genre by setting *Cold Comfort Farm* (1932), ludicrously, in the Sussex Downs. A A Milne immortalised his son Christopher Robin and some of his toys' adventures in Ashdown Forest in the *Winnie-the-Pooh* stories (1926–7). Brighton's disreputable side is depicted in Graham Greene's *Brighton Rock* (1938), though the razor-slashing at the racecourse is said to be based on an incident at Lewes.

More mobile novelist lifestyles were probably the reason why such a concentration of creativity did not re-form after World War II, but Lewes makes an unexpected late appearance in John Fowles' *The Collector* (1963), as the town where the novel's chilling central character does his shopping.

23 COMBE HILL

No nearby public transport

A grand viewpoint marking the northeastern culmination of the Downs, this sprawling hill is most easily reached via Butts Lane, which climbs from Willingdon, a suburb of Eastbourne, or walk up from Jevington village; a car park at the top makes for a straightforward stroll along its flat top – a favourite ground for dog walkers and kite fliers. The grassy humps mark what is termed a Neolithic causewayed enclosure, one of the very earliest constructions in Sussex (built around 3200BC), surrounded by a ditch in a series of segments, with access points or breaks through it. Such features are of unknown purpose, but this is thought to be a place of ritual rather than a dwelling. At the summit is a prehistoric tumulus, whose sunken top tells of digging-out by treasure seekers.

Look out for a small but prominent dressed stone by the track up from the west side, from the downland village of Jevington: it looks ancient at first sight but is actually a sad remnant, which somehow made it up here, of Barclay's Bank in Eastbourne, bombed to bits in World War II.

The award-winning Slow Travel series from Bradt Guides

Over 20 regional guides across Britain.
See the full list at bradtguides.com/slowtravel.

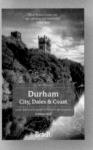

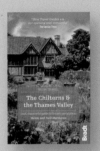

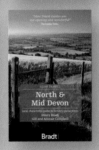

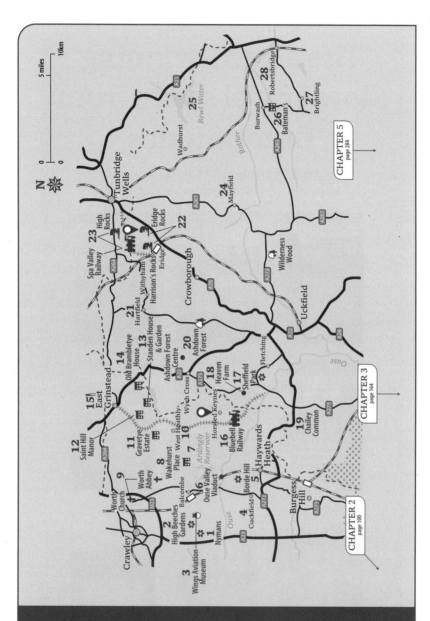

THE WESTERN HIGH WEALD

4

THE WESTERN
HIGH WEALD

East Sussex doesn't geographically extend north to south for any great distance, but this northern strip of sandstone scenery feels a world away from the more visited South Downs and coast. You need to get high up to piece together this remote-feeling and strangely impenetrable landscape of copses, hammer ponds, larger woodlands and sandstone outcrops. From churchyards such as those at Turners Hill, West Hoathly and Cuckfield you look over the tree tops towards the South Downs, bare-sloped and orderly.

You can get similarly grand views from some of the big estates that harbour world-class gardens such as Standen – itself my favourite Arts and Crafts house open to public view – and Borde Hill. Other great horticultural creations are more tucked away and secretive. Come here in late spring or early summer and the rhododendrons and azaleas put on a dazzling show. Nymans perhaps outdoes them all for sheer theatricality. Wakehurst Place and Sheffield Park are two vast and justifiably famed National Trust gardens. The latter, also celebrated for its stupendous autumn foliage, is most memorably reached by a vintage steam train on the Bluebell Railway. Among other architectural hallmarks, Horsham slates, hipped gables, medieval 'Wealden halls', pantiles and timber frames are seen in a plethora of ancient buildings in numerous villages – among them Mayfield, Wadhurst, Burwash and Rotherfield.

The term 'High Weald' isn't widely understood, even by some of its own residents. **High Weald Area of Outstanding Natural Beauty** is defined by its geology (sandstone, laid down during the dinosaur era 130 million years ago as what are known as the Hastings Beds) rather than its altitude. It's a rough triangle of land spilling into Kent and extending from just outside Horsham in the west to Hastings and Rye in the east, and bounded on its north side by the peripheries of

East Grinstead, Tunbridge Wells and Tenterden. It was never an area of aristocratic estates or rich farmland, unlike West Sussex: iron-ore extraction and smelting, seasonal swine grazing, and woodland activities such as charcoal making and forestry were more the norm in medieval times in this less fertile terrain, and the area has essentially changed its look very little in 700 years – effectively a rare survival of a medieval landscape.

The High Weald has numerous identifying features. Much of the tree cover is ancient woodland, preserving archaeological features such as raised boundary banks and charcoal-burning platforms. These wildlife-rich areas of woodland and the numerous unimproved meadows are found far more commonly than across the rest of the country: 70% of woodland in the High Weald is classified as ancient (that is, in existence at least since 1600), as compared to just 19% across the whole of Britain. Ferns and wild garlic are ancient woodland indicators. Oaks are the predominant tree species. Here and there you'll find 'gills' – steep-sided, fast-flowing streams carving out a course through ravines – the only part of southeast England that they exist. Fields often tend to be small and irregularly shaped – the result of peasants hacking out by hand little clearings in the Wealden forest. It wasn't a rich area, but somewhere folk eked out a rudimentary life grazing pigs or harvesting from the forest.

Some parts hereabouts have a distinctly un-Sussex look. **Ashdown Forest** is a large lowland heath that has almost a moorland character, carefully preserved by conservators for many years and almost a mini national park in itself. Wandering deer stray on to the lonely roads, clumps of Scots pines punctuate a skyline that might be in northern England, and *Winnie-the-Pooh* aficionados tackle a daunting maze of paths in search of literary landmarks. Further east **Eridge Rocks** is one among several rock outcrops in the vicinity that wouldn't look too out of place in the Peak District, although the luxuriant growths of bamboo hint at something more exotic.

GETTING AROUND

TRAIN & BUS

Travelling without a car is feasible, but rarely straightforward. Railway journeys won't get you close to many places of interest, and bus trips

ℹ TOURIST INFORMATION

Burgess Hill 96 Church Walk ✆ 01444 238202
East Grinstead Library Buildings, West St ✆ 01342 410121

tend to be long and convoluted. If you're car free, you'll probably find yourself combining the two.

The gardens that are most accessible by **train** include Borde Hill, which is within walking distance of Haywards Heath on the Brighton Main Line from London to Brighton and Lewes, and Sheffield Park, which is at the southern end of the Bluebell Railway, linked in turn to the main Oxted Line at East Grinstead. To reach Sheffield Park from elsewhere in the county, however, you'll need a car, unless you're travelling on a Saturday or Sunday, when Compass Bus 121 runs there from Lewes and North Chailey.

Bus routes to gardens include Metrobus 272 from Crawley to Brighton, which passes Wakehurst Place, and Metrobus 271 or 273 from Crawley, Brighton and Burgess Hill to Handcross, for Nymans and High Beeches. All three run several times a day, though less frequently on Sundays.

For other **attractions**, useful bus routes include Metrobus 84 (several daily Mon–Sat) from Crawley, Three Bridges and East Grinstead to West Hoathly and Standen, and Brighton and Hove Regency Route Bus 29 (three hourly Mon–Sat, less frequent on Sun) linking Brighton and Lewes to Tunbridge Wells via Eridge Green, for Eridge and the Spa Valley Railway. Compass Bus 231 (several daily, Mon–Sat) runs to Bateman's from Heathfield station.

Ashdown Forest is not at all well served; your best bet may be to take Metrobus 270 (hourly; less frequent on Sun) from Haywards Heath or East Grinstead to Wych Cross, at the junction of the A275 and A22, and explore the paths immediately south of the A22. Alternatively, Compass Bus 261 (several daily, Mon–Sat) travels to Wych Cross from East Grinstead, Forest Row and Uckfield.

Useful **railway stations for walks** are Eridge on the Oxted Line (for a walk taking in Eridge Rocks and Harrison's Rocks; page 270) and Balcombe on the Brighton Main Line, from where there are some excellent possibilities eastwards taking in Wakehurst Place, Ardingly Reservoir and the Ouse Valley Viaduct.

CYCLING

Very good cycling is here in abundance, but so are the hills. If you keep clear of the main roads, there are plenty of quiet lanes north of Haywards Heath and Uckfield. Note that off-road cycling isn't permitted on Ashdown Forest, except on the few bridleways that exist. The countryside north of Heathfield is outstanding too, but there is a lot of up and down in and out of small valleys. A much easier route is the Forest Way, part of National Cycle Network route 21, shared between cyclists, horseriders and walkers, and running ten miles along a disused railway track between Groombridge and East Grinstead, via Hartfield and Forest Row.

WEALDEN GARDENS & THE FOREST RIDGE

That such bucolic wonders should exist just a few miles from Gatwick Airport and Crawley is one of the paradoxes of the southeast. Within touching distance are a host of five-star gardens, the quaintest timewarp in the form of the Bluebell Railway, the astounding brick bravado of the Ouse Valley Viaduct, the Arts and Crafts delights at Standen and some very strange witchy goings-on at the Priest House in West Hoathly. So many people must whizz down the nearby M23/A23 without the faintest notion of what they are missing.

1 NYMANS

Handcross RH17 6EB ✆ 01444 405250; National Trust; Metrobus 271 or 273 (Brighton–Crawley; several daily Mon–Sat, less frequent Sun)

A more romantic garden than this would be hard to envisage. Located just east of the A23 at Handcross and some 500ft above sea level, on light acid loam, it is a secretive 30-acre series of spaces that entices the visitor round from one surprise to the next, very much more intimate than the likes of Wakehurst Place or Sheffield Park. In late spring and early summer its colour is quite startling. Paths continue into the more naturalistic park and stately pinetum and woodlands. Events held around the year, such as workshops and family activities, make Nymans worth visiting at any time of year, though it's worth avoiding the busier times as parking can be difficult.

It was begun by Ludwig Messel, who acquired the property in 1890 and brought in plants from around the world – he made a heather garden, sunken garden, raised pergola walk and pinetum, and planted azaleas and rhododendrons; his work was continued from 1916 by his son Leonard who planted the notable collection of rare magnolias and eucryphias and invested in plant-collecting expeditions in the Far East and South America, while his wife Maud created the rose garden, with old-fashioned varieties. Leonard also rebuilt the Victorian house in neo-Jacobean style only for it to be largely destroyed by fire, leaving all but one end a roofless ruin that has become part of the landscape in itself, complemented by sculptural topiary. After the National Trust took over in 1954, the Messels continued to oversee operations. Plans are afoot to create a new garden within the ruins of the great hall, though there's enough of the Messels' house intact to give an idea of the lifestyle of Anne, Countess of Rosse, who resided there during the 1980s.

2 HIGH BEECHES GARDENS

High Beeches Ln, Handcross RH17 6HQ ✆ 01444 400589 ⌖ highbeeches.com ⏱ late Mar–end Oct 13.00–17.00 Thu–Tue; Metrobus 271 or 273 (Brighton–Crawley; several daily, less frequent on Sun)

'He's seriously glamorous – there's just something about him; he simply glows on a sunny day,' said Sarah Bray, owner of this glorious 27-acre woodland and water garden just east of Nymans. She was pointing out an acer, a riot of autumn colour in mid-October, that to her stands out as a favourite. From the top with its vista to Devil's Dyke on the South Downs, the site slopes down through an intricate series of semi-open spaces between the trees; there are rhododendrons, champion trees, rarities from the Far East, a magnolia garden, redwoods and a pond reflecting giant rhubarb. 'We also have one of the best acid wildflower meadows in the southeast. It hasn't been cultivated in at least 60 years; we just mow it once a year. In late spring it's a mass of orchids, daisies, vetch, hay rattle and cowslips.'

Nothing remains of the original house that was reduced to a shell in 1942 after a Canadian plane carrying propaganda leaflets bound for Nazi Germany crashed into one of its chimneys. Sarah's parents, who live next door, bought High Beeches at auction in 1966, after the death of Colonel Loder; he created this, the first of the local gardens laid out by the Loder family – the others are Leonardslee and Wakehurst Place. As well as the landscape, the open spaces between the trees and the views, she rates the sense of continuity here as one of the garden's special attributes – Eric Stockton was the gardener here from 1927, and after the auction he was re-engaged and carried on until his death in 1979.

3 WINGS AVIATION MUSEUM

Brantridge Ln, nr Balcombe RH17 6JT ✆ 07769 688064 ⌨ wingsmuseum.co.uk ⊙ Tue–Sun; Handcross Community Bus (from Burgess Hill, Haywards Heath and Horsham; three times week); Balcombe railway station 2½ miles

The passion project of brothers Daniel and Kevin Hunt, this World War II museum is crammed with 1940s planes, equipment, uniforms and memorabilia, salvaged from old airfields in East Anglia and elsewhere. Among the exhibits are air-raid shelters, bombs and recreations of crash sites featuring rare, battle-scarred aircraft, complete with sound effects. The collection is constantly growing since, as well as running the museum, the Wings team conduct aviation archaeology, unearthing artefacts such as propellers and instruments from wartime locations.

4 CUCKFIELD

Metrobus 271 (Brighton–Crawley; several daily Mon–Sat, less frequent Sun)

A strikingly unspoilt large village/small town on the brink of the subtopia of Haywards Heath, Cuckfield is thought to take its name

A DINOSAUR DISCOVERY

A quarry at Whitemans Green, just north of Cuckfield, was where the Lewes-based geologist and palaeontologist Gideon Mantell began investigations of the fossil beds in 1819. Three years later his wife Mary found some quite gigantic teeth. Other experts pronounced them to be parts of a rhinoceros or a fish, but Mantell was convinced they were from a vast creature, some 60ft in length, from the Mesozoic (252–66 million years ago), now known to be the dinosaur era. The similarity to iguana's teeth – which they outsized by a factor of 20 – led him to name his hitherto undiscovered beast the *iguanodon*.

Dinosaur bones had been found before, but they had been thought to have been the remains of giant people. For the first time it was realised that they belonged to huge beasts. The Mantells never really got the glory they deserved, however. Mantell's nemesis Richard Owen, who hobnobbed with the Royal Family, had helped set up the Natural History Museum and was an outspoken critic of Darwin's *On the Origins of Species*, declared iguanadons God-created creatures rather than the ancestors of present-day species. He invented the word '*dinosauria*' ('terrible reptile'), which somehow stuck.

from the cuckoo, used as the village emblem. No single building stands out, but it is very pleasant to stroll around. The spacious churchyard has an expansive view of the Downs; among the gravestones is an unusual 1840 survival in the form of a wooden rail to commemorate Sarah Tulet, a faithful servant to one Mr Sergison. Within the Queen's Hall in the High Street, the **Cuckfield Museum** (𝒥 07857 815880 𝕙 cuckfieldmuseum.org ⊙ 10.00–12.30 Wed–Sat; free entry) has fossils, a dinosaur-era diorama and 18th-century clocks that were made locally.

5 BORDE HILL

Borde Hill Ln, nr Haywards Heath RH16 1XP 𝒥 01444 450326 𝕙 bordehill.co.uk ⊙ Feb–Oct; Haywards Heath railway station, then 1½-mile walk

Successive generations of the Stephenson Clarke family have developed this enchantingly diverse garden, which belies its proximity to Haywards Heath (actually only 30 minutes on foot from the railway station, though one might be tempted to get a taxi). Totally rural and blissfully tranquil, it surrounds a late 16th-century mansion built by Stephen Borde. The current family have been here since 1893, when Colonel Stephenson R Clarke created a ha-ha and planted shrubs and exotic and specimen trees. Of a host of rare tree and plant collections, many feature the original or the only examples in Britain, and were gathered on plant-collecting expeditions to exotic parts, particularly China but also other parts of the Far East and South America. The garden also contains 83 champion trees – that is, the greatest in girth or tallest of their kind in the UK. A further distinguishing feature is the rural views in various directions over the Weald, including the Ouse Valley Viaduct (page 240).

I was shown round by Eleni Stephenson Clarke, the Greek Cypriot wife of the great-grandson of the founder of the garden. She is passionate about this mini paradise, has an encyclopaedic knowledge of what grows where, and began the Jay Robin's Rose Garden – with its prized collection of David Austin roses – and Mediterranean garden (both designed by the eminent horticulturalist Robin Williams). She also developed the Italian Garden (on the old tennis court), with its rectangular, lily-filled pool and box hedging. Eleni walked me past the Garden of Allah, with its massive rhododendron sutchuenense from the forests of central China, a wildlife pond that encourages newts and dragonflies, and the Victorian greenhouses that have been restored with grant money from the Heritage Lottery Fund. A lot of visitors, she remarked, confine themselves to the garden and unfortunately miss out the magnificent woods, carpeted with springtime bluebells; the canopy of trees is spectacular.

Keen to follow in their forbears' footsteps, Eleni's son and daughter Harry Stephenson Clarke and Jay Goddard have now taken the reins, alongside horticulturalist Harry Baldwin.

Like the other local gardens, Borde Hill is utterly spectacular in May and June when the rhododendrons and azaleas are in bloom, and the roses present glorious shows of colour during summer. Outdoor events, including a food festival, gin festival, opera evenings and art classes, are held at regular intervals.

6 OUSE VALLEY VIADUCT

Not far from Balcombe, the insignificant Ouse is spanned by one of Britain's grandest railway viaducts, built in 1841 to carry the London-to-Brighton railway. If you approach by rail, you only get a hint of its architectural bricky swagger as the train briefly emerges into the open and passes fanciful pavilion-like structures at either end of the 37-arch, 95ft-high and 450ft-long viaduct.

To see it in its full glory, take the footpath that leads from the road. You're looking at 11 million Dutch bricks. Each pier has a huge oval void within it – which saved the need for millions more bricks – and by looking through all the oval spaces you gain a surreal view into a tame infinity.

There's a similar viaduct at Brighton, but as it curves there's no such nether-vista as that of Balcombe's structural wonder.

7 ARDINGLY RESERVOIR

Metrobus 272 (Brighton–Crawley; two-hourly) to Ardingly, then 1½-mile walk

This is one of the few large expanses of water in the southeast. Ardingly Reservoir extends across 198 acres between Balcombe and Ardingly – enough water to fill 15.9 billion drinks cans – and feeds the River Ouse.

---

1 The Ouse Valley is spanned by one of Britain's grandest railway viaducts. **2** Autumnal hues at the 27-acre High Beeches. **3** In June, the South of England Showground holds the biggest country event in the region. **4** Nymans' borders are filled with colour in spring and summer. ▶

Its V-shape positively graces the Wealden landscape, and footpaths around the southeast and northwest sides make an attractive strolling ground. The obvious starting point is from the car park beneath the dam at the south end; from there a trail heads past one of the reservoir's bird hides: kingfishers and great crested grebes may put in an appearance. Day fishing permits are available here through the **Ardingly Activity Centre** (⊘ ardinglyactivitycentre.co.uk), which also runs a programme of watersports including sailing, windsurfing and canoeing courses. They also hire out stand-up paddleboards and two-person kayaks; no experience or tuition required.

In June, the **South of England Showground** (⊘ seas.org.uk) on the B2028 just north of Ardingly hosts its namesake three-day show. It's easily the biggest event of its kind in the region, attracting tens of thousands of people, with show-jumping, a livestock parade, a Young Craftsman of the Year competition and apiary exhibits, among other country-related happenings. A two-day Autumn Show and Game Fair (Sep/Oct) features all sorts of rural crafts, sports and food-and-drink stalls, and, come November, there's a seriously festive Winter Fair. The showground also hosts the region's largest **antique fair** (⊘ iacf.co.uk) with up to 1,700 stalls, held over several days at various times of year.

8 WAKEHURST PLACE

Ardingly RH17 6TN ⊘ 01444 894066 ⊘ kew.org/visit-wakehurst; free entry for National Trust and Kew members; Metrobus 272 (Brighton–Crawley; two-hourly)

Be prepared for quite a lot of walking around this richly varied and hugely important semi-naturalistic garden, which spreads into a deep woodland valley and is of year-round interest. Managed by the Royal Botanic Gardens at Kew and accessed by the B2028 north of Ardingly, it occupies a large country estate around an Elizabethan mansion. The land is owned by the National Trust but has been leased to Kew since 1965. As a horticultural creation it owes its beginnings to Gerald Loder, who planted it from 1903 to 1936, after which Henry Price took over. It has national collections of skimmia, hypericum, betula and nothofagus. The daily guided walks led by volunteer guides are well worth catching, and the events calendar includes courses such as photography, willow-weaving and fungus forays.

Expansive and with more to take in than anyone could in a single visit, the site has a secretive nature, with no far-ranging views to speak of, and this whirlwind global tour of plants gets wilder as you proceed, beyond the island beds of more familiar perennials, round the sandstone crags of the Himalayan Glade, where you can appreciate the hilliness of the site to the full. The gardens merge into the **Loder Valley Nature Reserve**, a woodland, wetland and meadowland haven for Wealden wildlife such as dormice and kingfishers, with entry by free permit. Badger watches are periodically held here, using special hides.

In a contemporary barrel-vaulted pavilion-like structure at the top of the site, the **Millennium Seed Bank** is a project aiming to conserve the world's wild plants through the storage of seeds, enabling species to be kept alive for hundreds or even thousands of years. The project was begun amid predictions that half of the species on the planet could disappear in a century. To date, it has conserved over 2.4 billion seeds, representing thousands of plant species, the vast majority of which are native to the United Kingdom. The collection is stored at a constant minus 20 degrees Celsius in flood-, bomb- and radiation-proof vaults. Described as 'one of the most significant international conservation initiatives ever', the project has involved more than 90 countries. Within the atrium you can look straight into the areas where the scientific work is being done.

¶ FOOD & DRINK

Wakehurst's **cafés** serve fresh, locally sourced food. Seeds Café in the visitor centre at the entrance offers light lunches such as salads and sharing platters. In the former stable block (perhaps designed by Wren) within the garden, there's a larger restaurant and bakery, Stables Kitchen, offering pastries, sandwiches, hot dishes and teatime treats.

9 WORTH

No nearby public transport

Two very different religious establishments exist a couple of miles apart under the name of Worth, a few miles east of Crawley. **Worth Abbey** (Paddockhurst Rd, RH10 4SB ✆ 01342 710310 ⊘ worthabbey.net) is a modern Benedictine community of some 22 Catholic monks, who spend four hours a day in prayer and gather for worship in the striking 1960s Abbey Church six times a day. They observe a strict rule of silence from 21.30 until after breakfast the following day – one monk described the silence as 'like a wonderful spiritual bath which we invite you to get in to relax your spiritual muscles.' The Abbey Church is open to the public for services and private prayer, and the monks run the Worth Abbey Retreat Centre for men and women who want to experience a day or longer in this monastic community.

On the highest ground is a range of Tudorbethan stone and black-and-white buildings, once known as Paddockhurst and designed by Anthony Salvin in the 1860s. After the death of its owner Lord Cowdray in 1927, monks from Downside Abbey near Bath acquired the site and established a school there. The circular Abbey Church is tucked into the slope, while part of the Paddockhurst grounds have been restored to form a Quiet Garden open to all for contemplation.

To the north is the old village of Worth, at the fringes of Crawley. Soon after the northbound B2036 crosses over the M23, turn right into Church Road (signposted as the National Cycle Network). Here, within earshot of the motorway and approached from the lychgate by a narrow avenue of limes known as the Ten Apostles, the **Church of St Nicholas** is one of the finest surviving Saxon ecclesiastical buildings in the country. Edward the Confessor founded the present church, possibly as a centre for the court to worship while on hunting trips in the surrounding forest, but the site may have already been a minster, or early centre for Christian missionaries. The footprint of the church is identical to the original Winchester Cathedral, which was built in the 8th century. Inside, the chancel arch is – at 22ft high and 14ft wide – one of the largest Saxon arches anywhere in England. As you enter at the west end, look for the two blocked-in Saxon arches opposite each other on either side of the nave. Strangely tall and narrow, these are characteristic of Saxon church-building and are said to have been for knights on horseback to ride through and pay their respects without dismounting – like an early drive-thru church. In 1986 a workman's fire destroyed the Victorian roof, but this was by no means a complete disaster. The uncluttered design of the replacement is more in harmony with the form of the original Saxon timbers, and the acoustics are much improved, ideal for the many concerts that are performed here.

¶ FOOD & DRINK

Red Lion Lion Ln, Turners Hill RH10 4NU ✆ 01342 715416. An enjoyably unchanged, chatty rural local, run by the same people for many years. In an old tile-hung building looking over the village, it is just the place for a drink (Harvey's beers, including the seasonal brews) or for unpretentious home-cooked food; children and dogs are welcome, and there's a garden.

10 WEST HOATHLY

Metrobus 84 (Crawley–East Grinstead; several daily Mon–Sat)

This unspoilt backwater of a village a couple of miles east of Wakehurst Place has an extraordinary **churchyard**, falling in terraces down a precipitous slope, and looking towards the breach in the South Downs around Lewes. Opposite the churchyard is a conspicuously handsome manor house of 1627, symmetrically gabled and with mullioned windows.

What really makes West Hoathly worth seeking out is the **Priest House** (☏ 01342 810479 ⌨ sussexpast.co.uk ⊙ Mar–Oct Tue–Sun). This is a marvellously untouched 15th-century timber-framed cottage of the 'Wealden hall' structure – originally a buttery, pantry and upper chamber at either end, and a hall 23ft long and 27ft high (an open room with no chimney but with smoke from the fire going upwards through the ceiling). It's the same kind of arrangement as the much more visited Clergy House at Alfriston (page 213), but with considerably more to see

"The Priest House is a marvellously untouched 15th-century timber-framed cottage of the 'Wealden hall' structure."

inside. Unlike the Clergy House, where later changes have been stripped away to reveal the original, this has its later additions: chimneys and a central ceiling were added around 1580, but little has changed since then, apart from the division of the house into two cottages in the late 17th century. Antony Smith, the curator here since the late 1980s, lives in one part.

Despite its name, the building has nothing to do with priests, originating as an estate office for Lewes Priory. It might well have been forgotten were it not for its rescue by local man John Godwin King, who acquired it in 1905, restored it and opened it as a museum three years later. He gave it over to the Sussex Archaeological Society in 1935; many items from his collection of artefacts are still inside.

As you enter the house, notice the iron doorstep, made of local waste iron, and the Ws scratched into the front door: these are anti-witch devices (the iron being there because witches were supposed to be deterred by cold iron, and the W for Virgo Virginum, or Virgin of Virgins) and Antony will point out others inside, including circles, flower shapes and Ms, over the fireplace and elsewhere. 'They're not that rare,' he explained, 'but what is unusual is to find this many in one place.'

HORSHAM SLATES

The Priest House has a fine example of a roof made of Horsham slates. Also known as Horsham slabs, they are very local to the Weald – used since Roman times and coming from a series of sandstone quarries in the Horsham area. The natural cleave in the rock produces slates of different sizes and thickness; roofers (who were known as 'stone-healers' in medieval times) took advantage of this variation to create distinctive gradation patterns where the larger slabs are laid at the bottom, and become increasingly smaller towards the top. Various reasons exist for this, one being that the larger ones, which are typically 3ft sq, are easier to lay but harder to carry up to the top. It also makes sense in that the wall at the bottom provides support for the larger ones, and there are fewer joints for water to percolate through further down. Overall, though, it was probably done as a display of craftsmanship too.

The normal sort of thing to do if you didn't want witches coming in was to fill a bottle with nails, iron and urine, but the practices varied; Antony told me that another house locally has a cat's paw embedded in the mantelpiece, and that it's not uncommon to find similar marks on church doors (indeed the church door has more anti-witch markings).

There's a square piano of 1776, built when Beethoven was only six and Mozart was 20; a curator once found a man playing it without permission and realised it was Richard Burton, here with Elizabeth Taylor (according to Antony, 'the only visitors ever who put their address in the visitors' book as 'Hollywood'). Upstairs are some fine examples of samplers and embroidery, and a handkerchief embroidered with 65 signatures of Suffragettes imprisoned in Holloway in 1912. Very fortunately it was rescued in the 1960s by Antony's predecessor. 'It was about to be put on a bonfire with all the other remnants from a jumble sale. The custodian here obviously saw what it was, plucked it off the fire, and it's been here ever since.'

Antony's tasks also include attending to the garden, kept in the style of a Victorian cottage garden, rather than a medieval one, which would be less spectacular anyway. 'The plants are in control; I try to referee occasionally.'

SHOPPING

Plaw Hatch Farm Sharpthorne RH19 4JL ⊘ plawhatchfarm.co.uk ⊙ Mon–Sat. This community-owned biodynamic organic farm has been running its own farm shop for over

30 years. Its speciality is raw milk from its dairy cows, which are milked at 16.00 (you're welcome to watch); it also sells unpasteurised cream, kefir, small-batch cheese and yoghurt. Its polytunnels, fields and gardens produce an abundance of seasonal fruit, vegetables and flowers, and it champions other local growers, bakers and drinks-makers.

¶¶ FOOD & DRINK

Cat Inn North Ln, West Hoathly RH19 4PP ✆ 01342 810369 ⌕ catinn.co.uk ☉ closed Sun evening & Mon–Tue. Upmarket, highly acclaimed tile-hung dining pub serving Sussex beers, wines by the glass and elegant food such as hake with wilted spinach or aubergine with roasted plums, yoghurt and pine nuts. With four comfortable bedrooms and a sunny terrace, it's a good spot for a celebration.

11 GRAVETYE ESTATE

⌂ **Gravetye Manor**

Vowels Ln, West Hoathly RH19 4LJ

Frustratingly in this delectable scenery, the network of rights of way is limited, so it's hard to get to the heart of it. The luscious estate around Gravetye (pronounced 'grave-tie') Manor, a luxurious hotel, is a welcome exception, as it's largely open to the public. The small car park on the approach to the hotel, between West Hoathly and Kingscote station on the Bluebell Railway, is a good starting point for forest walks. Staff at the hotel have mapped

"It was designed by the great landscape gardener William Robinson, who lived here from 1884 until his death in 1935."

and waymarked several circular walks around the estate and its vicinity, exploring beautiful lakes and woods, and the manor's horticultural team offers tours of the **garden** three times a week from spring to autumn.

Designed by the great landscape gardener William Robinson, who lived here from 1884 until his death in 1935, Gravetye's garden has been restored after being neglected for many years. Robinson was a passionate advocate of gardening with hardy plants and wild flowers, with layouts becoming more natural-looking and wild further away from the house, in reaction to the artificial style of Victorian horticultural creations with dense bedding of hothouse-reared annuals. A white wisteria pergola and gorgeous herbaceous borders are set against the weathered stone of the Elizabethan manor house, and the orchard is strewn with daffodils. For a closer, leisurely look at it all, treat yourself to afternoon tea at the hotel or an overnight stay.

SPECIAL STAYS

Gravetye Manor Gravetye Estate, Vowels Ln, West Hoathly RH19 4LJ ✐ 01342 810567
⌂ gravetyemanor.co.uk. When it opened in the 1950s, Gravetye was one of Britain's
very first country house hotels, paving a new trend for weekend breaks in idyllic rural
surroundings. The house itself, which dates back to the late 1500s, is steeped in romance,
with grand fireplaces, panelled walls, intimate sitting rooms and supremely comfortable
bedrooms, most of which have luxurious bathrooms and sweeping views of the surrounding
lawns, lakes and woodland. The dining room was created by roofing in a courtyard and
adding picture windows on to the lovely gardens; serving Michelin-starred cuisine inspired
by Gravetye's own kitchen garden, it's very special indeed.

12 SAINT HILL MANOR

Saint Hill Rd, East Grinstead RH19 4JY ✐ 01342 317057 ⌂ sainthillmanor.org.uk; train to
East Grinstead (Oxted Line, London–East Grinstead), then two-mile walk

Glorious gardens, sloping down to a lake, with a fine manor house: it
sounds like all the ingredients for a typical country house visit. Only this
isn't. Saint Hill Manor, virtually next door to Standen (see opposite), is
the national headquarters of the Scientology movement in this country
– the controversial organisation established by the late L Ron Hubbard
and which lists Tom Cruise among its followers. It's certainly worth a
look, even if Scientology most definitely isn't your thing – free tours are
available if you book in advance, or you can stroll round the grounds at
leisure. Though you might want to take a deep breath first.

I wasn't at all sure what to expect when I ventured in here. It was a
hot, sunny day and the place felt like some hugely endowed university
campus in California. The collegiate part of it is the 'castle', actually built
in the late 20th century in a curious and somewhat surreal retro style,
all stone, battlements and Gothic windows. The guide took me to the
little building where they give students 'purification programmes' – a
rigorous schedule of up to three weeks, consisting of exercise, saunas
and dieting for up to five hours a day. It sounded a lot more Spartan than
a spa treatment.

A little further down and overlooking the rhododendron-embellished
grounds and goose-populated lake is the late 18th-century manor
house which Hubbard bought in 1959, and where he lived and ran his
Scientology empire. The library is devoted entirely to a set of his books
with their trademark garish covers: he started off in science fiction and
is the world's most published and most translated author of all time –

1,084 works in 71 languages. His office has been left as it was when he died, with a vintage dictating machine resembling an old-style record player, his two electric organs – a Wurlitzer and a very rare Mellotron, an early form of synthesiser – and desk complete with biros, stapler, a toy tiger and whatever other everyday bits happened to be there at the time. But the room that really drops the jaw (perhaps not for the right reasons) is the Monkey Room – with a quite bizarre mural painted by John Spencer Churchill, Sir Winston's nephew, for the former owner in 1945. Created for the American Ambassador's monkey-adoring wife, it depicts 145 monkeys of 20 species all sketched at London Zoo but given human roles – variously playing instruments in a bandstand, parading in clothes or diving into a swimming pool.

13 STANDEN HOUSE & GARDEN

West Hoathly Rd, nr East Grinstead RH19 4NE ✆ 01342 323029; National Trust; Metrobus 84 (Crawley–East Grinstead; several daily Mon–Sat)

For me this is the most pleasing and enjoyable National Trust house in the southeast. An Australian globetrotting friend who rapidly notches up National Trust properties when in England announced to me that he'd like to visit Knole House in Kent. I suggested that we ought to add on Standen, of which he'd never heard – so almost as an afterthought after visiting the impressively gloomy Knole House we cheered ourselves up by taking in this one, which he liked much more. Unlike most country houses, it's on a small and liveable scale with an almost contemporary lightness about the décor, though unmistakably in the style of its time.

Only a mile from the southern peripheries of East Grinstead but in a totally rural setting, the house is the Arts and Crafts masterpiece of Philip Webb (1831–1915). He was a close friend of the hugely influential designer William Morris, with whom he founded the Society for the Protection of Ancient Buildings in 1877; in 1858 Webb had completed Morris's Red House at Bexleyheath (on the Kent edge of London, and also now owned by the National Trust).

Webb's clients for Standen were the Beale family – James Beale was a wealthy London solicitor married to Margaret; they had seven children and an entourage of servants. This was their country weekend retreat until his retirement, after which they lived here permanently. After the last of the children died at the age of 92 it was left to the National Trust. Webb was at the forefront of technology, with the house built round a steel frame, with central heating and electricity, yet he also deliberately created something that harmonised with existing buildings and the physical setting. He used local Sussex materials, including sandstone quarried from the estate, bricks and tiles from Keymer, and timber from nearby oak woods.

The inside, presented as it would have looked ready to welcome guests for a weekend stay in 1925, is what makes it special, a million miles from the usual Victorian country house. Upon completion in 1894, Webb continued advising Margaret Beale about decorations, and the family used the firm Morris & Co for much of the wallpapers, fabrics and furniture. It's the small details one remembers – gorgeous lustre-highlighted ceramics by William de Morgan, a 'Decego' historic loo, ceramics by Dante Gabriel Rossetti, textiles and drawings by Edward Burne-Jones or the steel fireplace in the all-green dining room. Upstairs, Mrs Beale's embroidered bed hangings complement a bedcover by May Morris (daughter of the great William, whose wallpaper abounds here too) as fresh as it was when made in 1894 owing to its being stored away for a hundred years before being presented to the National Trust.

"The inside, presented as it would have looked ready to welcome guests in 1925, is what makes it special."

Webb, like William Morris, revered craftsmanship and the use of materials, and took much of his inspiration from nature. His architectural output was limited because of the detail he lavished on his projects, and his fastidious attention to detail was no doubt instrumental in the Beales engaging him in the first place. At Standen, electricity and central heating were installed from the start (the house's electrical generator was in the long, low building near the current car park). Indeed, the electric light fittings are very much part of the character of the house – admirably the Trust have gone to pains to get the original style of lightbulbs manufactured; the light is feeble but probably seemed pretty bright to those unaccustomed to electric light and certainly had the advantage over gaslight by not threatening to asphyxiate the inhabitants.

The gardens are not huge but have a wonderful variety. They spread in a series of sloping linked areas along the hillside, looking over Weir Wood Reservoir. The Beales brought back a host of exotic plants from their extensive travels, including a collection of Japanese maples. Ferns, mosses and liverworts thrive alongside toads and newts in a secretive sandstone grotto known as the Quarry Garden. You can stay overnight in The Morris Apartment, a one-bedroom holiday flat within the house, which enables you to explore at your leisure.

The adjacent shop stocks Arts and Crafts style homewares, as well as the sort of plants Mrs Beale originally had in her garden. There's a café in a converted barn, and various walks, children's trails and workshops are held in the house and gardens.

14 OLD BRAMBLETYE HOUSE

Brambletye Ln, nr Forest Row ♀ TQ416354; Compass bus 261 (East Grinstead–Uckfield; several daily Mon–Sat), Metrobus 270 (East Grinstead–Brighton; hourly Mon–Sat, less frequent Sun) or Metrobus 291 (Crawley–Tunbridge Wells; hourly Mon–Sat, less frequent Sun)

Very possibly Sussex's oddest ruin, Old Brambletye is a startling trio of upstanding chunks of a defunct mansion, standing to their original height and set out in a line like gigantic chess pieces. Grade II*-listed, they're set back from the lane, with the gatehouse to the fore; from some angles it almost looks as if might it still be functional. The date 1631 is emblazoned on the central entrance tower. The house was built for Sir Henry Compton, a lawyer and MP for East Grinstead; he died in 1649 and it appears the house was abandoned not long after.

There's no public access to the site by car, but you can reach it on foot via the Forest Way, a long-distance path following the trackbed of a former railway that passed through Forest Row en route between East Grinstead and Groombridge. At what was once the Brambletye railway crossing, turn south into Brambletye Lane.

15 EAST GRINSTEAD

Oxted Line (London–East Grinstead); Metrobus 270 (Brighton–East Grinstead; hourly Mon–Sat, less frequent Sun)

In the northeast of West Sussex, snug against the Surrey border, East Grinstead is not one of Sussex's major tourist destinations but has some status as a southern terminus of the Oxted Line from London and the northern terminus of the Bluebell Railway (page 252). There's not a lot of interest immediately around the station, but persevere to the **High Street**, which has some notably good-looking vistas, with timber-framed houses such as Cromwell House (1599), extending to the market square, itself divided into a couple of islands of houses, Middle Row –

which originated as market stalls. Further east are the gracious stone almshouses of **Sackville College** (✆ 01342 323414 ⌖ sackvillecollege. org.uk ☉ mid Jun–mid Sep), built in 1609 and still used for their original purpose. A statue of a snow leopard (easily mistaken for a dalmatian) – part of the Sackville coat of arms – perches on the top of its bell tower.

Behind the high street, the smartly modern **museum** (✆ 01342 302233 ⌖ eastgrinsteadmuseum.org.uk ☉ 10.00–16.00 Wed–Sun & bank holidays) on the site of the old cattle market houses a nicely set out local collection – including a mock-up of a hospital ward where New Zealand plastic surgeon Archibald McIndoe (1900–60) pioneered new techniques at the town's Queen Victoria Hospital in 1939, working on RAF casualties in World War II and rehabilitating them into normal life – his patients became the 'guinea pigs' and later established the Guinea Pig Club – and even had a pub named after them. McIndoe's innovations included the saline bath, for healing wounds. Elsewhere the museum displays an iguanodon footprint and items of local life, with touchscreen archives and an array of locally produced films featuring various carnivals and pageants, including one on Ashdown Forest in 1929 which very briefly starred the real Christopher Robin.

More guinea pig-themed mementoes are found in spacious **St Swithun's Church**, rebuilt in the 18th century, unusually in Gothic rather than the classical style of the time. Within the chapel to the right of the chancel is a black stone dedicated to Guinea Pig Club member Henry Standen, and in the clerestory light second from the end at the back of the church the stained glass includes a tiny flying guinea pig (not much more than a tiny speck to the right of the Holy Family – the church guidebook helps you pick it out). The Wealden iron industry left its mark in the form of some Tudor iron memorials, two set in the floor and one in the wall.

16 BLUEBELL RAILWAY

East Grinstead, Kingscote, Horsted Keynes & Sheffield Park ✆ 01825 720800 ⌖ bluebell-railway.co.uk; Compass bus 121 (Lewes–Sheffield Park; several daily Sat–Sun) or Metrobus 270 (Brighton–East Grinstead; hourly Mon–Sat, less frequent Sun)

Named after the bluebells that bring a vivid splash of colour to the views from the window in spring, this is in many ways the king of Britain's many heritage railways. It's run by an army of 700 volunteers, and unlike nearly every other heritage railway operates entirely on steam. In all the

Railway vividly evokes the feeling of travel through the countryside as it was in the steam era, and for the most part the views can hardly have changed in a hundred or so years.

In 1958 the line from East Grinstead to Lewes closed, but four men who had brewed the idea during their student days saw the possibility of reopening the line as a private railway. They got their act together, enlisted a band of dedicated enthusiasts, and a stretch reopened in 1960. This was at a time when steam engines were still operating on the national BR network, making this the first of Britain's heritage railways. And being first on board, they acquired a lot of the best railwayana – in addition to some marvellously antique standard-gauge railway carriages and locos, an impressive array of station paraphernalia, including wonderful displays of enamel advertising signs. Kingscote station is done out in 1950s style, while Horsted Keynes evokes the 1930s and Sheffield Park is a recreation of a country station in the 1880s. The line has been used repeatedly as a film location, including for *Downton Abbey* – Horsted Keynes station covered up its signs with 'Downton' for the purpose.

> *"They acquired an impressive array of station paraphernalia, including wonderful displays of enamel advertising signs."*

The latest chapter in the line's history was marked by the opening of the stretch from Kingscote to East Grinstead in 2013, finally linking the Bluebell Railway with mainline services, via a short walk across the tarmac. This restoration effort was quite a bit more than just rolling up sleeves and hacking down a few weeds, but a community effort of heroic proportions. What stopped the charitable trust from completing the final two miles from Kingscote to the BR station at East Grinstead was a mountain of rubbish, which was there thanks to an unfortunate decision by the local council to use Imberhorne Cutting as a landfill site. Reinstating this section of the line was something of an epic. In 1974 they began by purchasing the old station site in East Grinstead. Work began in 2008 to remove several thousands of tons of rubbish – a hugely costly job. Work to preserve the railway received backing from two Sussex councils, the Heritage Lottery Fund, and (predominantly) contributions from hundreds of volunteers. The deadline on the exemption from landfill tax which came to an end in 2011 galvanised people into action; donations sped up towards the end of the project with the Double Donations Dash bringing in £270,000 in four weeks, and 400 supporters did a sponsored Track Trail along the length of the track in question and raised a further £40,000. The total cost was £4.5 million. Chairman Roy Watts said 'the bringing of the line to East Grinstead has been the society's number one project for the past 40 years'.

So now you can travel from Victoria to East Grinstead in 55 minutes, change to platform 3 and saunter along the distinctly less express Bluebell for its 11 miles in 40 minutes. There's no prospect of reopening the line south to Lewes, but the Railway does own a stretch of track from Horsted Keynes to Ardingly, near Balcombe (the latter on the main London–Brighton line), which could well come into use again.

The carriages mostly date from the 1930s and 1950s, but there is a 1913 observation car as well as even older ones from 1890, and they're constantly renovating others that will eventually come into service. Virtually all were from the southern region, and have been rescued from all sorts of uses – including as hen coops, bungalows, holiday homes and even aviaries. The enamel advertising signs – of the likes of 'Redfern's Rubber Heels', 'Venus Soap: stops rubbing' and 'Virol, growing boys need it' – were mainly collected in the 1960s and came from auctions and from stations that were closing.

The railway's organisers welcome volunteers, skilled or unskilled, and will train people up for a range of tasks. A week's volunteering here would make a memorable holiday, and they even have accommodation in the sleeping cars on the sidings. You might start off cleaning and painting, then learn how to use a lathe, or make mortice and tenon joints. Not surprisingly, the volunteers are passionate enthusiasts and the lifeblood of the whole operation. Pop into the loco shed at Sheffield Park and you might meet some of them. David, who was in the workshop restoring old carriages, said, 'I'm a chartered engineer and am interested in seeing engineering artefacts preserved, especially steam locos, and getting them in working order. It can take ten years to restore one, and when you've finished it you really feel you've achieved something – I can say to myself "I've preserved the engineering heritage". Some volunteers

---

1 Sheffield Park is one of the greatest of all English gardens. **2** The morning room in the Arts and Crafts Standen House. **3** All aboard the Bluebell Railway. **4** The pioneering plastic surgeon Archibald McIndoe is very much remembered in East Grinstead. **5** The Church of St Nicholas near Worth has one of the largest Saxon arches in England. ▶

Horsted Keynes & the Bluebell Railway

❄ OS Explorer map 135; start: either Horsted Keynes village green ♀ TQ383282 or Horsted Keynes railway station ♀ TQ372293; five miles; easy. There's a free car park signposted at the road junction roughly opposite the Green Man pub. Metrobus 270 (hourly Mon–Sat from Brighton (Churchill Square), Haywards Heath & Lindfield) stops in the village. **Loos**: Horsted Keynes village & station. **Refreshments**: two pubs at Horsted Keynes (the Crown & the Green Man).

T his very easily followed five-mile route through Sussex's mini lake district (well, actually a chain of rather beautiful fishing ponds, but that will have to suffice) with rolling views for most of the way, includes a section alongside the **Bluebell Railway** (join the directions just before **5**), and takes in Horsted Keynes station, an alternative starting point (free car park), giving access from East Grinstead or Sheffield Park by steam train. For the first couple of miles you follow the thoroughly signposted West Sussex Border Path. **Horsted Keynes village** deserves a pause: an idyllic, long village green overlooked by two pubs.

1 From **Horsted Keynes village green**, at the road junction near car park and bus stop, walk along the green beside the road in the Dane Hill direction (signposted), then just after the Green Man pub and before the village sign turn left on a small lane (Church Lane, signposted to church and school), keeping right at the junction at the bottom. As its name suggests, Church Lane leads towards **St Giles Church**, where Harold Macmillan, prime minster 1957–63, is buried in the churchyard.

2 The lane leads to the left of the church: follow the bridleway signposts (avoiding a footpath to the left), now on an unmade track downhill. This is part of the West Sussex Border Path (intermittently signposted as such). You pass a tree-fringed fishing lake on the right, then a chain of smaller lakes and ponds on the left. Past the last pond, fork left as signposted, passing a black-and-white house, where the lane bends right and then left, near the gates of the imposing half-timbered **Broadhurst Manor**.

3 At the T-junction with a public road, turn left along it, then right at the next junction (towards East Grinstead). Turn left just before a thatched cottage, on an enclosed path (the West Sussex Border Path) which leads round the edge of a field, then drops through a wood, then skirts another field, turning left at the corner as signposted, then enters another wood at the next signpost. The path crosses the dam of a pond (care needed – only part of it has anything to hold on to). Go up a small field, to the left of a small brick outbuilding, to find a small gate in the top left corner, then turn left on the road.

4 After 60yds turn right at a signpost just before a stone-built house, on an enclosed path, then follow the top edge of two fields. The path then becomes enclosed again – the South Downs suddenly appear in the distance – and reaches a road by a **railway bridge** (a handy vantage point for the Bluebell Railway steam trains). Cross to the field path opposite, following the right edge, closely parallel to the railway. Cross the railway line at the next signpost, then turn left on the other side, beside the railway fence and close to the track. Eventually you are forced away from the railway, through a small plantation, then the path leads up over another railway bridge, with Horsted Keynes station visible to the right, beyond sundry **locos and antique rolling stock**, and three pairs of **railway-era cottages**. Carry

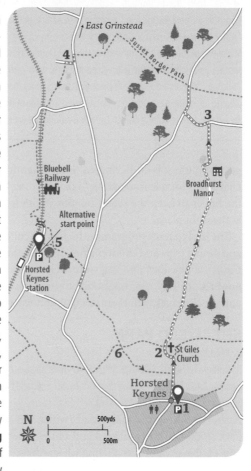

on along a gravel track to where it divides (above the car park and station) and fork left.
If starting from Horsted Keynes railway station Begin with the station on your left, follow the track uphill, then at the fork (by the old-fashioned 'no through road' sign) turn right.

5 This track soon peters out by a footpath signpost: take the direction straight on (avoiding the path signposted to the left), to pick up a path between fences at the edge of woodland. At the road, turn right along it for 80yds, then left on a signposted path, through a semi-open ▶

Horsted Keynes & the Bluebell Railway (continued)

◀ area, then down through woodland, following signposts and eventually dropping alongside a woodland gill to a T-junction with a track, with a lake just visible beyond the bank opposite. Turn right, past a sluice.

6 At the end of the lake keep forward at the next (four-way) junction (signposted); 30yds later another path joins from the left – keep forward, soon with a field up on the right. The path leads towards Horsted Keynes. At the road (Church Lane) turn right for Horsted Keynes village, keeping left at the next junction; if you started from the railway station and don't wish to visit the village, turn left along Church Lane and pick up the walk at **2**.

---

get the plum job of driving engines; Brian told me about some of the challenges for a learner driver – like needing to have sufficient water in the boiler to keep the steam up, not stopping too quickly and stopping at the right place.

The lively events programme includes a collectors' fair, various wining and dining trips and children's fun days. The full fare gives you unlimited travel for the day, and dogs are welcome; all the engines are steam-powered, though you might like to time your trip to coincide with the vintage carriages with their original upholstery and period adverts.

17 SHEFFIELD PARK

⟁ Wild Boar Wood

Nr Uckfield TN22 3QX ✆ 01825 790231; ◷ mid-Feb–Dec daily; Jan–mid-Feb Sat–Sun; National Trust; Bluebell Railway (East Grinstead–Sheffield Park); Compass bus 121 (Lewes–Sheffield Park; several daily Sat–Sun)

A short walk up the main road (which has a footway) from Sheffield Park station, at the southern end of the Bluebell Railway, leads to this, one of the greatest of all English gardens. Like many others in the Weald, this 120-acre garden and arboretum is renowned for its dazzling show of azaleas, kalmias, cherries, rhododendrons and other flowering shrubs in May and June, but the interest is year-round, with carpets of bluebells and daffodils in spring. In particular, the autumn colours rival those you might find in New England, when maples, tupelo trees, swamp cypresses, birches and eucryphias and others combine to make a mesmeric show of golds, reds, oranges and yellows. The four linked, broodingly silent lakes reflect the abundant and diverse foliage and shrubberies, providing exquisite vistas at every turn. High above stands the Gothic 18th-century mansion designed by James Watt for the Earl of Sheffield; it is now converted into very desirable flats.

The garden's master plan – including two of the lakes – was begun by Capability Brown in the 18th century, with further modifications in the 19th century. James Pulham, whose company specialised in water features and was responsible for some of the rock constructions in Brighton Aquarium, added cascades. In 1910 Arthur Soames acquired the property and added the magnificent collection of trees and shrubs, making the most of the sloping nature of the site.

"The garden's master plan – including two of the lakes – was begun by Capability Brown in the 18th century."

The estate includes a historic cricket field, where Australia began their tour between 1884 and 1896 against a team captained by W G Grace and put together by the hugely influential cricketing aficionado Lord Sheffield; admission was free and it drew a crowd of 25,000. He financed the England team's tour of Australia in 1891–92 and donated £150 to the New South Wales Cricket Association so that they could buy a plate and establish the Sheffield Shield, the same term used today for the first-class competition in Australia. He was also the longstanding president of Sussex County Cricket Club, to which he made a large donation so they could purchase Hove cricket ground, still the club's home. Nowadays the Sheffield Park ground is home to the Armadillo Cricket Club.

SPECIAL STAYS

Wild Boar Wood Horsted Keynes RH17 7EA ⊘ pegsandpitches.co.uk ☉ Apr–Oct. This small woodland glamping site has nine furnished bell tents tucked among the trees. Created in harmony with the natural surroundings and run with eco-friendly principles in mind, it's a couple of notches up from wild camping, with wardens permanently on site. Campfires, den building, birdwatching and bug hunts are positively encouraged. The location, which is kept secret (you're sent directions when you book), is within tooting range of the Bluebell Railway.

¶¶ FOOD & DRINK

The Griffin Fletching TN22 3SS ✆ 01825 722890 ⊘ thegriffininn.co.uk. In a lovely village street near the east side of the Sheffield Park estate, this warmly welcoming ancient beamed inn is one of the area's most celebrated dining pubs. The bar and restaurant food is not cheap but consistently good, with Sussex meat and seasonal vegetables. Excellent wine list, and Harvey's Best Bitter among the selection of real ales. Booking strongly recommended. It also has 13 very comfortable bedrooms.

The Old Dairy Farm and Shop Sliders Lane, Furners Green TN22 3RT ✆ 01825 790517 ⌂ theolddairyfarmshop.co.uk. Just south of Sheffield Park station is this unassuming general store run by the Barnard family, selling produce grown or reared on their farm, as well as artisan bread and groceries.

18 HEAVEN FARM

Furners Green TN22 3RG ✆ 01825 790226 ⌂ heavenfarm.co.uk; no nearby public transport

Just 1½ miles north of Sheffield Park, and south of Danehill, this 1830s farmstead turned Slow tourist attraction makes a very useful stopping point or a destination in itself, and is worth popping into just for the delicious rural, hilly views. The Stable Tea Rooms serves breakfast, light lunches and tea; in decent weather you'll want to sit outside at the tables amid roving chickens (a sign warns you that they may nick your food) and long-retired tractors. Youngsters can play mini-golf or lark about in the play barn, and in spring the woodland nature trail comes into its own with a magnificent show of bluebells. On the way are badger setts, the site of an ancient iron-smelting 'bloomery' and an area where the farm's own wallabies range about.

The food shop has locally sourced organic produce, including cheeses and apple juice, and there's also a Latchetts Farm ice-cream shop and a campsite.

19 CHAILEY COMMON

Compass bus 31 (Uckfield–Cuckfield; hourly Mon–Sat) and 121 (Lewes–Newick or Sheffield Park; hourly Mon–Fri, less frequent Sat–Sun)

Spanning both sides of the A272 on the western edge of the crossroads village of North Chailey, this is a miniature version of Ashdown Forest, a surprisingly heathery enclave in the rich green Sussex farmlands. Large enough to lose your bearings in, it's a very pleasant 450-acre strolling ground. It's also a designated **Site of Special Scientific Interest** and local nature reserve: species found here include blue marsh gentians, heath-spotted orchids, lizards and nightjars. The 1830s smock windmill on Red House Common, the section north of the A272 and west of the A275, is Grade II-listed, and contains a small Rural Life Museum (☉ Apr–Sep last Sun of month). The yew tree beside it is said to mark the centre of Sussex.

🛍 SHOPPING

Townings Farm Shop Plumpton Rd, North Chailey BN8 4EJ ✐ 01444 471352
✐ towningsfarm.co.uk ☺ Wed–Sat. Specialising in meat from the Uridge family's own heritage breeds, including Hebridean and Southdown sheep, this farm shop also sells seasonal fruit and veg and pantry essentials.

ASHDOWN FOREST & AROUND

One of Sussex's most wonderful open spaces, Ashdown Forest is among the High Weald's major treasures, thankfully untainted by development in spite of the *Winnie-the-Pooh* connections. Public transport, alas, is difficult unless you're prepared for a lot of walking.

20 ASHDOWN FOREST

Limited public transport access, but Metrobus 240 (Brighton–East Grinstead via Haywards Heath, hourly, less frequent Sun) stops at Wych Cross, 1 mile walk from Ashdown Forest Centre; charges payable for all car parks (pay via app)

A very surprising place in the heights of the Weald: this is 'forest' in the old sense of the word, meaning a deer-hunting forest enclosed in the 13th century. Like St Leonard's Forest (east of Horsham), it is a rare survivor of some 300 deer forests that existed in Sussex in medieval times. In late summer it's an absolutely glorious purple and yellow sight of heather and gorse, and humming with bees. I once brought an American visitor here who was amazed to find the forest devoid of gigantic fibreglass Pooh characters; that it has remained so clutter-free and unchanged is thanks in no small way to the Conservators of Ashdown Forest, who manage the area. You can pick up books and the excellent but otherwise hard-to-come-by Ashdown Forest map at its headquarters, **The Ashdown Forest Centre** (Coleman's Hatch Rd, Wych Cross RH18 5JP ✐ 01342 823583 ✐ ashdownforest.org). Here and there you encounter a stream flowing a deep rusty colour – because of its high iron content. This was a busy place at the height of the **Wealden iron industry**, which was going strong in Roman times, and saw the opening of Britain's first furnace at Newbridge in 1496; this material supplied the Roman navy and the British navy (cannons for fighting the Spanish Armada).

"In late summer it's an absolutely glorious purple and yellow sight of heather and gorse, and humming with bees."

The forest was enclosed by a fence, or **pale**, entered by **hatches** or gates (at points like Coleman's Hatch and Chelwood Gate). The peculiarly piecemeal shape of the forest today is the result of enclosures made 300 years back, which took parts of the original forest into private ownership. Centuries of activity of hunting and use by commoners have left the remaining area a **heathland**, though there's a fair amount of tree cover, especially further down the slopes. Lowland heath like this is internationally rare; it is a special haven for all sorts of flora and fauna, such as spiders.

Trees (especially the extra-persistent birch) are the biggest threat to this scenic microcosm. The Conservators of Ashdown Forest are charged with tasks of looking after visitors and protecting wildlife, and find chopping down trees is an emotive issue for some of the public, despite the fact that people have been doing this very activity for centuries. In places, woodland is coppiced for a variety of uses, including

STOOLBALL

Right outside the window of my home in Lewes, the Paddock hosts a weekly summer game of that strangely Sussex pastime, stoolball. It's a variant of cricket, played by both sexes, organised into leagues over much of Sussex and into western Kent. Instead of wickets there are posts with flat boards on them – a bit like estate agents' boards, and instead of bats there are wooden paddles like antique table-tennis bats to hit the semi-hard rounders-style ball. After I moved to Lewes, I watched this weekly ritual from my house, then wandered down to the ground and asked the players to explain. 'So do you fancy a bat? The Lewes Arms have bowled us out already, and we're batting again to play out time.' Thus wearing quite unsuitable indoor clothes and open sandals I began my extremely short career batting for the Sussex Flintknappers' Stoolball Team.

Stoolball has had a strange ride through history. Its origins are murky, but it is certainly from pre-industrial England. The 'stool' may have been the wicket or the bat, or may have referred to a tree stump in a woodland clearing. One theory is that it was played by milkmaids, with a milkstool as a wicket. It was known to have been played in Elizabethan times as a Shrove Tuesday game. In the 19th century it was taken up wholeheartedly, particularly in Kent and Sussex, by gentry and clergy, who organised female teams of upper-class ladies intermingled with village and farm women, with no age barriers. The rules were first codified in 1867: this way, women of all classes could exercise and socially interact. The sport became organised into a Sussex Stoolball League in 1903; soon men joined in, playing left handed against or with the women.

for firewood, for fencing material and as a wildlife habitat. Since 1945 the amount of tree cover has increased from 5% of the total to 40%. Left to its own devices the whole heath would become secondary woodland in 50 years.

The red deer have long gone, but **fallow deer** proliferate – hence the 40mph limit painted merrily on the road surface, which is there for a serious reason: deer don't have very good road sense and there are an awful lot of them about. More scarce are the sika, roe and muntjac deer.

With its uncluttered vistas and strangely disorienting topography, the heath displaces you to a different part of the country altogether – a London friend who knew nothing about it when I took him there thought he'd just woken up in the moors of Yorkshire.

For **walking**, prepare to be confused. The soil is highly acidic, and there's no farming or settlement up here to speak of. It's a rather magical maze of a place. The *OS Explorer 135* map is surprisingly useless here,

William Grantham, a wealthy Sussex lawyer and landowner from Chailey, popularised the game further, partly as a way of lubricating his social contacts. As Sussex became a place of hospitalisation for wounded soldiers in World War I, in 1917 he set up games of stoolball in the grounds of the Royal Pavilion in Brighton for officers whose injuries excluded them from more strenuous forms of sport: this proved a hit with patients and other hospitals in Sussex followed suit. As a member of the MCC he even got a demonstration stoolball match played at Lord's, and subsequently the game was even played on rough ground close to the trenches in the battlefields.

After World War I, Grantham revived the game for men and women and attempted to spread the sport further, promoting it in the spirit of reviving a folk tradition of old England. While playing, he donned the garb of a labourer of yesteryear – smock and beaver hat. It took off in Sussex in the 1920s at a time when such features of rural life were tangibly disappearing; by the 1930s stoolball was being played in the Midlands and northern England too, and he broadcast on television and radio, and travelled round the globe to the likes of Chile and Greenland, getting locals and expats to join in. Grantham fell out with what became the Sussex Federation, which adhered to 'Sussex rules' on positioning of umpires and allowing only 'clean' catches away from the body. Outsiders may find it astonishing as well as gratifying to learn that this quirkiest of pursuits still thrives. It was recognised as a sport by the Sports Council in 2008, and outside Sussex is played by women's leagues in Surrey, Kent and the Midlands.

as what few rights of way exist are indistinguishable on the ground from the dense network of other paths, and you can wander at will. Much more user-friendly is the *Ashdown Forest* map at the unusual scale of 1:30,000, obtainable from the Ashdown Forest Centre. It shows all the firebreaks and paths, and I've found it plus a compass the only way of finding my way around. Strangely, the handiest landmarks are the car parks, which are numbered and named on the map and at their entrances.

"What few rights of way exist are indistinguishable on the ground from the dense network of other paths."

Picking out a route to recommend above all others is hard, as it's all very pleasant, and however carefully I try to map read, I never quite end up where I'm aiming for. Favourite starting points in the forest are Camp Hill (a prominent clump of trees on the west side of the B2026) and the village of Fairwarp on the south side of the Forest (from which you could try following the ever-so-discreet wooden marker WW posts denoting the route of the Wealdway. Or begin anywhere and aim to circle the high ground – you'll soon realise the Ashdown Forest is donut-shaped, and the hole in the centre is the Old Lodge estate (with few public footpaths).

Some very good **walks leaflets** are available from Ashdown Forest Centre and from ⊘ ashdownforest.org/shop; these include the two Pooh Walks from Gills Lap which take you past the Enchanted Place, Heffalump Trap, Roo's Sandy Pit, Milne Memorial and North Pole, and skirt Eeyore's Sad and Gloomy Place. Another takes in the Southern Slopes and the Airman's Grave, starting from Hollies car park (♥ TQ462286) and getting views of the South Downs. You'll also find a series of **archaeology walks** pointing you to such recently discovered features as charcoal-burning platforms, saw pits, World War I and II practice trenches and Napoleonic-era field kitchens. These sites take a bit of spotting as most of them are well camouflaged by vegetation: the World War I practice trenches are zigzag in form, but by the time of World War II these would have been no defence against aircraft.

◀ **1** Ashdown Forest is one of the treasures of the High Weald. **2** The very bridge where Winnie-the-Pooh and friends invented the pastime of poohsticks. **3** Nutley Windmill is the only working open-trestle post mill in Britain. **4** The sandstone formations of Harrison's Rocks are a magnet for climbers.

'DRAWN BY ME & MR SHEPARD HELPD'

Thus wrote (supposedly) Christopher Robin on the map of the 'forest' at the beginning of A A Milne's immortal quartet of children's books which began with *Winnie-the-Pooh* in 1926, followed by *The House at Pooh Corner* (1928). Simply penned with pine trees and sandy tracks, and variously marked 'Pooh trap for heffalumps' and 'nice for piknicks', E H Shepard's map and the illustrations that follow perfectly evoke the Ashdown Forest landscape. Some names are only slightly changed: 'Hundred Acre Wood' in the stories is Five Hundred Acre Wood in reality, not far from Cotchford Farm near Hartfield where the Milnes had their country bolthole. Galleons Lap is really Gill's Lap, the 'enchanted place on the very top of the Forest' (close to which is thought to be where that Heffalump trap was set), easily picked out nowadays by an ice cream van that's often in the car park at a Y-junction of roads; just beyond, a memorial stone to Milne looks north across the Weald in celebration of what his stories gave to the world. Poke around further and you might find Owl's Tree or 'the North Pole'.

Easier to locate is the **Poohsticks Bridge** – officially known as Posingford Bridge – where Pooh, Piglet and Co invented the pastime of poohsticks. The wooden bridge is a replacement of the 1907 original – the Disneyland Corporation stumped up the cash for its rebuilding – but happily it is identical to what you might remember from the illustrations. To find it turn off the B2026 1½ miles south of Hartfield, and the Poohsticks car park is a short way along on the right. The little walk leads through woodland and down a track to the bridge, where you may well find that there's a conspicuous dearth of anything resembling a poohstick – so be sure to take your own supply of judiciously selected twigs.

Nutley Windmill (☏ 01435 873367 ☉ Mar–Sep last Sun of month & bank holidays), the only working open-trestle post mill in Britain (and one of only five such structures surviving in any form), is just outside the main-road village of Nutley. It's rather elusive, as you see it from a distance and then it disappears until the last moment. The easiest way to find it is from Nutley: take the A22 north, then turn east on the road towards Crowborough for a mile, until a car park appears on the left – the mill is a five-minute walk from there. Renovated in 1968 after 60 years of disuse, its age is uncertain; entrance is free of charge.

Another feature to include in a walk here is the **Airman's Grave**: a walled enclosure marks the spot where a Wellington Bomber crashed in 1941, killing its crew of six, including its 22-year-old pilot. It was on the way back from a raid on Cologne and got hit in the conflict, but struggling to make it on just one engine in atrocious weather conditions was unable to crash land and ended up here. A few years later the

The original Pooh, Kanga, Tigger, Eeyore and Piglet stuffed toys are now living in retirement in the New York Public Library. Of these, Eeyore is said to be the most identifiable and Piglet the least. Tigger and Kanga appeared on the scene later than the others – Christopher Milne, in his highly readable autobiography *The Enchanted Places*, speculates that these two may have been added partly for their literary potential. Roo was lost during Christopher Milne's childhood in a family outing from Cotchford Farm, and Owl and Rabbit never existed except in the creative mind of A A Milne. Shepard, who drew the original illustrations, drew Christopher Robin from life – unlike the animals, for which he used his imagination.

As a child I found the presence of Christopher Robin in the stories rather an irritating intrusion into a magical world. He seemed utterly wet and a weed. Having read *The Enchanted Places*, one gets the bigger picture. Christopher Robin was born in 1920; five years later the Milnes bought Cotchford Farm and came down for weekends from London, before moving in permanently. This must have been a very idyllic world for him to grow up in. His was certainly a happy childhood and at first he revelled in his celebrity status, though by the age of eight he dropped the 'Robin' and at boarding school he was not at all comfortable at being Christopher Robin; you can imagine the ribbing he must have got.

The Milnes' walks into Ashdown Forest took them to a little valley with the stream shallow enough to paddle across; it was here that the 'North Pole' was discovered by Pooh and his associates.

mothers of crew members set up a simple wooden cross on the site, and this was later improved with a stone cross. There's a ceremony on Remembrance Sunday each year, with poppy wreaths laid down and the Last Post bugled. Despite the name, no-one is actually buried in the 'Grave'.

¶¶ FOOD & DRINK

The snag about pubs in and around Ashdown Forest is that they aren't brilliantly located for walks, but there are a couple worth driving to.

The Foresters Arms Fairwarp TN22 3BP ✆ 01825 712808 ⌀ theforestersfairwarp.com. By a village green, with low beams, an open fire and a reliable selection of pub standards.
The Hatch Inn Coleman's Hatch TN7 4EJ ✆ 01342 822363 ⌀ hatchinn.co.uk. Even cosier, this pub, founded in 1430, serves stylishly presented dishes in an attractive weatherboarded building with a gorgeous garden.

21 HARTFIELD

Metrobus 291 (Crawley–Tunbridge Wells; hourly Mon–Sat, less frequent Sun)

North of Ashdown Forest, in Hartfield itself, the shop and tearoom **Pooh Corner** (see opposite) is the area's one concession to Milne commercialism, but on the gentlest scale; everything Pooh-related you might imagine is here, including the great books themselves.

Elsewhere the **village** has enough to justify a small potter around. Church Lane leads off the main street by the Anchor pub, a former workhouse, to the quaintest of lychgates – beneath a jutting-out 16th-century cottage. Beyond the churchyard spreads the Croft, the village's open space, cricket, football and stoolball pitch combined. By the B2026 at the northern end, Hartfield's long-

"Church Lane leads off the main street by the Anchor pub, a former workhouse, to the quaintest of lychgates."

defunct railway station stands by the former trackbed which is now the ten-mile Forest Way (East Grinstead to Groombridge) – offering an undemanding, sheltered walk or cycle ride; there are no views at all in the section around Hartfield, though. I've used it on several occasions to walk east to the hamlet of **Withyham** (and then up through the Five Hundred Acre Wood and on to the Ashdown Forest heathlands). Withyham has a popular pub, the Dorset Arms, a very comfy looking rectory and a memorable church. The church occupies an unevenly sloping, idyllically shady churchyard full of wonky, calligraphic sandstone tombs. Inside, the tomb of the gentry occupies the limelight – a most lump-in-the-throat memorial to the Sackvilles' 13-year-old son, with weeping parents, a frieze of skull-bearing children and a heartfelt epitaph 'What mother would not weepe for such a son…'

⍟ FOOD & DRINK

The Anchor Inn Church St, Hartfield TN7 4AG ✆ 01892 770424 ⌂ anchorhartfield. com. This dining pub offers classic dishes such as cottage pie, gammon and Sunday roasts. Upstairs, there are four guestrooms named after Pooh and his pals.

The Dorset Arms Withyham TN7 4BD ✆ 01892 770278 ⌂ dorset-arms.co.uk. Belonging to the Buckhurst Estate, this upmarket country pub with rooms is a free house with an ever-changing selection of cask beers and an above-average wine list. Thin on vegan options, the menu focuses on hyper-local meat and seasonal game.

Perryhill Orchards Edenbridge Rd, nr Hartfield TN7 4JJ ✆ 01892 770595 ⌂ perryhillorchards.co.uk. By the B2026 north of Hartfield, this farm shop sells its own apple juice, perry and cider from the adjacent orchard (tastings available), with a range of tastes to suit most palates. I find the cider from the barrel consistently good, and it goes very well with fish.

Pooh Corner High St, Hartfield TN7 4AE ✆ 01892 770456 ⊗ poohcorner.co.uk. This weatherboarded shop and café/restaurant serves family-friendly treats in Piglet's Tearoom and a rather posh afternoon tea in the E H Shepard Room.

22 ERIDGE ROCKS & HARRISON'S ROCKS

B&H Regency Route bus 29 (Brighton–Tunbridge Wells; three per hour Mon–Sat, less frequent Sun)

Quite an eye-opener in the gentle Wealden landscape, these are two lines of shapely greensand formations (free public access), both magnets for climbers – it saves them a hefty trip to the Peak District or West Country. They are in mixed woodlands that harbour woodland birds like great spotted woodpeckers and long-tailed tits; it is striking how trees cling to many of the rocks. Both sets of rocks are of soft sandstone that has been weathered into all manner of shapes, with fissures and bastions.

A variety of ferns, lichens and mosses – some rare – thrive in the damp conditions, the rocks absorb water and some are 30ft high.

Eridge Rocks is on Sussex Wildlife Trust land (⊗ sussexwildlifetrust. org.uk), at Eridge Green; turn into Warren Farm Lane from the A26 by a small church; a track leads to a car park (♥ TQ554355). Though tackling the rocks is definitely not for unequipped climbers, the walk along them is a delight – the views are rather better at Eridge, where the path goes beneath this strange inland mini-cliff for a fascinating half a mile, than Harrison's, but both deserve exploring. Eridge Rocks is designated a Site of Special Scientific Interest, with some rare mosses and liverworts, and a Regionally Important Geological Site, and is the only place in Sussex where you can see the Tunbridge slimy fern, if your eyesight is up to it (it is quite tiny).

"Eridge Rocks is designated a Site of Special Scientific Interest, with some rare mosses and liverworts."

It adjoins a larger forest called **Broadwater Warren**, an RSPB reserve. Graffiti scratched into the rock nearest the gate record that the trees were planted in 1811. There were also plantings of bamboo, which has gone somewhat out of control. Access at Eridge was restricted for many years, and surreptitious climbing went on invoking the wrath of local gamekeepers, but the SWT now runs it and has lifted the ban. Its climbs

Eridge Rocks & Harrison's Rocks

✲ OS Explorer map 135; eight miles, through undulating farmland & forest; numerous stiles.
Loos: Harrison's Rocks car park. **Refreshments**: The Boar's Head Inn (nr Crowborough TN6 3GR) just south of the start point is useful, as is The Nevill Crest & Gun (Eridge Green TN3 9JR), 100yds off the walk, reached by the footway along the A26, and The Huntsman (Eridge TN3 9LE), a good food option. There's also a drinking fountain outside the loos at Harrison's Rocks car park.

By car: start at Boarshead ♀ TQ535330 (signposted, just off A26 north of Crowborough, turn into Boarshead Road, then immediately left at a T-junction, and follow this old stretch of A-road to where it ends). There's plenty of roadside parking, and also a bus stop on the A26 at this turning.

By bus: B&H Regency Route bus 29 (Brighton–Tunbridge Wells, three per hour, less frequent on Sun) passes nearby. If you're using buses, it's easiest to start at Eridge Green (♀ TQ567356), where the bus stop is right on the walk where it goes down the lane between the black-and-white mock-Tudor building and the church. Join the walk at point **5**. Or you could get off at the Boarshead turning (and start the walk where the directions begin), which means you have to walk a quarter of a mile along the very quiet defunct stretch of A-road to start the walk, but this does have the advantage over starting from Eridge Green, as it means you get to the spectacular rock formations a bit later in the walk.

By train: start at Eridge (turn right out of the front of the station, take the first right and after 400yds turn left at a grassy triangle and join the walk at point **8**.

F or me this is one of the most enjoyably varied and surprising walks in the High Weald, with views of three of Sussex's sandstone rock outcrops that are the prime terrain for climbers in the southeast. The opening section from Boarshead gets quintessential Wealden views straight away, and there's a very beautiful, shady forest (RSPB Reserve) beyond Eridge Rocks. Allow four hours' walking: plenty to look at and three pubs to aim for. You could use the bus from Lewes or Tunbridge Wells and reduce the walk to four miles by starting at Eridge Green and following the walk as far as Boarshead, then pick the bus up from the stop on the A26 by the entrance to the Boar's Head pub: a handy way of seeing the walk's highlights without doing the whole thing.

It's quite well waymarked, but as this is complicated country you do need to follow the directions or the OS map carefully. Most of the road sections are very quiet, apart from the crossing of the busy A26 twice (good sight lines along the road make this safe enough though).

I have started at a point that has plenty of roadside parking; there's also a small car park at Eridge Rocks, and a larger one at Harrison's Rocks.

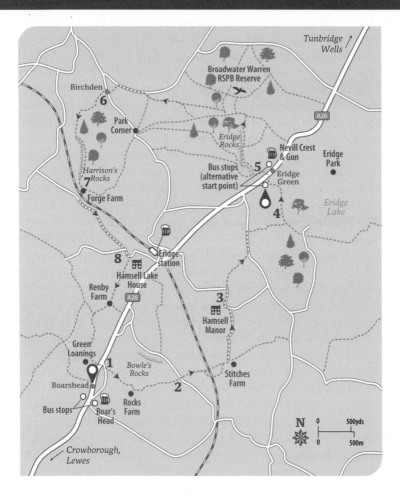

1 Facing the bollards at the end of the road, turn right by a tall wooden shed on a concrete driveway, which immediately bends right (you'll go past a tennis court on your left), and passes some back gardens, with gorgeous Wealden views on your left. At a farm (**Rocks Farm**), the track deviates round it to the left as signposted, and then drops down the edges of fields, with views over the hedgerow of **Bowle's Rocks** – the first sandstone outcrop seen on this walk – and its adjacent dry-ski slope. ▶

Eridge Rocks & Harrison's Rocks (continued)

2 ◄ At the bottom, go through a gate, cross a lane and continue on the path opposite and slightly to the right through another gate. This drops down alongside woodland, crosses a bridge at the very bottom of the valley (not to be confused with a small plank bridge on the right before you reach this: it clearly leads nowhere) and continues half right through a young plantation and under a railway bridge, then rises up the right side of the field. At a break in the hedgerow on your right, go right to a group of buildings around **Stitches Farm**. Turn left on the driveway in front of the red-roofed house (with a characteristic **catslide roof** that slopes down to the eaves – very much a Wealden feature). Follow this driveway as it drops and rises (passing two driveways joining to the left; you'll also see a fast-flowing stream running through a ravine to the right – one of several such features, termed as **gills**, on this walk, and again a High Weald speciality), and just after a pond away to the left, turn left at a T-junction where the view suddenly opens out ahead.

3 After 50yds turn right near **Hamsell Manor** (opposite the Coach House) on another driveway. This drops, and just as it is about to bend left, take a narrow path on the right side, crossing a small bridge and emerging into a large field. Cross the field diagonally to a waymarked stile, out of sight in the far right-hand corner, then go forward down a grassy track. Lying on the right side of the path is a mysterious iron object in the form of a hollow shaft, D-shaped in cross-section (a traction engine funnel or military hardware?). I've posted a photo of it on social media, and it generated interest from military historians and archaeologists, but no-one has identified its provenance. Carry on down across a field, and down to its bottom right-hand corner and on to a road. Turn left along the road for 300yds, and just before it crosses a stream and rises, take a path on the right, along the stream and at the bottom of fields.

4 At the end of the third field, turn left on a path just inside woodland (if you want a viewpoint over **Eridge Lake**, turn right here, through woods that are carpeted with bluebells in spring – in a few minutes you emerge on to an open hillside with a view over **Eridge Park** and the lake). Keep along the right-hand field edges all the way to the A26 at **Eridge Green**. Cross over carefully and turn right on the pavement for 100yds then turn left (signposted Park Corner) by a bus stop (where you'll start if you're coming by bus) and take the lane between a black-and-white mock-Tudor building and the church. The **Nevill Crest & Gun** pub is 100yds further along the A26.

5 Follow the lane to go through the entrance to **Eridge Rocks** on the right (marked by a sign; the first rock is just visible). Follow the path beneath the base of the rocks, which continue for half a mile, curving round slightly to the left. Where the rocks end, ignore a crossing-path and turn left at a T-junction in denser forest by an RSPB sign. This brings you into

Broadwater Warren, an RSPB reserve rich with bird species: at dusk you might see a nightjar in summer in pursuit of moths or in spring a woodcock, while winter is the season for lesser redpolls, suspended from birch and willow trees to find seeds, or chattering from the trees.

Ignore the first track on the right, but take the second one (by a fence corner), and after 70yds turn left through a gate on the track. After half a mile, where another track joins from the left, you see a field ahead and away to the left; carry on forward on the left-hand of two paths ahead (not the main track but the narrower path), just inside the forest and alongside the field. Emerge on to Park Corner Lane, turn right and immediately left (in front of a house with a bull in chains depicted on its gable) at the T-junction, along Station Road, marked as National Cycle Network route 18. Some 100yds before the Groombridge village sign turn left over a stile where the telephone wire crosses the road, and head up the field to a point between the two prominent gabled red-brick houses. Turn right on the road for 30yds.

6 Turn left into the lane with the Harrison's Rocks sign. After this enters woodlands and is about to drop, take a path to the left, soon dropping between banks. Cross over a track and take the waymarked path ahead (the car park, loos and a drinking water fountain are just to the right). The path emerges into a semi-open area, with the railway in view (maybe with some old rolling stock visible from the **Spa Valley Railway**); the railway later runs adjacent to the path. Eventually take a gate on the left by a sign for Harrison's Rocks and immediately turn right on the lower path beneath the rocks themselves. Later, fork right through a gate to resume walking close to the railway.

7 After a house (**Forge Farm**), turn right on a lane in front of an oast house, over the level crossing, and then turn left at the T-junction. After half a mile ignore a lane to the right signposted as a bridleway. The lane bends left over a stream (the white bridge parapets are more obvious than the stream itself), then 30yds later turn right on a driveway by a grassy triangle.

8 After **Hamsell Lake House** on the left (opposite which an attractive lake is glimpsed), this continues as a path, soon into a field: continue straight ahead, passing beneath **Renby Farm**, then joining a track at its corner and keeping forward. Turn left at a junction of routes with yellow marker arrows, up a sunken track. Go over a stile and keep right on a lane that becomes a house drive, passing a house called Little Renby. At the end, when you are just above the A26 as the driveway is about to bend left (by the entrance to **Green Loanings**), turn right on a narrow path. Cross the A26 with great care (fortunately the sight lines are very good) and take the path opposite up to the bollards at the end of the old road at the main starting point.

of 15 to 30ft feature challenges with names such as Sandstorm, The Crunch and More Cake for Me.

Harrison's Rocks was where the great Chris Bonington cut his climbing teeth – his introduction to rock climbing here is described in his book *I Chose to Climb*.

⟟ FOOD & DRINK

The Boars Head Inn Boarshead, nr Crowborough TN6 3GR ✆ 01892 660447. This roadside inn dates back to the 17th century, but has been much altered over the years: an extension with big windows offers splendid long-distance views. Real ale and good quality pub grub.

The Huntsman Groombridge Ln, Eridge TN3 9LE ✆ 01892 864258 ⌂ huntsmanpuberidge. co.uk ◷ Tue–Sun. Right by Eridge railway station, this has an appealing garden and an unpretentious, proper-pub interior, with no gimmicks or piped music. The menu changes daily and uses lots of locally sourced seasonal ingredients. Children are welcome.

Nevill Crest & Gun Eridge Rd, Eridge Green TN3 9JR ✆ 01892 864209 ⌂ brunningandprice. co.uk. A civilised, relaxed tile-hung dining pub, only a few minutes' walk from Eridge Rocks. It's spacious and rambling, with a traditional bar at the front and a large conservatory overlooking the back garden.

23 HIGH ROCKS & THE SPA VALLEY RAILWAY

B&H Regency Route bus 29 (Brighton–Tunbridge Wells; three per hour Mon–Sat, less frequent Sun)

More rocky wonders await just outside the western side of Tunbridge Wells in the form of **High Rocks** (High Rocks Lane, TN3 9JJ ⌂ highrocks. co.uk), where the sandstone crags are crossed by 11 footbridges, creating an aerial walk. There also used to be a maze, bowling green and cold bath here in its 19th-century tourist heyday. The Spa Valley Railway (✆ 01892 537715 ⌂ spavalleyrailway.co.uk ◷ check website) stops here on the way from Tunbridge Wells West to Groombridge, a line that closed in 1985 and partly reopened from 1996, and then to Eridge, glimpsing Harrison's Rocks on the way. Unusually, this heritage railway runs alongside a mainline track: Eridge is on the Uckfield branch of the Oxted Line from London. The ride is on steam or diesel-hauled services; the oldest carriages are 1932, from the Metropolitan Railway; the others are mostly 1950s and 1960s vintage. Themed events, such as murder-mystery specials, dining trains, ale and cider festivals and Thomas the Tank Engine days, take place throughout the year.

TOWARDS THE KENT BORDER

Some of the most lusciously secretive High Weald scenery is hereabouts, with a host of hamlets and villages tucked away in the folds of the land. A look at the OS map reveals numerous north–south tracks still in use. These originate from routes along which swineherds drove their herds to winter pastures in the forest in medieval times. The herds were led to the same places each year, to what were known as 'dens' – the suffix is found in many local place names.

24 MAYFIELD

Stagecoach bus 51 (Tunbridge Wells–Eastbourne; twice-hourly)

This is my nomination for the most perfect-looking Wealden village: Mayfield, three miles north of Heathfield, grew rich in medieval times on the iron industry – hence the Elizabethan cannon made in the local foundry and now proudly displayed in the High Street – and has survived the centuries remarkably well, with barely a hanging basket or pantile out of place.

The long High Street, with its raised brick pavements, has an eye-catching array of half-timbering, tile-hanging and cottagey front gardens; the most imposing are the 15th-century house known as Yeomans, Walnut Tree House, Middle House (a popular oak-beamed dining pub) and the Old Brewhouse. The church opposite Middle House has two locally cast iron memorial slabs in the nave, each to a Thomas Sands – the one of 1708 very well crafted but the earlier one of 1668 spectacularly amateurish and wonky, and with some of the lettering the wrong way round. On the High Street by the entrance to the churchyard, a red devil depicted on the bottom of the village sign is a nod to the village legend revolving around St Dunstan, who is said to have had a forge in the village and to whom the church is dedicated. The legend relates that the devil assumed the disguise of a young girl and attempted to seduce the saint who was then working at his forge; the plan didn't work and St Dunstan spotted the cloven hoofs beneath the skirt, tweaked the devil by his nose with red-hot pincers and lobbed him into a spring at Tunbridge Wells, which consequently gained sulphurous qualities.

Standing out among the tiles and half timbering is the Gothic stone façade of St Leonard's School, a Catholic girls' boarding school. This occupies the former palace of the archbishops of Canterbury; in 1617

THE SUSSEX BONFIRE TRADITION – BUT NOT IN LEWES

Lewes is justly heralded as the prime place to see the bonfire celebrations on 5 November (page 170). But what's less known is that the numerous other societies, mostly in East Sussex, start celebrating the bonfire season in September, and carry on each Saturday until late November. Many other societies come along on those days, and there are processions, bonfires and fireworks. In fact, these are generally more manageable and family-friendly than struggling through the crowds in Lewes in an atmosphere that certainly doesn't suit small children. The usual running order roughly falls into months as follows (though some may get switched around from year to year), with all events on Saturdays.

September: Uckfield, Crowborough, Mayfield, Burgess Hill. Note the Uckfield and Crowborough events are really carnivals with processions but no bonfires or fireworks, even though they are run by bonfire societies.

October: Rotherfield and Mark Cross, Eastbourne, Ninfield, Hastings, Hailsham, Seaford, Nevill Juvenile Bonfire Society (Lewes), Northiam, Fletching, Eastbourne, Staplecross, Newick, Littlehampton. Friday in late October: Lewes Bonfire Council Bonfire Costume Competition, Lewes Town Hall, with the costumes that will appear on 5 November on display.

November: Lindfield, Lewes (5 November, or on 4 November if 5 November falls on a Sunday). After 5 November: Battle, East Hoathly, Chailey, South Heighton, Edenbridge (Kent), Isfield and Little Horsted, Rye, Robertsbridge, Hawkhurst.

it fell into the hands of the Baker family, who owned several local foundries, and has been a school since 1872. Its restored 14th-century Great Hall is its most notable survival.

During the reign of Queen Mary in the 16th century, four Protestant martyrs from Mayfield were condemned for their religion and burned at the stake in Lewes. Perhaps partly for that reason, Mayfield's bonfire society continues to thrive to this day in a tradition that commemorates each of the 17 victims from various parts of Sussex with a burning cross held aloft during the bonfire celebrations.

¶¶ FOOD & DRINK

Middle House High St, Mayfield TN20 6AB ☏ 01435 872146 ⌂ mhmayfield.co.uk. Quite an eye-opener, this Grade I-listed house was built around 1575 for the Keeper of the Privy Purse to Elizabeth I and remained a private residence until 1920. Its dark-panelled rooms have changed little over the years, though it's now a very pleasant hotel offering elegant dining (everything's made on the premises), and you could just pop in for a drink or for afternoon tea.

Rose and Crown Fletching St, Mayfield TN20 6TE ✆ 01435 872200
🖥 roseandcrownmayfield.co.uk. By a triangular green at the bottom end of the village (a very pleasant few minutes' stroll down the hill from the High Street) and with seating out in front beneath a horse chestnut tree, this is a weather-boarded, convivial pub that welcomes children.

25 BEWL WATER

Nr Lamberhurst TN3 8JH ✆ 01892 890000 🖥 bewlwater.co.uk; no nearby public transport

Bisected by the East Sussex/Kent border, this naturalistic and undeniably landscape-enhancing reservoir is the largest body of water in southeastern England. Completed in 1975, it drowned a landscape – as evidenced by the little, ancient, sunken lanes to nowhere that approach it and abruptly fizzle out at the shore. It provides water to the Medway towns, Thanet, Hastings and elsewhere, and doubles as a major hub of outdoor activities. The Round Reservoir Route – open to walkers and cyclists (and horse riders May to October) – makes a varied 12½-mile circuit of the lake, all nicely varied and alternating between patches of woodland and open ground. The lanes on the south side around Three Leg Cross and Ticehurst onward make good starting points, with a number of paths leading to the water's edge.

On the north (Kent) side, the dam and visitor centre are the main starting point (with bike hire, watersports, a café and a campsite on offer). Unfortunately, there are no public transport routes nearby, but the pricey parking charge at the visitor centre can be avoided if you start from Ticehurst and follow paths leading to the very scenic south shore.

26 BATEMAN'S

Nr Burwash TN19 7DS ✆ 01435 882302; National Trust; Compass bus 231 (Heathfield–Etchingham; several daily Mon–Sat, pre-booking required)

> **Kipling strikes me personally as the most complete man of genius (as distinct from fine intelligence) that I have ever known.**
> Henry James

Built along a ridge and on the A265 east of Heathfield, the handsome village street of **Burwash** has tile-hung, timber-frame houses in the typical Wealden tradition. A short distance below it is **Bateman's**, the

17th-century country house where the Indian-born author and 'poet of Empire' Rudyard Kipling (1865–1936) moved in 1902, three years after the death of his daughter, purchasing the house, its outbuildings, its 18th-century watermill and 33 acres of grounds. It was a cherished escape for the author, who had become a huge celebrity in Edwardian England, as creator of the *Barrack Room Ballads*, in which he encapsulated the feelings of the British soldier, and the *Just So Stories*.

"Bateman's was a cherished escape for Kipling, who had become a huge celebrity in Edwardian England."

He had travelled much – including in the Far East – and after his marriage to Carrie Balestier in 1892 lived in Vermont where he revelled in the autumn colours. Prior to Bateman's, he lived at Rottingdean in Sussex, but the hordes of sightseers keen to catch a glimpse of the literary celebrity were becoming increasingly tiresome to him. At Bateman's he found privacy and seclusion: it was love at first sight. 'Behold us, lawful owners of a grey stone lichened house – AD1634 over the door,' he recorded, 'beamed, panelled, with old oak staircase, and all untouched and unfaked. It is a good and peaceable place.' He adored being driven by his chauffeur along the Sussex lanes: his beloved 1928 Rolls Royce Phantom I is displayed in the garage.

Inside, the **house** is strongly evocative of Kipling's day, his book-lined study seemingly unchanged, with pen and typewriter at the ready. His desk looks out to a splendid oak tree. The room is dark and rather snug, filled with mementoes of his time in the Far East. During his years here he wrote two connected collections of poetry and stories: *Puck of Pook's Hill* (1906) – the hill of the title is in view from the house – and *Rewards and Fairies* (1910), which contained the perennially popular poem *If*. He also wrote pamphlets in support of the aims of World War I, only to have his only son, John, die in the Battle of Loos in 1915. He continued to write into the last years of his life, but latterly his output declined in quantity and success. His wife survived him by seven years, and bequeathed Bateman's to the National Trust in 1939. Elsie, the only

1 The 25ft pyramid to 'Mad Jack' Fuller at St Thomas à Becket Church in Brightling.
2 Mayfield is arguably the most perfect-looking Wealden village. **3** Rudyard Kipling's writing desk in Bateman's, the house where he spent his final years. **4** Centuries-old Wealden fireplaces in the yard of a modern fireplace business in Robertsbridge. ▶

one of their children to live beyond the age of 18, died in 1976 and left the copyright of his works to the National Trust too.

The delightful **grounds** slope down to the River Dudwell and the watermill. Using money from the Nobel Prize for Literature which he won in 1907, Kipling laid out the pond, the rose garden and its yew hedges. In the watermill he installed a water turbine to drive an electric generator that gave modest lighting to the house.

Reputedly, Bateman's was built for an ironmaster, and this idea seemed to appeal to Kipling, who installed a splendid old Wealden iron fireback here, although the ironmaster connection has yet to be proven. **Burwash** was for centuries busy with iron-making – its village sign depicts a smithy and its church contains a remarkable 14th-century cast-iron tomb slab to one John Collins, one of a family of ironmasters who owned a forge nearby at Socknersh. Placed on the wall by the Lady Chapel altar, it is said to be the oldest such iron memorial in existence.

Bateman's stands on the threshold of some of the deepest, most unchanged landscapes in the High Weald. I have created a six-mile **walk** for the Royal Geographical Society Discovering Britain series from Burwash into the **Dudwell Valley**, leading through ancient woodland, across a wildflower meadow and highlighting such local features as shaws, granaries, oast houses, boundary dykes and iron-making sites. It was a fascinating project to get involved with – the walk instructions and details of what to look out for can be downloaded as a PDF or as an audio file (where I talk you through what's happening on the route) for free from ⏛ bit.ly/burwash-walk.

27 BRIGHTLING

Wealdlink Community bus 225 (Crowborough–Battle, limited service Tue & Thu)

The sheep-grazed churchyard around St Thomas à Becket Church here at Brightling, on lanes a couple of miles south of Burwash, has the aptly curious memorial to that stalwart among Sussex eccentrics, 'Mad Jack' (John) Fuller (1757–1834), the local Georgian squire and ironmaster who is commemorated in the form of a 25ft-tall stone pyramid; alas the popular legend that his skeleton was inside, dressed up in a top hat and eating dinner, turned out to be a complete fabrication when the structure was renovated and opened in 1982. He wasn't at all mad, in fact, but left his mark on the Sussex landscape in the form of many noble philanthropic gestures, purchasing Bodiam Castle so that it could be safeguarded for posterity, setting up Fullerian professorships in Chemistry and Physiology at the Royal Institution, sponsored Michael Faraday's pioneering work into electro-magnetism and endowed Eastbourne with its first lifeboat. He funded the recasting of five church bells at Brightling and the addition of a new treble one, and commissioned the barrel organ in 1820 – the largest in the country to be in full working order.

The churchyard pyramid was the apt finale for a man who embellished the locality with some notable follies. On Brightling Beacon he erected the unexplained **Brightling Needle**, a 65ft-tall obelisk that may or may not commemorate triumphs in the Napoleonic War, while his **Observatory** (visible from the road to Burwash) of 1818 originally housed a camera obscura, projecting an image of the surroundings on to a wall inside. Within his estate – Brightling Park – was a Coade stone summerhouse in the form of a Grecian **rotunda temple**, allegedly a venue for gambling and orgies (or perhaps not). The pointy-topped **Sugar Loaf**, seen on the road from Battle to Heathfield, is said to stem from a bet he made that he could see the spire of the Church of St Giles, Dallington, from his house: when it transpired that he was wrong, he had this mock-up of a spire built so that he would win the wager. His 35ft **Tower**, east of the road from Brightling

"The churchyard pyramid was the apt finale for a man who embellished the locality with some notable follies."

to Darwell Hole and easily accessed from a public footpath, was traditionally said to have been built so he could watch the workmen's progress on restoring Bodiam Castle – but it is thought to date a few years earlier from his Bodiam phase, and it seems more likely that he simply liked adorning the landscape with viewpoints.

28 ROBERTSBRIDGE

Hastings Line (London–Hastings); Stagecoach bus 1066 (Hastings–Tunbridge Wells; hourly Mon–Sat, less frequent Sun)

Another conspicuously handsome Wealden village, Robertsbridge, bypassed by the A21 south of Hurst Green, has a sloping main street with an eye-catching array of pantiles, half-timbering and weatherboarding. Just a few minutes north of Battle by railway, it's a former junction for trains from Bodiam, Tenterden and Headcorn in Kent. A budding heritage railway project, the **Rother Valley Railway**, is reinstating the

TRUG MAKING, SUSSEX STYLE

Robertsbridge is a key manufacturer of cricket bats, made by the renowned Gray-Nicolls company. An unexpected by-product of this comes in the peculiarly Sussex industry of making wooden open-topped containers known as trugs. Variously round, oval, rectangular or square, with a central carrying handle, properly made Sussex trugs are admirably sturdy and practical – useful for gathering fruit, carrying gardening materials or storing what you will. The trug developed where there were no suitable materials to make baskets, so instead willow was used from marshy areas like the Pevensey Levels and sweet chestnut from the woodlands. As a concept the trug is probably very ancient indeed, and comes from an Anglo-Saxon word 'trog': documentary evidence shows that its present design is basically unaltered in some 200 years.

Charlie Groves (⌀ thetrugstore.co.uk), based not in Robertsbridge but near Hailsham, north of Eastbourne, is one of the last trugmakers in Sussex. He told me that huge quantities of willow used to be burnt up after billets were extracted for the manufacture of cricket bats. Now he uses the remainder for trug making. He uses sweet chestnut for the frame and clefts of willow, which are soaked in water, as boards. Willow feet are added and a coating of linseed oil is applied.

Trugs are widely available across Sussex.

Robertsbridge Junction–Bodiam line, linking it to the Kent & East Sussex Railway (page 318), a steam enthusiasts' favourite.

A surprise awaits at the fireplace business **Ripleys Forge & Fireplaces** (Bridge Bungalow, Robertsbridge TN32 5NY ✆ 01580 880324 ⌀ ripley-fireplaces.co.uk), run by Kay Ripley and her son John at their home just outside the village near where the road crosses the River Rother. The front yard is crammed full of Wealden iron, most notably a unique and rare collection of locally made firebacks. Kay gave me a tour: the oldest ones are plain pieces of iron, then came simple ones with designs created by imprinting everyday objects and handprints into the sand moulds. Later designs were more elaborate and specially moulded, often with heraldic themes. She explained they have a much wider range of originals than you're likely to find anywhere else, and that her father-in-law started the collection after he settled here in 1920. 'The biggest fireback we have is the Ashburnham one – under that cannon,' she said, pointing to a cannon that originated from Woolwich Arsenal.

Heading north out of Robertsbridge, a choice of footpaths leads you along the River Rother to Etchingham, the next station on the Hastings Line towards Tunbridge Wells.

¶¶ FOOD & DRINK

The George Inn High St, Robertsbridge TN32 5AW ✆ 01580 880315
⌂ thegeorgerobertsbridge.co.uk. Stylishly modernised dining pub with rooms, run by
enthusiastic staff. As well as generously filled sandwiches, there's hearty pub classics and
homemade puddings, using ingredients from local suppliers. Children welcome; some
outdoor seating.

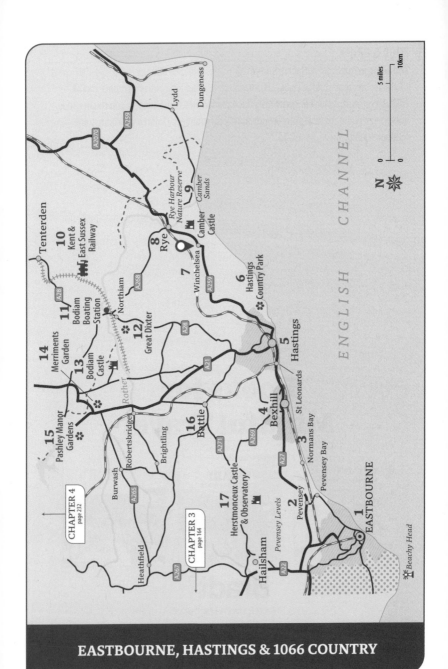

EASTBOURNE, HASTINGS & 1066 COUNTRY

5

EASTBOURNE, HASTINGS & 1066 COUNTRY

Where the South Downs end at Beachy Head, a stretch of coast extends eastwards to the Kent border, comprising the most diverse seaboard in Sussex. While researching this book, I took a boat cruise from genteel Eastbourne and strolled its gorgeous Victorian pier, tucked into fish and chips by the net houses of Hastings Old Town after an exhilarating walk over the adjacent sandstone cliffs, wandered through the cobbled streets of Rye and cycled my way along the unheralded coastline west of Bexhill's astonishing 1930s De La Warr Pavilion.

This region has numerous reminders of invasions both threatened and actual. Most famously it was the landing point of the Normans in 1066 in the last successful invasion of the mainland, from which they went on to defeat the English at what is now called Battle and change the course of English history. Then in medieval times it was a confederation of wealthy ports supplying naval craft and men to the monarch in return for certain privileges, including tax exemption and legal jurisdiction over criminals. These Sussex and Kent towns were known as the Cinque Ports, which originally numbered five, but the list later grew to include Hastings, Rye and Winchelsea. The area is instilled with a potent sense of the past, with Normans in evidence at Pevensey Castle (originally Roman) and Battle Abbey, and magnificent moated castles at Herstmonceux and Bodiam – the latter reached by the Kent and East Sussex Railway, and easily visited in conjunction with Great Dixter, the great 20th-century horticultural creation of Christopher Lloyd.

Camber Sands is by far the premier beach in East Sussex, and a bike ride away from Rye. Some former coastal settlements now stand well inland as the sea has silted up over the centuries, leaving expanses of rich, marshy farmland that have a quiet, brooding beauty – seen at its best around Rye Harbour nature reserve, the Royal Military Canal between Winchelsea and Cliff End and the Pevensey Levels. The **Coastal**

Culture Trail (⊘ coastalculturetrail.com) links three top art attractions: the Towner Art Gallery in Eastbourne, Bexhill's De La Warr Pavilion and Hastings Contemporary. Designed variously as an 18-mile route for walkers, cyclists and train travellers, it can be completed in a day but is easily made into a longer amble along the coast; the website gives lots of suggestions.

The High Weald Area of Outstanding Natural Beauty (page 233) extends across part of this chapter, including Bodiam, Great Dixter, Battle and Hastings.

GETTING AROUND

TRAINS

Eastbourne to Rye: The East Coastway Line from Brighton and Lewes to Eastbourne is good news for coastal explorers; it continues to Hastings, where it connects to the Marshlink Line to Ashford in Kent. The first stop east of Eastbourne, **Pevensey and Westham**, is within walking distance of Pevensey Castle. East of Normans Bay, the line runs very close to the coast and into **Bexhill**, just a few minutes' stroll from the De La Warr Pavilion. **Hastings** station is central, though a good ten minutes on foot to the Old Town. Kent-bound trains stop at **Winchelsea** (the station is just under a mile from the village) and **Rye**.

Tunbridge Wells to Hastings: Inland, options by train are far more limited. Hastings Line trains from London Charing Cross stop at Tunbridge Wells, then take a scenic route through the Weald via **Robertsbridge** and (more usefully for most visitors) **Battle**, from which it's a 15-minute ride into Hastings.

BUSES

Brighton and Hove Buses (⊘ buses.co.uk) offer regular, scenic bus services into the region from Brighton, Lewes, Newhaven and Seaford. Other buses to and around **Eastbourne**, **Bexhill** and **Hastings** are run by Stagecoach (⊘ stagecoachbus.com): you can make cash or contactless payments when you board, or buy smartphone tickets through the Stagecoach app.

Inland, buses cover more destinations than trains. Useful long-distance routes include Stagecoach bus 51 (Tunbridge Wells–Eastbourne; twice-hourly, less frequent on Sun), 54 (Uckfield–Eastbourne; hourly, less

i **TOURIST INFORMATION**

For most of this area see  visit1066country.com
Eastbourne Compton St, BN21 4BP ✏ 01323 415415 🖋 visiteastbourne.com
Hastings Station Approach, TN34 1BA ✏ 0303 003 8265

frequent on Sun), 98/99 (Eastbourne–Hastings; frequent services), 29 (Hastings–Tenterden, for the **Kent & East Sussex Railway**; hourly Mon–Sat) and 349 (Hastings–Hawkhurst via **Bodiam**; twice hourly, less frequent on Sun). The aptly named Stagecoach bus 1066 (Hastings–Tunbridge Wells; hourly, less frequent on Sun) calls at **Battle**, and bus 100/101 (Hastings–New Romney; hourly) gets you right into **Winchelsea**, saving you the slog up the hill from the railway station, then continues to **Rye** and **Camber Sands**, the best beach hereabouts.

CYCLING

The National Cycle Network has some quiet routes over the peaceful, flat and easily cycled **Pevensey Levels** between Polegate, Pevensey, Wartling and the western fringes of Bexhill. From **Eastbourne** National Cycle Route 21 is mostly urban, around the eastern fringes of the town, then joins up with the **Cuckoo Trail** (page 206) proper from Polegate to Heathfield. Along the **coast**, routes 21 and 2 are useful, taking in sections of road and seafront through Pevensey, Bexhill and Hastings, east of which it's appreciably hilly through Fairlight before dipping to shore level at Cliff End and heading on through Winchelsea and towards Rye. Further north in the High Weald, it can be very tough going, with a lot of ups and downs, although the scenic rewards are great; some of the main roads head along ridges, with not quite so much climbing but with more traffic to contend with.

 BIKE HIRE

Rye Hire 1 Cyprus Pl, Rye TN31 7DR ✏ 01797 223033 🖋 ryehire.co.uk

THE 1066 COAST

Curious travellers will be well served in the exploration of this coast, between the end of the South Downs and the Kent border. It's the mixture hereabouts of history, architecture and character that perhaps impresses most of all. The mood changes almost bewilderingly from one moment to the next: Eastbourne's Victorian and Edwardian stucco, lines of modern villas perched by the shingle around Normans Bay, Bexhill's architectural curios, St Leonards' ocean liner-shaped block of flats, the fishing fleet drawn up on Hastings's hugely atmospheric beach, the medieval street layout of Winchelsea and the foodie paradise of historic Rye. Then just inland, Pevensey Castle asserts a brooding presence on the vast expanses of Pevensey Levels. At Sussex's far southeastern tip, Camber Sands is a glorious sandy beach, with a distant backdrop of the otherwordly shingle expanse of Dungeness, over the border into Kent.

1 EASTBOURNE

Brighton Main Line (London–Eastbourne) & East Coastway Line (Brighton–Hastings);
regional bus hub

Beneath the South Downs' spectacular termination, Eastbourne is on the coastal plain, but its western edges creep up to the chalky downland slopes towards Beachy Head. There's not a lot that is ancient about the town, although it has Saxon origins: well into the 19th century it wasn't much more than a dot on the map. By 1813 it was noted in *The Beauties of England and Wales* as having lately become 'a fashionable bathing place' but apart from a villagey cluster known as the Old Town, well inland around St Mary's Church, you'll struggle to find anything pre-Victorian.

With the arrival of the railway in the 1840s things took off. Much of the resort was developed by the seventh Duke of Devonshire – the family that owns Chatsworth and prospered out of Derbyshire mining ventures – and this was done with considerable style that still graces the town today. Its plan is neat and organised: ample-looking streets, leafy suburbs and above all a little-blemished stucco-sporting period-charmer of a seafront, resplendent with flowerbeds that are in the best municipal seaside tradition.

The composer **Claude Debussy** came here to stay in the Grand Hotel in 1905 when his personal life was in turmoil: he was having an extramarital affair with one Emma Bardac, who was pregnant with his child. The couple managed to avoid the public gaze. He had recently completed his astonishing impressionistic masterpiece *La Mer* and worked on the final proofs here ahead of the first performance. It is often said that he wrote the music here, but this is not the case: 'The sea unfurls itself with an utterly British correctness', he declared, so evidently the scene was poles apart from the sonorous complexities of the three tone paintings that this, his most famous orchestral work, comprises. Yet some of his piano music might have been inspired by the town: *Reflets dans l'eau* may have been a result of his observations of sun and cloud in a pond in a park, while buskers on the streets of Eastbourne are said to have inspired his marvellous little comic-grotesque piano prelude called *Minstrels*.

Rather unfairly, Eastbourne sometimes gets saddled with a reputation for dullness; 'it's a little English seaside place, silly as these places sometimes are,' remarked Debussy dismissively. But more than a century on from his visit, the town has kept much of its dignified, neatly prosperous look. Towering above, **Beachy Head** (page 228) looks positively mountainous and other-worldly. Paths zigzag their way up through the undercliff to the very top; or you can get one of the frequent buses, including City Sightseeing buses (☉ Easter–end Oct).

"Towering above, Beachy Head looks positively mountainous and otherworldly."

Sussex doesn't seem to have a lot of luck with its piers. Hastings's was attacked by an arsonist, and Brighton's splendid West Pier fell into long-term neglect before burning down in mysterious circumstances. Eastbourne's **pier**, opened in 1870 and one of the most delectable you'll find anywhere, bristling with elaborate ironwork all picked out in blue and white, suffered a major fire at the height of the summer-holiday season in 2014, when the dome-shaped amusement arcade (originally called the Blue Room) was reduced to an iron skeleton. Not that any newcomer to town would necessarily know that now, as it's all been admirably tidied up. The efforts of some 80 fire-fighters saved the rest and the damage was restricted. The owners reportedly got the insurance money and sold up without completing the restoration; hotelier Sheikh Abid Gulzar stepped in and bought it, hanging a banner that spelt out the inevitable pun: 'thank you for visiting Sheikh's pier'. He caused controversy over saying he might charge for entrance, and painting bits of its domes gold, but happily the overall scheme of blue and white remains. Now the amusement arcade is no longer and Eastbourne's pier has gained a welcoming open space: a marked improvement on what was.

In 2010 the pier was selected to feature as Brighton's Palace Pier in the filming of *Brighton Rock*, starring Helen Mirren, Sam Riley and Pete Postlethwaite. Production designer James Merifield found Eastbourne's pier had far more period ambiance. 'We came to Eastbourne to recce the

Grand Hotel, and looked east to see this incredible piece of architecture and we asked ourselves why are we not filming here instead of Brighton; here it already feels like we're in the 1950s. So we had a wander down and went on to the pier, and it unravelled itself – it had the right feel and the right architecture with very few modern influences on the pier, and we found we had the right canvas.'

The extraordinarily long **prom**, its flowerbeds bursting with colour in summer, heads westwards past the pier, the little **Lifeboat Museum**

ERIC RAVILIOUS

**The colour of the landscape was so lovely
and the design so beautifully obvious**
Eric Ravilious, while writing about the South Downs

The Sussex artist Eric Ravilious (1903–42) captured the character and beauty of the Downs landscape like no other artist. His paintings date from his rediscovery of the area where he grew up; when he was a boy his family moved to Eastbourne, where his father ran an antiques shop. In 1925 he began teaching at his old school of art in Eastbourne after studying at the Royal College of Art in London. He would take students to sketch Saxon downland villages like Alfriston, Wilmington and Jevington.

In 1934 his friend Peggy Angus invited him to stay at her cottage – Furlongs – beneath Beddingham Hill on the Firle estate. He felt at home in an area he had never explored in detail, selecting familiar subjects like the Long Man of Wilmington from new angles. A perfectionist, he destroyed two thirds of his watercolours. He died in his prime in 1942 when as a war artist he flew to Iceland to draw planes of the Norwegian squadron and his aircraft went missing in bad weather.

His works have been described as the calm before the storm, done at a time that witnessed a revival in English landscape painting, spurred on by the uncertainty of the European political situation and the awareness of fragility of the national way of life. Often there is an element of ambiguity and mystique within the everyday in his pictures, and some seem to have a foreboding sense of imminent threat that all is about to change. In 1939 he painted a series of chalk hill figures, including the Long Man, whom he thought of as a giantess. These he considered 'symbols of Englishness and defiance as well as an evocation of the manmade in a natural setting.' The Towner Gallery in Eastbourne has the finest public collection of Ravilious paintings anywhere.

Cricket aficionados will almost certainly be familiar with one of his works: the woodcut depicting the duo of behatted Victorian cricketers that has graced variously the cover and title page of *Wisden* each year since 1938. His story is memorably told in the 2022 feature film *Eric Ravilious: Drawn to War*.

and **Wish Tower**, one of 47 of the 103 Napoleonic-era Martello towers still standing and decommissioned as late as 1973 (occasionally open for tours see ⌀ wishtower.org.uk), around which spreads an exotic 500ft-long border of palms and succulents. Nearby, the Holywell Tea Chalet serves outside winter months as the eastern terminus of a land train (the Dotto Train) which trundles along the seafront to **Sovereign Harbour**, Europe's largest manmade marina, very Docklands in feel, with ship-shaped apartment blocks and several waterside eateries for alfresco dining.

Eastbourne has four **theatres**, including the Victorian, supremely lovely **Devonshire Park Theatre**, and takes its onion-domed **bandstand** very seriously: amid a sea of deckchairs, it offers a busy programme of concerts ranging from 1812 nights to film music or rock 'n' roll; fireworks are held here in the evening in summer. My favourite Eastbourne interior is the **Winter Garden**, which stages various concerts and events. Built in the spirit of the Crystal Palace, it's rather ramshackle from outside, but its period charms reveal themselves within.

Next to the Congress Theatre and backing on to the tennis courts of Devonshire Park is the **Towner Gallery** (College Rd BN21 4JJ ✆ 01323 434670 ⌀ townereastbourne.org.uk ⊙ Tue–Sun & bank holidays). Adorned in 2019 with a dazzling geometric mural by German artist Lothar Götz, this is a sleekly modern setting for high-standard seasonal exhibitions of historical, national and international art; it hosted the Turner Prize in 2023. More than 4,000 items from the permanent collection are shown on a rotating basis, including a notable array of paintings by the incomparable Eric Ravilious (see opposite), as well as works by Alfred Wallis, Picasso, Duncan Grant, Vanessa Bell and others. On alternate Sundays are hour-long Art Store Tours, and they can also arrange exclusive private tours.

In a turreted Victorian building opposite the Winter Garden, the volunteer-run **Eastbourne Heritage Centre** (2 Carlisle Rd, BN21 4BT ⌀ eastbourneheritagecentre.co.uk ⊙ Easter–Dec Sat–Sun; Dec–Easter Sat), home of the Eastbourne Society, takes a look at the town's evolution from its beginnings to the present, with archive films, maps, photos and changing exhibitions, well worth the modest entry fee.

Further east along the seafront on Royal Parade is the **Redoubt**, a fine example of an early 19th-century circular fort. Unlike Seaford's Martello tower, however, it can only be viewed from outside.

Boat trips from Eastbourne

For the best cliff views of all, take a speedboat trip from Sovereign Harbour. One of the busiest operators, Kraken Rib Tours ($\mathscr{D}$ 01323 700168 $\mathring{\vartheta}$ kraken-rib-tours.co.uk), offers a choice of routes, one of which skims out to the remote Royal Sovereign Light Tower (built in the 1970s and often mistaken for an oil rig). Another scoots beneath the Seven Sisters, scanning for dolphins, porpoises and seals. From the sea, the cliffs' crumbly qualities are much in evidence.

These waters hide numerous local World War I and II wrecks, which are habitats for abundant sea life, such as lobsters, crabs and sponges. They include the *Alaunia*, south of Sovereign Harbour, a massive liner almost the size of the *Titanic*, and which sticks up 65ft from the sea bed.

ACTIVITIES & EVENTS IN EASTBOURNE

Swimming is pretty good here, with a large, safe shingle beach which extends into a substantial expanse of sand at low tide. If you want a swim but it's too nasty outside, beat a retreat to the Sovereign Centre (Royal Parade, BN22 7LQ $\mathscr{D}$ 01323 738822) which has a flume, bubble pool and wave machine. There's an outdoor paddling pool nearby at Treasure Island (Royal Parade, BN22 7AE $\mathring{\vartheta}$ treasure-island.co.uk), a small beachfront adventure park.

For frivolous pursuits and pottering about, **Princes Park** takes some beating, with a lake for sailing model boats, putting green, rose garden and two playgrounds.

Eastbourne is prized territory for **windsurfing**. Buzz Active (Royal Parade, BN22 7LD $\mathscr{D}$ 01323 417023 $\mathring{\vartheta}$ buzzactive. org.uk) run taster sessions and weekly courses for all ages; Princes Park Lake is the beginners' spot. They also teach sailing, kayaking, stand-up paddleboarding and raft building. Armchair windsurfers can watch Britain's top talent in action during Eastbourne's Beach Life festival in July.

Eastbourne International Airshow (aka **Airbourne** $\mathring{\vartheta}$ eastbourneevents.org), a four-day air fest of historic and military planes, Red Arrow flyovers and parachuting displays takes place in August; you can see it from miles around, but the seafront between the pier and the Wish Tower and Beachy Head are particularly fine vantage points. Entry is free.

Tennis enthusiasts should beat a path to Devonshire Park in June for the Rothesay International tournament that precedes Wimbledon fortnight, featuring many of the big guns. Some tickets may be available on the day, but booking is strongly recommended; see $\mathring{\vartheta}$ lta.org.uk.

During October, the **Eastbourne Beer Festival** ($\mathring{\vartheta}$ visiteastbourne.com/beer-festivals) showcases over 100 beers, ciders and perries from Britain and overseas, with live entertainment from local bands.

The largest wreck in Sussex waters, the *Alaunia* hit a German mine in October 1916 and sank, but all except two of the 166 passengers survived.

Also operating from Sovereign Harbour, **Channel Diving** (℘ 07970 674799 ⊘ channeldiving.com) has diving, fishing and sightseeing boat trips.

¶¶ FOOD & DRINK

Deliciously Gorgeous 12 Cornfield Rd, BN21 4QE ℘ 01323 749794 ⊘ deliciouslygorgeous. co.uk. This French-inspired café takes its coffee very seriously and offers simple meals such as jacket potatoes, plus indulgent afternoon teas.

Gelato Famoso 30 Marine Parade, BN22 7AY ℘ 01323 722128 ⊘ gelatofamoso.co.uk. Reassuringly retro Italian ice-cream shop and cappuccino bar on the seafront.

The Lamb 36 High St, BN21 1HH ℘ 01323 720545 ⊘ thelambeastbourne.co.uk. Cosily traditional Old Town inn, with a log fire, Harvey's beer, pub grub and occasional live music. Four bedrooms upstairs.

Skylark 52 Grove Rd, BN21 4UD ℘ 01323 417000 ⊘ skylarkeastbourne.co.uk. Café and restaurant championing fresh Sussex produce. Particularly good for brunch, with classics such as granola with compote, eggs Benedict and buttermilk pancakes.

2 PEVENSEY

Train to Pevensey & Westham or Pevensey Bay (East Coastway Line, Brighton–Hastings); Stagecoach bus 99 (Eastbourne–Hastings; frequent services)

It was somewhere in Pevensey Bay, between current-day Bexhill and Eastbourne, that William the Conqueror landed on longboats from St-Valery-sur-Somme in what was the last successful invasion of mainland Britain in 1066, the best-known date in British history.

The focal point here is **Pevensey Castle** (Pevensey BN24 5LE ℘ 01323 762604; English Heritage). It has always been a practical building and never a residence, repeatedly used for military purposes, falling into disrepair and being renovated and adapted; it has been besieged four times in its long history. The castle originated as the last of the late-Roman chain of fortifications known as the Saxon shore forts, begun in the mid AD290s, when the marshes and the sea were adjacent enough to be the defences. Little is known of what happened here between AD310 and 1066, although the *Anglo-Saxon Chronicle* records raids after the Roman defences were removed. It was apparently abandoned after a massacre, but is thought to have been inhabited again by the 7th century. William the Conqueror erected a wooden fort within the outer walls of the Roman fortifications, making it a strategic base and communication centre with Normandy after his invasion, then strengthening it into a stone castle. It was rebuilt in the 13th century, then as the harbour silted up it became less strategically important and was abandoned by around 1500. Remarkably, it became an important stronghold on this long, vulnerable shoreline during World War II, and is one of the few Norman castles to sport a 1940s gun emplacement.

The outer walls of the castle force a sharp road detour in the village of Pevensey. Most unusually these are substantial portions of standing Roman walls – though the turrets are medieval. Inside you enter a huge, enclosed grass oval, where in places you can see where the outer wall has been excavated, and it's easier to spot the Roman parts – look for the pinkish cement and flat red bricks around the West Gate for instance; most of the original facing has been removed to reveal rubble beneath.

A reedy moat surrounds the medieval castle, with its rounded towers, arrow slits and massive walls that are 10ft thick in places. The informative audio tour takes you round what is an intriguing mixture: a Tudor gun, a spiral staircase down to a dark, vaulted dank-floored dungeon cell, a glimpse into a grim oubliette prison – a deep, dark hole which prisoners were thrown into and left to die – piles of excavated stone balls used for trebuchets (medieval stone-throwing catapults), and concrete and brick rooms used by British and Canadians as pillboxes in World War II. In the exhibition room a map lights up the coastline as it was before 1100 and during medieval times.

Among Pevensey village's other historic buildings, the **Court House Museum** (℘ 01323 760581 ♦ pevenseycourthouse.co.uk ☉ May–Oct) occupies what was the smallest courthouse and jail in England, in use from 1540 until 1886. The Victorian beadle's uniform is displayed in a glass case, and in the judge's changing room are scales used for weighing imported goods. They have a few Roman bits and pieces, and the volunteer on the desk told me she has unearthed Roman coins in her garden. Pevensey's former method of dealing with criminals wasn't too lenient: regular felons were hanged, while murderers were marched down the high street, had their hands tied and were chucked in the river. Downstairs, the whitewashed prison cell looks suitably spartan.

Just north of Pevensey are the fen-like **Pevensey Levels**, with a quiet beauty of their own. It is an important site for flowering water plants, dragonflies, damselflies and aquatic beetles, and the rare fen raft spider, which is the largest arachnid to be found in Britain. This is rewarding cycling country: a very quiet unfenced road wiggles its way around this reed-fringed expanse of drained marshes, past the hamlet of Rickney.

¶ FOOD & DRINK

Castle Cottage Tea Room Church Ln, Pevensey BN24 5LE ⊘ castlecottagetearoom.com. Right by the castle entrance, and ensconced by the Roman wall, this quaint cottage serves teas, sandwiches and cakes.

Sharnfold Farm Hailsham Rd, Stone Cross BN24 5BU ⊘ 01323 768490 ⊘ sharnfoldfarm. co.uk ⊙ Tue–Sun. This farm has a seasonal shop with own-made and local produce, pick-your-own (including apples, blackcurrants, gooseberries, redcurrants and strawberries), a café and plenty of farm animals to encounter.

3 NORMANS BAY

East Coastway Line (Brighton–Hastings)

Named after the supposed arrival point of the Normans in 1066, this village, a couple of miles west of the fringes of Bexhill, is a seaside curio. It's almost entirely a product of modern times, apart from a Martello tower converted into a private house. Seen from the reed-fringed unfenced lane that wends its way through the Pevensey Levels from Pevensey itself, it looks quite surreal: a long line of detached seaside houses, all pointy-roofed and standing close together, side by side, on the shingle ridge. Virtually every house has been adapted in its own way, and on the beach side many sport their own flagpole and pebble garden. Here and there the odd pre-war villa survives unaltered, its piles dug straight into the shingle bank. One development, **Beachlands**, created by noted inter-war architect Thomas Cecil Howitt, extends inland in the form of an estate of flat-topped bungalows of seemingly unique appearance; some are 'oyster bungalows', so called because of their oval shape. Marine Avenue, a dual carriageway with virtually no traffic, pierces into this strangely quasi-American 1930s utopia.

4 BEXHILL

East Coastway Line (Brighton–Hastings); Stagecoach bus 98/99 (Eastbourne–Hastings, frequent services)

The seventh Earl De La Warr was the local landowner who got Bexhill started back in the 1880s by naming it Bexhill-on-Sea, just in case anyone had any doubts as to its status. It's hardly a pulsating resort –

but very pleasingly unhurried, benign and cared for, looking along the coast towards its more raucous neighbour, Hastings. The **beach** here is pleasantly divided up and sheltered – good for families.

In the 1930s lucky Bexhill gained Britain's first building in International Modern style, the airy, light **De La Warr Pavilion** (Marina, TN40 1DP ⌀ dlwp.com). It was built in 1933–35 under Bexhill's first socialist mayor, the ninth Earl De La Warr, who decided the town needed a palace for the people. He turned to the designs of Erich Mendelsohn, a highly regarded Jewish architect who'd fled the Nazis, and architect and designer Serge Chermayeff; together they created a masterpiece. The Pavilion looks younger than its years: the sleek curves and ship's-deck railings have been much imitated in far more recent buildings. It is a centre for contemporary arts, with events, concerts and exhibitions, but you can just step inside to visit the café, take in the sea views from the sun terraces and admire the supremely elegant staircase encircling a vertical chandelier of chrome disks and neon tubes which runs the full height of the building. Volunteers occasionally lead architectural tours of the building. Note the supremely inappropriate brown-and-white signs as you enter town, signposting the De La Warr Pavilion with the standard classical mansion symbol.

There's a lively cultural war among the architectural styles on the seafront, with white Victorian stucco frontages contrasting with the Pavilion, and the extraordinary houses of **Marina Court Avenue** and **Marina Parade**, built 1903–07, where Moghul details such as onion domes and flamboyant chimneys are more reminiscent of India than of the Sussex coast.

Most of the buildings in the town centre went up between 1895 and 1905; in 1911 the **Colonnade** was erected in honour of George V's coronation – its playful cupolas and balustrades an engaging contrast to the De La Warr Pavilion that appeared later.

A scale model of the Pavilion, along with costume displays and copious local history material, is on show at the nearby **Bexhill Museum** (Egerton Rd, TN39 3HL ✆ 01424 222058 ⌀ bexhillmuseum.org.uk), where a gallery of vintage motor-racing cars pays a nod to Bexhill's early

---

1 Bexhill's striking 1930s De La Warr Pavilion. **2** The Red Arrows fly past Eastbourne pier during the town's international airshow. **3** Hastings Old Town features cliff railways and a maze of lanes. **4** Pevensey Castle has been besieged four times in its long history. ▶

links with the sport – around the turn of the 20th century the town hosted the first motor races in Britain. It also was ahead of every other seaside resort in the country by allowing mixed bathing in 1901.

5 HASTINGS

East Coastway Line (Brighton–Hastings) and Marshlink Line (Hastings–Ashford); regular buses from Bodiam, Camber Sands, Eastbourne, Rye, Tenterden, Tunbridge Wells, Winchelsea

It's always an event arriving here, particularly by train: Hastings has terrific atmosphere thanks in part to the extremely strong physical presence of its towering cliffs and its beguiling, precipitous Old Town – the original and remarkably unspoilt fishermen's quarter – exuding plenty of fishy charm of the thankfully untidied-up sort. It feels further from London than it actually is, and there's something intangibly West Country about the whole place: the higgledy-piggledy nature of the Old Town has something of a Cornish persona, and the cliffs lying to the east are strongly reminiscent of the Dorset or Devon coast. The newer, and far less distinctive, part of the resort lies further west and metamorphoses into St Leonards. The TV series *Foyle's War* was set in Hastings, to the lasting gratitude of the town's tourism industry.

"It feels further from London than it actually is, and there's something intangibly West Country about the whole place."

Hastings has Saxon origins, and boasted its own mint in AD984. It is most famous for a battle that actually took place elsewhere, seven miles inland, but from Norman times was of military importance as William the Conqueror set up a castle on a headland – possibly on the site of an already existing Saxon fort, impregnable on three sides – and made the town the premier Cinque Port. In the 13th century storms ripped the town apart, destroying the harbour and causing large chunks of the castle to be undermined and to collapse seawards. The town lost its military role, but lived on as a fishing village in a quarter known as the Old Town. From the 19th century it spread beyond, with the seafront developing westwards towards St Leonards: there are the usual trappings associated with a resort along here, but the town's real distinction lies on its east side.

The seaside resort fun extends to the likes of go-karts, a boating lake with swan pedalos, a miniature railway and mini golf. The semi-derelict **Hastings Pier** has about as chequered a history as possible. Dating from 1872 and designed by Eugenius Birch, who also created Eastbourne

Pier and Brighton's West Pier, it kept going until 1990 when a storm damaged it, then closed completely in 2008. In 2010, it was subject to an arson attack and virtually destroyed. Its £14.2 million restoration – partly funded by 3,000 people buying shares – was completed in 2016 after years out of action, and all looked rosy. There were announcements of live music, art events, farmers' markets, a summer circus and sky watching; its phoenix-like reappearance won the 2017 Stirling Prize for architecture. But the sums didn't add up and it closed the same year. Despite being rescued by Sheikh Abid Gulzar, the same private buyer who snapped up Eastbourne Pier, its future remains uncertain.

A bit of a way from the centre of things, the free **Hastings Museum and Art Gallery** (Bohemia Rd, TN34 1ET ✆ 01424 451052 � hmag. org.uk) has permanent displays covering some of its most celebrated former residents – the socialist and author of *The Ragged-Trousered Philanthropists* Robert Tressell, the TV pioneer John Logie Baird, the 'concrete king' Sidney Little and the intriguing Grey Owl (the Hastings boy who adopted the persona of an indigenous American and became an early campaigner for conservation causes). Other exhibits feature bathing in Hastings, natural history and dinosaurs, indigenous American artefacts, temporary exhibitions and the splendidly ornate Durbar Hall, created for the Colonial and Indian Exhibition held in South Kensington in 1886, and carved from teak, Himalayan cedar and shisham by Indian craftsmen.

The Old Town

For unstructured wandering, the Old Town is a joy, snuggled as it is into and around the mouth of the valley between West Hill and East Hill – with **cliff railways** making the ascent to the top of each. The West Hill Lift climbs up through a tunnel, while the East Hill Lift, opened in 1903 and the steepest in the country, rises up from the fishing area on to the clifftop heights of Hastings Country Park.

Members of the Old Hastings Preservation Society lead free **walking tours** (� ohps.org.uk) around the Old Town and the Stade. The Society's archive in the Hastings History House (21 Courthouse St, TN34 3AU ☉ Thu–Sat) has a comprehensive range of photos of the town stretching back over the decades. It is largely thanks to the efforts of the Society that Hastings Old Town has survived so well. The council began demolition to make way for the new road in the 1930s and carried on until the

1950s. Further 'improvements' might have taken place were it not for the campaigning efforts of the group.

One of the great pleasures of Hastings is that fishing and boats are still so much part of the scene. **The Stade**, Hastings's joyously un-tidied up fishing district, is very much a place of work. After a massive storm in 1287 diverted the River Rother, causing a cliff collapse, Hastings's original port was no longer operational, and the fishing fleet operated instead from the beach, where it has remained ever since. It's currently the largest beach-launched fishing fleet in Britain. This is a precarious business, as a choppy sea prevents boats from being launched. And quite where Brexit will lead to is a contentious issue, with 80 percent of the catch being sold to EU countries. Meanwhile, it's ideal pottering territory with a camera in hand: a photogenic mishmash of lobster pots, tattered flags, winching equipment, boat skeletons and crab shells. Fresh, smoked and cured fish is sold from an assortment of stalls around the **net shops**, a cluster of tall, tarred wooden sheds erected to store fishing equipment, and now preserved as historic structures.

"One of the great pleasures of Hastings is that fishing and boats are still so much part of the scene."

Hastings Contemporary (Rock-a-Nore Rd, TN34 3DW ⊘ hastingscontemporary.org) opened on this stretch of seafront in 2011. Originally called the Jerwood Gallery, its critics considered it an intrusion on the Old Town, but it looks very fitting with its carefully chosen black/grey tiled exterior that sensitively complements the greys and textures of the adjacent net shops and winch sheds. As a gallery for changing exhibitions of modern British art, it functions extremely well: the windows from the smallish gallery rooms frame vistas of the Old Town, which effectively becomes part of the exhibition. The building ticks all the boxes for sustainability: heated and cooled through ground source probes, solar power used for heating the water, and recycled rainwater used in the loos.

Looking over the whole scene from just above street level, **Pelham Crescent** is Hastings's most elegant piece of Georgian streetscape. Its centrepiece is St Mary in the Castle, a crisply proportioned church with a striking circular auditorium, designed by Joseph Kaye in 1823.

Further along Rock-a-Nore Road, just beyond the net shops, lie an absorbing trio of maritime attractions. **The Shipwreck Museum** (TN34

3DW ⊘ shipwreckmuseum.co.uk; free entry) holds an absorbing array of items recovered from the depths of the ocean. On display are items from the *Thomas Lawrence*, a Danish ship sunk in 1863, including rusting muskets, gin and brandy bottles, a chunk of what is thought to be the original London Bridge built in Roman times, and part of an iguanodon skeleton that was the best-preserved dinosaur fossil ever found when discovered in 1834. It also tells the story of the *Amsterdam*, the shell of which can still be seen from the beach off Bulverhythe at low tide. On her maiden voyage to Java in 1749 she became marooned on a sandbank, and there was plague on board – and when the crew was quarantined while this happened, mutiny broke out, with drunkenness, violence and death; some finds were recovered and are exhibited, including clay pipes, brass guns and fortified wine. Opposite, the **Hastings Aquarium** (TN34 3DW ⊘ hastingsaquarium.co.uk) has native and tropical species and features a walk-through viewing tunnel and large, child-friendly tanks, all well elucidated by hourly talks; a ticket lasts a whole day so you can re-enter during feeding times when the creatures are at their liveliest. The aquarium breeds seahorses here – the females produce the eggs, then the males carry them and give birth from a special pouch. You'll also see a range of reptile life, including bearded dragons, iguanas and snakes. Housed in the old Fishermen's Church (which still does baptisms), the appealingly unchanged **Fishermen's Museum** (TN34 3DW ⊘ ohps. org.uk; free entry, donation requested), has the *Enterprise* (1912), the last sailing lugger in Hastings, as its main exhibit – you can climb on board. The museum is stuffed with well-loved mementoes, including a model of the Stade and paintings and sepia photos of smocked, whiskery fishermen. Also commemorated is Biddy the Tubman, who performed a surfing act in a half barrel on the beach, was awarded a medal for his feats of bravery in saving people from a watery grave, and took his boat to rescue troops stranded at Dunkirk.

"The museum is stuffed with well-loved mementoes, including paintings and sepia photos of smocked, whiskery fishermen."

Immediately inland, **George Street** and the **High Street** contain an appealing mix of eateries, junk shops (particularly in Courthouse Street), boutiques and jewellers. Narrow, private-looking passages rise from the High Street and All Saints Street, making up a maze characterised by stepped alleys, tiny gardens, snoozing cats and unexpected vistas over the rooftops. Seek out 10 Starr Cottages (next to 60a All Saints Street), known as the Piece of Cheese Cottage – painted bright yellow and thinly wedge-shaped as its name suggests; triangular furniture must be very useful inside.

At 58a High Street is a unique little factory and shop, the **Shirley Leaf and Petal Company**, which manufactures cloth flowers and leaves that are supplied to theatres, opera houses and movie-makers worldwide: they have supplied the props for movies such as *Gladiator*, *Mamma Mia* and *War Horse*, as well as Glyndebourne operatic productions, and individual items are also sold in the shop for a few pounds a go. Carrying out a trade traditionally taught to women with disabilities, including those missing an arm, it is now the last-surviving establishment of its kind in Europe. Sometimes it receives vast orders – for example 100,000 vine leaves to recreate a vineyard, but individual items are on sale too. They have some 10,000 tools of the trade, and stock antique velvets dating back to the 1930s. The workshop is a working museum, using cutting-tools made with blacksmith's skills. All the dyeing is done by hand. 'Yes, we're training up young people, but it's difficult. It's not computer oriented, and it takes a lot of skill and patience – we tend to find that a lot of retired and semi-retired people enjoy this sort of work. Basically we do cut-outs here, and home workers put it together and then we do quality checks here. We're very attentive to detail.'

> "The Shirley Leaf and Petal Company manufactures cloth flowers and leaves for theatres, opera houses and movie-makers."

The **West Hill Lift**, completed in 1891 and the older of the town's two funiculars, ascends through a tunnel to the open, sloping lawns of West Hill. From here, a path leads to a crumbly-looking headland on which stands the **castle**, dating from the arrival of the Normans in 1066. Four years later William had it rebuilt in stone. Much of it fell into the sea following an almighty battering by storms in the 13th century and as a result of subsequent erosion – and King John ordered it to be dismantled in 1216 for fear of it falling into French hands – but the setting is still terrific. The most substantial part to survive is the Collegiate Church of St Mary in the Castle, founded around 1069, which became the King's Free Chapel of Hastings in 1272; its chapel was an important place of pilgrimage, only to be dissolved by Henry VIII. The castle site declined into use as farmland, then started attracting tourists in Victorian times.

During World War II it housed an anti-aircraft gun and was used by commandos as a training ground. Today, within a recreated siege tent a 20-minute audiovisual show, the 1066 Story, presents a rollercoaster of English history from the Norman invasion to World War II.

Just beneath the castle, **St Clement's Caves** are partly natural and partly manmade and have served a variety of purposes – smugglers' caves (of course), a Victorian tourist attraction carved out with arches and pillars (hence the niches for candles to go in), a ballroom, and air-raid shelters in World War II. They're now run as Smugglers' Adventure – with lashings of mock-Gothic spookiness. The commentary doesn't take itself too seriously, with Hairy Jack the Smuggler introducing it, and there are sundry low-tech games, ghost effects and the like; small children might find it either entertaining or scary.

Another underground attraction is the ultra-grisly **True Crime Museum** (White Rock, TN34 1JP ✆ 01424 430115 ⬧ truecrimemuseum. co.uk) on the seafront roughly opposite the pier, with abundant tales of murders, spectacular heists and sundry other nasty goings-on together with ghoulish mementoes such as the bullet produced in the trial against the Krays and a noose used at Lincoln Prison.

St Leonards
East Coastway Line (Brighton–Hastings)

The western part of Hastings merges into St Leonards, named after a medieval church but entirely 19th century in origin. James Burton bought land in 1828 and saw the development potential, which he and his son Decimus realised over the ensuing decades. The hinterland has some rewarding strolling grounds, with handsome hilly streets of opulent Regency villas and grandiose turreted, stepped-gabled Scottish baronial Victorian mansions. For a sample, wander along Highland Gardens, Maze Hill and Upper Maze Hill, around the deep quarried ravine of St Leonards Gardens.

"The hinterland has some rewarding strolling grounds, with handsome hilly streets of opulent Regency villas."

In the 1930s, St Leonards had a futuristic phase. The borough engineer, 'concrete king' Sidney Little – later to be involved in constructing the Mulberry floating harbours used in the 1944 D-Day landings – transformed Hastings and St Leonards into a veritable

WATCHING SEAWARDS

During the months from March to September, bottlenose dolphins come close to the shore and to boats along the coast from Bexhill to Rye Harbour. When the water is calm, you have a good chance of spotting them from land early in the morning and later in the evening at high tide. They have a tall hooked-shape dorsal fin and grow up to 13ft long. During winter and early spring you might glimpse harbour porpoises or seals.

symphony of concrete and chrome, and ripped up tramlines to make a promenade. The tram rails he recycled as reinforcements for Britain's very first underground car park in 1931. He created a double-decker prom between the two resorts; the lower portion gives surreal, concrete perspectives embellished with wall decoration made of broken glass set into concrete and known as Bottle Alley. His curvaceous concrete wind shelters look amply capable of withstanding nuclear fallout. Above this, and dominating the entire stretch of coast, rises the sleek, 14-storey Marine Court (completed in 1938), inspired by the *Queen Mary* ocean liner. It's been a bit messed around with of late, alas, with balconies glassed in.

Also along the prom is an engagingly old-fashioned weather station set up in 1875 and sporting cartoon Normans, gilded lettering and a mechanical thermometer with gull and yacht pointers showing the land and sea temperatures respectively. In 1926 change-resistant residents petitioned for a 10mph speed limit along the seafront. I don't believe they succeeded.

🎭 ENTERTAINMENT & EVENTS

Hastings has two **theatres** – the White Rock (⏁ whiterocktheatre.org.uk) opposite the pier stages commercial productions, while the Stables Theatre and Arts Centre (⏁ stablestheatre. co.uk) is a small venue for quality amateur theatre. On the High Street, the **Electric Palace** (TN34 3ER ⏁ electricpalacecinema.com) is an enchantingly quirky and intimate 50-seater arthouse cinema, showing an excellent selection of world, classic and locally connected films. You can watch with a glass of craft beer or organic wine in hand.

Major **events** include Hastings Fat Tuesday (a five-day music festival in February); Jack in the Green (a folk festival featuring morris dancing and traditional parades, May Day bank holiday weekend); the extremely lively Old Town Carnival (with wellie throwing, a pram race and a terrific procession, early August); the Seafood and Wine Festival (September); and the Bonfire Celebrations (October).

🍴 FOOD & DRINK

Produce markets are held at Wellington Place (2nd and 4th Sat of the month), and on Trinity Street (Sun; monthly). There is also a market on Kings Road in St Leonards (Apr–Oct first Sat of the month).

The Crown All Saints St, TN34 3BN ⊘ thecrownhastings.co.uk. An excellent, characterful Old Town dining pub with bare floorboards, leather armchairs and an open fire. Serves quality food and real ales from a roster of local breweries.

Farmyard 52 Kings Rd, TN37 6DY ⊘ farmyardwine.com. St Leonards is the foodie end of town, with upbeat places such as this sustainability-conscious bistro and natural wine bar leading the way.

First In Last Out 14 High St, TN34 3EY ⊘ thefilo.co.uk. Atmospheric, family-run pub serving ales from its own brewery, FILO (⊘ filobrewing.co.uk), based in a Grade II-listed former stable just up the road. Menu of well-presented classics, plus occasional tapas evenings.

Judges Bakery 51 High St, TN34 3EN. Tasty cakes, brownies and additive-free bread from a bakery that's been in business since 1828.

Land of Green Ginger 45 High St, TN34 3EN. A nice daytime café with a courtyard, offering local and seasonal produce, free-range eggs and fair-trade coffee.

Maggie's Rock-A-Nore Rd TN34 3DW ⊘ maggiesfishandchips.co.uk. In a town with plenty of very good seafront fish-and-chip spots, this is the most celebrated spot, tucked away up steps by the net shops. A spokesperson for the local Fishermen's Mission rated it the best place for fish and chips on the south coast, so who can argue with that?

Penbuckles Delicatessen 50 High St, TN34 3EN. Specialising in artisan cheese and wine from Sussex and beyond, this cosy little deli also serves great coffee.

6 Hastings Country Park

Stagecoach bus 101 (Hastings–New Romney; hourly)

On a coast that's best known for white cliffs, the eastern fringes of Hastings are unique. Here, sandstone buttresses – the oldest rocks in Sussex – jut out of the sea. They mark the west end of **Hastings Country Park**, much of which lies within a Site of Special Scientific Interest and looks rather like a chunk of the West Country, adrift in Sussex. Paths lace through gorse-clad, heathy tracts above the East Hill Lift; from here, it's top-drawer coastal scenery all the way to **Fairlight Glen** and the village of Fairlight Cove. The wildlife is richly varied, with breeding birds such as Dartford warblers and stonechats, sizeable numbers of dormice, stoats and weasels, rare ant-eating spiders, bee-devouring

ROYAL MILITARY CANAL

Although this waterway is no longer navigable for craft, you can walk its entire 28-mile length, from Hythe in Kent to Cliff End. It is a haven for wildlife: you have a good chance of spotting kingfishers here in summer. This canal was built between 1804 and 1809, during the Napoleonic Wars, as a third line of defence, with the Royal Navy patrolling the English Channel and a string of 74 Martello towers erected along the coast. Cannons were placed every 500yds along the canal, and there were station houses manned by guards to control smuggling. It was a construction project riddled with problems, and was completed four years late. To speed things up they built the final sections half as wide and deep as the earlier ones, and it was much criticised as a waste of public money. Nevertheless, it survives as the third longest defensive structure ever built in the British Isles – after Hadrian's Wall and Offa's Dyke.

wasps and an outsize weevil known as *Lixus algirus*. The park's wooded coombes include Fire Hills, at its best when carpeted with bluebells.

East of the suburban roads of Fairlight Cove, the coast is undeveloped for half a mile as you drop to shore level at Cliff End, on the edge of the flat farmland of Romney Marsh. The Saxon Shore Way, a long-distance path from Hastings to Gravesend in Kent, has perhaps its finest moment as it follows this coastline.

7 WINCHELSEA

🏠 **Strand House**

Marshlink Line (Hastings–Ashford); Stagecoach bus 100/101 (Hastings–New Romney; hourly)

Spaciously ranged on a neat crisscross of streets and on a rise a couple of miles southwest of Rye, Winchelsea has an incongruous sense of grandeur, and although an ancient town it exudes a village-like calm. Three town gateways and substantial remains of town defences hint that events were once much headier here. In medieval times it flourished as an industrious port planned by Royal command and became one of the Cinque Ports; only King's Lynn was a more important centre for shipbuilding. In its heyday it imported wine at the rate of up to four million bottles a year, and it could have become a great maritime city like Southampton or Portsmouth. Then seemingly everything conspired against it.

There's no trace of **Old Winchelsea**, the earlier sea-level settlement beneath the present hilltop site: it was washed away in a series of storms after 1250. In 1283 Edward I ordered the **new settlement** to be rebuilt on its present hilltop site, with a wall and gateways, and streets laid out on a **grid plan** with 39 rectangular plots of buildings between. He appointed Commissioners to lay out a new town of Winchelsea, which became one of England's top ten ports. If Old Winchelsea had been in this league its loss must have been a strategic disaster. This – and perhaps the fact that subsequent rents went to the Crown – might explain why the King was so generous in his support for his new royal town.

But further disaster followed: in the early 14th century Winchelsea seamen were prone to thuggish behaviour, raiding and burning boats in English ports as well as in France. The French had their revenge in 1360 with a massive attack, which compounded the effects of the Black Death and caused Winchelsea's decline. Then the sea began to recede, and by the early 16th century the harbour had completely silted up. This was the final blow. By 1565, of the 800 plots there in the 1300s, only 109 houses were left standing; by the mid 17th century the number had dropped to 40. Writing in around 1725, Daniel Defoe described the place as 'rather the skeleton of an ancient city, than a real town'.

Today an influx of retired people and commuters has brought a modest amount of redevelopment to Winchelsea, and in contrast to some unfortunate experiences in the 1960s and 1970s every building site is closely watched by archaeologists. The subsoil is dense with reminders of the great past of this once Royal port.

In the very centre, the early 14th-century **Church of St Thomas the Martyr** fills one of the squares of the grid: its incompleteness stands as a poignant reminder of the village's past torments. All that survives are the chancel and ruined transepts of a much larger church, the tower of which survived into the 18th century, but the tracery and canopied tombs indicate massive wealth in centuries past. As an example of the Decorated style it has few rivals in Sussex: judging from the wealth of stone carving, elaborate canopied tombs and tracery, there was plenty of money to employ stonemasons and builders, and to import Caen stone from Normandy. Just opposite the church, the **Winchelsea Court Hall Museum** (✆ 01797 226642 ⌂ winchelsea. com/museum) incorporates the former gaol, and has a model of Winchelsea as it was.

Winchelsea's **defences** were under construction by 1322 and re-planned on a smaller scale around 1415. The most obvious relics are

The great coastal walk: Winchelsea to Hastings

✤ OS Explorer map 124; start: Winchelsea, near New Inn and church ♀ TQ904175 (bus stop; plenty of free on-road parking); 11 miles; substantial ups and downs, and a level section over marshland. If starting from Winchelsea station, leave the level crossing on the far side of the platform & walk a half a mile to the A259, along which turn right up into the village. There are **loos** at Winchelsea, Cliff End and Hastings. For **refreshments**, Winchelsea has a pub and Hastings has plenty. **Shortened version (five miles)**: walk the most scenic part of the walk, from Fairlight Cove to Hastings. From Hastings station catch the 101 bus (hourly; every two hours on Sun) to the Commanders Walk bus stop in Fairlight Cove (♀ TQ876117). From there walk a few paces up past the traffic roundabout and up Shepherds Way to the T-junction with Channel Way, where you turn right and pick up the directions at **5**.

I t's quite an effort to do this stupendous full-day walk, but it is amply rewarding, reflecting this corner of East Sussex in all its dramatic changes of mood. The strange thing is that a walk of this calibre isn't conspicuously waymarked throughout its length; part of it is the **Saxon Shore Way**, but even those sections are poorly signed in places. It starts in historic Winchelsea, leaving through an abandoned town gateway and leading beneath the sea cliffs of the Saxon shore – now a long way from the sea. The two-mile stretch along the swan-patrolled Royal Military Canal has an East Anglian-like beauty, reaching the beach at Cliff End before rising on to the sandstone cliffs that continue to Hastings. After you are diverted inland at Fairlight Glen the finest part of the route begins – an energetic three miles of up and down through the lushly vegetated cliffs around Covehurst Bay and through the Hastings Country Park. Only at the last possible moment does Hastings Old Town suddenly appear as you emerge by the East Hill Lift.

1 From the centre of Winchelsea with the New Inn on your right and the churchyard on your left, follow the road out of Winchelsea, past the public loos on your left. Where the main road bends right (ahead is Wickham Rock Lane), keep right alongside it for a few yards, then just after the jagged ruin of the west wall of medieval **St John's Hospital**, take a stile on the left. Go diagonally right down to the bottom of the field and walk along it to find another stile; do not cross the stile immediately beyond this but turn left between field boundaries. Grass lumps on the left mark abandoned buildings of medieval Winchelsea, when the village was larger than it is today. Turn right on the lane, under the **New Gate** (another of the village's entrance gates; you see the big defensive ditch on the right just after the gate). Some 300yds later (where woods are about to start on the left) turn left on a signposted public footpath. The wooded bank up on the right is **Wickham Cliff**, marking the former shoreline.

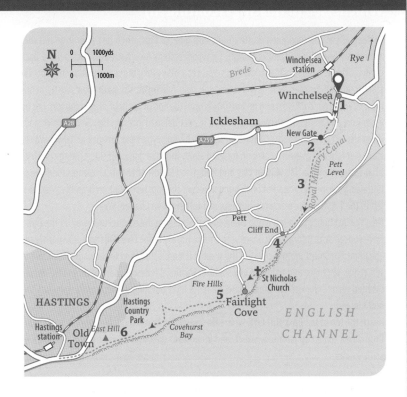

2 Very soon leave the woodland edge as it veers away right and continue forward to a prominent wooden enclosure around an electric sub-station by the **Royal Military Canal**. Cross the bridge and turn right to follow the canal towpath two miles to **Cliff End**.

3 At a junction by a bridge, turn left to leave the canal and cross the road and continue along the path at the top of the beach, passing the back gardens of some very swish contemporary houses. You pass the Pett Level Independent Rescue hut on your right, where there's a way down to the tiny **St Nicholas Church**, in a shed called the Rocket House, originally housing rocket-launching equipment to aid mariners in difficulty; it was made a church in 1935. Carry on past a mobile-home park on the right, then take steps on the right (passing 'private' signs that deter access into the mobile-home park), turn right on the access road and turn left on the public road, past the end of the canal and public loos. ▶

The great coastal walk:
Winchelsea to Hastings (continued)

4 ◄ Keep left at the road junction (the right turn goes to Pett), then just after it go left into a driveway and immediately keep right up wooden steps on a path that rises behind back gardens. Where a break in the trees allows, you get a view along the coast to Dungeness power station in Kent. Further on it opens out as you near **Fairlight**. The path then shortly bends right inland around a field; carry on for 100yds until the end of the field, where you turn left by a signpost and through a barrier, and on to a residential road junction (Sea Road, which goes off to the left, is permanently closed because of cliff falls; you keep forward on Lower Waites Lane, not labelled as such). Carry on forward along the road, ignoring side turnings (such as Briar Close, Primrose Hill, Clinton Way and Rockmead Road). After half a mile this road bends left, rising steeply up a road of brick bungalows. At the top, turn right on Bramble Way. Turn left at the T-junction to reach the cliff-top, and turn right on Channel Way.

5 Near the last house keep left along a fenced path, avoiding the parallel driveway on the right. Once you reach an information board with a map, you are in the **Fire Hills** area. The path leads ahead into the most dramatic part of the walk. It is simplest to keep to the path closest to the sea at any junctions, and to follow any signs for Hastings. It descends three times into deeply wooded glens – for each of these there are more level but longer alternatives that skirt the glens inland.

6 Reach the top of the **East Hill Lift**, where **Hastings Old Town** suddenly appears below you. Drop down the steep path to a street, and wend your way to the very bottom. The railway

Pipewell Gate (by the main road) and Strand Gate (on the edge of a cliff, with a terrific view of the coast); the New Gate crosses a country lane outside the village (reached by following the waymarked 1066 Country Walk). During his research, historic buildings archaeologist David Martin spotted the remains of an 85ft length of town wall and two D-shaped turrets on the cliff side of Winchelsea, which incredibly had remained unrecorded.

Winchelsea had a thorough makeover in the 17th and 18th centuries, but many of the houses reveal far older origins. Beneath many buildings, garages and even under a cricket pitch are 32 medieval **vaulted cellars** that originally served to store wine from Gascony at a time when the wine trade was thriving here. These cellars were built to be seen, presumably by buyers visiting to try the wares. Only Southampton has a comparable number of vaulted cellars.

station is about ten minutes on (inland, on the far side of the shopping centre) and is well signposted from the town centre.

GETTING BACK FROM HASTINGS

The 100 bus is the best option, as it runs hourly (every 2hrs on Sun) from Hastings railway station to the centre of Winchelsea (then on to Rye). Another option is the train from Hastings to Winchelsea, which is less frequent; Winchelsea station is half a mile outside the village.

GETTING FROM WINCHELSEA STATION INTO WINCHELSEA

It's just over ¾ mile, but this route is far superior to slogging along the busy and unappealing A259: leave the station, turn right over the railway tracks. After half a mile reach the hairpin bend with the A259: instead of walking up the A259 into the village, turn immediately right (signpost for 1066 Country Walk) on a track passing sewage-treatment works, and then becoming a path. Enter a field, turn left as signposted, along the edge. Soon the path ascends and you go through a small gate. Carry on up a sunken grassy track, passing just to the left of a fire beacon, view indicator and trig point, marking the site of a windmill that blew down in the 1987 storm. There's a fine view from here over the Brede Valley. Go on past houses at the edge of Winchelsea, cross the A259 and take the residential street opposite, past 1 & 2 The Orchards on your left, and take the next right to The New Inn in the village centre.

 SPECIAL STAYS

Strand House Tanyards Ln, TN36 4JT ℰ 01797 226276 ◈ strandhousewinchelsea.com. Just below the town, this mid-priced B&B in a 600-year-old former Wealden hall has neck-craningly low ceilings and delightfully wonky rooms, with lots of timbering and character – all much cosier than its former days as a workhouse. Outside, there's a charming cottage garden with meadow views.

 FOOD & DRINK

The New Inn German St, TN36 4EN ℰ 01797 226252 ◈ newinnpubwinchelsea.co.uk. Situated in Winchelsea's historic heart, this reasonably priced dining pub with rooms is the best place to eat in town. Everything is prepared from scratch, and the chefs take pride in sourcing their ingredients locally.

Queen's Head Inn Parsonage Ln, Icklesham TN36 4BL ℰ 01424 814552 ◈ queenshead. com. Deservedly popular village pub two miles west of Winchelsea, with a rustic interior and terrific views over the Brede Level from the back garden. Good selection of real ales, cider and pub classics. This is a handy objective for walks from Winchelsea, following the waymarked 1066 Country Walk past Icklesham windmill and Icklesham's striking Norman church, then returning via the Brede Level and arable fields.

8 RYE

♠ Jeakes House

Marshlink Line (Hastings–Ashford); Stagecoach bus 100/101 (Hastings–New Romney; hourly)

A more perfect small medieval hilltop town would be hard to find: indeed, Rye is thought to have retained a higher proportion of historic buildings than any other town in Britain. It only takes minutes to walk across the centre, but it is certainly not a place to rush. Every house differs from its neighbours, yet the blend of Tudor, Georgian and other architecture could hardly be more harmonious, most famously along the ankle-threatening cobbles of Mermaid Street with its venerable old inn, but there's more of the same standard in West Street, Church Square, Watchbell Street and elsewhere. Rye scores highly as a place for **shopping**, with a surprisingly comprehensive choice of independent retailers for such a small town. Thankfully it's too small for chain stores but it serves a large, prosperous hinterland, and browsing here is part of the pleasure of the place – with the pleasingly unchanged High Street frontage of Britcher & Rivers' retro sweet shop alongside a range of shops selling crafts, pottery, clothes, books and antiques. Rye's evergreen appeal to visitors also means it has a disproportionate amount of places to eat and drink for a town of its size.

From its hilltop site, all seems a very different world to the surroundings. You can see a long way across flat expanses that were once under the sea which formerly lapped three sides of the town; a Cinque Port in medieval times, Rye lost much of its former importance as the coast receded. However the tidal River Tillingham still accounts for a hub of modern industry along its opposite bank towards the sea; a century or so ago the river would have been much busier, with boats exporting Wealden timber and bringing in coal for the town's gasworks.

1 Rye is thought to have retained a higher proportion of historic buildings than any other town in Britain. **2** Gateways and defences are a reminder of Winchelsea's illustrious past. **3** Rye Harbour Nature Reserve includes the remains of Henry VIII's Camber Castle. **4** Camber Sands is the premier beach in East Sussex. ▶

DMITRY NAUMOV/D

SUE MARTIN/D

STEVEN D POTTER/S

LILLY TROTT/S

Rye's fortifications survive in part, with an extant chunk of town wall parallel to Cinque Ports Street and more spectacularly in the form of the **Landgate**, one of three gates built under Edward III. The 13th-century **Ypres Tower** (TN31 7HE ⊘ ryemuseum.co.uk; pronounced 'Wipers') served as the town gaol for 400 years, and its claustrophobia-inducing interior reveals the prisoners' appallingly cramped conditions. In the 20th century it served as a mortuary for 60 years, and in World War II corpses of RAF and Luftwaffe officers washed ashore were brought here, sometimes poignantly laid out side by side. In front, cannons stand outside on a terrace known as the Gun Garden, with a view stretching downriver to Rye Harbour.

> "Rye's fortifications survive spectacularly in the form of the Landgate, one of three gates built under Edward III."

Within the picture perfection that is Church Square, **St Mary's Church** crowns the town's highest point. A mixture of Norman and Early English, it is on a grand scale. As you enter, the pendulum of what is England's oldest church town clock swings above, over 450 years old and still working well, with its Quarter Boys chiming on the quarter hour. The bells were stolen when the French ransacked and destroyed the town in 1377, but were recaptured in a later raid on Normandy. You can climb the top of the tower for the best view in town, as well as close-ups of the clock's mechanism. Abutting the churchyard is a curious oval brick water tank, where water used to be stored after being pumped up Conduit Hill.

Rye Heritage Centre (Strand Quay, TN31 7AY ⊘ ryeheritage.co.uk) organises walking tours and displays a painstakingly researched town model depicting Rye in 1872, made over four years in the 1970s by retired local history teacher Joy Harland and her husband. It was done very much on the cheap, with polystyrene for building blocks and tapioca for road surfaces, but looks astonishingly good. The centre's 15-minute sound-and-light show, *The Story of Rye*, is worth catching (proceeds go to the town), while upstairs there's an entertaining collection of antique penny-arcade machines. A pound gets you seven old pennies to try out shooting cats, activate a scene of Charlie and Mabel in the Park (his hat self-tilts politely as he hitches her skirt ever so slightly) or view Davy Jones's Locker, with a shipwreck revealing mermaids watching TV.

The **Rye Castle Museum** (East St TN31 7JY ⊘ ryemuseum.co.uk ⊙ Apr–Oct Sat–Sun) has among its local-history items maps showing how the coastline has changed over the ages; one wonders how similar to present-day Chichester Harbour it must once have looked. Also on display are the town's hand-pumped fire engine that was in service from 1745 to 1865, E F Benson's recipe for poison pancakes supplied as a joke for a recipe book being compiled locally, and examples of a very striking local wood mosaic known as Tunbridge Ware, using a technique revived by one Tom Green of Rye – but the secret reputedly died with him in 1959.

Lamb House

West St, TN31 7ES ℰ 01580 762334 ⊙ Mar–Oct Fri–Tue; National Trust

In the centre of town, Lamb House was home to the American writer Henry James. Built in 1723 and now owned by the National Trust, it plainly suited James down to the ground. He lived here from 1898 to 1916 like an 18th-century man of letters, far away from the social pressures of London, and entertained many other literati, including Rupert Brooke, Joseph Conrad and H G Wells – who proclaimed it 'one of the most perfect pieces of suitably furnished Georgian architecture imaginable'. Inside

"H G Wells proclaimed it 'one of the most perfect pieces of suitably furnished Georgian architecture imaginable'."

are James's walking sticks, photos and manuscripts, and in the walled garden are memorials to his dogs. He wrote such late works as *The Ambassadors* and *The Golden Bowl* in a garden house, one of Rye's few buildings to be destroyed by bombing in World War II. His friend E F Benson later rented the house with his brother, and penned his Mapp and Lucia stories – set in Rye (called Tilling in the stories).

Rye Harbour Nature Reserve

Rye Harbour Rd, TN31 7FW ⊘ sussexwildlifetrust.org.uk; 40-min walk from Rye railway station, or Stagecoach bus 313

Southeast of Rye, beyond the riverside industrial estates where, from the 1860s, tar from gasworks was distilled into products such as creosote and paint thinners, is the Sussex Wildlife Trust's largest reserve. Around a third of its 4,275 species are found in none of its other reserves. Appealingly wild and remote, Rye Harbour Nature Reserve protects a rare shingle habitat, where little terns, curlews, ringed plovers, avocets and oystercatchers coexist alongside plants such as yellow-horned poppy. The reserve's wheelchair-accessible Discovery Centre, close to the mouth of the Rover Rother, has excellent displays on history and natural history, and a modern café with sweeping views. From here, paths shared by walkers, cyclists and wheelchairs lead out through saltmarsh and past pools created by gravel extraction towards the bird hides and beach.

The sad relic of the **Mary Stanford Lifeboat House** stands on the shore, intact and Grade II-listed but disused since November 1928 when the lifeboat *Mary Stanford* was called out to rescue a steamer which was in trouble in gale-force winds. As it happened, the steamer recovered and returned safely, but there was no means of sending a signal to the lifeboat: the next day the vessel was found upside down on the water, and none of the lifeboat crew of 17 survived.

The reserve includes the impressive hulk of **Camber Castle**, built by Henry VIII around an earlier circular tower, which apart from its gentle decay is totally unchanged since then. It didn't have a long service: within a hundred years of its erection the coast had silted up, stranding it far inland. The sheep graze right up to the walls and footpaths lead to it; though it's not manned, you can peep through the windows and doorways.

🎭 ENTERTAINMENT & EVENTS

Rye's literary and artistic connections account for a thriving **Arts Festival** (⌂ ryeartsfestival. org.uk) – featuring some big-name speakers and tantamount to a mini-Hay – over two weeks in September. **Kino Rye** (Lion St, TN31 7LB ⌂ kinodigital.co.uk/rye), a stylish independent cinema, has daily screenings.

🧳 SPECIAL STAYS

Jeakes House Mermaid St, TN31 7ET ☎ 01797 222828 ⌂ jeakeshouse.com. A few steps along the cobbled lane from The Mermaid Inn, this house was visited by numerous literary figures in times past and has served as a Quaker Meeting House, then Baptist Chapel. Now a supremely comfortable B&B, where the bedrooms are gorgeously old-fashioned with lots of soft furnishings, and the breakfasts sumptuous. Reasonably priced and much acclaimed over many years thanks to the care and thought that the owner puts into it.

🍴 FOOD & DRINK

Rye's **weekly market** takes place on Rope Walk on Thursday mornings. There's also a small **farmers' market** on Cinque Ports Street on Wednesday mornings.

Cobbles Tea Room 1 Hylands Yd, TN31 7EP ✆ 07485 437893. In an alley off The Mint, this deliciously quaint place serves sandwiches, scones, cake and everything else you'd expect from an ultra-traditional tea shop.

Fletchers House 2 Lion St, TN31 7LB ⌂ fletchershouse.co.uk. This contemporary restaurant in a historic building has a superb reputation for modern British cuisine, featuring top-quality local ingredients such as Romney Marsh lamb and fish from Hastings and Rye.

Hayden's 108 High St, TN31 7JE ⌂ haydensinrye.co.uk. An attractive spot for lunch or tea, this café and restaurant offers local, organic and fair-trade produce, in two airy rooms with a plant-filled terrace behind. They also do B&B.

Mermaid Inn Mermaid St, TN31 7EY ✆ 01797 223065 ⌂ mermaidinn.com. The obvious choice for a drink or meal in historic surroundings, this stupendous medieval timber-framed pub is full of comfortable corners. It offers reliably decent standards, from bar meals to special-occasion fare.

Rye Deli 8–10 Market Rd & 28B High St, TN31 7JA ⌂ ryedeli.co.uk. Handy for picnics, this pair of shops sells tasty quiches, salads, pastries, cheeses and wines from local producers.

Rye Fish Market & Seafood Bar Simmons Quay, TN31 7HJ ⌂ ryefishmarket.co.uk ⊙ Feb–Nov Tue–Sat. Locally caught fish, oysters, lobsters, crabs and whelks, served with artisan bread, beer and wine. In February, it acts as an unofficial hub of Rye Bay Scallop Week, a food festival championing local shellfish.

Standard Inn The Mint, TN31 7EN ⌂ thestandardinnrye.co.uk. In a double-gabled building that dates back to 1430, this dining pub serves seasonal dishes such as catch of the day with fennel and samphire or root-vegetable and dahl pie.

Ypres Castle Gungarden ✆ 01797 223248 ⌂ yprescastleinn.co.uk. Right beneath Rye's stone tower, this historic inn proudly declares itself a drinkers' pub, with real ale on tap, real cider and good wine. There's no kitchen, but they'll rustle up a cheese board on request, and there's a delightful garden.

9 CAMBER SANDS

Stagecoach bus 100/101 (Hastings–New Romney; hourly)

The best beach for miles around, and the only place in Sussex apart from West Wittering (near Chichester, page 32) with extensive, ever-present sand. It's a huge seven-mile expanse backed by dunes, but does get very crowded in high summer, when the nose-to-tail stop-start traffic jams aren't much fun. A much better way to arrive is by bike: it's an easy three miles from Rye, along the signposted off-road cycle path. Swimming is good and family-friendly. Dog owners should be aware that some parts of the beach are not dog-accessible in summer.

INTO THE WEALD

This chunk of terrain is part of the High Weald Area of Outstanding Beauty (page 233), where although the bus services are not super-frequent there are one or two outstanding opportunities for Slow travellers. The Kent & East Sussex Railway from Tenterden trundles through the landscape, linking in nicely with the possibility of taking a boat trip along the canalised Rother to Bodiam Castle. The river silted up over the centuries and attention was focused instead on draining the fertile marshland for grazing. Today, the surrounding pastures with their reed-filled ditches and channels are a wetland habitat. In places the sandy, loamy soils and south-facing slopes create the perfect conditions for growing vines, producing clean-tasting, distinctive wines.

I have devised a guide to Slow travel around the Bodiam area for the High Weald AONB website: it can be downloaded from ⊘ bit.ly/SlowTravelBodiam.

10 KENT & EAST SUSSEX RAILWAY

Tenterden, Northiam, Bodiam ⊘ 01580 765155 ⊘ kesr.org.uk; Stagecoach bus 29 (Hastings–Tenterden via Northiam; hourly Mon–Sat); bus 349 (Hastings–Hawkhurst via Bodiam; twice hourly Mon–Sat, less frequent Sun)

One way to arrive in style at Bodiam Castle, this preserved railway gives a 10½-mile trip through the Rother countryside from Tenterden station to Bodiam, via Northiam. A mixture of steam and diesel locos run here; the oldest steam engines date from 1872. Note that you can park only at Tenterden and Northiam, and that Tenterden station is some way outside Tenterden itself. The films that have been shot on this line range from *Nineteen Eighty-Four* and *Cold Comfort Farm* right down to an all-dog cast for a TV commercial for 'New Bakers' Gravy Bites – don't miss the gravy train!'.

"This preserved railway gives a 10½-mile trip through the Rother countryside from Tenterden station to Bodiam."

The Kent & East Sussex was the first of 16 light railways created by Colonel Stephens and was much used to bring hop-pickers down from London for their annual working holiday. The term 'light railway' refers to a type of line constructed at a time when regulations were relaxed, and instead of striding across viaducts and through cuttings as they were obliged to do in the early days of railway building, new lines were allowed to wiggle about following the lie of the land. Stations on the line are mostly trademark corrugated iron. Tenterden station has a display paying homage to Stephens' achievements.

Over the border into Kent, **Tenterden** is well worth a wander round. With its broad leafy street of grass verges and white weatherboarded houses this little town reminds me strongly of some of the villages in New England, though its amiably wonky architecture lacks the regularity of its American counterparts.

11 BODIAM BOATING STATION

A28 at Newenden TN18 5PP ℰ 01797 253838 ⊘ bodiamboatingstation.co.uk ☺ Mar–Oct; Stagecoach bus 349 (Hastings–Hawkhurst via Bodiam; twice hourly Mon–Sat, less frequent Sun)

And here's the other memorable method apart from train of arriving at Bodiam Castle: just a few minutes' walk from Northiam station on the Kent & East Sussex Railway, and next to 18th-century Newenden Bridge, the boatyard offers 45-minute cruises in a 24-seater former lifeboat, ferrying passengers along the Rother to Bodiam Castle, and you can get a one-way ticket to Bodiam and return by train, or vice versa, or take a three-hour sunset cruise to Iden Lock (just outside Rye) and back. Vanessa, who runs the service, told me there's a good chance of spotting barn owls and herons – and kingfishers if you're lucky – while in the water you could well glimpse carp or pike. They also hire out rowing boats, Canadian canoes and kayaks so you can make the journey under your own steam and at your own pace (they'll pick you up at the other end and take your craft back on a trailer). The campsite here gives scope for leisurely exploration.

12 GREAT DIXTER
🏠 Swallowtail Hill

Northiam TN31 6PH ℰ 01797 252878 ⊘ greatdixter.co.uk ☺ Mar–Oct Tue–Sun & bank holidays; nursery all year; Stagecoach bus 29 (Hastings–Tenterden via Northiam; hourly Mon–Sat)

Even among the world-class gardens of Sussex, Great Dixter – actively managed to promote biodiversity – stands out as one of the very finest. On the edge of Northiam village east of Bodiam Castle, it's not large or grand, but laid out in an intimate, almost disorienting series of outdoor 'rooms' that change in mood from one surprise vista to the next. Wealden barns and oast houses overlook an octagonal pond in the middle of the sunken garden, and there is a wildflower meadow speckled with ox-eye daisies and orchids. Shapely yew hedges, neatly clipped, enclose gardens that shift level and are punctuated by spectacles of blooms and foliage. It was the creation of the late, great Christopher Lloyd (1921–2006), whose parents moved here in 1910; a few fruit trees survive from the early days, but his remodelling was dramatic. The buildings form an important backdrop, with a weatherboarded barn wall and oast houses. Colour and contrast were keynotes of his densely planted garden design.

It all surrounds a half-timbered house of the medieval 'Wealden hall' design, restored and extended by Edwin Lutyens for the Lloyd family in 1910: Lutyens opened up the main room to reinstate its medieval form, with a ceiling the full height of the building, by removing the first floor inserted in Tudor times. With its huge bay windows and central heating it feels much more light and comfortable than it would have done originally. The parlour beyond, where Lloyd wrote, has a cosier feel with books and piano. Upstairs the solar, originally a private room for the ladies, with its medieval squint window for looking down at the goings on in the Great Hall, also has a very personal atmosphere. The furniture includes examples of Lloyd's collection of modern wooden furniture – sculptural and somewhat incongruous in this setting, but he believed they would blend in within a hundred years.

"The nursery Lloyd began in 1954 is an excellent place to stock up for your own garden, and you can order by post."

The nursery Lloyd began in 1954 is an excellent place to stock up for your own garden, and you can order by post. Throughout the year, study days are held here – into such subjects as meadow gardening, exotic gardening, propagation and preparing borders for spring and summer, and the shop sells local products, garden tools and related books.

🧳 SPECIAL STAYS

Swallowtail Hill Hobbs Lane, Beckley TN31 6TT ☎ 01797 260890 ⬧ swallowtailhill.com. Small-scale rural eco-glamping on a private nature reserve, six miles northwest of Rye, with six cute cabins neatly kitted out with kitchenettes and woodburners. To help guests switch off, they're deliberately free of TV and Wi-Fi. The surrounding farm is a long-established conservation project, run purely for sustainability and eco-diversity, with wildflower meadows and semi-ancient woodland. Families welcome; large parties can book the entire site.

13 BODIAM CASTLE

TN32 5UA ✆ 01580 830196; National Trust; KESR steam railway (Tenterden–Bodiam); Stagecoach bus 349 (Hastings–Hawkhurst via Bodiam; twice hourly Mon–Sat, less frequent Sun)

Swans paddle around the lilies in the water-filled moat surrounding this most perfect-looking of medieval castles, in the Rother valley about four miles southeast of Hawkhurst and the same distance east of Robertsbridge. Although a ruin, Bodiam Castle is a substantial one, and has retained much of its original appearance from outside. A knight of Edward III, Sir Edward Dalyngrigge, began it in 1385, justifying it by fears of a French invasion – though it seems to have been built more for display than defence, at the centre of an early 'designed landscape' featuring sheets of water: the car park was once the 'flote' or harbour, and the low-lying area between the car park and the castle was a mill pond fed by a leat. Dalyngrigge created the quadrangular plan with massive drum towers at each corner, two gate towers and the top robustly crenellated, using heavy military symbolism. The portcullis is thought to be the oldest in England. Bodiam wasn't exactly top-notch as a fortification when built though, as the concentric forms favoured elsewhere were much better at dealing with an attack.

"Although a ruin, Bodiam Castle is a substantial one, and has retained much of its original appearance from outside."

Fortunately for posterity the castle did not see any serious military action, surviving the Wars of the Roses and then serving as a Royalist stronghold in the Civil War until being partly dismantled. It then languished in a state of picturesque decay until careful restoration in the 19th century and again in 1916 by Lord Curzon, who left it to the National Trust in 1925. Its history continued beyond then though: a pillbox in the grounds acts as a reminder of the site's renewed military importance in World War II.

Though it's roofless inside, the castle is a most evocative structure, and spiral staircases take you up to a higher level for a different perspective among the battlements. I have yet to see a child there who hasn't been transfixed by it. On a warm day the lawns surrounding the site make ideal picnicking terrain.

The Kent & East Sussex Railway (page 318) has steam and diesel services that most conveniently end at Bodiam station.

14 MERRIMENTS GARDEN

Hurst Green TN19 7RA ✐ 01580 860666 ♿ merriments.co.uk; Stagecoach bus 1066 (Hastings–Tunbridge Wells; hourly Mon–Sat, less frequent Sun)

Back in 1988 this spot just east of Hurst Green was just an orchard and a field; then David Weeks and his family ingeniously transformed the heavy clay site into a four-acre show garden. 'The biggest challenge was the soil', says David, 'but it's a lovely south-facing aspect.' His creation features ponds watered by a stream, a bog garden, a rock garden and a bridge inspired by Monet's garden at Giverny. They grow herbaceous perennials and sell them in the nursery, adjacent to which is a café offering local fruit juices and Rother Valley beers, and food from Wealden ingredients.

15 PASHLEY MANOR GARDENS

Ticehurst TN5 7HE ✐ 01580 200888 ♿ pashleymanorgardens.com ☉ Apr–Sep Tue–Sat & bank holidays; Stagecoach bus 1066 (Hastings–Tunbridge Wells; hourly Mon–Sat, less frequent Sun) then 1½-mile walk

By the B2099 just over a mile southeast of Ticehurst, a timber-framed Tudor ironmaster's house stands in a glorious formal garden renovated by Mr and Mrs James Selick since 1981. It is largely a renovation of a Victorian garden, with distinguished foliage and colour, spring-fed ponds, herbaceous borders, contemporary sculptures and a series of enclosed spaces. Paths wind round rhododendrons and camellias and the fountain looks over the High Weald towards

"Paths wind round rhododendrons and camellias and the fountain looks over the High Weald towards Jack Fuller's obelisk."

Jack Fuller's obelisk. In late April to early May the tulip festival is quite a spectacle, with over a hundred varieties on show.

---

1 Mighty Bodiam Castle was begun in 1385. **2** The 1066 Battlefield holds re-enactments of the Battle of Hastings. **3** The former Royal Observatory near Herstmonceux Castle is now a science centre. ▶

16 BATTLE

Hastings Line (London–Hastings); Stagecoach bus 1066 (Hastings–Tunbridge Wells; hourly Mon–Sat, less frequent Sun)

Northwest of Hastings and linked to it by rail, Battle is a typical Wealden town – with an attractive if traffic-spoilt High Street sporting plenty of the tile-hanging and timber-frame buildings one expects to find in the Weald, and its own railway station, bonfire society, choral society and bowls club. But the name of the place makes it unique: where else do you find a town that is there solely because of an abbey that was the first thing to be built there, and it was only built there because of a battle?

HAROLD'S DOWNFALL

The Battle of Hastings (at what was then called Senlac) on 14 October 1066, the most famous date in English history, was decisive in the last successful invasion of the British mainland. The full story behind the conquest is extremely complex: the succession to the throne was not at all a simple matter. But the key points are that Harold II was Edward the Confessor's brother-in-law rather than his son (as one might assume), while William of Normandy was Edward's cousin and claimed Harold had sworn to uphold his right to the throne – though this oath, if it existed, may have been extracted under duress when Harold was rescued from a shipwreck in France.

When Harold took the English throne on Edward's death, William of Normandy claimed that he had reneged on a promise, and decided to enforce his side of the bargain. Harold's men had already defeated an invasion by another would-be successor, King Harald Hardrada of Norway, at the Battle of Stamford Bridge in Yorkshire on 25 September, and then had to march rapidly south to deal with William, who had landed at Pevensey Bay on 28 September. It was not the ideal prelude for the second battle as far as the English were concerned.

All the same, this was a battle that Harold probably should have won, though it is the subject of endless conjecture. The shield wall of the English was doing its job on top of the hill – the Norman horses could not muster enough speed to get up the slope and breach it, and the slope was slowing down the rate of their arrows (also, the English weren't firing a lot of arrows, so there were very few to return). However, when William's men (in three flanks: Normans; Bretons; French and Flemish) retreated, some English made the mistake of descending in pursuit – they were then surrounded by mounted Normans, who were skilled in fighting in small groups in open countryside and hacked the Saxons to bits. In a hail of Norman archers' arrows into the now vulnerable shield wall, Harold was killed. William's army saw how this retreat

The key point of interest here is obviously Battle Abbey and the 1066 Battlefield. Elsewhere in town, within the medieval Almonry is the **Battle Museum of Local History** (High St ✆ 01424 775955), with an absorbing survey of the town's past from prehistoric to modern times, and featuring the area's gunpowder making (hence Powdermill Lake, a mile's walk south of town). A Saxon battle axehead found in 1951 is possibly a relic of the famous battle itself. The Guy Fawkes effigy is the very one used in the town's ebullient Bonfire Procession each year and is said to be the oldest in existence; Battle, as elsewhere in Sussex, has a flourishing bonfire society which joins those from other towns for the grand procession in Lewes

had worked to its advantage and so feigned to do it again – and the hapless English pursued only to be systematically annihilated. The battle took all day – the facts that William's army had never encountered a shield wall and the Saxons had never faced cavalry were instrumental in prolonging the struggle. Then many of the Norman cavalry perished in a watery ditch pursuing the fleeing Saxons.

All the English really needed to have done was to hold out until nightfall and wait for reinforcements. Or they could have waited a little longer to regroup for battle in the first place. But it was not to happen, and at the end of that fateful day, when some 7,000 perished, William had won. William's army of under 10,000 had thus invaded a country of 1.5 million.

As an act of contrition, William decided to build an abbey on the very spot where Harold fell. At first monks started building the abbey elsewhere, on a more practical site (with decidedly useful things like level land and a water supply), but this did not please the new king, who ordered the whole project be moved here.

It is not known if Harold really died by an arrow in the eye. The Bayeux Tapestry, which can be viewed as a contemporary strip cartoon informed by an eyewitness (if you'll forgive the pun), does indeed have the word 'Harold' above a man killed by an arrow apparently in the eye; but there is another adjacent man, who might be Harold, being killed by swords. Either way, he had been so hacked about that only Edith, his mistress, was able to identify him.

It all leaves you wondering what might have been. Had the Saxons won, our laws, language, politics and architecture would have been very different; the feudal system that the Normans set up would not have happened in the way it did. Harold was an experienced soldier, and a popular monarch. He had the reputation for being rash; so perhaps William goaded him into battle when it might well have been more prudent for him to have bided his time and rallied new troops.

on 5 November (page 170). The garden outside, at the back, is a wonderfully semi-secret place for a picnic.

Battle Abbey & 1066 Battlefield
✐ 01424 775705; English Heritage

Ironically, the setting for the horrific events of 1066 is very beautiful today. The **Visitor Centre** sets the scene by presenting a reverse timeline, starting from the present and ending at 1066, and showing an excellent film narrated by David Starkey, featuring animated bits of the Bayeux Tapestry.

In the impressive **Battle Abbey Gatehouse**, there's an exhibition and multimedia guide revealing the abbey's origins, as a passion project of William the Conqueror, and its role in medieval England. A flight of 66 steps leads up to the rooftop for panoramic views of the site, amid Wealden and coastal landscapes.

Beyond the gatehouse, you can explore the abbey ruins and stand on the spot where King Harold is said to have breathed his last. In 2016, Harold's tomb was moved a few yards to its historically correct spot, at the high altar. The adjoining stately home (now **Battle Abbey School**) was created out of the site after Henry VIII's Dissolution. The former abbot's residence now forms part of the school, and one side of the cloister now constitutes one of its walls. Of the abbey buildings, just the sleeping quarters and latrines remain, impressive for their size and state of preservation. The monks' common room and novices' chamber are both intact, with vaulted ceilings and columns of Sussex marble; head-bangingly low doorways lead into the undercroft, with one former storage room leading off another, and where bats roost in winter. Steps lead up to the dormitory.

"You can explore the abbey ruins and stand on the spot where King Harold is said to have breathed his last."

The last abbot here cursed future owners with ill health and misfortune, and the family who took it on after the Dissolution suffered vast gambling debts, leading to the estate falling into decline. Things got better in the 19th century when the Duchess of Cleveland took it over: she added garden features, and the thatched dairy and icehouse. The original layout of her tranquil garden paradise has been recreated.

From the abbey, you can choose between a short walk along a paved terrace looking over the battlefield, close to where Harold's men stood

SUSSEX MARBLE

Italian-style marble is one rock not extant in Britain's uniquely diverse geology, and although Sussex marble isn't the real thing, it has filled a useful gap for many centuries of building. Also known as winkle stone or Petworth marble, it is found only in Sussex and southern Kent, and is formed from fossilised winkle shells in shallow salt water – hence the spiral shapes. When cut and polished it makes a very fine building material not that dissimilar to its more prestigious namesake. It has been used for many high-status buildings in Sussex, including as chimneypieces in Petworth House, interior columns in Battle Abbey and pillars in Chichester Cathedral.

(this shortcut is a good option if you're visiting in bad weather; the audio tour helps fill in what you're missing), or a longer (one mile) battlefield tour, which drops into a typically lush, green, hilly Wealden landscape, winding around via a series of chainsaw-carved wooden sculptures depicting the likes of Saxon knights and Norman archers. Beyond the site, you can see a lake where gunpowder mills once operated. Historians are still arguing about the precise location of the battle according to the lie of the land and other evidence. It's believed that the top part of the site was levelled off for the building of the abbey, so the hill would have been even more formidable an obstacle for the Norman invaders.

The **shop** has a well-chosen selection of Saxon and Norman-themed items and **children** are well catered for throughout the site, thanks to special exhibits, trails and an outdoor play area with 1066-themed wooden apparatus to scramble about on.

₩¶ FOOD & DRINK

Battle Deli & Coffee Shop 58 High St, TN33 0AG. Useful for light lunches and picnics, with pork pies, home-made cakes and local cheeses like Sussex Charmer.

Carr Taylor Wines Wheel Ln, Westfield TN35 4SG ℘ 01424 752501 ⊘ carr-taylor.co.uk. This vineyard just east of Battle offers guided tours and wine tastings, and has a shop and small café.

Sedlescombe Organic Vineyard Sedlescombe TN32 5SA ℘ 01580 830715 ⊘ sedlescombeorganic.com. When Roy Cook set it up back in 1979, this was England's very first organic (or 'biodynamic') vineyard. He goes for the traditional approach: hand picking and no chemical nasties. Bees, butterflies and birds thrive in the wildlife-friendly conditions. Sedlescombe also produces liqueurs, fruit juices and cider. Vineyard tours, shop and café; on the trail you'll pass a World War II 'dragon's teeth' tank trap.

17 HERSTMONCEUX CASTLE & OBSERVATORY

There are two very different education-linked sights a couple of miles south of the village of Herstmonceux: a massive castle and gardens and the former Greenwich Observatory, which now offers a broad programme of workshops, courses and drop-in events for aspiring space-gazers. Paths and bridleways skirt the rolling landscape around the castle, observatory and Herstmonceux's remote church, which is also south of the village. For an extended walk of around five miles, start at Windmill Hill, east of Herstmonceux.

Herstmonceux Castle

Nr Herstmonceux BN27 1RN ℘ 01323 833816 ⌖ herstmonceux-castle.com ☉ castle, grounds & Chestnuts Tea Room early Apr–end Oct; Stagecoach bus 98/99 (Eastbourne–Hastings, frequent services)

Not at all a conventional country-house visit, although it looks supremely imposing from outside, Herstmonceux Castle now houses the International Study Centre for Queen's University, Ontario, and has a wholly collegiate atmosphere. It closed for repairs in 2023, but if all goes well it will re-open in 2024 or 2025. It stands on a rise above the north extremities of the Pevensey Levels. In its previous incarnation the estate was home to the Royal Observatory from 1946, and the BBC pips were broadcast here for 40 years until the scientific establishment moved out because of light pollution and went to La Palma in the Canary Islands. Happily, plans for a leisure centre were thwarted by the early 1990s property crash, and Queen's University took over the castle in 1993.

"The estate was home to the Royal Observatory from 1946, and the BBC pips were broadcast here for 40 years."

Inspired by French châteaux of the period, the castle was the very first brick building on such a large scale anywhere in England, with Flemish bricklayers brought in for their expertise. It was completed in 1446 after Sir Roger Fiennes, Henry VI's treasurer, was granted licence to improve his manor. It is quite a sight, with its brick turrets high above a lily-filled moat.

At first sight it's hard to fathom how such a complete brick building should have survived in a near pristine state. It was abandoned in the 18th century when it was thoroughly stripped out for the building of a new mansion called Herstmonceux Place and remained ruinous until

1910. Then Lieutenant Colonel Claude Lowther began restoration, while his tame ram – a mascot of his territorial battalion – was given the run of the castle. The **tour** is not quite what you might expect from outside – you're taken round classrooms, the chapel and a panelled Elizabethan room, and there's a brief glimpse down into a dungeon; an en-suite stone toilet was positioned to empty into the moat, and there's an alleged siege tunnel.

The whole place comes to life very entertainingly each August bank holiday weekend with a huge **medieval festival** featuring cannon-firing, knights in armour, archery, falconry, a traders' market and medieval food and ales. Other **events** include outdoor plays and concerts.

The Observatory Science Centre

Nr Herstmonceux BN27 1RN ✆ 01323 832731 ⌂ the-observatory.org ☉ end Jan–early Dec

A short way east of Herstmonceux Castle, the former Royal Observatory is now an interactive science centre. The great green telescope domes, which have been collectively likened to the poor man's Taj Mahal, are a feature of the East Sussex skyline and are Grade II-listed. Carefully laid out and exuding a strange sort of 1950s period charm, they evoke a mini university campus – the design may not have been appreciated by some astronomers, who tended to find it somewhat hazardous at night and kept stumbling over edges and falling into the lily pond. Science exhibits bring in the school parties – with microscopes to look into, a clock to assemble and any number of experiments to try. Although the South Downs National Park is now a designated Dark Sky Reserve, the official stargazing in this part of Sussex ceased in 1979, and the lab left in 1990, but its 1896 telescope – the venerable 12-tonne, 26-inch Thompson Refractor – is still one of the largest in the world. One area chronicles the story of the Royal Greenwich Observatory. See the website for details of open evenings and astronomy courses; to come here at night and scan the skies through the telescopes makes the ultimate Slow experience.

INDEX

Entries in **bold** refer to major entries; *italics* refer to maps.